# THE
# POWER
## OF
# ADRIENNE RICH

## ALSO BY HILARY HOLLADAY

*Herbert Huncke: The Times Square Hustler*
*Who Inspired Jack Kerouac and the Beat Generation*

*Wild Blessings: The Poetry of Lucille Clifton*

*Tipton: A Novel*

*The Dreams of Mary Rowlandson (poems)*

*Ann Petry*

# THE
# POWER
## OF
# ADRIENNE
# RICH

### A BIOGRAPHY

# HILARY
# HOLLADAY

NAN A. TALESE · DOUBLEDAY

NEW YORK

www.nanatalese.com

DOUBLEDAY is a registered trademark of Penguin Random House LLC.
Nan A. Talese and the colophon are trademarks of Penguin Random House LLC.

Jacket photograph copyright © Estate of Betty Lane; courtesy of Schlesinger
Library, Radcliffe Institute, Harvard University
Jacket design by Michael J. Windsor

Library of Congress Cataloging-in-Publication Data
Names: Holladay, Hilary, author.
Title: The power of Adrienne Rich : a biography / by Hilary Holladay.
Description: First edition. | New York : Nan A. Talese, [2020] | Includes
bibliographical references and index.
Identifiers: LCCN 2019060247 | ISBN 9780385541503 (hardcover) |
ISBN 9780385541510 (ebook)
Subjects: LCSH: Rich, Adrienne, 1929–2012. | Poets, American—
20th century—Biography.
Classification: LCC PS3535.I233 Z66 2020 | DDC 811/.54 [B]—dc23
LC record available at https://lccn.loc.gov/2019060247

FOR ROBERTA CULBERTSON

*with love and gratitude*

# CONTENTS

# PREFACE

Adrienne Rich was a powerful woman. Throughout her long life and career, she marshaled the power of her formidable mind in the service of art and social justice. Her father, a brilliant scientist and scholar, made sure she understood the power of knowledge and the power of language. It was implied throughout his many years of insistent, bullying tutelage that if she could write better than everyone else of her generation, she would have his undying respect and a place in the annals of immortal literature. An assimilated Jew who declared himself a deist, he held out to her the possibility of life after death, if only she would devote her entire being to the art form he had chosen for her. Dr. Arnold Rich's message was so irresistible, she could hardly distinguish between his directive and her desire to fulfill it.

She gladly gave her life to writing, especially the writing of poetry, for poetry was as close to a religion as anything she would ever know. From a young age, she saw herself as a chosen person whose life mattered a great deal. She had her self-doubts and vulnerabilities, but she knew she was smart and, if she followed orders (her father's and her own), she was certain she could achieve her lofty goals. Her supreme self-confidence was an early source of strength that translated to power as she began moving methodically up the rungs of literary recognition while she was still an undergraduate at Radcliffe.

Although she was diagnosed in her early twenties with rheumatoid arthritis, which chased and whipped her for the rest of her days, Adrienne Rich also possessed the power of enormous energy—a gift of untold value to someone of her acumen and ambition. Her sister, Cynthia Rich, told me in the first of hundreds of email messages we traded over a period of five years, "Like my father, my sister was a genius who didn't need much rest and wrote many letters every day while writing essays and books and lectures and reviews [and also] writing poetry while teaching and cooking (and raising children and dealing with physical pain)—and more."[1]

In addition to her intelligence, willpower, and energy, she had the imagination and curiosity she needed to develop and sustain her creative powers for a lifetime. Well into early middle age, the fruits of those creative powers were almost enough to satisfy her. But when her writing flagged in the face of the burdens and responsibilities of motherhood, she began to take a fresh look at her life as an artist. She wondered what it would be like to stop pretending that a "universal" voice meant anything other than masquerading as a man. She noticed that, yes, the literary canon was full of poems about women, but they were almost exclusively by men. She would work to change that by taking up the subject herself. This decision prefigured her life as a radical feminist by nearly a decade.

In "Snapshots of a Daughter-in-Law," composed sporadically from 1958 to 1960, she wrote in the third person of how her choices differed from her passive mother's: "Nervy, glowering, your daughter / wipes the teaspoons, grows another way." And at the end of that poem, the first unmistakable harbinger of the feminist powerhouse she would eventually become, she sketched out a new kind of woman who was "long about her coming," as she phrased it, but drawing nearer all the time:

> Her mind full to the wind, I see her plunge
> breasted and glancing through the currents,
> taking the light upon her
> at least as beautiful as any boy
> or helicopter,
>
>                 poised, still coming,
> her fine blades making the air wince

but her cargo
no promise then:
delivered
palpable
ours.[2]

It was almost as if these lines were composed in retrospect, so sure was Rich of her eventual transfiguration. But she was right about being long about her coming. Eight years passed before she limned the changes she was undergoing, in a poem called "Planetarium." Through the isolate figure of Carolyn Herschel, the rare woman in the male world of astronomy, Rich remained at a remove from her true subject. But in the closing lines, she speaks for herself:

I have been standing all my life in the
direct path of a battery of signals
the most accurately transmitted most
untranslateable language in the universe
I am a galactic cloud so deep      so
involuted that a light wave could take
15 years to travel through me      And has
taken      I am an instrument in the shape
of a woman trying to translate pulsations
into images      for the relief of the body
and the reconstruction of the mind.[3]

This was Adrienne Rich in 1968: an instrument poised to change her life and many minds, including her own.

At the peak of her fame, in 1978, on the first page of *The Dream of a Common Language,* the greatest poetry collection of her career, she published "Power." In mounting certainty and dread, the poem works its way toward the controlling metaphor of her life and the central argument of this book. To get underneath the skin of this poem's pain is to know the bones and sinew and heartbeat of this singular woman, who devoted her entire life to writing.* The poem begins solemnly, the clusters of words spread out as if awaiting inspection:

Living     in the earth-deposits     of our history

Today a backhoe divulged     out of a crumbling flank of earth
one bottle     amber     perfect     a hundred-year-old
cure for fever     or melancholy     a tonic
for living on this earth     in the winters of this climate

The story appears to describe something that happened in the poet's neighborhood, perhaps on her own property.[4] For most, the bottle would be of only passing interest, but in Rich's mind, it is caked in irony, streaked with meaning. People long gone needed the cure the tonic purported to offer and would have wanted to believe it could help them. They were willing to be fooled. In the absence of editorial commentary, the poem's empty space seems to weigh their naïve hopes against the inevitability of their suffering.

The third stanza is much more conversational and direct as Rich suddenly announces her presence in the poem:

Today I was reading about Marie Curie:
she must have known she suffered     from radiation sickness
her body bombarded for years     by the element
she had purified
It seems she denied to the end
the source of the cataracts on her eyes
the cracked and suppurating skin     of her finger-ends
till she could no longer hold a test-tube or a pencil

Led along by the poet's horrified revelations, we see a driven woman, a genius of a scientist, who appears to value her work more than her own life. In her laboratory experiments, Curie was handling raw sources of power that could be used to treat cancer and identify

* Her California death certificate specifies "Occupation" and "Years in Occupation." Rich, who died at age eighty-two, is identified as a poet who worked for seventy years.

illnesses through X-rays. Though she may not have been quite as heedless as her chroniclers have made her out to be, she entered popular imagination as a woman so deep into her investigations, she refused to read the awful lessons written on her body.

The first part of the poem tells of the human suffering embedded in history and the innocent yearning for a cure-all that will take away earthly pain. The second part turns to Curie, who knew nothing came easily and gave up her life in pursuit of actual cures. She seemed to deny her suffering, the point on which the poem comes to rest:

> She died     a famous woman          denying
> her wounds
> denying
> her wounds  came     from the same source as her power[5]

What was literally true for Curie, whether she denied it or not, was figuratively true for Rich. She carried the wounds of a strange childhood, during which she tried to live up to her father's impossibly high expectations and received no meaningful support from her emotionally absent mother. All the while, her parents clearly favored her over her younger sister, Cynthia. The weird, inexplicable dynamic turned the two sisters against each other; they were never friends and ended up estranged for the last three decades of Adrienne's life. Cynthia has said she grew up feeling as if her sister viewed her as impossibly weak and insignificant. She and Adrienne had both been wounded in childhood, but their wounds were different.

There were other wounds in Adrienne Rich's life, but the one that most consumed her and pushed her toward ever-greater achievement was the gnawing sense she lacked a definitive identity. She took on the role of writer as a young child, but a role is not the same as an identity, and an identity was what she craved. In the early 1970s, she came out as a radical feminist and soon thereafter as a lesbian. There would be further pronouncements and calibrations in the years after that.

In researching the story of her life, I found that the absence of a fully knowable self was her deepest wound and her greatest prod. In "Sources," her sequence poem from the mid-1980s exploring her origins and linked by its title and content to "Power," she writes:

*With whom do you believe your lot is cast?*
*From where does your strength come?*

I think somehow, somewhere
every poem of mine must repeat those questions

which are not the same. There is a *whom,* a *where*
that is not chosen     that is given     and sometimes falsely
    given

in the beginning we grasp whatever we can
to survive[6]

And so the story of her survival begins as she grasps the pencil with which she will write her name for the very first time.

# THE
# POWER
## OF
# ADRIENNE
# RICH

# CHAPTER I

# BABY GENIUS

Adrienne Rich's first volume of poetry was published when she was six years old. Bound in a stately blue cover by Joseph Ruzicka Bookbinders of Baltimore, *Poems* begins with "The Tree" and ends with "Evening Star."[1] The thirty-seven poems in the book are well put together; the sentiments sincere, if conventional. Borrowing Emerson's famous response to Whitman's *Leaves of Grass*, one might have said with a smile to the child author, "I greet you at the beginning of a great career, which yet must have had a long foreground somewhere, for such a start."[2]

Adrienne Cecile Rich's father, Dr. Arnold Rice Rich, had arranged for the book's publication, and the foreground for her nascent career had begun taking shape in the months leading up to May 16, 1929, the day she was born at Johns Hopkins Hospital in Baltimore. Dr. Rich, a rising pathologist at Johns Hopkins University's medical school, had decided his firstborn would be a genius; he would make a project of it. All eagerness when the baby arrived, he came up with her distinctive name. Though not the hoped-for boy, she would have a given name beginning with *A*, like Arnold. He chose Adrienne (pronounced with a short *A* and equal emphasis on each syllable), a tribute to Adrienne Lecouvreur,[3] a renowned French actress of the eighteenth century who died mysteriously at age thirty-seven. Possibly Arnold Rich and his wife, Helen Jones Rich, had seen the 1928 film about her, *Dream of Love*, starring Joan Crawford. Adrienne's middle name honored Arnold's sister and only sibling, Cecile.

A few days after the baby's arrival, Arnold wrote to his father-in-law: "Miss Rich is gradually assuming a human appearance. I think that she is going to be quite a girl and I hope that we shall make you proud of her. Rumor about here has it that she was born speaking Greek and Sanskrit fluently, and with a most unusual and polished pianistic technique, but I assure you that that is all somewhat exaggerated."[4]

No one had to wait long before the proud and determined father's jesting hyperbole gave way to a series of astonishing facts. Dr. Rich made a second job out of tutoring Adrienne during his free time, and Helen Rich, a pianist and composer trained at the Peabody Conservatory in Baltimore, began teaching her music as soon as the toddler was able to sit upright at the piano and extend her plump little hands to the keyboard. When Adrienne was three, Helen wrote in a notebook, *"This is the child we needed and deserved."*[5] By four, the solemn, rather testy child with the round cheeks and penetrating dark eyes was dictating stories and playing Mozart with a prodigy's ease. The poems would soon follow.

Her father transcribed her stories in a book containing a blank page opposite each of a dozen fanciful illustrations. With her parents hovering close by, Adrienne composed the stories over a period of several months. The first, titled "The Kitty Story," is dated "March 31, 1933 at 12:05 midnight"; the last, "The Fish Story," was dictated on May 18, 1933, two days after Adrienne's fourth birthday. On that date, Dr. Rich took pains to write a note at the beginning of the book, which he addressed "To Adrienne in Later Years."

His daughter had written her first name in capital letters, with backward *n*'s, on the cover of the book and the title page. But since the stories were in his precise, highly legible script, he didn't want her to doubt that they were her original creations. Her advanced vocabulary, he told her, "can readily be traced to your passion for fairy stories, several of which Mimi has read to you every day for a year." Her mother ("Mimi") treated her to a steady diet of poetry, mythology, and fairy tales by Hans Christian Andersen and the Brothers Grimm. Adrienne also listened to her mother read *Alice's Adventures in Wonderland*. Dr. Rich also wanted the adult Adrienne to know that as a young child she would ask her mother to define unfamiliar words. "And so my dear, you may accept the contents of this book as being a faithful mirror of the workings of your own child mind, completely unsullied by any vulgar parental attempt to make you appear more accomplished than you actually were by helping you with little suggestions or by slyly inserting improving words or phrases."

At the bottom of this letter of validation he signed himself "Your Father," with a period at the end.[6] Once she was grown and writing hundreds of letters each year, Adrienne Rich often put a period after her name—a distinctive touch she evidently picked up from her father, her first literary mentor and the person who shadowed her youthful progress every step of the way.

In her fourth year, she learned to read and write. By five, she was practicing her handwriting every day by copying out passages from Blake and Keats, among other poets her father wanted her to know. Describing her assignments in the third person, the adult Rich wrote:

> [H]er father sets her a few lines of poetry to copy into a ruled notebook as a handwriting lesson. . . . She receives a written word in her notebook as grade: "Excellent," "Very good," "Good," "Fair," "Poor." The power of words is enormous; the rhythmic power of verse rhythm meshed with language, excites her to imitation.[7]

This was the way Arnold Rich wound the clock of Adrienne Rich's mind. Looking back on her early years from the vantage point of middle age, she said, "It was in many ways a privileged childhood. It was also a childhood under a lot of pressure because my father was a very intense, very complicated man."[8] Like Elizabeth Barrett Browning, with whom she would later identify, she had her father to thank for her early indoctrination into the literary life. But both poets suffered as a result of their fathers' controlling ways.

If she'd been the rebellious sort, Adrienne might have turned her attentions elsewhere just to spite her father. But she genuinely enjoyed writing and the praise she earned for it. In a letter dated September 17, 1935, her maternal grandmother, Mary Gravely Jones, wrote from New York to her daughter: "Don't forget to send me more of Adrienne's poems, and be sure to save them all."[9] On the same day, she wrote to the widowed Hattie Rich, who stayed half the year with Arnold's family: "I am deeply interested in Adrienne's poetic outpourings, I do hope Helen is keeping every one of them, I thought the ones she sent me remarkable, because they were so clearly pure poetic inspiration. The unfolding of her intelligence is certainly an interesting study, and I feel sure that we will have cause for great pride in her achievements, whether it be music, literature or poetry."[10]

Her unusual upbringing became the subject of some of the adult Adrienne Rich's most revealing and emotionally complex poems and essays. In a 1993 essay, she described the excruciatingly advantaged world of her childhood: "My parents require a perfectly developing child, evidence of their intelligence and culture. I'm kept from school, taught at home till the age of nine. My mother, once an aspiring pianist and composer who earned her living as a piano teacher, need not—and must not—work for money after marriage. Within this bubble of class privilege, the child can be educated at home, taught to play Mozart on the piano at four years old. She develops facial tics, eczema in the creases of her elbows and knees, hay fever. She is prohibited confusion: her lessons, accomplishments, must follow a clear trajectory."[11] What appeared to come easily, even naturally, was the result of enormous pressure she could never escape, even when her physical symptoms sent clear messages of distress to her doctor father and her seemingly attentive mother. For the rest of her life, she would look back in wonder, grief, and fury at the strange mix of privilege and unacknowledged suffering that defined her childhood.

Once it was set in motion, the interdependent machinery of instruction and accomplishment would never cease. Her mother taught her the basic lessons a child learns in the early grades (while going light on math), and her father pushed her ever harder in literature, history, and writing, when he wasn't at Johns Hopkins teaching medical students or conducting research. At the age of seven, she completed a fifty-page play titled "The Trojan War." Another early play is titled "Suicide, an Allegory in One Act by Altis Spenth." By age eleven, if not before, she was typing her own stories on a manual typewriter. In deference to the weighty keys, she pounded away with her index fingers.[12] At these times, deep in her thoughts, she was rehearsing the activity that would consume her for a lifetime.

Always, it seemed, she was doing what one parent or the other wanted her to do. When she wasn't writing stories or poems or plays, she was seated at the piano, practicing classical music. In "Solfeggietto," the first poem in *Time's Power: Poems 1985–1988*, she shows how distant she felt from her mother and how little pleasure she got from the lessons both her parents insisted on:

Piano lessons     The mother and the daughter
Their doomed exhaustion     their common mystery
worked out in finger-exercises     Czerny, Hanon
The yellow Schirmer albums     quarter-rests     double-holds
glyphs of an astronomy     the mother cannot teach
the daughter because this is not the story
of a mother teaching magic to her daughter
Side by side I see us locked
My wrists     your voice     are tightened
Passion lives in old songs     in the kitchen
where another woman cooks     teaches     and sings
*He shall feed his flock like a shepherd*
and in the booklined room
Where the Jewish father reads and smokes and teaches
Ecclesiastes, Proverbs, the Song of Songs
The daughter struggles with the strange notations
—dark chart of music's ocean flowers and flags
but would rather learn by ear and heart     The mother
says she must learn to read by sight     not ear and heart[13]

The magic of the household lies in the kitchen, where the family cook, likely based on Annie Bowie, a black woman who worked for the Rich family for many years, sings Christian hymns, and in the study, where the "Jewish father" pores over several poetic books of the Old Testament. They teach by example, through their love of spiritually inflected song and literature. Although Rich's father did not practice the faith of his ancestors, he was a lover of poetry and knowledge of all kinds. There is no hint of love or warmth coming from the mother toward her young daughter, who would clearly rather be with her father or the woman singing in the kitchen.

🎵

At age sixteen, Adrienne decided she wanted to make a career out of writing, not playing the piano. It was a wrenching decision because she knew she was an extremely talented musician. In her journal, she wrote as if for posterity that she'd been immersed in music ever since birth: weekly performances of chamber music at home, her father often playing violin or viola, her mother playing piano and composing music, and her own daily piano lessons ever since she was three years old. She worried she might regret passing up a career as a successful pianist, but there was a major sticking point. She just didn't love it the way she thought she should. Her mother believed she could fix that by practicing diligently and perfecting her technique. Adrienne didn't see things that way and felt it was time to announce her full commitment to writing.

In her journal, she recalled a long-ago dream in which her piano suddenly transformed into a desk. Although young Adrienne typically scoffed at prophetic dreams, this one was right on the mark. Since about the age of twelve, she'd wanted to be a writer, not a musician.[14]

A writing life was not just what *she* desired, however, but what her father had in mind for her. In this, he seems to have set himself in competition with his wife. While her mother pushed Adrienne to practice the piano, he spent hours every day tutoring her in writing. Though overbearing, he was by far the more charismatic and engaging parent. As an adult, Adrienne recalled that he spoke "with driving intensity," though she never knew what he was feeling.[15]

Once she had declared her plans to be a writer, her literary ambitions intensified. In a later journal entry the summer she turned sixteen, she wrote with relish of the mountain of writing she had done from childhood through the present—poems, letters, journals, diaries, essays, and partially drafted plays and novels. She imagined that if she ever became a prominent author, someone would publish a three-volume set of her juvenilia featuring a facsimile of her handwriting and a photograph of her as a child. But if she died without achieving greatness, surely all her papers would be burned in a backyard bonfire after the funeral.[16]

She was joking, sort of. There was no doubt in her mind that she was a writer; the question was, Would she become an important one whose words would outlive her? She knew better than to aspire to mere fame, what her high-minded father considered a gauche and meaningless measure of success. Her identity was so bound up in her achievement that she expected no one to keep her juvenilia, though clearly precious to her, unless it contributed to a greater understanding of her as an illustrious author. And since her father was the one pushing her to write, it was his opinion that truly mattered. If she failed to become a notable writer, Arnold Rich, or some avatar of him, would be the one stoking the flames of the trash pile after her death. At sixteen, full of adolescent hubris leavened by caustic wit, she could not imagine a middle ground in which her intrinsic value was distinct from her posthumous literary reputation.

Decades later, long after he had died, Adrienne Rich gave her father credit for his heavy hand in her formative development. "The message I got was that we were really superior," she wrote. "[N]obody else's father had collected so many books, had traveled so far, knew so many languages. [. . .] My father was an amateur musician, read poetry, adored encyclopedic knowledge. He prowled and pounced over my school papers, insisting I use 'grown-up' sources; he criticized my poems for faulty technique and gave me books on rhyme and meter and form. His investment in my intellect and talent was egotistical, tyrannical, opinionated, and terribly wearing. He taught me, nevertheless, to believe in hard work, to mistrust easy inspiration, to write and rewrite; to feel that I *was* a person of the book, even though a woman; to take ideas seriously. He made me feel, at a very young age, the power of language and that I could share in it."[17]

This was heady brew for a child, and Adrienne Rich drank it for many years without question. Yes, she could have become an accomplished pianist, but her mother never had a chance at winning the familial battle for Adrienne's artistic soul. No one could compete with the narcissistic genius of Arnold Rich, certainly not the subservient wife who quietly met her husband's every need while stifling her own talent and desires. In her long-sleeved black crepe dress based on a pattern her husband designed for her, Helen Rich was present but barely visible. Dr. Gerald Spear, a family friend and colleague of Dr. Rich's, remarked years later, "As for Mrs. Rich, as well as I knew her I am embarrassed to say I cannot provide a detailed enlightening description other than to say she was charming."[18]

Looking from one to the other, the young Adrienne threw her lot with Arnold Rich, the more powerful parent, the one with the study filled with books and antique maps, a microscope, and stacks of manuscript pages. He was "no feminist, believe me," she said in an interview many years later. "I see him as the embodiment of patriarchy. But he was interested in the achievements of women in the arts."[19]

Throughout her youth, he was interested in her artistic achievements more than anyone else's. To become Adrienne Rich the poet, essayist, intellectual, teacher, feminist champion of women's rights—perhaps even to become a lesbian—she would have to internalize this man, this patriarch, and then face him down. To know herself, she would have to know him. To grow into the woman, the writer, the Jew she wanted to be, she would have to denounce what he stood for and then reclaim him on her own terms. As for her mother, the enigma, the confounding mystery in the black crepe dress, she tried to find meaning in the earliest days of their relationship, when she was an infant suckled at Helen's breast and nothing stood between them. But Arnold's dominating presence could not be ignored, and it was obvious Helen's first allegiance was to him.

Both mother and daughter yearned for the patriarch's acceptance, approval, and love. Helen had the odd disadvantage of being a fully formed adult. The child, Adrienne, was the work in progress, and she knew that no matter how much she irritated him with her occasional fits of temper, her potential renown as a writer riveted his attention like nothing else. Call it fate, coincidence, or capitulation to psychological abuse, but she wanted for herself precisely what he wanted for her. Together, Arnold and Adrienne would do everything they could to transform the barely marked slate of her young life into an immortal tome.

CHAPTER 2

# THE PATRIARCH AND THE WOMAN IN THE BLACK DRESS

Arnold Rich was the central figure in Adrienne Rich's family drama. Although she knew him as an all-powerful figure controlling her every move, the patriarch of her youth had once been a small Jewish boy, the spoiled darling of his family. Born in Birmingham, Alabama, on March 28, 1893, Arnold Rice Rich was the son of Samuel Rich, a prosperous businessman who owned a shoe store, and Henrietta "Hattie" Rice Rich, an inventive, practical woman who was good at carpentry and enjoyed fishing. His sister, Cecile, was three years older than he was and doted on him. The family lived comfortably on a hill overlooking Birmingham.

Samuel Rich's transition from European immigrant to American southerner had happened while he was still a teenager. As a young man, he left behind his hometown of Kassa, Hungary, an ancient trade city in Austria-Hungary, and made his way to the United States. A cousin who preceded him had changed the family name from Reich to Rich, settled in Atlanta, and founded Rich's department store, which became a successful enterprise and prominent city landmark. Samuel also changed his name.[1] Although it is unclear why or precisely when Samuel Rich ended up in Birmingham, a new industrial city was a sensible choice for a young merchant: The miners, factory workers, and their families all needed shoes.

Samuel waited until middle age before marrying, probably to make sure he could provide for a family. In any case, Hattie Rice, eighteen years his junior, was well acquainted with the life of a shopkeeper. She had grown up in Vicksburg, Mississippi, the daughter of David Rice, a Bavarian immigrant who owned a furniture store, and Pauline Cromlein Rice, a New Yorker whose ancestors were from Amsterdam. It is unclear whether Arnold knew of Amsterdam's place in his maternal family tree. If he had, the detail would have pleased him, since Western European origins were a point of pride among American Jews of his and his parents' generations. In the 1940s, filling out a faculty questionnaire for Johns Hopkins, Arnold Rice Rich wrote that his father was born in Austria, though it would have been more accurate to say Austria-Hungary or just Hungary.[2]

Founded in 1871, during Reconstruction, Birmingham embodied a new industrial South very different from the old agrarian one. With its rich deposits of ore, it became home to iron mines and steel factories. The merchant class included Jews like Samuel Rich who sold essential goods to the larger community. In acknowledgment of his service, Samuel was invited to sit on the board of a local bank, a fact Arnold Rich proudly shared with his daughters.

There is no record that Arnold Rich had formal religious training. When he decided as a youth that he was an agnostic, his parents did not object. He could not change his ethnicity, but his identity would be as much of his own choosing as he could make it. For Cynthia Rich, Adrienne's younger sister, Arnold Rich was part of "a generation that felt on the one hand some shame and need to dissociate from the 'ghetto' Jewish immigrants, and on the other had a genuinely idealistic streak of wanting a Larger Life—to be a 'citizen of the world,' unconstrained by 'narrow, clannish' ways."

Whatever he knew and denied as an adult, Arnold was a pampered child during his formative years. He was rambunctious and into everything. The Irish nanny, Mamie, couldn't control him, and the family's pet parrot picked up her ineffectual rebuke: "Arnold, you're the devil! Arnold! You're the devil!" But she coddled him, as did his mother and sister.[3] The spoiling ended, however, when Hattie and Samuel sent Arnold to a place that would make a man out of him: the Bingham School in Asheville, North Carolina. "With whatever conscious forethought, Samuel and Hattie sent their son into the dominant southern WASP culture to be an 'exception,' to enter the professional class," Adrienne Rich wrote as she contemplated the erasure of Jewish identity in her family.[4]

Very likely the only Jew in his class, if not the whole school, Arnold Rich had fond memories of his time at this military preparatory school in the mountains of western North Carolina. Its hardships and rigor became part of the lore he passed down to his daughters. In the winter, the place was so cold that he and the other boys had to break the ice on the washbowls before washing their faces. Old Colonel Bingham lectured them on the proper use of all things, even toilet paper: "One wipe, one sheet."[5] As part of the military regimen, Arnold learned to march and stand up straight. His time at Colonel Bingham's school imbued him with good posture and a strict self-discipline that he applied to his future life and career.

Arnold then enrolled at the University of Virginia, where the breadth of his talents and abilities began to come into focus. Although he had thought about becoming a mining engineer, a profession that would have served him well in Birmingham, he changed his mind after realizing he didn't like math and decided to pursue a career in medicine instead. Wasting no time, he completed his bachelor's degree in three years, got elected to Phi Beta Kappa, and earned a master's degree in biology a year later. His graduate work in zoology resulted in a study published while he was in medical school,[6] a harbinger of his future professional success. All the while, he kept up his interest in the arts. He filled book after book with beautiful drawings for his botany classes. He published poems in a student literary publication, including at least one for Helen Jones, the young woman from Atlanta whom he would eventually marry. He practiced the viola, violin, and piano. This was the modern Renaissance man in his young manhood.

He was the only Jew in his class at the University of Virginia, according to Helen Rich. Like many other colleges both public and private, the school informally capped the number of Jewish applicants it admitted. Anti-Semitism became official policy at Mr. Jefferson's University in the 1920s, when the school set up a quota system "to limit the number of Jewish students, especially New York Jews, as children of Jewish immigrants applied to elite colleges in droves."[7] None of that stopped Arnold Rich from loving his alma mater, which he recalled with pride and affection in conversations with his wife and daughters. "Never in describing [his experiences in prep school or college], did he speak of having suffered—from loneliness, cultural alienation, or outsiderhood. Never did I hear him use the word *anti-Semitism*," Adrienne Rich observed from a remove of many decades.[8]

Early in her college career, she came across Karl Shapiro's poem titled "University," about the University of Virginia, where Shapiro had briefly studied before World War II. The devastating poem begins, "To hurt the Negro and avoid the Jew / Is the curriculum." The narrator approves of Jefferson, "the true nobleman," but believes the school that the author of the Declaration of Independence founded is deeply flawed in its present form.[9] This, then, was the university Arnold Rich had attended and spoken of so affectionately. The teenaged Adrienne Rich was shocked. Why had her father withheld the truth from her?

But Arnold Rich's truth was not the same as Shapiro's. He was by nature an achiever, not an activist, and he did not complain. Whatever prejudices or exclusions he faced at the University of Virginia or elsewhere, he worked to overcome through diligent application of his intellect and work ethic. His astonishingly sharp mind and encyclopedic range of interests would be his calling card; his dazzling accomplishments, his entrée into the meritocracy that he, like Thomas Jefferson, believed in.

In the fall of 1915, as a first-year medical school student, Arnold Rich walked through the doors of the institution that would become his professional home for the rest of his life. Johns Hopkins University served as the great offstage character in Adrienne Rich's complicated childhood. Just as she would later cherish Harvard, her father loved Johns Hopkins. Its medical school was prestigious and, in his time, retained a gentility that was important to his sense of himself as a southern gentleman. Its small size allowed for close working relationships and an intimate esprit de corps, both of which he would champion as essential to a successful medical school.

After completing his degree, he could have gone any number of places, due to his superior record as both scientist and instructor, but Hopkins had his heart. In a memoir describing his career as dean of the medical school at Hopkins, Dr. Thomas B. Turner offers telling glimpses of Arnold Rich, whom he remembered as "a quiet nonconformist, sleeping late in the morning when classes permitted and doing his best work around midnight." When the two men collaborated, Turner would go to Rich's lab at 8:00 p.m., long after most faculty members had gone home for the day. "Stretching across the wall of his laboratory was a vast chart in the process of development, designed to show the interrelationships over time of great events and great persons in different fields—art, music, exploration, medicine, inventions and so on. With this as a conversation piece his scintillating mind and talk would range widely for about two hours, when he would say abruptly, 'Well, let's get to work.'"[10]

Lurking behind his friendly and witty persona was a scholar in deadly earnest. Dr. Rich did not hold back when it came time to point out what was accurate and true and what was utter nonsense. Though his advice and guidance were much in demand, even admiring chroniclers acknowledged his criticism could wound. Dr. Ella Oppenheimer, who studied with Dr. Rich and became a fellow Hopkins pathologist, knew him for decades and saw him in all his enigmatic complexity: "His trim appearance was pleasing in spite of his perpetual pallor, which mirrored a sedentary life. His most characteristic expression was a quizzical smile, whether in accord or dispute with his companions."[11] After his death, another colleague wrote that while some would remember him as "an intellectual fountainhead," others would recall "a ruthless critic, impatient with carelessness and slipshod thinking."[12]

Although Arnold Rich was clearly the dominant parent who molded Rich's personality, drive, and career goals, her mother's influence on her, or lack thereof, had its own significance. The poet in middle age, much preoccupied with empowering relationships between women as well as the deleterious influences of the patriarchy, looked back on her childhood and searched in vain for a mother she could love and empathize with. But if Arnold Rich were the sun, then Helen Jones Rich was neither the Earth nor the moon, but a faint star whose vague outline never came into focus. No one could say she wasn't a dutiful mother throughout Adrienne's childhood. The problem was, no one could say much of anything about her. She had a vested interest in her older daughter's piano playing and shared her husband's enthusiasm for Adrienne's literary success, but her innermost thoughts and feelings stayed hidden. She "was in twilight sleep from the time of my birth," wrote her aggrieved and resentful daughter in 1975.[13] Adrienne could not escape a dialogue with her exacting, highly verbal father, with whom she argued in her head.[14] She found it much more difficult to have any kind of exchange, in person or in her imagination, with her opaquely smiling mother, who lived to the age of 102.

Helen Jones Rich couldn't win. In attempting to be exactly the wife Arnold Rich demanded that she be, she fell short as a mother and role model for her sensitive, high-strung daughter. Born in Wilmington, North Carolina, in 1898 to two Virginians, William Jones, a traveling tobacco salesman, and Mary Gravely Jones, an amateur poet and playwright, Helen Gravely Jones grew up in Atlanta, a middle child with two brothers, Willis and Lawrence. Her father was a jovial alcoholic who reportedly squandered the family money buying drinks for his friends. Mary Gravely Jones was a literary woman educated at a convent in Virginia. When her husband was heading out of town on business trips, she always asked him to bring back books. Clinging to gentility by her fingernails, Adrienne's maternal grandmother suffered from migraines and private grief. Her poem "To a Still-Born Babe" appeared in a 1909 issue of *Watson's Jeffersonian Magazine*, an Atlanta publication. Her unpublished play about Aaron Burr and Alexander Hamilton combined her interests in literature and history. She and Helen were not close.

Mary Gravely Jones encouraged her daughter, however, to develop her musical talents, perhaps in hopes that Helen would succeed in ways she had not. Helen showed such promise that Alfredo Barili, a noted piano teacher in Atlanta and nephew of the opera star Adelina Patti, took her on free of charge. Her abilities then earned her a scholarship to the Peabody Conservatory, where she studied musical composition as well as piano. Although she maintained her ties there later in life, Helen's student days were marred by the egregious sexism of her male instructors, at least one of whom made unwanted sexual advances. From Baltimore, Helen moved to New York City, where she lived with her mother while studying with a new teacher. By now, Helen's parents were separated. Mary was working as a real estate agent, and money was tight. Both mother and daughter clearly believed Helen had potential; otherwise, there would have been no reason to bother with continued musical training. Unfortunately, Helen again ran into a wall of boorish male behavior. She later wrote, "For me, at that time, these experiences were merely personal. I thought only that somehow, mysteriously, things had not worked out for me. Only later did I begin to wonder."[15]

Throughout her years in New York, Helen was corresponding with Arnold Rich, an ardent suitor whom she had encountered during a chance meeting at the University of Virginia in 1915. While playing the piano for friends, she had so charmed the slim young graduate student from Birmingham that he fell instantly in love. Nominally an Episcopalian, she had no objection to his Jewish ethnicity, nor did her mother, who saw great promise in him. But with other young men in pursuit and career ambitions taking up much of her time and thought, she didn't return his affections right away. It took him a couple of years to win her over with love poems and lively letters. Since Arnold was in medical school in Baltimore and Helen lived in New York, theirs was mostly an epistolary romance.

In August 1917, Arnold wrote to Helen from Danvers State Hospital in Massachusetts, where he was conducting research. He was worried Helen would miss out on her youth while waiting for him to marry her ("The years between nineteen and the middle twenties—how much they mean to a girl!") and feared Helen hadn't fully considered the social difficulties she might experience as a Gentile married to a Jew. He wrote, "For myself, my religion is to do that which I believe to be right and most consistent with my innate desires—These, if I am of worth, will guide me nearer to the idealistic goal of self-perfection—. . . . I am unhampered by religious formulae or prejudices—It is a product of my liberal bringing up." But he wanted his fiancée to know their life together might be hampered by biases coming from both sides of the Christian-Jewish divide. She would have to decide whether to take the gamble.[16]

Helen was willing to wait for Arnold and risk discrimination after their marriage. In the remaining years before they married, she continued along her path as a working artist and began teaching piano lessons at a couple of girls prep schools in New England as a way to support herself. The work wasn't rewarding. Desperate for a taste of happiness and adventure, she saved her money so she could spend a year studying in Paris. She and Arnold arranged it so her studies coincided with his in Vienna. It was 1921, six years after their first meeting, and the two were eager to be together. When Helen visited Vienna, Arnold got her a private room and they made love for the first time. In the aftermath, the double standard dug its hooks into Helen. Years later, she confessed that at the time she felt no other man would want her after she had been with Arnold.

Their courtship lasted an amazing ten years. Finally, with little fanfare, they were married on June 3, 1925, by a justice of the peace in New York City. Helen's mother was present. The absence of other family members wasn't evidence of disapproval; all signs indicate both sides of the family were happy about the union. Afterward, Helen and Arnold sailed separately to Paris, an odd way to begin a honeymoon after so much time apart. As Helen prepared to board the ship, Arnold gave her a letter to read about his expectations of a wife. The letter was so long, detailed, and dreadful that Helen tossed it in the ocean.[17] She may not have liked what she read, but there was no turning back, literally or otherwise. Arnold's demands and expectations would be with her for the next forty-three years. As Adrienne wrote in 1973, "The woman / I needed to call my mother / was silenced before I was born."[18]

Yet to all appearances, Helen Rich had gotten very lucky. With no prospect of a successful career in music and no money of her own, she needed a husband, and Arnold Rich had a magnificent future ahead of him. She could have done worse, or so she must have told herself many times. Their exotic honeymoon partially righted the wrong of the awful letter Arnold had written her. They reunited in Paris and sailed (together) to Morocco, rode camels by moonlight, and sat around a campfire while Arab men in long white robes played music. The trip was so magical and absorbing, despite the punishing daytime heat, that they returned to North Africa the following summer.[19]

On the home front, the magic swiftly faded. Although Helen didn't have to wear a veil like the Arab women did, Arnold insisted she wear a long-sleeved black crepe dress he designed for her. She wore it everywhere, not just in Arab countries. They jokingly called it her "uniform" (though one wonders which one of them laughed at that joke), and she wore a version of it virtually every day of her marriage until his death, in 1968. The dress was stark evidence that her married life had everything to do with her husband's wishes and commands and practically nothing to do with her needs or desires. She continued to play the piano every day, but Arnold rarely listened unless he was performing with his wife on his viola or violin as part of an amateur musical group.

Early in their marriage, when she had the opportunity to share some of her musical compositions with a well-known composer in New York, Arnold insisted, in spite of her pleadings, that she take along some of his compositions, as well. The meeting came off as planned, but Helen never heard another word from the composer.[20] Her professional career was over.

There was little time for anything besides following Arnold's instructions anyway. His salary was adequate for their needs, but he required her to economize and account for every expense. In the early years of their marriage, she recorded every penny she spent, and she and Arnold went over her checkbook every month. A strong swimmer, she gave up the sport because of her husband's peculiar aversion to exercise. Because he thought pregnant women were ugly, she avoided going out in public while pregnant with Adrienne. The long and painful labor that she endured, and talked about for years afterward, was likely worsened by many months of inactivity.[21]

This, then, was the woman Adrienne gazed upon when she opened her eyes to the world: a southern WASP. The daughter of an alcoholic father and melancholy, migraine-prone mother. A thwarted musician and composer. A wife who obeyed her husband's every command. The maddening, perplexing, barely visible woman to whom Adrienne's thoughts would repeatedly return, at midlife, as she embarked on a searing, ferociously unsentimental exploration of motherhood, the subject she said "radicalized" her.[22] She never gave her mother much credit for anything. But just as she wrote both for and against her powerful, overbearing father in her poetry, so did she write for and against her emotionally absent mother in her greatest work of prose, *Of Woman Born: Motherhood as Experience and Institution*. In retrospect, the inverse of Helen Rich's comment about the three-year-old Adrienne was true: They were the parents the future feminist needed and deserved.

# CHAPTER 3

# KINGDOM OF THE MIND

## *1933–1947*

Adrienne Rich's first home was a comfortable fourth-floor apartment across the street from Baltimore's Wyman Park. It was here, a couple of months before her fourth birthday, that she became a big sister on March 12, 1933. The day should have been a joyful occasion for the whole family, but Arnold Rich had again hoped for a boy and, alas, he and Helen had to make do with a beautiful baby girl they named Cynthia Marshall Rich. Friends of the family actually sent condolence cards to Helen because they felt so bad that she had produced yet another daughter.[1] The Riches would not try for a third child. Instead, they redoubled their efforts with Adrienne, their gifted stand-in for a son, while Cynthia was left to feel like a pretty little afterthought.

Adrienne was jealous of the new baby, who elicited her share of coos and took the spotlight on occasion. When they were grown, she told Cynthia in all seriousness that giving up her status as only child was "like losing the Garden of Eden."[2] But it wasn't Cynthia's birth alone that made 1933 a hard year for her. That was the year her mother taught her to play Mozart concertos, and her father was already grooming her for a career as a writer. The pressure to achieve was intense, and sometimes the only way she could release tension was to scream and cry. On one occasion, when she was unable to keep her anger and frustration in check, her mother obeyed Arnold's command and locked her in a closet. The horrifying episode, forever sealed in her memory, would show up decades later in a poem called "Tear Gas," in which Rich wrote, "Locked in the closet at 4 years old I beat the wall with my body / that act is in me still."[3] Perhaps it was inevitable that her complex and confusing relationships with her parents became jumbled in her mind with Cynthia's arrival on the scene.

The adult Adrienne looked back on herself as "an angry child."[4] She was perceptive and eager to learn, fully able to meet the intellectual and artistic challenges Arnold and Helen put before her, but there was much that she was too young to understand. As an adult obsessively looking to her childhood for insight into larger social patterns, she better understood the family dynamic: "Tin shovel flung by my hand at the dark-skinned woman caring for me, summer 1933, soon after my sister's birth, my mother ill and back in the hospital. A half-effaced, shamed memory of a bleeding cut on her forehead. I am reprimanded, made to say I'm sorry. I have 'a temper,' for which I'm often punished; but this incident remains vivid while others blur."[5] She knew she had been wrong to strike out at the nurse, Annie Bowie,[*] who had always treated her gently and affectionately, and the fact that Bowie was black made the adult Adrienne feel even worse: They were reprising the old pattern of the cruel white mistress and the defenseless enslaved woman. But it was her mother, not the nurse, with whom little Adrienne was actually angry. Helen was the one who had temporarily abandoned her.[6] Her impetuous act was evidence of a child's vulnerability and fear.

As she grew older, she learned to modulate her tumultuous feelings or at least hide them. She was moody but obedient, not one to make trouble. Arnold clearly believed she had real promise, even though her father's nonstop teaching made it hard for her to relax. He liked to hold forth about history and literature from his bed while Adrienne sat at the foot and absorbed lesson after lesson. Cynthia watched and listened from a nearby chair.

Helen didn't intervene or call attention to the blatant favoritism.[7] Her mother noticed it early on, however, when Cynthia was a toddler and Adrienne was six years old. In her 1935 letter to Hattie Rich praising Adrienne's precocious talents, Mary Gravely Jones hinted that the imbalance in attention was a potential problem for both girls: "If one can keep [Adrienne] always as natural as she now is & and let her development be spontaneous and un-influenced,—Precious little Cyn-

---

* Identified by Cynthia Rich. Adrienne doesn't name Bowie in the essay.

thia will not be overshadowed, you can see interesting things in her big eager eyes."[8] That prescient warning, unfortunately, had no impact. Throughout her childhood, Cynthia outwardly worshipped her older sister while never feeling at ease around her. Like Adrienne, she stored away memories that caused her great pain in later years.

In 1939, as the war began in Europe, the Riches left their apartment for a house reminiscent of an antebellum mansion. They came as renters, but two years later, Arnold was able, with his mother's financial assistance, to buy the property at 14 Edgevale Road in Roland Park, an upscale neighborhood in Baltimore. For the Jewish doctor and his young family, this was a bold move, since Roland Park had a documented history of segregation.

In the 1890s, Edward H. Bouton, the general manager of the Roland Park Company, transformed a hundred wooded acres north of Baltimore into one of the nation's first planned suburbs. Reflecting its remove from the city, Roland Park was sometimes called a "streetcar suburb" or "garden suburb." In time, Bouton acquired more land and added two neighboring developments, Homeland and Guilford, to the enclave. With the aid of landscape architects, he worked with the hills and woods rather than against them. Mature trees were left in place whenever possible, and Bouton himself gave thought to the flowers that were planted. In 1918, Roland Park and its sister suburbs were incorporated into the city of Baltimore.

Appearing quite visionary, Bouton promoted Roland Park as a clean and healthy alternative to the city's grit and noise, but in key respects he was a man of his times. In 1912, Roland Park Company's property deeds began including a category called "Nuisances," which spelled things out very clearly: "At no time shall the land included in said tract or any part thereof, or any building erected thereon, be occupied by any negro or person of negro extraction. This prohibition, however, is not intended to include occupancy by a negro domestic servant."[9] Although a 1913 "Deed and Agreement" pamphlet for homes in nearby Guilford repudiated that clause,[10] Bouton had other ways of enforcing discrimination—namely, his company's "exclusion files." Of particular relevance to the Rich family, Bouton's salesmen placed in these files information on would-be home buyers they knew or suspected to be Jewish. In the 1930s, Guilford had but one Jewish household, and the owner, a man named Julius Levy, was hardly made to feel welcome: "[T]he newspaper man, the bread man, and the milk man wouldn't deliver to him."[11]

When Arnold Rich brought his wife and daughters to 14 Edgevale Road in 1939, he would have known the racist and anti-Semitic lay of the land. Yet this was where he wanted to live: a stately brick house with white columns, a place that looked like it belonged on the movie set of *Gone with the Wind*. The house was situated on a steep hill in a tree-filled neighborhood that epitomized his idea of southern gentility, Baltimore-style.

In 1941, on the eve of the United States' entry into World War II, his purchase went through without complication. Perhaps his two years of renting served as a sort of probationary period, during which the distinguished doctor and his family proved to neighbors that they could behave just like respectable Gentiles. Maybe the war had distracted the Roland Park home owners' association, or Arnold's status at Johns Hopkins overrode his ethnicity in the eyes of its members.

Roland Park Country School, "attended by the daughters of socially prominent Baltimoreans,"[12] was the logical place for the Riches to send Adrienne and Cynthia after their early years of being tutored at home. At the time, the small private school enrolled both boys and girls through fourth grade. Beyond that, it was for girls only, and they were expected to study hard, learn Latin and ancient history, take part in numerous extracurricular activities, and go on to prestigious colleges. Arnold Rich served on the board of directors; Helen Rich was a chaperone at school dances and gave occasional guest talks there.

The teachers, all women, quickly realized they had an unusually gifted child in their midst and did all they could to nurture Adrienne's talents. They adored her, but she struggled to fit in with her classmates and make friends. One of her classmates was Peggy Webb, now Peggy Webb Patterson, who got to know her well. In fourth grade, Peggy watched as the less than athletic Adrienne stood on the sidelines and complimented the other girls as they performed on the exercise bars. The girls then competed for Adrienne's attention by showing off all the tricks they could do. "She was immediately popular," said Patterson, but it may have been in her sympathetic eyes only, since Adrienne never felt that way.

More than seventy years later, Peggy had many other memories from those long-ago school days. In grade-school conversation, Adrienne confidently used the word *insinuating*—a word Peggy had not heard before. Adrienne's vivid imagination was evident when she proclaimed, "I felt like I was flying!" after a lackluster attempt at ice-skating. Whenever Adrienne came for a visit, Peggy's mother would ask her to play the piano. Patterson remembered how "cute" it was when the young Adrienne swayed above the keyboard in rapturous affinity with the music. She also recalled funny little cartoons Adrienne had drawn, at least one of them especially for Peggy.

Peggy was aware that Adrienne's parents wanted her to use her time wisely. Recreation and relaxation were allowed, but only of the right kind. They were irritated with Peggy for teaching Adrienne to play solitaire, a card game the Riches (that is to say, Arnold) thought only an idler would cultivate. Little did Arnold and Helen Rich know that when Adrienne and Peggy walked across the street to the Baltimore Country Club's golf course, they weren't just taking a leisurely stroll. No, they headed to the club's deep and unfenced garbage pit and ran around it in wild circles, barely avoiding a perilous tumble into its fetid depths. That, too, might have been characterized as a waste of time, and a heedless risk of life and limb, but the protective Riches had no idea.[13]

Looking back on her early years, Adrienne wished she had taken more risks. In college, engaged to be married and thinking about the three sons and the daughter she intended to have, she told her parents she didn't want those future youngsters to feel anxious about competing in sports or to shy away from outdoor adventures. "I'll want them to learn caution and commonsense but I think a couple of broken collar-bones would have done me good in my childhood."[14] She was beginning to have her own ideas about what childhood should be like, and those ideas pointed toward a much more spontaneous and carefree existence than what she had experienced in the leafy confines of Roland Park.

Still, there was much to like about growing up there. In her youth, Adrienne wrote many journal entries expressing contentment with her home life. If those were the only basis for an understanding of her childhood, one would think it was very nearly idyllic. She wrote with delight of family birthday celebrations and appeared to savor her time at home during the summer. The family typically went on vacation in August, when Baltimore was hot and uncomfortable, often to Long Island,* but she spent most of her school vacation at home. She watched as the iceman slowly climbed the hill to deliver dripping blocks of ice to the back door of 14 Edgevale Road. When the grass grew high on the steep front lawn, she helped her father scythe it—a bit of exercise for the man who claimed to loathe it. She rode her bicycle around the neighborhood and played on her own or with friends. On sweltering days, sometimes she and Peggy Webb cooled off beneath the garden hose. As much as Arnold Rich pushed her to work hard at her writing and her studies, neither he nor Helen attempted to monitor her every move—hence, she had her chance to think her own thoughts and occasionally run around that garbage pit. But there were no broken collarbones, and she always dutifully returned home to her books and her writing, just like a little adult.

On the surface, young Adrienne belonged in Roland Park and cherished her family life in the "Wrennery," as Arnold Rich called their home, which was surrounded by trees full of chirping birds. The house was unostentatiously decorated with solid furniture that would last a long time and antique maps that Arnold had purchased during his travels. There were plenty of places where one could sit quietly and read. The family had pet cocker spaniels, a popular breed of the era, which sat at Helen's feet while she played the piano. The neighborhood was all that it promised to be—safe and beautiful. In a show of independence, Adrienne rode the streetcar to school each day. She thrived academically. She played the piano and wrote.[15] She should have been happy, and often she was. It was only years later that she began writing about the invisible pressures that found their way between the elms in the front lawn and snaked their way up the many steps, between the white columns on the porch, and through the front door of 14 Edgevale Road.

Whatever anxiety and anger she felt growing up in a household that was outwardly comfortable but quietly and insistently demanding, her sexual identity was not a source of confusion or pain. She was wildly enthusiastic about boys. In the "Vital Statistics of Adrienne Cecile Rich, female (as of Summer, 1944)," compiled when she was fifteen, she announced her fondness for handsome, assertive men under

---

* Before World War II began, the Riches sailed to France on several family vacations. Arnold's mother accompanied them and paid for these leisurely trips.

twenty-five. The same summer, on the way home from a shopping trip with her mother, she met a tall and attractive young Southerner whom she considered an ideal beau. The next day, she asked the Ouija board, a gift from her father, about her marriage prospects. With her fingertips guiding the wedge-shaped pointer across the alphabet and a row of numbers, she learned that in six years she would marry a man with the initials "U.E." and that she would die at age eighty.[16]

Time proved the Ouija wrong about these important matters*—after all, how many men named Ulysses was she likely to encounter?—but Adrienne's innocently posed questions showed what was on her mind. She hoped her mother would talk to her about sex and sexuality, but Helen did not seem to know how. Later in life, Adrienne wrote, "When I was a young girl desperately needing to understand sexuality the last thing I needed was to be told it was 'mysterious,' as my mother liked to do out of her own sexual ignorance and confusion."[17] Helen had her own sexual life to draw on for information, but she was not used to being an authority on much of anything in her own household. Arnold, the doctor and scientist, would not presume to teach sex education to his daughters, and Helen was disinclined to fill the gap. The school was not going to help, either. This was a subject that would go untaught.

Adrienne was eager to record her adolescent romantic attractions. The summer of 1945, she had a crush on a boy named Ted Davis. She thought he looked patrician in a tux and positively godly in a summer shirt. In one of the more spontaneous passages in her girlhood journals, she wrote about how she fell ill with the mumps only a day after realizing she was in love with him. It was June of her sixteenth year, the perfect season for young love; why did she have to endure a double chin sliding into the side of her neck? And what would she do if Ted called up and asked her out? The thought of declining because she had the mumps was unbearable.[18]

She recovered. The two began dating, and, as late as her freshman year in college, he was still flickering in the background. Cynthia wrote to her sister, wondering whether Ted might propose marriage when Adrienne came home for Christmas.[19] By then, however, Adrienne had lost interest. The summer of 1950, when she was engaged to a Harvard

---

* The Ouija wasn't far off on her life span, however. She lived to be eighty-two.

graduate student whose mother, coincidentally, taught at Roland Park Country School, she looked back on Ted with bemused detachment.[20] He was a brief infatuation, nothing more.

As a teenager and well into middle age, Adrienne's conscious romantic thoughts and physical passions were focused on men. She didn't acknowledge until many years after the fact that her love for a college friend had the makings of a lesbian attraction. In her later years, when she had identified as a lesbian for about two decades, a Stanford colleague asked her whether she had known she was a lesbian as a young girl. Adrienne shook her head no.[21] The notion of homosexuality had barely dented her consciousness while growing up. "I had a wonderful childhood in many ways, but there was so much I just didn't know about," she told a *Baltimore Sun* reporter in 1993. "You know, I never heard the word 'lesbian' and the word 'homosexual' then, except for a few men who people called names and intimated there was something wrong with them."[22]

Interestingly enough, it was the ever-vigilant Arnold Rich who wondered about her sexuality long before Adrienne did. When she was only ten years old, he had his suspicions when she wrote poems from a male point of view. Recalling this line of inquiry, Helen Rich wrote that, "like most men," Arnold "had lesbianism on the brain." But even from the vantage point of 1978, when both of her daughters had come out as lesbians, Helen didn't hear a Sapphic lute strumming in Adrienne's juvenile verse: "Now how could she have written in any other gender when all of the poetry that she had read, had been written by male poets?"[23] Adrienne would not identify as a lesbian until 1974. That year, she wrote to her friend Susan Griffin, the recipient of many of her most intimate revelations, that becoming a lesbian wasn't a political decision. Instead, it was something that gradually evolved after she stopped having sex with men. She felt she was just becoming acquainted with her lesbian self at the same time she and her lesbian lover were getting to know each other.[24]

Her choice of words is telling. Sexuality and identity politics aside, Adrienne Rich was on a lifelong quest to know herself and the world. The process of discovery always motivated and energized her. In another letter to Griffin, she mulled over her plans for an upcoming lecture. Her subject, the entwined nature of racism and misogyny, deeply engaged her. But it wasn't just the content that held her attention: "[T]here is something in this very process of exploration which is exhilarating to me, an excitement of seeing certain configurations I had been blind to, the old electricity of making connections. It is this, as much as the necessity for justice, that I wish I could convey."[25]

That electricity had begun early in her childhood, when she fell deeply in love with learning, thanks in part to her parents, especially her father, and in part to her innate intelligence and curiosity. By the time she was a teenager, she was already seeing herself as a writer of great promise, just as her father wanted her to do. She didn't need his frequent exhortations to work ever harder, because she wanted to work, to write. Above all else, she wanted to learn. Arnold instilled in her, through his example and instruction, a tenacious desire to dissect and connect. Illumination was everything. She, too, would push away the darkening curtains and welcome in the light, even if it made her wince in pained surprise.

Learning is not the same as being taught, a distinction that became enormously important to her in the years after she grew up and left 14 Edgevale Road. She spent much of her adult life thinking about the fault lines in her education at home and at school. There was so much about discrimination and injustice, some of it directed at her and her family, that she hadn't been taught or made aware of. She found her otherwise-hyperarticulate father's silence on anti-Semitism particularly mystifying and galling. It was her gift that she was able to look back on her youth and convey, in her poems and essays, what she had belatedly learned from the silences and omissions. And in seeing what she had learned, others might also learn and grow: That, too, was important to this woman who fervently believed in the power of knowledge.

The teacher she was closest to, Margareta Faissler, had a Ph.D. in history from the University of Chicago and taught European history at Roland Park Country School for more than three decades. A dedicated scholar and an independent, self-possessed, and kindhearted woman, she provided a significant counterpoint to Helen Rich. Radiant with her love of learning, she inspired Adrienne, and later Cynthia, to read widely and think deeply about the human dimensions of history. Cynthia recalled, "Adrienne's eyes would shine when she spoke of her." As for Cynthia herself, it eventually became obvious she had developed a schoolgirl's crush on her beloved teacher. A worried Arnold Rich discouraged contact between his younger daughter and the one person who made her feel as if she had value all her own.[26]

After graduating from high school, Adrienne corresponded with Faissler for the rest of her mentor's life and hosted her for visits, as well. Faissler introduced her to the principles of social justice, and Rich was forever grateful to her for that.[27] Since Faissler had never married, the adult Adrienne eventually asked her whether she was a lesbian. The answer came back negative, but Adrienne maintained that Faissler was no less a lesbian role model for that. Ever since she was a child, she had loved her teacher's intelligence, wit, physical well-being, and her obvious desire to connect with and help other people. As a lesbian, she felt a strong affinity with Faissler, who embodied so many qualities she admired in strong, capable women.[28]

The teacher's pet never wins any prizes for popularity. Though her classmates eventually voted her wittiest and most intelligent (she tied with another student in each category) in their graduating class, she was not a class favorite. "When girls at school are hostile to me I try to get in the limelight as much as possible in classes, by coming forth with brilliant answers," she wrote when she was fourteen.[29] Since she couldn't figure out how to join them, she would beat them. The strategy worked in most subjects but not in math and science. Her mother had taught her basic computation, but her father disliked math and couldn't imagine girls studying science. Hence, she didn't have the advantage of his tutoring in these subjects—and it showed. On one occasion, a science teacher asked her, "Which weighs more, a pound of lead or a pound of feathers?" She was slow to reply, and her teacher's face grew red with suppressed laughter when Adrienne said, "I know there's a trick to this."[30]

For all the effort she put into her study of the arts and humanities, and her desire to best those classmates who were unfriendly to her, Adrienne could not be bothered to excel in subjects she didn't find interesting, the same ones her father didn't press on her. Although she would later read up on the lives of prominent women scientists and study astronomy on her own, she earned a shocking D in chemistry during her senior year of high school.[31] Her chemistry partner, Margaret Louisa "Lou" Dukes, now Lou Pine, said the two of them muddled their way through the course. "She was as dumb as I was," Lou recalled. "She was not a mathematician and certainly not a chemist." But Lou didn't worry about failing the class. The teachers "wouldn't flunk me because they wouldn't flunk Adrienne—they realized Adrienne was a very brilliant person in other fields. Everybody loved Adrienne. I think they knew she was going places."[32]

When she reached the upper grades, Adrienne was immersed in extracurricular activities. She sang in the glee club, wrote for student publications, starred as Juliet opposite a female Romeo, and played the title role in *Elizabeth Bennet,* based on Jane Austen's *Pride and Prejudice.* The student newspaper, *The Red and White,* offers glimpses of her life at school. In the May 1945 issue, her poem "Sonnet in a Time of Battle" appears along with other school entries in a statewide contest for the best "Poetic Toasts to the Boys Overseas." The fifteen-year-old Adrienne wrote that American soldiers fight "Not for glib phrases coined with careless ease," but instead "for familiar things, that tell the story" of their hometowns.[33]

By December 1945, the middle of her sophomore year, she was the paper's literary editor. The war finally over, the issue has a lighthearted tone. Although the article is unsigned, its wit and personal details indicate that Adrienne wrote "Backstage of 'Romeo and Juliet,'" an account of the play's dress rehearsal. A moment of startling comedy occurred right after Romeo's suicide: "Emily had died and Adrienne was on the verge of killing herself when she discovered to her horror that the dagger was not revealing itself to the eye as before planned. Ad's line went, 'Yea, noise? Then I'll be brief, oh, happy dagger—Emily, for Pete's sake *where's* the dagger?' However, born with the motto of 'Carry on,' Ad substituted the poison vial's cork, stabbed herself with it and slumped to the ground registering much pain."[34]

Adrienne also wrote for the yearbook, *Quid Nunc* (translated "What Now?"). For the 1946 edition, she appears in a group photo taken in front of a small pond on school grounds. With all of the girls in long-sleeved blouses and skirts, Adrienne sits front and center, turned slightly sideways in a model's pose, her reflection mirroring her from below.

Classes above fourth grade were called "mains," with the eleventh grade known as the Seventh Main. Adrienne wrote a page of text accompanying this group photo of the Seventh Main: "Who are these ardent souls conducting yelling contests in cheer practice! The ear-splitting Sevens. Who graced our stage last November in every conceivable capacity from lovesick hero to footlight screwer-in? The Shakespearean Sevens. . . . Who makes the lunchroom a discussion-place for every subject from Latin scansion and the foreign policy of Napoleon to 'the most adorable boy I ever saw'? The versatile Sevens." In a prescient nod to her own future, she wrote, "Around about 1967, civilization may begin to acknowledge its debt to certain gifted artists, politicians, musicians, mathematicians, social leaders, writers and thinkers, all sprung from RPCS' class of '47."[35]

As a teenager, she thought a great deal about the future, a subject that would interest her for the rest of her life. In a humorous essay in the 1947 edition of *Quid Nunc* imagining a class reunion in the distant future, she pictured her classmates rushing in from various points around the globe. The girls, all identified by name, will surely be famous painters, writers, stage actresses, and dance instructors; the descriptions are appropriately frothy and flattering. But, like the school newspaper article about *Romeo and Juliet*, this story ends with a description of Adrienne herself:

> And here finally is the last of the party. Adrienne Rich has left her inkpots and proofsheets to make a last appearance among her old companions. When her latest historical novel was attacked for "inaccuracy and inadequacy of material" by a certain learned specialist in European history, Adrienne, in frustration, decided to retire to Europe to spend her declining years in a houseboat on the Rhine. As she glances at the assembled company, her sole comment is—"I may be hazy on the past, but I certainly could prophesy the future!" Any further remarks are drowned out as the familiar strains of the Whiffenpoof Song rise above the conversation and we know that the party has really begun.[36]

If there was any doubt as to the authorship of the unsigned story, Adrienne cleared that up with the clever quote attributed to her. She also worked in an allusion to Miss Faissler, her history teacher. As in the newspaper article, she gave herself a good line and got the last word. That desire to get the last word, which she shared with her father, was to become a defining characteristic as she came into her own as a poet and feminist leader.

The page about her in the 1947 *Quid Nunc* further reveals how the young Adrienne Rich wanted to be seen. She gives her slogan as "My mind to me a kingdom is," a line drawn from a poem about intellectual self-sufficiency by Sir Edward Dyer. Interestingly, for someone who would achieve international acclaim as a poet, she describes herself as "Continually beginning the Great American Novel." Her abomination is "routine" and her weaknesses are "the sea and chamber music." She says her "by-word" is "Let's not be subtle"—a pronouncement her future friends and adversaries would not have found surprising. And she completes the phrase "Wants to be . . ." with "remembered." That motivation lay behind virtually everything she wrote for the rest of her life.

In a journal entry written during her junior year at Radcliffe College, Adrienne admitted she still got angry and upset recalling her high school experience. She had received an invitation to an alumnae event that she initially decided to turn down. On reflection, she decided to go because she didn't want her resentment to influence her actions. Although there were teachers such as Miss Faissler and her French teacher, Miss Emerson Lamb, whom she liked and admired, she wasn't fond of her peers. She bitterly recalled times when she loathed them, and she assumed they would bore her if she tried to befriend them now.[37] Memories of her prep school cast a pall over her, yet she was determined to face down those memories. She thought skipping the reunion would be an admission of defeat.

Heading into her final year at Roland Park Country School, she wanted to be editor of the yearbook and was disappointed when Jane Troxell, who also had literary aspirations, was elected to the position. Being denied the honor by her classmates pricked her sensitive ego. At some point during her teen years, she confessed to her father that she didn't feel popular at school. Arnold Rich consoled her by saying this was a common problem for those who would go on to achieve great things later in life. Perhaps drawing on his own experience, he said that once gifted people made their contributions to the world, they had lots of devoted fans.[38] This message comes through in Adrienne's senior yearbook, not just in her story about a future class reunion but also in the blurb accompanying her graduation photo. The unsigned tribute imagined what it would be like to look back on this girl of so many talents:

> Sometimes we wonder what our class would have been like without Adrienne, and we shudder to think. Of the twenty-seven members, we are positive that this one will be famous so that we can say "We knew her when"; but the question is, for which talent she will win her fame. Perhaps in writing, we say, because hasn't she continued to make all A's in English, and haven't we been held spellbound many a time by her compositions? Or perhaps it will be acting. Can we ever forget her superb performances as Juliet and Elizabeth Bennet, and her moving way of reading poetry? And then, we would not be surprised to see her sitting on a piano bench on a concert stage, playing some concerto brilliantly, or giving famous lectures on European History. Yes, we're proud of Adrienne, and we want to wish her all the success in the world for a colorful future.[39]

Perhaps her aura of future fame made her hard to approach. When she described herself in her journal a few years later as "but a second-best sort of friend," her thoughts clearly echoed her father's words. She didn't feel actively disliked, but she wanted more from her friends than she was getting.[40]

The classmates who signed her high school yearbook confirmed this assessment. A girl named Charlotte Gailor Cleveland, who had played Darcy to Adrienne's Elizabeth Bennet, wrote, "I'll be proud to say 'I knew her' when your fifth book is published." Emily Lanning Tompkins, who was Romeo to Adrienne's Juliet, had this to say: "Well A.R. I'm sure gonna miss my old rival in the hymns, plays etc. Maybe someday we'll meet on Broadway. [. . .] It's really been wonderful knowing a gal like you (daughter & lover) Loads of luck & love, Emily." Still another, Rebecca Hopkins Cromwell, painted this vivid picture: "To Addy, a heck of a swell gal. She'll smoke Pall Mall's, dance gracefully resembling a horse just like I do, and all in all you're super Addy—love and good luck to a far more talented writer than I—Becky." Her yearbook rival, Jane

Bradley Troxell, weighed in more guardedly: "Dear Ad—I'm not much good at this, but this book couldn't have been without you—[. . .] I'll never forget you & someday will be proud to have known you."[41]

Adrienne knew she was gifted and believed it was just a matter of time before great success came her way. But a pervasive sense of social inadequacy persisted alongside her abundant self-confidence. Both insider and outsider, she felt important to the world, even essential, yet somehow not fully embraced or loved.

The *Quid Nunc* staff photo shows Adrienne dressed in saddle shoes and a dark school blazer with white piping. She has one leg propped on the arm of a chair in an assertive pose and smiles faintly at the camera. Her facial features are darker than those of her fellow staff members. Her nose is prominent, and she has her father's deep-set eyes. Just as Arnold Rich's appearance was recognizably Jewish, in this picture Adrienne herself looks Jewish.

Although the school had no formal church affiliation, she and the other girls sang Episcopal hymns, recited Episcopal prayers, and "read aloud through the Bible morning after morning." She also attended St. John's Episcopal Church on Sundays and became a baptized, confirmed member, though she did not believe what the church taught and went only because her mother wanted her and Cynthia to have the social imprimatur of a church affiliation. As far as Adrienne could tell, Jews were consigned to history: "I gained the impression that Jews were in the Bible and mentioned in English literature, that they had been persecuted centuries ago by the wicked Inquisition, but that they seemed not to exist in everyday life. These were the 1940s, and we were told a great deal about the Battle of Britain, the noble French Resistance fighters, the brave, starving Dutch—but I did not learn of the resistance of the Warsaw ghetto until I left home." A great prober of silences of all kinds, she looked back on this omission in her education with angry amazement.

These were her reflections years after the fact, in her essay titled "Split at the Root: An Essay on Jewish Identity." At the time, the silences at school and at home left her unable to formulate the questions about identity and bias that would later preoccupy and possess her. In "Split at the Root," she recalls rehearsing her part as Portia for *The Merchant of Venice*:

> Whatever Jewish law says, I am quite sure I was seen as Jewish (with a reassuringly gentile mother) in that double vision that bigotry allows. I am the only Jewish girl in the class, and I am playing Portia. As always, I read my part aloud for my father the night before, and he tells me to convey, with my voice, more scorn and contempt with the word "Jew": "Therefore, Jew . . ." I have to say the word out, and say it loudly. I was encouraged to pretend to be a non-Jewish child acting a non-Jewish character who has to speak the word "Jew" emphatically. Such a child would not have trouble with the part. But I must have had trouble with the part, if only because the word itself was really taboo. I can see that there was a kind of terrible, bitter bravado about my father's way of handling this.

Her parents had taught her that polite people didn't allude to someone else's race or ethnicity: She was not even to say "Negro" in the presence of black people. "In a parallel way, the word Jew was not used by polite gentiles."[42] What was presented as good manners was part of the family pattern of evasion and silencing that later troubled her so much. Although her father held forth on a myriad of topics and encouraged open debate, he said practically nothing about what it meant to be or not be Jewish, and it seems he said not a word about anti-Semitism, at least not in her earshot.

The young Adrienne was always thinking, her mind bent on interpreting and understanding everything that crossed her path. At sixteen, she contemplated the end of World War II and noted that it had begun when she was twelve: "What could be further apart than those two ages—the beginning and end of adolescence. The things that made a difference to me then don't even matter, now. Whether or not you could get skates or go in the car to Carlin's Amusement Park. And that was just <u>our</u> war. Britain got in in '39, when I was only ten." She strained to imagine how peace would change her life: "Lipsticks in metal cases, nylon stockings, more boys to dance with?" Now, perhaps, she could travel outside the United States as much as she wanted, but she wasn't thinking just of herself: "And 'the Parliament of Man, the Federation of the world'—if such is possible—I'd like to see grow and thrive. The rest doesn't much matter."[43]

Around this time, probably after she wrote about the war in her journal, she went alone to a Baltimore movie theater to watch "stark, blurry, but unmistakable newsreels" showing "the Allied liberation of the Nazi concentration camps."[44] The reality of the Holocaust shocked her and everybody else viewing the footage in their hometown movie theaters. Returning home to discuss what she had seen, she discovered that her parents "were not pleased. I felt accused of being morbidly curious, not healthy, sniffing around death for the thrill of it. And since, at sixteen, I was often not sure of the sources of my feelings or of my motives for doing what I did, I probably accused myself as well. One thing was clear: there was nobody in my world with whom I could discuss those films. Probably at the same time, I was reading accounts of the camps in magazines and newspapers; what I remember were the films and having questions that I could not even phrase, such as *Are those men and women 'them' or 'us'?*"[45]

In fact, such questions had already come up. But the silences in the household were so profound that at times both she and her sister blocked out what little they knew of their Jewish ancestry. On one occasion, ten-year-old Cynthia consulted her about prejudice, the subject of a book she was reading. In regard to prejudice against Jews, Cynthia said she didn't think she knew any Jewish people: "At which point [Adrienne] replied, 'How can you be so stupid! Don't you know that Ah-dear was Jewish?' " "Ah-dear" was the family nickname for Arnold's late father, Samuel Rich. Adrienne made no mention of the other Jews in the family—their father, their paternal grandmother, nicknamed Anana, who spent half of every year with them, their aunt Cecile, her husband Leonel Weil, and the Weil cousins. Even though their mother was a Gentile, many people would have considered the Rich girls Jewish, as well. But that possibility was not to cross either Adrienne's mind or Cynthia's for a long time to come. Like her father speaking to a befuddled medical student, Adrienne had set her little sister straight on the volatile matter of Jewish identity. "By this measure," Cynthia wrote years later, "the only Jew in the family was dead."[46]

For all of the changes she later made in her life and dramatized in her art, there was much about Adrienne Rich that never changed. The "Vital Statistics" she compiled when she was fifteen reveal not only the girl she was but also the person she always would be. She hated "Mathematics, crowds, bugs, snobs." She loved the color green, Saturdays, poplar trees, melons, the lily of the valley, *War and Peace*, pearls, and the sight of "the postman stumping down the path." She wished she had green eyes. Her "Head Interests" were "Literature, music, drama, history, languages, art." Her chosen occupation was writing; her favorite pastime, writing letters. Her favorite feeling was "that of having accomplished something." Most telling of all, her favorite motto was "Noblesse Oblige." At age fifteen, drawing on ideas she had learned from her father, the pathbreaking pathologist, and from her favorite teacher, Miss Faissler, she was beginning to see herself as someone who should help those less privileged and fortunate than she was. It was a ways off, but eventually she would dedicate much of her energy and thought to precisely that end.

At sixteen, Adrienne imagined her family making a bonfire of her personal papers if she died a nonentity, her stories and poems and journals not worth preserving. In fact, a fire was in her future, but not at home. In a startling turn of events, Roland Park Country School caught fire on the night of June 4, 1947, a day after her graduation. Most of the school burned down, and the cherry trees on the grounds were charred. When it was safe to enter the buildings, Adrienne returned to haul out what she could, including a bust of Patrick Henry she removed from Miss Faissler's classroom—little else remained. The fire had quite literally consumed her life as a schoolgirl, a life she had found alternately exhilarating and maddening. Like Patrick Henry, she would eventually have her liberty—and she would fight for it. That same evening, she happily dined at the home of her friend E. C. Speers, who was headed to Wellesley College in the fall.[47] Though the fire no doubt occupied much of the night's conversation, Adrienne was moving on.

As the citizenry of Roland Park worked to rebuild the small prep school where she had tied for the honor of wittiest girl and most intelligent girl, and was surely the most ambitious, Adrienne Rich turned her gaze toward New England. On the last day of school, shortly before it burned down, she had learned of her acceptance to Radcliffe College, the women's division of Harvard University. The men's undergraduate school, Harvard College, was the oldest college in the nation and, in many people's eyes, the most prestigious. Radcliffe offered a passageway to that locus of male privilege and power, a whole new kingdom of the mind. It was the opening she had been waiting for.

# CHAPTER 4

# THE GIRL WHO WROTE POEMS

## *1947–1950*

When Adrienne Rich arrived at Radcliffe College in the fall of 1947, she wanted to make good use of her every waking minute, and the record shows she very nearly did so. With each successive year as a Radcliffe student, she earned more recognition as a writer. By the time she graduated, she had published a prizewinning book of poems that earned praise from *The New York Times Book Review*, *The New Yorker*, and *The Atlantic Monthly*. She had come north from Baltimore wanting to be accepted into Harvard University's inner circles of artistic and intellectual power, and she pursued inclusion in those circles with the same energy, skill, and resolve she applied to her writing. The ambitious girl and the nation's oldest university were well-matched dance partners, each twirling the other with grace and aplomb. Not long after her graduation, the fledgling literary star credited Harvard, quite rightly, with making her who she was.[1]

Throughout her four years of college, she regarded Harvard with wonder and carefully concealed desire. Her dorm mates saw a self-possessed and proper young woman who spoke with precise diction and wore heels to class, while the other girls wore loafers or saddle shoes. She fussed over her stocking seams, making sure they were straight, and complained about a dormitory shower curtain that didn't close all the way. Her biting sense of humor only added to an overall impression of high seriousness and propriety. The other girls detected ambition in her, but even as late as her junior year, when she was writing many of the poems that would appear in her first book, few knew she was already a writer of deeply serious intent. They didn't give any thought to the sound of typing that frequently emanated from behind her closed door, nor were they aware that every morning after breakfast she wrote for at least an hour.[2] Engaged by the end of her junior year to a pleasant but staid Harvard graduate student, she seemed to casual observers like a typical, if rather more driven, Radcliffe girl. Her friends and acquaintances had little reason to suspect she would make her name as a poet. The possibility she also might become a pathbreaking lesbian feminist activist was ludicrously remote.

Reserved though she appeared to be, she was nevertheless on a conscious quest for fulfillment that began anew each morning. As a freshman, she settled into dorm life with ease. Her roommate, Priscilla Thayer, was a New Englander who had graduated from Garrison Forest School, a suburban Baltimore girls prep school not far from Roland Park. Adrienne slept in the upper bunk of the room they shared in Whitman Hall. In those years, introductory courses were segregated by sex, so she attended several classes alongside other young women in Longfellow Hall in Radcliffe Yard. But for her, the true "Yard" was Harvard Yard. Having been exempted from taking introductory freshman writing, she made the long walk from her dorm to Harvard Yard for her advanced composition class, which was coed. Leaving Whitman, which faced Radcliffe Quadrangle, she walked along Garden Street or perhaps cut across Cambridge Common, and entered Harvard Yard via one of its several gates. Hurrying along the brick walkway, she gazed up at the statue honoring John Harvard, a bronze rendering based on a long-ago student rather than on the great benefactor himself, whose seventeenth-century visage was unrecorded. She passed among students and faculty members also on their way to class and happily greeted the people she recognized. Alert to cliques, she was aware that admission to Radcliffe College didn't necessarily mean acceptance at Harvard University. She longed to be fully vested in the male-centered community of influence and privilege.

Early signs pointed to a deeply rewarding undergraduate career in the making. Her classes in writing, humanities, government, and philosophy engaged and challenged her; she was a member of Radcliffe's Choral Society, which performed on campus and in an annual concert with the Boston Symphony Orchestra; and she was meeting and dating interesting young men. She loved it so much that it wasn't until well into October of her first semester that she briefly felt tired. To her family, she wrote, "From half past seven in the morning, I am thrown upon a day of strong swift feelings and ideas and experiences—new ones constantly appearing, old ones constantly changing. Just walking through the Yard is an event which, daily as it may be, never loses the excitement of a first impression."[3] Like Coleridge's Aeolian harp, she was joyfully responsive to all the new sensations passing through her. Harvard felt like just the right place for her to learn and to be.

Although she and her sister were never close, they enjoyed a period of epistolary warmth during Adrienne's first year of college, when sibling rivalry yielded to their shared love of books and letter writing. In an October 1947 letter to Cynthia, Adrienne wrote enthusiastically about Thoreau's Walden. The part she wanted to discuss came from the conclusion, specifically the passage about being true to one's principles and heeding the beat of one's own drummer. "You know my favorite bit—'If the condition of things for which we were made is not yet, what were any reality which we can substitute? Etc.' I've come to the conclusion that after some years of rejecting 'desperate enterprises' I've actually reached the 'condition of things for which I was made.'" She assumed she hadn't reached her peak just yet, but she thrilled to the sensation that she was on her way.[4] This, too, sent the message that Harvard was now her home.

There was still her father to contend with. She was grateful to him for all he had done for her, but his meddlesome ways irked her no end. On the evening of October 29, 1947, she sent him a generous, openhearted tribute. "Tonight, coming up from dinner, I paused on the landing to look out of the window and across the quad, at all the lighted windows gleaming through the dark fog. I couldn't help thinking how terribly lucky I've been to come from a home like the one you and Mum and Anana have made for us." She added a few more lines of fulsome gratitude to Arnold alone.[5] In another letter sent during her freshman year, however, she chided him for snooping in her desk at home in search of love letters. She told him to poke around in Cynthia's desk instead if he got "really bored."[6] In other missives, she told both of her parents to stop pestering her with unsolicited advice and guidance. She tartly assured them their admonitions were never far from her mind and that they had no reason to think her anything but a loyal and obedient daughter.[7]

Her father's close monitoring of her budget was another source of provocation. Later in her college career, in response to a sudden cut in her allowance, she spelled out her expenses in detail and insisted on a fair allotment: "When I was playing the field I recklessly allowed young men to squander their old fathers' savings on me, but that day is past."[8] In all of these instances, she deployed wit in the name of keeping the family peace, but there was something of the smart-mouthed child in her tone. She didn't always succeed in sounding like the reasonable adult she wanted to be.

Her father's continued investment in her writing, especially her poetry, was a delicate and complicated matter. She craved his approval but not his alone; she wanted to write for the world, to leave an indelible mark. These swirling desires came through in her first free-verse poem, composed during the fall of her freshman year. She wrote it for the composition class she was taking with Kenneth Kempton, a tight-lipped New Englander, whom Rich very much wanted to impress. In a letter to her parents and sister, she described "To a Young Minstrel," which concerned that "point in the artist's life when facility and abandon aren't enough, when he comes to the edge of decision—and the alternative is labor or oblivion."[9] The poem ambitiously addressed the artistic impasse that was bedeviling her. She told her father she was afraid she'd "fallen between two stools" in leaving her old style of writing behind without mastering anything new.[10] The subject matter required a recalibration that frightened and exhilarated her.

By the time she finished revising the poem and submitted it to Kempton, "To a Young Minstrel" aptly reflected her state of suspended animation. Written in the second person, chock-full of adjectives, the poem imagines a universe in which past generations wait expectantly for the poet to make an interesting move. They are not listening, but watching, and the poem conveys Rich's fear that if she never produced work of lasting value, she would forever remain a mere child, seen but preferably not heard, in the existential judgment of those whose opinions mattered.[11] "To a Young Minstrel" was a lavish note to herself, her father, and her professor, showing she knew the high stakes and solemnity of her task. It also showed how alone she felt, and as yet unheard.

A meeting with Kempton in late April of 1948 ended up being the high point of her freshman year. As their conversation about her semester's work wound down, the dour professor invited her to apply for admission to his advanced short story writing course. Enrollment was limited to twenty, and competition to get in would be fierce. In response to her bubbling gratitude for his invitation, Kempton cracked a smile. It was obvious he wanted her in the class.[12]

His encouragement was manna from the Cambridge heavens. Her Roland Park friend Peggy Webb Patterson remembers Rich complaining that her professors didn't always take her seriously as a writer; it was as if they were "patting her on the head," an infuriating situation for her.[13] But that wasn't how she felt on this particular April day. In a daze, she left Kempton's office in Warren House, trotted downstairs, and paused before stepping out on Quincy Street. The habitually reserved young woman then began simultaneously laughing and crying—a fit of hysterics that would have amazed her dorm mates, who thought of her as supremely self-controlled.

Spilling everything to her father not long after, she described her brief, friendly conversation with Kempton as enormously important, something akin to a religious conversion. In exultant tones designed to please and impress, she promised her father she would do everything in her power to get into English 2a.[14] Like Arnold Rich, she worshipped at the altar of intellectual and creative accomplishment. From a young age, she had dreamed of the literary immortality he held out as a possibility for her if only she worked hard enough for it. Ever since she could apply pencil to paper—even before, thanks to his transcription of the stories she composed as a toddler—writing was second nature to her. As difficult as it was to live up to his endlessly high expectations, she never stopped trying. So it wasn't the prospect of the advanced class alone but, rather, the chance to prove herself worthy of Kempton's favor, and Harvard's—and her father's—that transported her. The vision that hovered before her was one of patriarchal recognition on a par with actual paternal love. Maybe she could be more than a speck spinning in the void.

Wiping her eyes, Rich left campus and bought a pink rose at Sage's flower shop on Brattle Street to mark the day. Then, as she gazed up at the city's imposing buildings silhouetted against the sky, her emotions came into focus. She felt she might actually have some worth—and be supported and recognized in this grand place. The steeples and towers of Cambridge symbolized the kingdom to which she wanted so much to belong; Kempton had offered her the toehold she needed to begin her ascent in earnest. As she clutched the rose, she thought of how much this sudden turn of events would please her father,[15] who had made it a life goal to become an insider at Johns Hopkins. Surely he would appreciate what she was up against at Harvard and how hard she was working.

Yet there were beginning to be other people whose opinions counted as much as his—and they weren't just the paternal proxies who peered at her from every lectern. In May, as she put the finishing touches on the fourteen-page story that formally earned her admission to Kempton's advanced course, her friend Eleanor Pearre stopped by her room and asked to read it. Adrienne was happy to oblige and even took Eleanor's suggestion for a title—"Amateur."[16] A native of Frederick, Maryland, the blond and attractive Eleanor was the object of her intense interest the whole time they were at Radcliffe. In an April 1948 letter home, she praised her new friend "Ellie" and wrote unself-consciously about the care they had taken to get to know each other slowly and carefully.[17] And thus the crush began.

Over the next several years, she and Eleanor were frequently seen together. Mutual friends considered the owlish Adrienne the leader and the lovely Eleanor her devoted acolyte.[18] Foreshadowing Adrienne's later interactions with close female friends, the relationship was rocky. She fumed when Eleanor didn't ask to read her poems; she ached when her friend kept her feelings to herself. When Eleanor finally confessed her affection for her, Adrienne inwardly rejoiced and wrote her father about the momentous conversation.[19]

Decades later, after she came out as a lesbian, Adrienne told an interviewer she hadn't known what to do about her feelings for the woman she had fallen in love with during college.[20] That is, she didn't know how to *act* on her feelings. During her junior year, she wrote a seventy-five-line poem based on her friendship with Pearre: "Stepping Backward," a highlight of her first book. With insight beyond her years, the speaker realizes she and her friend (whose sex isn't specified) know each other too well ("crack and flaw, / Like two irregular stones that fit together") and see each other too often to take the other's full measure. But both have the sense there is much more to know, if only they could get to that point of knowing:

> You asked me once, and I could give no answer,
> How far dare we throw off the daily ruse,
> Official treacheries of face and name,
> Have out our true identity? I could hazard
> An answer now, if you are asking still.
> We are a small and lonely human race
> Showing no sign of mastering solitude
> Out on this stony planet that we farm.
> The most that we can do for one another
> Is let our blunders and our blind mischances
> Argue a certain brusque abrupt compassion.

In short, there would be no throwing off the daily ruses anytime soon. Unable to move forward, the hovering narrator twice tries out the word that pulls her every which way:

> Perhaps the harshest fact is, only lovers—
> And once in a while two with the grace of lovers—
> Unlearn that clumsiness of rare intrusion
> And let each other freely come and go.

When it comes time to say good night, she steps back for a lingering glance at her friend. With the keen anticipation of the future that was to mark her whole career, she imagines measuring future friends and lovers against the standard the object of her devotion has set:

> Your stature's one I want to memorize—
> Your whole level of being, to impose
> On any other comers, man or woman.
> I'd ask them that they carry what they are
> With your particular bearing, as you wear
> The flaws that make you both yourself and human.[21]

A beautiful, brainy love poem with Sapphic fingerprints all over it, "Stepping Backward" was a triumphant leap forward in Adrienne's poetic growth. She had come quite a ways since "To a Young Minstrel," but it would be more than twenty years before she took her own full measure and declared herself a lesbian.

During this period of her literary development, Adrienne had the good fortune to live in a community flush with poets and lovers of poetry. Robert Frost, the nation's most prominent poet and a future friend of hers, lived on Brewster Street, near the campus. Her poems eventually appeared in *The Harvard Advocate* alongside those of fellow students Donald Hall, Frank O'Hara, Robert Bly, and John Ashbery, all future luminaries. Poetry readings, such as Dylan Thomas's performance at the Brattle Theatre in 1952, drew excited crowds. The Harvard Coop, the Grolier Poetry Book Shop, Phillips Book Store, and the Harvard Book Store were among the numerous bookstores stocking contemporary and classical poetry, and the Harvard English department offered a number of literature courses on poetry. In addition to Kempton, the English department's creative writers included Theodore Morrison, John Ciardi, Archibald MacLeish, and May Sarton. Morrison was a poet, novelist, Chaucer scholar, and the director of the Bread Loaf Writers' Conference at Middlebury College. Ciardi was a rising poet and anthologist who later became poetry editor of the *Saturday Review* and succeeded Morrison as director of Bread Loaf. MacLeish and Sarton wrote in several different genres, poetry prominent among them.

Sarton didn't hold the rank of professor, nor was she on the tenure track. The university's only female professor during Rich's time, in fact, was the distinguished historian Helen Maud Cam, who arrived from Cambridge University in 1948 and retired in 1954. As late as 1970, Harvard's Faculty of Arts and Sciences had no tenured women.[22] In hindsight, Rich was grateful for her female teachers at Roland Park Country School, the place she was once so desperate to escape. "There I was taught by women, many with Ph.D.'s, who would have been teaching in colleges, but who, in the Depression, ended up teaching high school. They were very ambitious for us intellectually if we showed any promise," she said in an interview. "All the time I was at Harvard, on the other hand, I never had a female teacher. There was none of the female mentoring, the female intellectualizing or care-giving: very few Harvard professors were prepared to give that kind of consideration to women."[23]

Rich, however, was unusual in that she had an energetic and devoted mentor in Ted Morrison, her writing instructor during her last two years of college, and the support of several Radcliffe deans, all women, whose friendship she assiduously cultivated. Although she didn't take a class with Sarton, the two became friends after Rich graduated. Adept at charming older people, who warmed to her polished manners and meticulously groomed appearance, she was the beneficiary of a great deal of encouragement and aid from women and men alike.

In her letters home, she sounded like a typical boy-crazy coed, despite the occasional off-message tangent about Eleanor Pearre. As a freshman, she made a show of complimenting Henry David Aiken, her philosophy professor, and Paul Ylvisaker, the section leader for her government class, whose height, blond hair, blue eyes, and general handsomeness reminded her of the English poet Rupert Brooke.[24] Her male classmates were a further source of pleasure. On the first day, when the section leader for her philosophy class looked around for "Mr. Rich" during roll call, she thrilled to the sound of her male classmates' chuckling when she tentatively made the correction.[25]

Of all the professors she studied with, the only one she lionized in later years was the literary critic F. O. Matthiessen. A Rhodes scholar with a Ph.D. from Harvard, Francis Otto Matthiessen was the renowned author of *American Renaissance: Art and Expression in the Age of Emerson and Whitman* and other major works of criticism. He also was the editor of *The Oxford Book of American Verse* (1950), the later editions of which would include selections of Rich's poems. She took two classes with him, the first in the spring semester of her freshman year and the second during her sophomore year. In letters to her family she fondly called him "Matty" and commended his sensitive treatment of poetry and dry sense of humor. A gay man and socialist who made his political convictions known in the classroom, he was someone she looked back on later in her life with compassion and profound gratitude.

Although at the time she didn't share his political views, she drank in his every word and filed away the breadth of his perspective for future reference. Decades later, she said his class on the poetry of Blake, Keats, Byron, Yeats, and Stevens "perhaps affected my life as a poet more than anything else that happened to me in college." He required his students to memorize and recite poems, which she greatly enjoyed. (Recitation would prove to be excellent training for the countless poetry readings and public lectures she soon would begin giving.) The exercise was part of a full-body immersion in poetry, which involved soaking up politics, too. Adrienne noticed that Matthiessen "spoke of the current European youth movements as if they should matter to us."

At a time when English departments routinely taught great works of literature as intricate, self-enclosed globes of meaning, her professor's discussions of "a world beyond the text" captured her attention. Rich realized he was quietly acknowledging the military veterans attending his classes. They were there on the G.I. Bill, these "men who might otherwise never have gone to college, let alone Harvard, at all."[26] The world and the poems, stories, and plays that attempted to describe it came together every time a literature class convened, so why not talk about the overlap? Matthiessen did, and Adrienne listened. Unlike her other professors, he was not a proxy for her father. He taught her to see literature in historical and political contexts, a lesson that would inform her thinking and writing for the rest of her life. In hindsight, she realized the enormity of his gift to her. Late in life, she dedicated a book of poems to his memory.*

Matthiessen provided her with invaluable scaffolding for her study and writing of poetry, but it was Ted Morrison who critiqued her poems (and stories) during her junior and senior years and did all he could to bring her to the brink of fame. Although she later said she took creative writing classes mainly so she would have time to write, that belies the importance of Morrison's role in her early success. Her journals and letters indicate she was actively seeking constructive criticism beginning with Kempton and continuing throughout her college career. She was extremely receptive to the opportunities Morrison provided her and eager to learn from him. The proof is in her first book, which he helped her call into being and which she dedicated to him.

When he became her instructor in the fall of 1949, the handsome, buttoned-up Morrison had been teaching at Harvard for nearly two

---

* *Telephone Ringing in the Labyrinth: Poems 2004–2006* (2007) is dedicated to Aijaz Ahmad, a poetry translator, scholar, and friend of Rich's, and "in memory of F. O. Matthiessen, 1902–1950."

decades. As director of Bread Loaf, he was well connected in the world of poets, publishers, and literary magazine editors, and counted Robert Frost as a close friend and Bread Loaf colleague. His wife, Kathleen, was Frost's personal secretary. (She also was Frost's lover, a liaison Rich probably didn't know about until after she graduated.) Gentle and personable, less severe in demeanor than Kempton, Ted Morrison advised Rich on her poetic language and challenged her to shake off the spells Yeats and Frost had cast on her. He went out of his way to make sure she and Frost met each other on very nearly equal terms.

Primed by her intensive study with Kempton and Matthiessen, the twenty-year-old Rich arrived in Morrison's writing class a versatile, preternaturally disciplined writer. She would write fiction and verse dramas under Morrison's tutelage, but it was her lyric poetry that showed the most promise. Her early study of meter and verse forms had set her on this path; her lifelong training in music, thanks to her mother, aided the cause. It helped that Morrison loved her writing and saw no end of potential in her. In a 1953 interview with *The New York Herald Tribune Book Review*, the seasoned author and educator called her "the most gifted young person" he had ever taught.[27]

Morrison's receptiveness to Rich seems almost heroic in comparison to the message other young women of the era were receiving from their English professors. In *Minor Characters*, Joyce Johnson (née Glassman) writes about the creative writing class she took at Barnard College, the women's college at Columbia University. It was 1953 and the course was required for students concentrating in writing. The professor began the semester by asking how many of his students planned to become writers. In response to a unanimous show of the young women's hands, including Glassman's, he said he was "sorry to see this" because "first of all, if you were going to be writers, you wouldn't be enrolled in this class. You couldn't even be enrolled in school. You'd be hopping freight trains, riding through America."[28] No matter that he had discredited himself as a writer and teacher of writing (since he wasn't out hopping trains), his point was they couldn't be writers because they were female.

Rich was spared that idiotic pronouncement, but sexism was rampant at Harvard, too. The university wouldn't allow Radcliffe students to use the luxuriously appointed Lamont Library (designated for Harvard College's male student body) unless they had a special dispensation, and *The Harvard Advocate* restricted its staff to male students.

Although there were gestures made toward balance—Radcliffe had its own library, and there were student publications solely for Radcliffe students—it was obvious that the Harvard men were the ones who counted; they were the ones for whom professional and social opportunities would present themselves as if by magic for the rest of their lives. It was precisely because she saw this so clearly that Rich moved in Harvard's circles of male privilege whenever she had the chance. She didn't necessarily like what she saw, but she knew she deserved the same pathways to success that her male peers had.

Rich had the good fortune of coming of age just as the 1950s were beginning, not in the midst of them. Before the era's institutionalized sexism fully took hold, she already believed she was a real artist. She would fall prey to the insidious messages infiltrating the culture at large, like most other women and men of her generation, but at her core, she knew her writing would only get better with time and continued hard work. She would never give up her career as a poet, and her unshakable commitment to writing and her faith in her ability would never leave her.

One could say she was a born writer, due to her father's early and endless tutelage, but she was not a born rebel. She had an idea of what a conventionally popular college girl should be and do, and she was determined to fit that mold even as she aimed to break molds in her writing. Her friend Jane Williams had the room next to hers in Eliot Hall during the 1949–1950 academic year. Jane liked Adrienne and enjoyed her acerbic sense of humor, but at times she found her exasperating. One afternoon, Jane went to her family home in Cambridge and discovered that, unbeknownst to her, her mother was hosting a tea party for Adrienne and Eleanor Pearre. At the moment she walked in, the visitors were inspecting nightgowns from Jane's trousseau. There was embarrassment all around as Jane realized she was crashing a party in her own home.

It was no wonder Mrs. Williams liked Adrienne. The young lady from Baltimore was polite, fastidiously neat, and interested in what other people had to say; her intelligence and wit improved any social interaction. She was so self-possessed, however, that Jane Williams found her intimidating and a little hard to take. Her ambition was palpable, her eventual radicalism as yet unimaginable: "While I knew she was going places, it was not at all clear she was going to break out of her properness or speak out on any issue."[29]

Rich was on the lookout for an equally proper boyfriend. During her first two years in college, she went to countless parties, concerts, and dances on the arm of one date or another, mostly Harvard men but sometimes young men from other prestigious colleges. She relished the rush of male attention, which had been in short supply in Baltimore. During her sophomore year, she met a Harvard Ph.D. student in American Civilization, bearing the wondrously elegant name of Sumner Chilton Powell. By the fall semester of her junior year, they were a couple; by the spring, engaged. Sumner's arrival in her life brought her great pleasure while also complicating her career plans.

Powell was born in Northampton, Massachusetts. His father was an Amherst College English professor who had died of cancer when Sumner was a toddler. His Mississippi-born mother, Theodora Duval Sumner Powell, then moved with her young son to Baltimore, where her late husband's family lived. Her father-in-law, Arthur Chilton Powell, was a prominent Episcopal rector and became an important influence in young Sumner's life. In 1929, the year Adrienne was born, Theodora Powell took a teaching job at Roland Park Country School; she eventually met her son's future fiancée when Adrienne was a student there. There is no indication, however, that Adrienne knew Sumner in Baltimore. He was a few years older and attended the Taft School, a prep school in Watertown, Connecticut. By the time he and Adrienne met in Cambridge, he had served for three years as a lieutenant in the U.S. Naval Reserve, earned his bachelor's degree from Amherst College, and was making good progress toward his Ph.D. at Harvard. He appeared to be a perfect WASP catch with a pedigree that no one, not even Arnold Rich, could find wanting. None of that would have mattered if Adrienne hadn't adored him, but she did—and expected to spend the rest of her life with him.

Brown-haired and plump of face, of medium height, Sumner Powell typically wore a suit and tie and had the look of "an older person," according to Adrienne's dorm mate Jane Roland. He frequently came by Eliot Hall to take Adrienne out on dates, and the two of them appeared well matched in their dressy attire and seemingly even temperament.[30]

A photo of them in the summer of 1950, at Jane Williams's Cambridge wedding, shows a radiantly happy young couple, both of them smiling widely.

By her junior year, she was well known among her English professors as a rising literary talent, but her anticipated life with Sumner had begun to consume her thoughts. Her dual ambitions were very much in conflict, and for a while she told herself that if she had to prioritize, her marriage to Sumner would come first. If she ever feared her writing might fall permanently by the wayside, as her mother's career in music had done, she kept those thoughts at bay.

Her plans were in keeping with the way many young women of her age and social class had begun mapping out their lives. According to the 1951 Radcliffe yearbook, "After graduation, the 'typical' Radcliffe girl would like to combine marriage with a career and raise a family of three or four children. As a housewife, she would enjoy cooking, but would prefer not to do her own ironing. The qualities she looks for most in a husband are (1) consideration; (2) intelligence; (3) sense of humor; (4) popularity; and (5) good looks." This composite portrait resulted from a lengthy poll of the student body conducted in the fall of 1950. Of nearly a thousand young women, about a third responded to the yearbook's questions about family background, academic major, outside reading, hobbies, religion, spending habits, and plans for the future. Those plans leaned heavily toward the domestic. Asked their "intended vocation," 13 percent of those responding from Rich's class and 21 percent of those in the class behind her listed marriage. About a fourth of the respondents in her class were either engaged or already married. Eleven percent of all the respondents wanted to have five children; another 14 percent, six or more.[31] Rich herself wanted to have four children, three boys and a girl as her youngest.[32]

In love with Sumner Powell and planning to marry him, she had no intention of shelving her writing, but Harvard's politically liberal climate had evaporated by her senior year. In its place, a stultifying conservatism had emerged, one that she wasn't yet willing or able to question. As she wrote decades later, "There was nothing overt in the environment to warn me: these were the fifties, and in reaction to the earlier wave of feminism, middle-class women were making careers of domestic perfection, working to send their husbands through professional schools, then retiring to raise large families."[33] She, too, was temporarily caught up in the illusion that women existed primarily to serve men and children, even women who had tremendous talents and ambitions like hers.

In a journal entry written in January 1950, Rich went so far as to lambaste women who dared to challenge the patriarchal order. She was certain that all women wanted to "subordinate" themselves to powerful, admirable men. Whenever a man proved smarter, stronger, or more accomplished, a woman could take comfort (and perhaps mentally even the score, though Rich didn't spell that out) on those occasions "when he comes to her like a little boy and rests his face on her breast. Any woman who says she would trade this for sovereign 'equality' simply doesn't speak truth, or else her emotions are distorted by unhappy experience."[34]

This was exactly the kind of rhetoric that would infuriate her in years to come, but Rich was hardly alone among emerging female poets in thinking this way. Her contemporary Sylvia Plath wrote in her journal a few years later: "I long to permeate the matter of this world: to become anchored to life by laundry and lilacs, daily bread and fried eggs, and a man, the dark-eyed stranger, who [. . .] goes around the world all day and comes back to find solace with me at night."[35] As young women, Rich and Plath both bought into a submissive feminine ideal. That they accepted this, even longed for it, shows just how pernicious and insistent the stereotyping was.

It was around this time that Rich's lifelong penchant for judging others came more sharply into view. She admitted in her journal that physical beauty was very important to her. It wasn't just that she admired good-looking people but also that she recoiled from those who were physically unattractive: "I seem subconsciously to hate them for not being beautiful. No great looker myself, it matters to me immensely that I at least never look my worst to others. I think it is more than vanity, since I am equally delighted to see anyone else looking particularly attractive."[36] Unconsciously mimicking her father, she wanted perfection in everybody and everything around her. She took it personally when people fell short, even when they couldn't help it. She thought they should all work as hard as she did.

This attitude helps explain why she sometimes felt less popular than her peers. Her friends had reason to pull back if they sensed she was passing judgment on them, but she didn't make this connection and ended up feeling bruised even as she longed for close friendships that didn't materialize.[37] There was, it turned out, a great deal of insecurity beneath her remarkable poise—both bred into her by her demanding father.

Not yet able to address his complex influence on her, she sought to fuse her identity with another man's as soon as she reasonably could. Perhaps it felt like the only socially acceptable way to break free from Arnold Rich's control. In February 1950, she recounted a conversation with a friend who asked whether she would publish under her birth name or her married name. Without giving it any thought, she replied, "Adrienne Rich Powell." She had come to believe that her identity was completely fused with her boyfriend's.[38]

Like her thoughts on the sorry fate of women seeking equality of the sexes, these reflections were stunningly at odds with the position that would later make the name Adrienne Rich (with no other surname attached) synonymous with radical feminism. For the time being, she mouthed the language of the patriarchy with the same vehemence that would later characterize her efforts to expose and dismantle that very institution.

Before the start of the spring semester in 1950, in the midst of her junior year, she took Sumner Powell home to Baltimore to meet her parents. It is unclear whether word of their daughter's imminent engagement had reached 14 Edgevale Road in advance. Suffice it to say that Sumner didn't impress either of her parents. Although Adrienne was relieved that her father gave the appearance of approval, she was incensed at her mother for avoiding the topic of engagement during this important visit. They made amends only after Adrienne returned to Cambridge. In response to Helen's letter complaining that Adrienne had ignored her and behaved childishly during the visit, Adrienne said her petulance was proof that she cared what her mother thought; she had only wanted Helen to welcome her future son-in-law the way Arnold had done.[39] But Helen would never have expressed anything counter to her husband's views. Her tacit message of disappointment and disapproval spoke for both of them.

It was not the smoothest start to an engagement, but it would have to do. In subsequent letters home, Adrienne marveled over her fiancé, whom she described as "an incredible phenomenon," an angel with just the right human traits. Her effusive praise of marriage strained hyperbole to its breaking point: "I don't see how the human race, with its talent for making itself miserable, ever invented such a heavenly thing as marriage," she declared. "We are a miraculously perfect pair—no two people ever could have fitted together so well."[40] At twenty, she wanted so much for it all to be true.

# CHAPTER 5

# THE MAKING OF ADRIENNE RICH

*1950–1951*

With Sumner Powell never far from her mind, Adrienne Rich continued to write poems of increasing skill and depth. She had now reached the point where she could realistically pursue publication in national journals. Most young poets overestimate the maturity of their writing, and the proof is in the rejection letters that quickly pile up. That was not her experience. In February 1950, not yet twenty-one, she had her first major literary coup. *The Virginia Quarterly Review* wanted to publish "Aunt Jennifer's Tigers," "Undimensional," and "A Clock in the Square."[1] The first of these, describing a woman whose artistic legacy of embroidered tigers is sharply at odds with her submissive, wifely status, became one of her most famous and frequently anthologized poems.

Rich calmly noted the *Virginia Quarterly Review* acceptance in her journal. A few days later, after the accomplishment had sunk in, she allowed herself to dwell on her success, incidentally in the same entry in which she declared that she would take Powell's name and her identity would forever be fused with his. Here was proof of the split Rich later recognized between the "girl who wrote poems" and the one who defined herself through her relationships with men.[2] That looming contradiction aside, the year was going exceedingly well. To borrow the passage from *Walden* that she quoted to her sister during her freshman year of college, she had once again reached the condition of things for which she was made. Averse though she was to bragging, she could exult privately in her journal. She wondered what she would have thought if someone had told her four years earlier that at the age of twenty she would be an academic success at Radcliffe, happily engaged to an academic star in the making, with three poems slated for publication in an important journal. Not only that but she would also have the guidance of an ideal mentor and feel secure in her sense of who she was. Her sixteen-year-old self would have been astonished by all of this largesse, but she told herself it was only the truth.

Something registered in her mind as she wrote this journal entry. Changing tack, she credited her success to "an unusual background, some hard work, a good deal of idealism and a lot of luck. I hope I can keep it and still remain a decent person. I want above all things to remain human—a creature recognizing my own foibles."[3] It was an admirable sentiment and a rather transparent admission that she was feeling very full of herself. At sixteen she had wondered if someday her juvenile writings would be published in a three-volume set. At twenty that possibility didn't seem entirely farfetched. There was no getting around the fact that a great many of her wishes were quickly coming true. She wouldn't gloat, but her heart sang.

She envisioned her future as a writer and married woman with steady resolve and little idea of the difficulties the combination would entail. In a meeting with Ted Morrison in March 1950, she told him about her marriage plans. If she and Powell couldn't afford to marry right after her graduation, she would take a job. In response, Morrison suggested she apply to the Radcliffe Publishing Procedures course, which would prepare her for a career in editing and publishing.[4] It was this sort of recommendation that made his concern for her obvious. He continued to strategize, with her career interests in mind. A practical course in publishing would expand her connections in the world that meant so much to both of them.

During this time period, Sumner Powell was preparing for his Ph.D. oral exams and had little thought for anything but this tremendously important moment in his academic life. Feeling left out, Rich watched from the sidelines and anxiously contemplated her dependence on her fiancé. She decided her neediness was a characteristic and "selfish" flaw in all women: "Men can really shut everything else out and think of intellectual problems; a woman's mind gets constantly infused with emotions."[5] Such truisms blended her father's doctrinaire thinking with the sexism synonymous with the decade. Perhaps the clichés provided her with a modicum of comfort. Later on, she would regret being so enmeshed in Powell's life. For now, she rejoiced when he passed his orals with highest honors and his professors declared him "one of the best men they ever examined!"[6]

The day after her fiancé's triumph, in the midst of an eventful semester, Rich reeled from the news that her favorite professor, F. O. Matthiessen, had killed himself. He had been in a long relationship with Russell Cheney, a much older painter, who died in 1945. Despondent over Cheney's death and upset by postwar politics, Matthiessen made a dramatic exit by jumping out a twelfth-story window at the Hotel Manger in Boston. *The Harvard Crimson* reported the horrifying news on April 1, 1950, just hours after the suicide occurred. "The 48-year-old professor was an outspoken advocate of Christian socialism," a student reporter wrote. "The note found in Matthiessen's room at the Hotel Manger read in part: 'I am depressed over world conditions. I am a Christian and a Socialist. I am against any order which interferes with that objective. I would like to be buried by the side of my mother in Springfield, Massachusetts.'"[7]

As a child, Adrienne had written an allegorical play about suicide, a subject that continued to interest her philosophically, but Matthiessen seems to have been the first person she knew who took his life. Eulogizing him as if they were peers, she wrote, "Pathetically blind though he was in his misplaced political ideas, I shall always feel the depth of his influence on me, as critic and teacher."[8] She rationalized his suicide as horrible but inevitable in a difficult historical moment. In a letter to her family some months later, she continued to keep her grief at a remove. "I might think that poetry couldn't be given in a course if I hadn't had two courses under Matty both of which increased my insight and stirred me to creative efforts which I might never have attempted otherwise."[9] She seemed to think that her growth as a writer was the only way to justify his importance to her.

The shock of Matthiessen's death receded as Rich's future blossomed before her eyes. Robert Frost was going to give a reading for Radcliffe students, and Ted Morrison had invited her to a postreading party in his honor. It would be her first meeting with the poet whom she most admired. Ecstatic, Rich wrote to her family, "I've wanted this so much—not for the sake of Meeting a Great Man, but because something touches fire when you are trying for the same heights and can glimpse them a little through one who has made them."[10] For all of her talk about the necessity of a woman's taking a subordinate role in marriage, Rich saw no reason to subordinate herself to any other poet, not even Frost. She was that self-confident. Frost was her elder by many decades and as grand an American poet as the twentieth century had yet to see, but she knew she could hold her own with him. The fire, the passion, of his genius would stoke her own.

The night in Frost's company was another pearl in the strand of Rich's fantastic junior year. Unable to contain her ebullience, she wrote to her family immediately after she got back to Eliot Hall that evening. This wasn't the first time she'd heard Frost read, but her familiarity with his engaging public manner only added to her pleasure. On this night, however, the reading was prelude to the main act. She and Frost's granddaughter, Lesley Lee Francis, were the only two Radcliffe undergraduates present at the intimate gathering the Morrisons hosted afterward. Adrienne had ample opportunity to establish a warm rapport with Frost, who greeted her with friendly interest.[11]

Alert to the importance of his every word, she wrote down a generous sampling of his remarks. Irascible and quotable as always, Frost told the small gathering of students and English professors that what made him happiest in life was "never having majored in anything." Furthermore, he was not impressed with contemporary education, which, he said, "fills the mind with a lot of inert matter." This was Frost playing the contrary old gent who could say whatever he pleased, no matter who was pouring his drinks. But beneath the familiar, rather clichéd crustiness lay a mind as coldly luminous as a brand-new scalpel. When that mind lit on poetry, Rich very nearly swooned. "He talked so acutely and honestly about poetry that I sat there swelling inside with a great and joyful assent," she wrote to her family.

Frost then made an unexpected connection between his preoccupation with language and Matthiessen's recent death, confessing that he couldn't help but judge everything he read, even a suicide note, by the same exacting standards he applied to literature. Coming from a poet whose son had committed suicide, this was an extraordinarily telling admission. His unsentimental eye made him who he was: a poet who never went off the clock. His observation would reverberate in Rich's life two decades later.

During the party, Rich found out Morrison had given copies of her poems to Frost. The author of *North of Boston* and *New Hampshire,* among many other volumes, said he didn't read poems by just anyone but was intrigued by hers because they came so highly recommended. As usual, Rich maintained her admirable poise. The antithesis of the giddy coed, she nevertheless exuded a feminine charm in the presence of men she admired, and that heightened the laudatory effect of her desire to engage with Frost and others who stood high on the literary mountain she had begun to climb.

She easily won over Frost, whom she would get to know well in the ensuing years. But equally significant, he gave her a glimpse of something she craved. She saw, as she had hoped, a luminescent twinkling of her own future: "I suppose the truth of it is that poetry will nag me till I'm old and can't even remember lines—though I'd like to be old as Frost is old—and that wherever I meet the embodiment of poetry I am going to be struck by it as by few other things in life. And I have certainly met it tonight." One more thing had made the evening very special, something Rich blithely confessed to her family. In talking with Frost, she felt herself "getting to the fringe of a world I want; it's the good talk and the magnificent humanity of such a man, and what he does to people around him."[12] Frost was difficult and egotistical, but Rich responded to the pure poet in him. The poet in her wanted few things more than to join the circle of poets whose minds had the fire, and the ice, that she saw in Frost.

In the midst of this social and literary whirl, Sumner Powell gave her a diamond ring on May 16, 1950, her twenty-first birthday. The ring made official what they had told her parents months earlier. The diamond was a Powell family heirloom and the gold setting was one she and Powell had picked out together on a trip into Boston. The day before her birthday, she solemnly reflected on her legal coming of age and credited Powell with the maturity she had gained in the past year.[13] The day after her birthday, she wrote about the significance of coming of age while also wearing an engagement ring, both of which she considered enormously significant responsibilities.[14] She did not permit herself even a single day of autonomy. Although she didn't see it this way at the time, the ring signified a continuation of the status quo, her subordination to a man.

Meanwhile, Ted Morrison, another man of influence in her life, had an ace up his literary sleeve. In a move that would dramatically accelerate her career, he encouraged her to submit a collection of her poems to the Yale Younger Poets competition for a debut volume. Morrison was not working alone. A journalist named Bill Stucky, a Nieman Fellow on leave from his job as city editor of the *Lexington* [Kentucky] *Leader*, knew Rich and her poetry from his participation in Morrison's writing course. Stucky spoke highly of Rich to the Yale University Press editors, who, in turn, asked that Rich submit a manuscript.[15] The prospect was thrilling, but Rich was not going to enter unless she thought she could win. In a letter to her father, she alluded to an "extraordinarily exciting" opportunity without sharing the particulars. In a small show of independence, she added that she would not be consulting him about this mysterious matter but would inform him when she had made a decision.[16] Morrison and Powell, however, were allowed to weigh in. After talking with each of them, she worried that she didn't have enough good work to meet the minimum requirement of forty poems. She worked feverishly at revision but remained unsure what to do. Following Morrison's lead, Powell encouraged her to enter the competition.[17]

As the deadline neared, Rich continued to weigh her odds. Perhaps by now she knew the current Yale Prize judge, W. H. Auden, had found no one worthy of publication in the series in 1950. It would be hard to lose out to another poet but harder still to be lumped in with two years' worth of losers. Yet the competition was just the sort of thing she relished: During her first year in college, she had been hysterical with joy when Kempton asked her to apply for admission to his advanced fiction-writing class. Since then, her self-confidence as a writer, in particular as a poet, had soared. She wouldn't let this opportunity slip away.

In due time, she completed a manuscript, titled simply "Forty Poems." On June 15, 1950, she wrote in her journal that she had entered the competition but received no notice from the press other than a letter of acknowledgment. In the same journal entry, she reported that *Harper's* had accepted two of her poems, "Storm Warnings" and "Boundary." This was a good omen as well as good news in itself. On July 6, she wrote that she had earned four A's for the semester and won Radcliffe's Caroline I. Wilby Prize for her poetry.[18] The ever-helpful

Morrison had nominated a selection of her poems for the honor, which recognized the best original work in any department and typically went to a Ph.D. dissertation. Rich was the first undergraduate to receive the prize, which had been awarded annually for more than fifty years.

The news was about to get even better. On July 31, she received a letter from Auden. Writing from Italy, he informed her that "Forty Poems" would be published in the Yale Series of Younger Poets the following year.[19] His transatlantic missive meant the twenty-one-year-old poet was already moving swiftly beyond "the fringe" of the world she had touched in Frost's company and into its very midst.

Over the next several weeks, she corresponded regularly with Auden, who advised her on diction and word choice and recommended that she replace several poems that he didn't think worthy of inclusion in the book. One of those was "Undimensional," which *The Virginia Quarterly Review* had accepted; he thought it sounded too much like Frost. In regard to a line in "Sunday Evening," describing "leather benches in the lethargic car," he wrote, "Can one say that the car is lethargic, when one means the people sitting on the benches?" In case he came across as too picky, he asked Rich to forgive him "for being such an old governess" and do whatever she saw fit. This reassured Rich her judgment of her own work mattered more than anybody else's.

An editor at Yale University Press had told her to choose a more specific title for her book. Here was an instance where Auden thought she should stand her ground; he considered it "a pity" that publishers insisted on specific titles for collections of short poems covering many different subjects.[20] It was a good point, but Rich decided on *A Change of World*. The title of a minor poem in the collection, it held portent in the postwar era. It also provided a touchstone for Rich's eventual renown as an artist capable of great changes in her writing style and worldview.

During this period of mounting success, Rich was at home in Baltimore. She didn't hold a summer job during her college years and went on family vacations as usual. This particular summer, Arnold Rich had contemplated taking the family to Paris, as he had enjoyed doing in the prewar years, but in the end, the trip was postponed until the following summer. Adrienne was restlessly awaiting the start of the new academic year. The same day in early July that she wrote about the Wilby Prize and her excellent report card, she noted, "Papa is already planning for atomic bomb attacks in the next war. [. . .] Cynthia is going out with a lot of college boys and behaving very normally. Mum is, as always, rather confused, worries, but gets things done. Anana has not yet arrived."[21]

It was a cool reckoning. By the end of August, after she won the Yale prize, her feelings for her father had turned distinctly cold: "Papa is like Communion or the Catholic Church—people are drawn to him because he is a sort of absolute authority—a system, left in a world of flux and confusion. For my part I have other sources of order."[22] Arnold Rich had shed his ancestral faith long ago, and Adrienne was neither religious nor, according to one condescending journal entry, willing to take seriously anyone who was.[23] Yet the bond she and her father shared had a distinctly sacred dimension. Arnold embodied power, ritual, and rectitude, and she had spent her life as his disciple. To step outside his force field and view him objectively was akin to heresy. Turning away from him, she could find "other sources of order" in her writing, her studies, and her relationship with her fiancé. But leaving the church of Arnold was no simple task: It would eventually require a mutual excommunication.

In September 1950, Rich returned to Harvard for her triumphant senior year. Far from the constraints of 14 Edgevale Road, she was once again able to write expansive letters home about the joys of living in Cambridge, a place she obviously preferred to Baltimore. Her college town was "heaven,"[24] and Radcliffe College's fall convocation in the First Congregational Church, her version of a religious experience. With a scholar's reverence, she wrote "that the black folds of an academic gown enfold the real trustees and wardens of civilization and the people to whom I would rather belong than any other."[25]

Her selection as winner of the Yale prize reinforced her conviction that she'd found the place she truly belonged. She told herself not to get swellheaded, but there was no reason not to enjoy the attention. *The Harvard Advocate* solicited poems from her; Mary Churchill Small, a Radcliffe dean, invited her to give a poetry reading in a college-wide speaker series; and the editor of *Radcliffe Quarterly,* the alumnae publication, wanted to interview her and publish a selection of her poems.

There was even talk of a feature story about her in *Life* magazine, which would have increased her name recognition exponentially and no doubt helped sales of her forthcoming book. However, Harvard English professor Kenneth Murdock fended off the reporter, whom he didn't like, and shared his paternalistic decision with Powell. When Rich learned from her fiancé that Murdock had intervened on her behalf, she exhaled with relief.[26] She told her parents that during her upcoming meeting with the editor of *Radcliffe Quarterly,* she would keep her comments brief rather than risk saying something that could be misinterpreted.[27]

Her myriad literary successes emboldened her. Though thoroughly enamored of academia, she was no longer in awe of her professors the way she had been as a first-year student. Now, they had to earn her approbation. One who fell far short was Pulitzer Prize winner Archibald MacLeish, the distinguished poet, playwright, and essayist who had preceded Auden as judge of the Yale competition. Rich had signed up for his poetry course in her senior year. In a letter home dated October 28, 1950, she wrote that she had expected the class to be easy but not without merit. Alas, MacLeish was "the greatest wind-bag stuffed shirt, poseur and fraud I ever saw on a Harvard rostrum." She raged against his "overblown personality," "infantile approach to Yeats," and "inept and shoddy" organization of his course. The saving grace, "the greatest single piece of luck I ever had," was that during the previous year she had chosen Morrison, not MacLeish, as her mentor.[28]

The only thing to do was make her dissatisfaction known, so she sought out John Simon, MacLeish's teaching assistant. Like Rich, the Ph.D. candidate in comparative literature was headed toward fame, in his case as an arts critic for *Esquire* and *New York* magazine. Simon's account of his meeting with Rich captures her in youthful high dudgeon: "Back in 1951, I was one of three assistants in Archibald MacLeish's poetry course at Harvard, and a student named Adrienne Rich came to me with an acrimonious complaint. W. H. Auden had just chosen her Yale Younger Poet of the year, yet MacLeish was not paying special attention to her. She had hoped for advanced, personalized treatment, and here she was being denied privileged status. I tried to remonstrate gently, but the Yale Younger Poet-elect indignantly dropped the course."[29] Thinking back decades later on MacLeish's class and his conversation with Rich, Simon observed, "It was a perfectly respectable course in essentially three poets, Rimbaud, Rilke, and Yeats. There was nothing elementary about it, but it wasn't quite a seminar. She had a point, but it wasn't a very good point or a strong point. In any case, the course could proceed quite well without her."[30]

Unable to get anywhere with Simon, Rich turned to Radcliffe's Dean of Instruction, Wilma Kerby-Miller, for help. Happy to oblige, the dean allowed Rich to drop the class and complete the semester with three courses rather than the usual four. Reporting the news to her family, Rich said Kerby-Miller told her she "didn't believe in 'being inflexible with the exceptional person—particularly one who had done a lot for the college'—an aspect that never occurred to me, frankly."[31] Although Radcliffe's class of 1951 would produce two other famous writers—Rona Jaffe and Ursula K. Le Guin—Rich was the known quantity already making good on her early promise. She had sought out the women who ran Radcliffe and they liked her tremendously. It is not surprising they would bend the rules in her favor.

If Rich hadn't anticipated that sort of quid pro quo relationship, now she knew it was possible. In later years, although she repeatedly benefited from good deeds done on her behalf, she refused to feel obligated to return favors. Her resistance was a matter of principle, which could make her seem cold and ungrateful even as it reminded the people around her that she could not be co-opted or bought.

Her book's imminent publication was much on her mind. In November she received the proofs, the sight of which reassured her that *A Change of World* was a worthy effort. To her family, she wrote that it helped her see a direction for her future poetry and that she didn't think she would feel the need to apologize for the book later in her career.[32] In fact, eight years later, she would tell a Yale editor she was no longer satisfied with most of the volume's poems. In the mid-1960s, she would choose only a handful for publication in a selected volume of her verse published in the UK.* But in the months leading up to publication, she had no qualms about the debut she was about to make.

On December 13, 1950, in the living room of Cabot Hall, a Radcliffe dormitory, she had a foretaste of the book's reception. This was the poetry reading Dean Small had arranged, and Rich was delighted with the turnout of about sixty people, including Radcliffe administrators, Eleanor Pearre, other friends from her dorm, Helen Maud Cam (the lone female professor at Harvard), her fiancé, and "a good sprinkling of Harvard men." She read for only twenty-five minutes and offered

---

* Later still, however, Rich would come around to liking the book again and point out that some of the poems foreshadowed her later focus on women's lives.

no comments between poems. The result was a polished performance that made it seem as if Rich had been giving readings for years, or so people in the audience told her afterward. "The response," she wrote to her family, "was very reassuring; a really warm one but not in the least forced." She was pleased that an emotional Eleanor approached her afterward and indicated she knew several of the poems grew out of conversations the two of them had had.[33] All in all, it was a grand evening, the first of many hundreds of readings she would give during her long career.

Aware every word could go for or against her, the determinedly cautious Rich sought to strike just the right note in her interview with *Radcliffe Quarterly*. The published result is so carefully and unspontaneously worded that it seems likely she submitted her comments in writing: "This year I have continued working at both poetry and fiction. I hope to grow more skilled at prose forms, and I keep discovering how much more I need to learn about poetry. That's the general plan for work ahead. My college years have given me more opportunities and more varied stimulation than I could have believed possible four years ago, and I'm deeply grateful to the sources of criticism, encouragement and enrichment that I've found here."[34] With her unerring ability to inspire admiration and trust in her elders, she had intuited what Radcliffe's matronly alumnae would want to hear from one of their own. To borrow the pundit Michael Kinsley's line about Al Gore, the undergraduate Rich was an old person's idea of a young person.

For anyone who wanted to peek beneath that façade, the two poems on the opposite page of the magazine offered compelling material. "The House at the Cascades" echoes Frost's "Directive" in its energetic and ominous depiction of an abandoned house subsumed by the natural world. The man-made structure is no match for the "riot of green" that overtakes it at every turn. It is a poem about the fecundity of loss, the devouring wild beauty that cares nothing for man-made objects in its path. Though it is unsettling, the other poem, "Prisoners," is by far the more malevolent. Its anguished lines describe persons with "faces stiff as mourners," "suffering in one identity" and "lonelier than alone."[35] Written in the first person plural, it conjures a couple or perhaps a family unable to transcend or make sense of a suffocating, rival-making closeness. Was this all a fiction, or was "Prisoners" spinning a dark tale about Adrienne and Sumner, or perhaps pointing an accusatory finger toward 14 Edgevale Road? The seething tensions in the poems, neither of which appeared in *A Change of World*,[36] made one look twice at the author's photo accompanying the two-page spread. Behind the dark gaze and small smile lay a fierce, roiling mind.

❧

*A Change of World* was published on April 18, 1951, in the middle of Rich's final semester at Radcliffe. The first edition is a small hardback with a plain cover; the author is identified by her full name, Adrienne Cecile Rich. Beginning with "Storm Warnings," a measured study in suppressed danger, the poems are elegant and serious, though Rich's intellectualized wit occasionally shines through. The elevating influences of Yeats, Frost, and Auden are clear, though Rich later disavowed their impact and instead identified Louis MacNeice, Stephen Spender, John Crowe Ransom, "and Wallace Stevens to an extent" as the main influences on the book.[37] In addition to "Stepping Backward," the poem based on her friendship with Pearre, a handful of poems stand out as especially lucid and well made: "Aunt Jennifer's Tigers," "Storm Warnings," "For the Felling of an Elm in the Harvard Yard," "A View of the Terrace," and "At a Bach Concert." Given its portentousness, the title poem is a surprisingly slight effort, and some of the longer poems feel like the ambitious undergraduate efforts that they are.

Along with "Aunt Jennifer's Tigers," which shows a female artist subordinated to her husband, several of the poems touch on themes of enduring importance to Rich. In "Air Without Incense," the speaker reveals her inability to believe in organized religion while still yearning for a system of meaning beyond the intellectual and material. "By No Means Native" explores the restless feelings of an outsider, perhaps based on Rich herself, who wants to fit in but can't understand the native ways of the place in which he lives no matter how hard he tries. "An Unsaid Word" initially seems to reflect the antifeminist sentiments that colored Rich's thinking in her twenties, as it imagines a woman nobly choosing not to draw "her man" away from his preoccupying thoughts.[38] But given Rich's belief in the importance of solitude, it can be interpreted more broadly as a poem of fidelity. The woman's respect for the man's need to think his own thoughts does not mean she has no meaningful ideas of her own.

As virtually all of Rich's critics have noted at one time or another, Auden's brief foreword to the book, a convention required of him as series editor, is not especially kind to her. It has gone largely unnoticed, however, that he expected little from *any* poet writing at the midpoint of the twentieth century, other than honesty and an aversion to taking up more space, literally or emotively, than was warranted. In his introduction, he compares reading a poem to meeting a person. While one could make discrete judgments on appearance, intelligence, and character, "these different aspects are not really separate but an indissoluble trinity-in-unity," and in the end, character matters the most. The pretentious, dishonest poem is not to be tolerated: "In art as in life, truthfulness is an absolute essential, good manners of enormous importance."

What he considered a period of stasis in poetry is central to his discussion. The twenty great elder statesmen in modern poetry and other art forms (whom Auden did not name) had responded with a new style to "changes in our civilization" occurring in their youth and early middle age. He predicted that something momentous would have to happen before younger poets would have reason to stake out new ground. Time would prove him right. In the United States alone, the civil rights movement, the Vietnam War, the women's liberation movement, and the gay and lesbian movement would lead to all kinds of new writing across all genres. Without knowing what was to come, Auden argued it would be wrong for poets to manufacture new attitudes just for the sake of breaking from tradition.

In closing, when he turned at last to Rich and *A Change of World*, he wrote:

> Miss Rich, who is, I understand, twenty-one years old, displays a modesty not so common at that age, which disclaims any extraordinary vision, and love for her medium, a determination to ensure that whatever she writes shall, at least, not be shoddily made. . . .
>
> . . .
>
> I suggested at the beginning of this introduction that poems are analogous to persons; the poems a reader will encounter in this book are neatly and modestly dressed, speak quietly but do

not mumble, respect their elders but are not cowed by them, and do not tell fibs: that for a first volume, is a good deal.[39]

His comments uncannily conveyed the appearance and demeanor of the young woman he had not met, the one in heels with straight stocking seams. The description hurt Rich's feelings and maddened her later devotees, but Auden would go no further than the truth as he saw it. In contrast to the decision he had made the previous year, when he refused to select a winner, at least he thought her book deserved to win the Yale competition and be published. His observations amounted to praise in the context of his discussion and, it must be said, despite the permeating cologne of sexism, he was right about *A Change of World*. It was a good and candidly written debut by a young writer: no more or less. Given his low expectations for poetry in an era he considered anticlimactic, it would have been odd if he had raved over Rich and her elegant gems.

His qualified praise notwithstanding, an introduction by Auden was a real boon to Rich's career. His name had the power to attract reviewers and readers who otherwise might never have picked up the book, let alone read it. She knew this, and she also recognized a spur when she got one. In a letter home written May 29, 1951, she declared that she hated seeing the word *neat* applied to her poems. In a letter home written May 29, 1951, she declared that she hated seeing the word *neat* applied to her poems. From now on, she would aim for extravagant messiness like that of Wagner's operas or Leonardo da Vinci's *The Last Judgment*.[40] Few things irritated her more than being patronized, but she intended to put Auden's pronouncements to good use. In the ensuing decades she would gradually move away from her youthful neatness and devote herself to long, discursive sequence poems no one would call quiet or modest. And in keeping with Auden's edict, she would make truthfulness the bedrock of her art.

The reviews that appeared in the weeks and months after *A Change of World* came out were largely complimentary. The consensus was that the young author was very nearly a fully formed poet, someone to watch. In the May 13, 1951, issue of *The New York Times Book Review*—three days before Rich's twenty-second birthday—Alfred Kreymborg wrote, "Miss Rich at 21 is a poet thoroughly trained by masters of verse whom she echoes at times but never slavishly. Thanks to her search for perfection she has composed her poems with an almost flawless perception and sound ear. While one might say that she belongs to an age in which youth is skeptical of a world unmade by tottering elders she is clearly aware of the artist's place in society, and this without special pleading or self-defenses. She is, in short, the kind of neo-classical poet who relies on true form."[41]

In her *New Yorker* review of several women poets, Louise Bogan gave the lead notice and the most space to Rich, of whom she wrote, "She is well read and has a sense of humor and a feeling for variety and proportion. Each of her poems has its own shape and tone; if she is modest, she is not monotonous. And she nowhere succumbs to that urge toward the poetic chic that dates so quickly and now mars certain pages of Edna St. Vincent Millay and Elinor Wylie with a faded modishness."[42] These were two of the most prominent notices and likely the most widely read, but there were many others in small magazines and regional newspapers that warmly greeted Rich as a new talent.

With the book in print and selling at bookstores, including those she frequented around Harvard Square, Rich happily turned her attention to graduation. On the surface, it may seem surprising that her parents chose not to attend, but Arnold Rich couldn't be bothered with pomp and circumstance. Adrienne's artistic achievements were all that mattered to him.[43] And perhaps as a proud southerner, he had no desire to see his daughter so at ease in the northern academic enclave she pointedly claimed as her own. If Cambridge was "heaven," as she insisted, then what was Baltimore? He had wanted her to attend Radcliffe, but he also mocked it as " 'that cow-college in New England.' "[44]

Cynthia Rich represented the family at the festivities. In a letter to Arnold and Helen from Cambridge, she described a busy week, during which Adrienne was "running around in her little black gown and mortar-board to all sorts of impressive ceremonies." Cynthia loved the evening walk she took with Adrienne and Sumner Powell along the Charles River and around campus. She got to go with Adrienne, a new member of Phi Beta Kappa, to hear William Carlos Williams read the Phi Beta Kappa poem at Sanders Theatre. Cynthia didn't like his poem, "The Desert Music," and loyally told her parents that her sister would have done a better job.[45] Adrienne would have her chance in 1966, the year she was named Harvard's Phi Beta Kappa poet.

Radcliffe's graduation speaker in June 1951 was Archibald MacLeish, whose advanced course Adrienne had dropped in the fall. Her journals and correspondence from her undergraduate years suggest her brief time in his presence was the only trouble she ran into during four splendid years at Harvard. One can imagine her narrowed eyes and small, ironic smile as she listened to his speech.

At twenty-two, she was ready to take on the world. In keeping with her pattern of forecasting her biography while her life was still in the draft stage, she paused to acknowledge how she had become the person she currently was. To her father, she wrote, "[T]his place has been my life—remove Harvard and you'd have no Adrienne Rich—all the strands that don't emanate from you and Mother have been woven here, in those intensely significant years of one's maturing."[46] Begun at Arnold Rich's knee, her identification with the male halls of power was now complete, or so it seemed.

She would eventually come to see how problematic that identification was. She would talk about it privately with friends for years and eventually direct her anger and disappointment directly at Harvard, a target she knew extremely well. In a 1973 interview with *The Harvard Crimson,* she spoke in the blunt terms that characterized her feminist proclamations: "Radcliffe girls are a well-to-do, well-educated elite group of women. They are expected to be grateful because they're supposedly getting the same juicy 'carrot' as the men at Harvard. But these equal chances, equal opportunities, this ready acceptance—it's all an illusion and a lie. They're not nearly aware of the ways in which they're being taken. Harvard is an intensely patriarchal institution, in every way."

The mature, darkly meditative Rich saw much to criticize about the school she once said had made her who she was. Even during her time as a student, she claimed later, she knew she wasn't truly "a part of the whole literary and intellectual 'scene' at Harvard, because I was a woman. Women couldn't be on the *Advocate* then, but I was invited to their parties—and felt like some kind of hetaira in the midst of a bunch of condescending men. I always sensed that I was an outsider in a man's literary world."[47] An educated female companion, a step up from an ordinary prostitute, the hetaira could hold her own among powerful men in ancient Greece, but that didn't mean she was having a good time.

In spite of all her successes and all the ebullient letters she wrote home, Adrienne wasn't quite as delighted with her circumstances as she made herself out to be. The internal split between the girl who wrote poems and the one who defined herself by her relationships with men prevented her from speaking up at the time. Eventually, she would look back on the Adrienne Rich of 1951 through a prism of grief and amazement: "I was like someone walking through a fogged-in city, compelled on an errand she cannot describe, carrying maps she cannot use except in neighborhoods already familiar. But the errand lies outside those neighborhoods. I was someone holding one end of a powerful connector, useless without the other end."[48] Creating versions of herself that she could love and respect would be one of the great errands of her lifetime.

# CHAPTER 6

# TOUTE LA GLOIRE

## 1951–1952

During her senior year at Radcliffe, Adrienne's father had encouraged her to continue her studies at the University of Oxford, an ambitious plan he knew would require her to leave Sumner Powell behind at Harvard. She had been intrigued by Oxford for a long time, but in a letter to Arnold Rich in May 1951, she said she'd changed her mind and didn't want to study there after all. She and Sumner had numerous interesting friends in Cambridge, Massachusetts, and she saw no reason to uproot herself when she was beginning to feel like part of the community rather than a student passing through.

Father and daughter had evidently talked at length about Oxford and the advantages it would offer her, and he had agreed to continue paying her bills. Now she was rejecting the opportunity. In her letter, she said nothing about wanting to stay by Powell's side while he wrote his dissertation. Instead, she asked Arnold to understand her feelings and accept her decision.[1]

Determined to put down roots in her college town, she rented an apartment near Harvard and dug into her writing once again. She had a part-time job as a secretary and researcher for Ralph Barton Perry, a Harvard philosophy professor, which allowed her plenty of time to write. She finished a verse drama that Ted Morrison critiqued for her. Longer forms had captured her interest, even as her gifts as a lyric poet were being recognized. A letter from Yale University Press in late July informed her that nearly 400 of the 550 copies of A Change of World had sold, and the press was already preparing a second printing.[2] Although the first printing was small in number, it was standard for a poet's first book. Library sales would put Rich's collection into the hands of countless additional readers.

Encouraged by the book's sales and critical reception, the Yale editors approached T. S. Eliot at Faber & Faber about releasing a British edition. Although Eliot declined, pointing out it would be better to wait until Rich had established her reputation and could command an international audience, he admired A Change of World and went so far as to suggest that in a few years Faber & Faber would consider publishing a selected volume of her verse.[3] Rich would not forget this tantalizing missive. It would take sixteen years, but she eventually would publish her selected poems in Great Britain—though with Chatto & Windus, not Faber & Faber.

At the end of the summer, she rose from her desk and stepped away from her routine. The reason for the hiatus was a trip to France, the last of the Rich family's leisurely vacations, a mainstay of her childhood. Without the financial help of Anana—her paternal grandmother, Hattie Rich—there would have been fewer of the trips abroad, perhaps none at all. As it was, Adrienne shared the family's love of European art and culture. She was comfortable traveling first-class and dressing in a formal gown for dinner aboard an opulent ocean liner. On this occasion, however, neither her parents nor her grandmother nor her sister could jolly her out of the bad mood she brought overseas with her. Cynthia Rich recalled that Adrienne "was determinedly miserable that summer in Paris—which made my father miserable, which made the family miserable."[4] Stewing and glowering, she counted the days until she could be on her own again.

Back in New York on September 19, 1951, she disembarked from the Queen Mary and returned to Cambridge. In October she began researching the application process to Oxford. The Oxford plan was on again, because her engagement was off. At some point during the fall, she had ended things with the studious young man she once described as the perfect combination of angelic and human qualities. Her old friend Peggy Webb Patterson recalled the story Adrienne told her about the breakup: "They went out on a boat together. She was very swept away by the sights, and he wasn't, and that just kind of did it. He wasn't as sensitive as she was. She didn't want to spend her life with someone who was less sensitive."[5] Had Sumner known he could have kept his beloved's heart if only he'd inhaled the salty air and praised a seagull, he surely would have done so. But it would not have mattered, for Adrienne had now fallen decisively out of love.

She soon realized she and her ex-fiancé could not remain friends. On November 5, 1951, she wrote her father that she had ended the relationship after a difficult conversation with Powell about love and the lack thereof. She knew she had hurt her ex-fiancé but didn't think she had harmed him. Continuing in this vein, she explained a key objection. It seemed he didn't know how to be alone with his thoughts; he was incapable of the deep solitude that she considered essential to a truly fruitful intellectual life.[6] Her comments echoed a paper she had written during her freshman year for Kenneth Kempton's writing class. In "Alone," she observed that people who adopt a herd mentality may come to fear the contemplative nature of solitude. She wrote in the essay that if she ever had a child, she would want to cultivate in him the ability to be alone and self-sufficient, because that would lay the groundwork for a balanced, self-confident adulthood.[7] Four years after writing "Alone," she returned to its principles in making her case against Powell. She told her father that the hard-working graduate student lacked the wisdom and judgment she associated with the capacity to be deeply, productively alone.[8] She didn't say the turning point came when Powell undervalued the pleasures of a scenic boat ride. Arnold Rich required a loftier explanation than that.

Describing the relationship's dissolution could not have been easy, especially since Arnold's "I told you so" hung in the air between Cambridge and Baltimore. She wrote him that she knew he had expected her engagement to end. In severing ties with Powell, furthermore, she said she had realized that "one has to hurt the people one would most want to leave intact."[9]

She sounded calm and philosophical, but the fact remained that she had cut all ties with the man with whom she'd planned to spend the rest of her life. During March of her junior year, she had written in her journal about lying in bed with Powell in a vacated dorm room and feeling a deeper peace and contentment than she had ever known.[10] Now the relationship was over, and she was left with the knowledge that she had done exactly what her father hoped she would do. In her letter she made a point of telling Arnold she hadn't postponed the breakup purely out of stubbornness. That in itself showed how enmeshed, and obliquely competitive, she and her father were.

Elsewhere in Cambridge, Sumner Powell was not doing well. Adrienne's rejection of him seems to have coincided with, and exacerbated, the beginnings of the mental illness that would afflict him for the rest of his life. He was deeply depressed after she called off the engagement and, according to a confidant's description, "despaired of all things truly and dangerously."[11] In a year's time, his depression would give way to mania. He would talk excitedly about his plans for a career in politics and imagine Adrienne by his side when he kicked off his first campaign. He would tell his confidant that Adrienne had compared him unfavorably to her artistically inclined doctor father, whom Powell considered the driving force behind her decision to spurn him. As if that wasn't bad enough, she was unconvinced (Powell alleged) that he earned enough money to support her and pay for a household servant in the bargain.

Although he may not have been in a wholly rational state of mind when he made these claims, they are plausible nonetheless. Later on, once she was married and had children, Rich insisted on household help. More to the point, no matter what Powell had done or not done on the ill-fated boat ride, no matter his ability to be alone with his thoughts, he was not the man Arnold Rich would have chosen for his daughter, and Arnold's unenthusiastic opinion of him had become Adrienne's own.

D etermined to get on with her life, Rich applied to Oxford in October 1951. The possibility of an accompanying Guggenheim Fellowship beckoned brightly. Without the publication of *A Change of World,* its many favorable reviews, and her national journal publications, she would have had no reason to apply for this award typically bestowed on older, more seasoned scholars and artists. Energized as always by the challenge of proving herself worthy, she sounded out Henry Allen Moe, the Guggenheim Foundation's secretary, in an understated query letter. Giving only the bare facts of her background, she said she wanted to request a year to write and study at Oxford. Upon learning she was eligible, she applied for a fellowship that would begin in September 1952. Her characteristic earnestness comes through in a draft of her application, in which she asserted her desire "to write poetry addressed to men's hearts as well as their minds; veering in the direction neither of uncontrolled and undisciplined emotion nor of pure coldly educated intelligence." For references, she listed Ted Morrison, Bill Stucky, Dean Wilma Kerby-Miller, and Rollo Brown, a local writer and former Harvard faculty member.[12] Stucky, the Nieman Fellow and newspaper editor who had recommended her work to the Yale University Press editors, had turned out to be an exceedingly loyal friend. His favorable review of *A Change of World* in the *Lexington Herald-Leader* predicted that Rich "may become one of the really first-rate poets of her generation."[13]

While waiting to hear back from both Oxford and the Guggenheim Foundation, Rich wrote steadily and added books on astronomy to the many volumes of history and literature that she was reading for edification and pleasure. When not absorbed in her work, she was lonely, but it was the love *she* had brought to the relationship, not the presence of her former fiancé, that she keenly missed. She realized how much her engagement had shaped her views: "I have for three years felt I was fulfilling myself as a woman, as a passionate being—I pitied old maids, damned sterile feminism, saw in marriage the frame for my whole conception of life. And now I sense that fulfillment no longer."[14]

Even with that insight into herself, she didn't yet see how destructive and ultimately self-defeating her attitude was. What she called "sterile feminism" may have referred to Simone de Beauvoir's *The Second Sex,* first published in French in 1949 but not yet in Rich's library. By the late 1950s, she was excitedly quoting the famed feminist philosopher to Robert Lowell. But in 1951, though she hovered at the edge of a revelation about internalized biases, her main concern was that she no longer felt fulfilled as a woman.

A round this time, the twenty-two-year-old Rich experienced some pain and swelling in her left thumb and forefinger and in her left foot. A doctor diagnosed the worsening symptoms as the onset of rheumatoid arthritis. Now in the grips of a debilitating disease, a chronic autoimmune disorder that would cause her untold misery for the rest of her life, she wrote home about how well she was responding to treatment and how pleased her doctor was with her progress. In her letters she seems to take the bad news with equanimity. She went so far as to tell her father that she viewed her affliction "as a sort of insurance policy" guarding her against "the tumbling of other things" in a time when so much else was going exceedingly well.[15] Yet there were signs that she knew what she was in for. Once, when Cynthia asked her about the affliction, Adrienne responded by screaming at her never to bring up the subject again.[16] The disease was a sign of weakness she could not bear to discuss with her sister.

Over the ensuing years, Rich came to feel that people in physical pain were "used, objectified." She confided to a friend that she had put enormous energy into "hiding my pain because I felt it was a kind of handle on me people could get, in a very superficial way."[17] Though she would have periods of remission and several surgeries that improved and preserved her mobility, physical hardship was now an integral part of her life.

Back in Baltimore, Arnold Rich was devastated. As a pathologist, he knew his vibrantly energetic daughter was in for a lifetime of physical pain and endless medical appointments. The periods of remission would be a blessing, but a flare of acute suffering could occur at any time. The typically ebullient Arnold sank into despair. Cynthia Rich characterized his reaction as one of three bouts of depression that she knew of. The first occurred before his daughters were born, when his sister, Cecile, got married and he was left in a desolate state of mind. On that occasion, Samuel and Hattie Rich had sent their son north from Birmingham to a Canadian ranch where he could ride horses and recuperate in the fresh air. Arnold's third depression would occur in 1953 and again involve Adrienne.[18]

Adrienne, however, had much to distract her from her new medical condition. On February 6, 1952, she received word of her acceptance to Oxford's Merton College. Again, she was experiencing "euphoria," her favorite way of describing the rushes of joy that accompanied her collegiate and postcollegiate successes. She was quick to share the news with her father, whom she addressed as "Joe," a playful nickname for him that she and Cynthia sometimes used. She told him she'd already sent a copy of her Oxford acceptance letter to the Guggenheim Foundation, in hopes that it would strengthen her fellowship application. Excited though she was, she paused to acknowledge her father's willingness to pay for her studies abroad. With Cynthia headed to Radcliffe in the fall, she thought "it might mean something to have me revelling away on Guggenheim's $3500 instead of yours!" But she was careful to add that she didn't expect to win a fellowship; the Oxford acceptance was amazing largesse unto itself.[19]

Her broken engagement was behind her, and she was trying to regain her old footing with her father. Once again she could present herself as the perfect daughter, a model of talent, hard work, thoughtfulness, and girlish insouciance. It was a persona she had adopted a long time ago. She was sick of it, but it wasn't easily set aside without a replacement of some sort. Pleasing and impressing her father was practically a full-time job, one that required not just endless writing and revising but also careful anticipation of his reactions.

She continued to report her news to him. As a girl she had loved his gift to her of a Ouija board, and now she rushed to tell him that her future had become the stuff of premonitions. That very morning, when she received the letter from Oxford, she had stopped by the Radcliffe dean's office to share her happy news with Wilma Kerby-Miller, who was, predictably, thrilled for her. Then, as she hurried out of the building, she saw—or thought she saw—her name in large letters on the wall. Taking it as a sign of what her future held, she felt a rush of emotion at all the good things that had happened to her in so brief a time.[20] This was destiny writ large; this was the way the world looked to Adrienne Rich at age twenty-two.

To her taskmaster of a father, she hastened to add that she suddenly realized that she still hadn't "worked half hard enough." What she had written was only "half as good" as she wanted her writing to be in the future. "For the devil of this success business is that you begin to tell yourself that to be a second-stringer isn't enough; that you won't be satisfied to be a Karl Shapiro or a Dylan Thomas or [Richard] Wilbur— that you want it all—toute la gloire—and if not public gloire, then to leave things behind you that will blaze their way into the minds of men after you're gone."[21]

Poetry was her lifeblood, and she was determined to climb to Yeatsian heights, not dawdle on the low plains conquered by well-known poets of her own era—men who would have been very surprised to hear they were "second-stringers" in her coolly discerning eyes. Yet for all of her triumph, she was still vulnerable in ways she barely understood. She confessed to her father that she had "needed" all her recent good news, culminating in the acceptance letter from Oxford. Failure would have been educational in its own way, "but artistically I should have been left raging with doubts and lack of self-justification. I don't expect things to go on happening so beautifully; but at least now I know where I stand."[22]

She had grown up in a household where all of her actions and desires were subject to her powerful and charismatic father's approval. Although she was fully capable of losing her temper and talking back, she routinely capitulated to him in the end. She had no choice, and the rewards of obedience were generally irresistible. Earning his approval always boosted her self-confidence: She was fine until the next time she had to pass muster.

It was only natural, then, that she would crave the approval of Harvard and Oxford, patriarchal seats of knowledge that were in the business of bestowing favor on their chosen acolytes. These universities were the institutional expression of her father's rule. When they welcomed her into their respective folds, she felt honored and validated, fully alive and real.

In her moments of triumph she ran to her parents, especially her father, with her good news and then quickly reined herself in. Her journals from high school and college are rife with passages of reflexive humility. When her mother chastised her for letting all the attention surrounding the publication of A Change of World go to her head, she responded furiously. Nothing, she insisted, could be further from the truth: She was an exemplar of humility, someone who always kept her ego in check. Although neither she nor her mother put it into words, both of them knew that gloating over her success would be in poor taste, a violation of Arnold Rich's strict code of behavior. And his approval, in the end, was what really mattered. Until that was secured, nothing else counted. And because Adrienne sensed that her father might someday withhold his approval and turn against her, her "self-justification" was always tenuous.

For her and perhaps for him as well, uncertainty was worse than outright rejection. In a poem called "Double Monologue," published a decade later in Snapshots of a Daughter-in-Law, she wrote, "Since I was more than a child / trying on a thousand faces / I have wanted one thing: to know / simply as I know my name / at any given moment, where I stand."[23] Her father had named her and thus defined her in that most fundamental of ways. Well into adulthood, when she was "more than a child" but not quite a self-defined woman, she wanted the results of his endless up or down votes. For lack of unconditional parental love, she would take what information she could get. It was not the same as self-knowledge, but it would offer clues as to which of her thousand faces she would do well to preserve.

On February 14, 1952, Rich gave her second poetry reading in Cambridge. This was a grander occasion than the dormitory reading Radcliffe had hosted before *A Change of World* was published. Archibald MacLeish, whom Rich considered a "wind-bag stuffed shirt," did her the favor of inviting her to participate in a new series presenting young poets, sponsored by the Morris Gray Poetry Fund. *The Harvard Crimson* announced the event in a news item headlined "Rich, 'Cliffe Poetess, Will Read Work Today."[24]

A recording of her reading in Harvard Hall captures loud applause before she began to read. Her belief in the significance of her own work comes through strongly in her self-confident performance. She continued her practice of saying little between poems. As the evening progressed, her witty lines drew rippling murmurs of laughter. She read in a high-pitched, emphatic voice, with an air of theatricality not heard in her first reading or in later years, when she calmly enunciated her poems with spine-tingling gravitas.

The reading was another triumph, yet the audience's reception was not uniformly positive. MacLeish's graduate student assistant, John Simon, was predisposed to dislike Rich's performance as a result of her heated complaint about MacLeish's poetry course. He went to Harvard Hall to confirm his opinion rather than to listen to her poems: "Knowing my skepticism about this reading, Dean Wilma Kerby-Miller of Radcliffe, a charming woman, asked me as we were leaving for my opinion. 'To appreciate it fully,' I replied, 'one would need the combined attributes of a Homer and a Beethoven, namely blindness and deafness.'"[25] It was a memorable zinger, characteristic of the lines Simon would deliver later in his career as a boldly opinionated and highly quotable arts reviewer. But what he'd said about Rich was dripping in misogyny. He could hardly wait to tell the "charming" Radcliffe dean, who helpfully set up his punch line, that a "'Cliffe poetess" was not so special after all.

Rich was, mercifully, oblivious to their exchange. It would be a long time before she realized that men, fronted by male-run institutions, often did whatever they could to silence women and prevent them from making names for themselves. Sadly and ironically, she herself didn't particularly like women during this period in her life or for many years to come,[26] even though she wanted the companionship and validation of female friends. Her tormented friendship with Eleanor Pearre suffered from her ambivalence toward her own sex. She felt more at home in the company of intellectual men, whose minds and attitudes she had been taught to admire and emulate.

In the months after she broke her engagement, she had numerous dates but didn't go out with anyone who captured her interest. On February 21, 1952, a week after her reading, her luck changed. She spent an evening with a Harvard graduate student in economics, Alfred Conrad, who warranted a hopeful mention in her journal. He may have been an acquaintance she had known for a while, since her journal does not recount a first meeting. After their first date, she began seeing him frequently and writing about him at great length. Their shared interests in art, music, and literature, combined with a mutual spark of attraction, filled her with happiness.[27]

Known as "Alf" or sometimes "Al," her new beau was handsome and carried himself with authority. With his heavily lidded eyes and large facial features, he was more virile in appearance than the boyish Sumner Powell. In her journal Rich wrote excitedly of her physical attraction to him. On the brink of a dramatic love affair, she looked in the mirror and saw herself transformed: Her eyes were brighter than usual, her cheeks flushed, her whole demeanor more sharply alive.[28]

Their second date took place on a romantically snowy night at Alf's apartment. Rather than trudging through the snow to a restaurant in Harvard Square, they made a meal of scrambled eggs, rye bread, bean soup, cake, and coffee, which Adrienne pronounced the best she'd had. For entertainment, they listened to classical music on Alf's record player and talked with great ease.[29]

As the evening progressed, Alf began to tell her about his past, and Adrienne listened with rapt attention. To her astonishment, she learned that the attractive man serving her eggs and coffee was married. Not only that but his wife was manic-depressive and confined to a mental institution. Hearing these startling revelations, the very proper young lady from Baltimore might well have grabbed her coat and angrily headed out into the snow. But to her own surprise, she was not put off. Perhaps his unusual story was part of Conrad's appeal. He was by all rights unavailable to her, yet there he sat, his green eyes lingering on hers, his tastes similar to hers, and sexual tension vibrating between them. She would see him again as soon as she could.[30]

The elder of two sons born to Emanuel Cohen and Anna Frank Cohen of Brooklyn, New York, the twenty-eight-year-old Alfred Haskell Conrad came from an upwardly mobile and affluent family. His father had worked his way up in the bedding and pillow business to become co-owner of National Feather and Down. For many years, Emanuel Cohen was an active member, and eventually president, of the Brooklyn Jewish Center. Alfred had graduated from Boys High School in Brooklyn and, while still using the family surname of Cohen, enrolled at Harvard. During World War II, he was an advanced foreign languages student in the Army Specialized Training Program. He went on to earn his bachelor's and master's degrees in economics at Harvard.[31] In the midst of his doctoral studies, he suffered a blow when his original dissertation director, the formidably brilliant Joseph Schumpeter, died unexpectedly in January of 1950,[32] just a few months before Rich endured the loss of F. O. Matthiessen, one of her favorite professors.

Although his family was Orthodox, Conrad was not a practicing Jew. Rich later quoted him as saying of his abandoned faith, *"There's nothing left now but the food and the humor."*[33] At some point before she met him, he had changed his name from Cohen to Conrad and had cosmetic surgery, which made his nose appear less recognizably Jewish. Considering the escalating discrimination American Jews faced after World War II, his actions were not unusual, though rhinoplasty was more common among women than men. Cynthia Rich recalled Alf saying he made the changes at the insistence of his first wife, Annette Strum, though Annette's family disputes that claim. Annette herself had rhinoplasty when she was a young woman, apparently around the time she married Alf.[34]

He had married Annette possibly while he was still an undergraduate at Harvard. Born in 1923, she was a dancer and choreographer—a willowy, beautiful young Jewish woman with a distinctive streak of gray in her long dark hair. She was also very smart. Nettie, as her friends and some of her family members called her, graduated summa cum laude from Brooklyn College, where she was well known for her academic success and creative talent. She and Alf lived in married-student housing at Harvard and rode their bicycles around town. Like Alf, she was in graduate school at Harvard, though her area of study is not known. Her youngest sister, Frances Strum Gilmore, remembers visiting Alf and Nettie and observing that they were part of a young, fun-loving, intellectual crowd.

The fun abruptly stopped when Nettie experienced a manic-depressive episode early in the marriage. Around the same time, Alf was diagnosed with tuberculosis. He was not getting along well with his parents, who didn't accept his new wife. (Annette's family was under the impression that the Cohens had wanted a wealthy daughter-in-law rather than a middle-class dentist's daughter.[35]) His life felt hopeless. After a period of convalescence at the Trudeau Sanatorium in Saranac, New York, he recovered and completed college. But he was now deaf in one ear, possibly as a result of the medication he took for the TB, and his wife, who had studied at the Martha Graham studio in New York, continued to suffer from manic depression. She had been hospitalized several times over the past eight years, initially at an expensive private institution in Maryland and later at McLean Hospital near Boston, her time at the latter facility possibly overlapping with Sylvia Plath's.[36]

Alf provided the broad outlines of his story on his second date with Adrienne. Quick to conclude that Nettie had treated Alf badly, she did not concern herself with Nettie's acute suffering. Instead, she observed in her journal that her exciting new relationship with Alf had put an end to her loneliness. His interest in her made her feel vital and womanly. Letting her heart lead, she decided his marital status was no reason to stop seeing this man in whom she saw "warmth, gaiety, sensitivity and, I think, a growing strength." A sense of destiny having taken hold of her, she decided dating him was right, not just "all right."[37]

The evening after her second date with Conrad, Rich went out with another young man, a graduate student in classics. While seated at Young Lee's, a Chinese restaurant in Harvard Square, she saw Conrad walk in. Several excruciating minutes passed; her interest in the classics student plummeted. Eventually, Conrad came over to her table and told her, sotto voce, to call him later on. With that, her spirits revived. At the end of the dinner, her companion asked if she was always so lively. Rich confided to her journal that her animation was a new development: "I was under something beyond my control—that's how it has felt—and yet <u>this</u> is how I thrive!"[38]

With no time to waste, she called Alf, who invited her to his apartment. Once again, they listened to classical music, this time over steaming cups of coffee laced with brandy. Then the conversation turned to Alf's newly acquired book of drawings by European masters. It was all very proper, but when their hands touched or he kissed her hair in the midst of helping her with her coat, Adrienne inwardly shivered with delight. These small gestures helped keep the sexual tension from becoming more than she could bear.[39]

A week later, she was imagining what a future with Alf would be like. They had spent another wonderful evening together, beginning with dinner out in Cambridge, followed by a literary salon at the home of the literary critic R. P. Blackmur. She knew that being seen with a married man left her vulnerable to speculation and gossip. She was prepared to deal with that in Cambridge, but her parents' reaction was another matter. She had told them about Alf, as she told them about all of her friends, but his inconvenient marital status defied sharing. Perhaps seeing her new boyfriend through her father's censorious eyes, she admitted in her journal that their differences in background potentially posed another problem. And yet she had no intention of breaking things off. Though she wasn't religious, she yearned for the guidance of a higher power.[40]

The next night, after a concert, Alf declared he was in love with her. They had been dating just over two weeks. Rich resisted saying the words back to him, but the next day they talked at length about all that was good about their situation and all that was complicated. Alf, of course, would have to divorce Annette before they could make solid plans, and that would take time.[41] As a means of protecting her heart, Adrienne resolved to continue accepting invitations from other young men rather than committing to one who could not fully commit to her.

No one else had a chance. There were parties and concerts and readings to go to, and Adrienne chose to attend these events with Alfred.

Just as she had promised herself, there was nothing "furtive" in her approach to their courtship.[42] Yet for all her forthrightness, she was privately worried about their long-term compatibility. He had suffered traumas greater than any she had known, but she rationalized that these experiences had imbued him with strength and sensitivity. More of a concern to her, Conrad's striving Jewish origins in Brooklyn contrasted sharply with her "unquestionably Gentile environment in Baltimore." Alf, she believed, "has been a Jew, and I have not, in any real sense."

It would be decades before she claimed her Jewish heritage and ethnicity and in effect came out as a Jew. For the time being, she had no meaningful understanding of Jewish identity, her own or anyone else's. That was by her father's design but also a result of her own lack of investigation. All that Arnold had suppressed and all that she had chosen not to think about rose up before her in the person of Alfred Conrad. Even though he had made an obvious effort to assimilate into secular society, he was still undeniably a Jew. Contemplating his upbringing, Adrienne had to confront issues central to her own: "It would seem to me that Father's attitude—an unspoken one, nearly always—was the right one. That to get the broadest range of experience from life and people one should lose rather than try to preserve a racial consciousness. Yet that consciousness does flare up in the children of a Gentile and a Jew, at some time. And it has to find some expression or articulation—which is what I never had at home."[43] By allying herself with Alf, Adrienne would eventually provoke her father into expressing his views on Jewish consciousness. When that time came, his opinions would stun and sicken her—and force her to choose between him and Alf.

For now, her concerns did not slow the romance, and she continued to mention him in her letters home. As preoccupied as she was with her love affair, she was still thoroughly devoted to her life as an artist. She and Alf attended Dylan Thomas's reading at the Brattle Theatre, "an electrifying experience" that she could hardly wait to describe in a long letter.[44] Even if she couldn't share all the details about her boyfriend, she could certainly tell her parents and sister about her exciting night of poetry at the Brattle Theatre.

Positioned in front of a black screen, the large and dour-faced Thomas had read from John Webster's *Duchess of Malfi,* Shakespeare's *King Lear,* and Christopher Marlowe's *Dr. Faustus* before turning to his own poetry. He read just three of his poems to close out the performance. Along with everyone else in the packed house, Rich hung on every word of "Poem on His Birthday," "When I Was a Lad," and "Do Not Go Gentle into That Good Night." She took note of his heavy face and thick black hair and marveled over the two-octave range of his melodious voice. His total absorption in his art impressed her: Perhaps he was not a "second-stringer" after all. In her letter home, Rich declared that "there is something in his poetry that other poets today are straining for, and achieve only rarely—he has it, it is his native idiom. The auditory imagination!"[45]

With his beautiful voice and carefully planned program of readings, Thomas earned the awe that Rich and others felt as they listened to him. If some people came to see a literary celebrity, they left knowing they had heard a great poet. These were object lessons for Rich, who would go on to give countless powerful readings. Her own incantatory voice enhanced her reading of her poems. Although she needed solitude to write and regain the physical energy that her chronic illness took away, she was extroverted by nature and comfortable in front of an audience. She had played the piano for most of her life and performed in choirs; she had gladly taken lead roles in high school theater productions. During her first public reading at Radcliffe, her well-modulated voice had drawn praise. As she realized anew while listening to Thomas, a melodic voice and a strong stage presence were gifts to be cultivated.

Thomas was not the only one drawing attention that evening. Before the show began, two young men seated next to Rich were engrossed in books of Thomas's poetry when a friend joined them. Glancing their way, she couldn't help reading a note the newcomer had passed to the man beside her: "'You're sitting next to Adrienne Rich!'" Her initial amusement gave way to discomfort: The scrawled comment "made me feel like not myself but a Thing."[46] Although there were many poets in Cambridge, Rich was the young breakout star whose prizewinning book was for sale all over town. She wanted acclaim and recognition, both of which she was beginning to get. She didn't want to be a mere celebrity—someone known, in Daniel J. Boorstin's phrase, for being well known. But her abundant talent, combined with a deep reservoir of ambition and steely charisma, would eventually make her truly, deservedly famous.

About a month after Thomas's reading, on April 10, Rich opened an acceptance letter from the Guggenheim Foundation. The decision was hardly surprising, given her run of professional good fortune. Had she asked a judge or committee for the moon in those days, who knows but she wouldn't have come home to find a cratered chunk of it glowing on the street in front of her apartment. The fellowship would cover not only her expenses at Oxford but also her desired travels across Europe. She was quick to call home with the thrilling news and follow up with a letter the same day: "I could kiss the hem of St. Gugg—it's a very noble largess indeed."[47]

That evening, she and Alfred celebrated with a cocktail party at his apartment. The guests included his dissertation director, Wassily Leontief, and his wife, Estelle; a young Harvard economist named Robert Solow, who would go on to win the Nobel Prize for Economics in 1987, and his wife, Barbara; and Alf's brother, Morris Cohen, a lawyer who would later make a name for himself as one of the nation's preeminent law librarians.[48]

Bob and Barbara Solow had previously socialized with Conrad and his wife, Annette Strum. Thinking back more than half a century about their younger friends' marriage, Bob Solow said, "Alf and Nettie appeared to us to get along fine. She was fragile and he was caring. I don't remember tension. Nettie did 'modern dance' though I imagine she had had ballet training." He and his wife never learned the details of her illness but were aware when she was hospitalized. Nettie struck him as "a little remote," someone who "didn't relate well with other people. She tended to be in her own world."

As for Alfred, the Solows liked him and enjoyed his company. Bob Solow remembered him as a friendly man who smiled frequently. "He was wry, humorous, liked to be agreeable. Not self-effacing exactly, but definitely not attention-grabbing." In time, he and Barbara got to know Adrienne and Alfred together. "I think that when we first knew Adrienne she was on the whole cheerful and ebullient, with little of the darker intensity that came later. Her poetry was no secret, but not much of a topic of conversation. I thought of them as a fine couple."[49]

Dating Conrad brought Rich into contact with a new set of Harvard intellectuals, including the Solows and Leontiefs. They were significantly older than Rich, sophisticated, and experienced in the ways of the world. Her Guggenheim likewise expanded her circle of friends and acquaintants. Among the other eight local winners, all men, were the poet Richard Wilbur, whom she already knew and liked, and Vladimir Nabokov, a visiting lecturer, whose fame would grow exponentially a few years later after he published *Lolita*.

The poet and critic Randall Jarrell would later compare Rich to a princess in a fairy tale, and she had reason to feel like one as she mingled with great writers much older than she was. At a cocktail party honoring Wallace Stevens following his reading at Harvard, she chatted with the modernist luminary, whom she would later cite as an important influence on her poetry. Writing home about his stage performance, however, she criticized his "very monotonous" and hard-to-hear voice, which had irritated her throughout his reading. As for Stevens the party guest, she declared him "somewhat of a stuffed shirt," a term previously reserved for Archibald MacLeish. Fortunately for her, there were other people to talk to, including Nabokov. With unabashed delight, she wrote to her family, "Vladimir Nabokov hailed me with a joyous— 'Hello, my sibling!'"

The great novelist was not the only one who recognized Rich as a fellow Guggenheim winner. Renata Poggioli, wife of Slavic studies scholar and Guggenheim recipient Renato Poggioli, gaily told Rich she should spend her whole fellowship period in Italy, as she and her husband planned to do. Rich also chatted amiably with Harvard professors who were stars in the local literary firmament. Among them was Perry Miller, the renowned intellectual historian and expert on American Puritanism. She wrote that the "terror of the graduate students" had "leered charmingly" at her and said he'd been hearing about her for a long time, presumably from Sumner Powell, whose academic specialization was the Puritan era. Refusing to let Miller's insinuations rattle her, she responded by praising his lectures on Kierkegaard. The forty-seven-year-old historian had "quite melted" at the praise.[50]

It was this sort of occasion that Rich had in mind when she later recalled feeling like "some kind of hetaira in the midst of a bunch of condescending men" during her formative years at Harvard.[51] Though she performed her expected role with Miller, she was perhaps not as amused by her conversation with him as her letter to her family would suggest. In her journals and letters home (which her parents saved for her), she stored away incidents and impressions she would revisit and analyze later on. As readers of her later essays would find, the telling moments in her life were vivid touchstones in her discourses on women's history. Her understanding of her experiences helped her identify patterns of social injustice that historians of her era, most of whom were white men, were unable or unwilling to see.

In the spring of 1952, Rich pushed onward with her writing, but she had a lot to juggle and think about: a new love affair, an accelerated social life, potentially debilitating arthritis, and the chasm opening up between her and her parents. She couldn't bring herself to tell them the extent of her feelings for the man she kept mentioning in her letters. She was essentially hiding in plain sight, and at times worry and guilt overtook the thrill of the romance.

Perhaps even if Alfred's marriage hadn't stood in their way, she would have hesitated to reveal her feelings for him to her parents. For she continued to have doubts about this man she had known only a couple of months. She was aware of being on the rebound and still not convinced she and Conrad were well suited. She wanted to throw caution aside, but her concerns kept up a steady drumbeat in her head. The differences in their backgrounds could not be ignored, and now in her journal she added "ill health" to her list of worries—presumably a reference to her rheumatoid arthritis, though she also may have been thinking of Conrad's experience with tuberculosis. Those issues were on one side of the scale. On the other was the love between them, which she felt transcended quotidian logic. The scales teetered precariously from side to side as Rich braced herself for the decision she knew she had to make. In a moment of pained candor, she wrote that she knew their marriage would be hard.[52]

In July she returned to Baltimore and began preparing to leave for England. Just weeks earlier, Baltimore had seemed like the seat of her troubles. Now, when she looked back on Cambridge, the city she had once called heaven, she thought of the extreme emotions, not all of them celestial, that had beset her while living there. She told herself that Cambridge had made her who she was; she had once given that credit to Harvard, but now she allied herself with the larger city. Her understanding of Cambridge in relation to her own identity was a work in progress that would continue for many years, but one thing was certain: She had outgrown 14 Edgevale Road. Even a brief stay upset her. She wrote in her journal of feeling stifled in the house where she had spent her youth. Her bedroom was a particular source of irritation. As "a sort of palimpsest" of her high school years, it revealed nothing about the person she had become in the time since then.[53] She could not reasonably expect her childhood room to reflect her more mature identity, but sleeping in that room, that house, squarely confronted her with the girl she once was. Her presence added a living, breathing layer to the palimpsest. She could not divorce her old self, nor could she go back and rescue that self, but she could express her discomfiture in the privacy of her journal. Her anguish circled back to her father, "so wide in thought and so narrow, so cruel and so benign, so possessive and so generous, so disturbing always to me." Due in large part to his dominating ways, she could not relax around him or fully articulate her thoughts and feelings in his presence. "He <u>has</u> dominated me, and yet I am his daughter, and perhaps more like him unconsciously than he or I know."[54] Her resemblance to him was one of the great revelations of her life. In her mature writings, she would come back to it again and again, surprised, pained, and newly unburdened with each retelling. Arnold Rich was as inescapable as her shadow. To rage against him was to rage against an integral part of herself.

By now she was sure that she would marry Alf. She knew it would be a mistake to announce their plans to her parents when Alf still had a divorce to arrange (a daunting prospect, since the law at the time made it difficult to divorce a mental patient). But her mother's nervous questions were edging ever closer to the love affair no one dared talk about openly. Adrienne's imminent departure for England made the circumstances all the more strained. Though she was loath to keep secrets from her parents, as evidenced by her prolific and detailed correspondence with them, Adrienne could not bear the confrontation with her father that would accompany full disclosure of her feelings and her plans.[55]

While trouble simmered at 14 Edgevale Road, Adrienne turned her thoughts to her first public lecture. On September 18, 1952, shortly before she departed for England, she gave a lecture and poetry reading for the Maryland Historical Society and the English-Speaking Union. Her hosts had suggested her topic, "Some Influences of Poetry Upon the Course of History," which Rich took up with enthusiasm. The occasion in Baltimore marked her debut as a public intellectual, a career that was to run parallel to her life as a poet and later as a college professor. The speech was published in the December 1952 issue of the *Maryland Historical Magazine*. Rich's audience expanded further still when a writer for *The New York Times Book Review*, J. Donald Adams, used her essay as the basis for a 1953 column on the value of reading contemporary poetry. In "Speaking of Books," Adams lauded Rich for her lucidly argued essay.[56] Although she conceded that few poems had changed the course of history, she argued persuasively that poetry and history were closely tied and that great poetry captures the spirit of life and social interaction in ways that are of enormous value to a collective understanding of history and human nature. No doubt glad for the distraction from her private worries, she poured her intellect into this reflective and engaging talk.

The fortuitously assigned topic stayed with her. In her later years, she came to new conclusions about the lasting impact of poetry and her own ability to shape political discourse and therefore influence history. In a 1982 reading, for instance, she asserted that "the earliest poetry, which was tribal and passed down through oral traditions, was political. It gave warnings and advice and helped structure society. I want my poetry to be political in that sense."[57]

Whatever anxiety she felt about giving her first formal lecture, Rich put on a confident face. In a profile published the day before her talk, *The Baltimore Sun* quoted poems from *A Change of World* and described the author as "tremendously excited" about her upcoming talk. In the reporter's admiring estimation, the twenty-three-year-old Rich was a "svelte brunette" with a "clear, light voice." The accompanying photo shows her in a dark blouse with a small brooch at her throat; her hair curls away from her face. A study in hard-won perfection, she is no longer quite the dewy young woman of her yearbook pictures.

As was the case with so many of her photos, her gleaming dark eyes seem to look far beyond the photographer in front of her. It is as if she is returning the searching gaze of posterity. As curious as she was about her future, she was equally curious about how future generations would see her. In unimaginably distant years, she wondered, would she be remembered for her poems? In February of that year, on the glad day of her acceptance to Oxford and not long before meeting Alfred Conrad, she had suddenly glimpsed her own name looming mystically before her in large black letters. Would *toute la gloire* cling to her name like a wreath of laurels? Leaving her father's house, she set out to make it so.

# CHAPTER 7

# CLEOPATRA OF OXFORD

## *1952–1953*

W hen Rich embarked on her year as a Guggenheim Fellow, she left behind Harvard, the oldest American college, for Oxford, the oldest university in the English-speaking world. Its many colleges and gardens were integrated into the city to dazzling effect. Beyond the city, the countryside was peaceful and beautiful. It was all new to her. She beheld Oxford and its environs with awe, just as she had Cambridge, Massachusetts. Though she couldn't block out anxious thoughts about her engagement, the Old World beckoned. She had won the right to be there and soak up all the knowledge and experience that she could.

She took up residence in the Oxenford Private Hotel on Magdalen Street, where a Miss Barton served as proprietress, and set about exploring the Bodleian Library, known locally as the Bod or the Bodley. Her beloved Harvard Yard receded from her thoughts as she made her way around the imposing Mob Quad and the Fellows' Quadrangle, both part of Merton College and among the many quads integral to Oxford's constituent colleges. Women were not officially admitted to Merton until much later, but, as a visiting student, Rich was assigned a Merton don as her tutor. Among her Merton contemporaries was track star and future neurologist Roger Bannister, who, in 1954, was the first to run a mile in under four minutes. Literary eminences who preceded her at Oxford included Matthew Arnold, Lewis Carroll, Oscar Wilde, T. S. Eliot, and W. H. Auden. Yet again Rich was in a rarefied patriarchal world. Yet again, she flourished.

Ancient and wondrous though it was, Oxford was a college town through and through. Its community of literary scholars and young poets offered Adrienne a new take on what she had known and cherished at Harvard. Her letters to May Sarton give a glimpse of her first months studying abroad. In response to Sarton's inquiry about her work, she wrote in February 1953 that she'd been afraid she would arrive in Oxford only to discover she had nothing to write. But instead she had been extremely productive in the fall and was delighted with the "intensively literary environment" at Oxford. "Even at Harvard there's nothing quite like it, as I'm sure you know—the concentration of people and ideas and careers in London, Oxford and Cambridge."[1]

It didn't take long for her to find her way into the university's literary circles. Among the poets she got to know was Elizabeth Jennings, an Oxford resident who was a few years older and already making a name for herself. Jennings biographer Dana Greene writes that Rich joined a circle of young writers, including Geoffrey Hill, Paul West, Anthony Thwaite, and Donald Hall, who gravitated toward Jennings and humorously called themselves "the Elizabethans."[2] Rich also became good friends with Jenny Joseph, another young Oxford poet, who later became famous for "Warning," a whimsical poem that inspired an international social group for older women, the Red Hat Society.

Rich was delighted to meet up again with Hall, who had taken her out a couple of times during their undergraduate days. Now in his second year at Oxford, where he would earn a B.Litt. in 1953, he was busily publishing his poems, networking with other poets, and continuing the editing career he had begun at Harvard. As an undergraduate, he had edited *The Harvard Advocate Anthology,* thanks to John Ciardi, who in his capacity as Twayne Publishers' poetry editor asked Hall to take on the project. While at Oxford, Hall was literary editor of *The Isis,* a student publication. He gave pride of place to Rich's long narrative poem "Autumn Equinox" in the magazine's Christmas supplement of 1952. (Perhaps drawing on Rich's soured view of Sumner Powell, the poem is a Frostian tale of a woman looking back without fondness on her long marriage to a dull and predictable English professor.) While in Oxford, Hall and Rich developed a close bond, which they kept up by correspondence once Rich returned to the States.

In Hall, Adrienne had found a poet friend she trusted and admired. She had long wanted such a friend with whom she could share drafts of poems and trade literary news and gossip. Her interest in him was strictly platonic, and it was the rare note from her that didn't include warm greetings to his wife, Kirby, yet the avidity and strenuous good cheer of her letters reflect a desire to please and impress. It was as if now that the epistolary relationship with her father was in decline, she craved an intellectual man to fill the void. Her letters to him, and to other male poets later on, were a form of courtship, a pursuit of the approval she once had from her father, and often were written in the jocular style she sometimes used when writing to Arnold Rich.

A note to Hall in February 1953 was typical. She sent him a poem she said reflected his influence and that of Gerard Manley Hopkins—a pairing clearly designed to flatter her friend. "Now I want you to look at it and tell me what is the matter with it. It's only a verse exercise really but I need advice from a master of translingual prosody." And in May 1953, when her time in Oxford was winding down, she wrote him a valedictory letter pronouncing him the conduit of "all the best of Oxford" that she had known, "directly or indirectly." Going still further, she wrote him "that of all the clever and sensitive young men you seemed the only person who really cared passionately about poetry— the thing itself, not Being a Poet or poetry as drawing-room gambit or any of the other things that most people stop at."[3]

Hall's rising status as a poetry editor made him a particularly valuable friend for her to cultivate. As founding poetry editor of *The Paris Review*, he published Rich's "Snow Queen" in the second issue, in the summer of 1953. The journal quickly became a plum publication credit for writers on both sides of the Atlantic. Her "Recorders in Italy" appeared in the fall/winter issue of 1954–1955, which also featured poems by A. Alvarez, the English poet and critic who later wrote eloquently about the suicide of his friend Sylvia Plath. In addition to Rich and other Harvard friends, including Robert Bly and Richard Wilbur, Hall published Jennings and Hill, whom he considered his best friend at Oxford. University connections were paying off for all of them.

Not only did Hall publish Rich in *The Paris Review* and *The Isis*; he also chose a selection of her poems for a pamphlet in the Oxford University Poetry Society's 1953 Fantasy Poets series. In a review of the series, *The Times Literary Supplement* identified her as one of "the young Oxford poets" using formal meter and stanza patterns reminiscent of Yeats. The reviewer commended her "moderation of aim and the confidence with which she handles the admirable form" in "Versailles," a poem in her Fantasy pamphlet. Although the writer had good things to say about the other three poets, including Geoffrey Hill, it was Rich who received the lead notice.[4] Readers could reasonably conclude she was the most promising of the lot.

While in Oxford, Rich also became a regular contributor to *The New Yorker*, a rare coup for a poet in her early twenties. She had seen an opening when *The New Yorker*'s longtime poetry editor Louise Bogan favorably reviewed *A Change of World*. In response, Rich sent a batch of poems directly to her. Bogan wrote back that she admired the poems and was forwarding them to Katharine White, the magazine's current poetry editor. In due time, White also wrote. It seems there had been a lapse in communication, since the magazine had been waiting to hear from Rich. White thought Howard Moss, the assistant poetry editor, had already solicited poems from her.[5] Over the next several years, there were other lapses: Rich's submissions were occasionally misplaced or her accepted poems were slow to be published, matters that irritated her and made for awkward exchanges between her and various editors.[6] Still, her *New Yorker* years raised her profile considerably and boosted her self-confidence.

A punctilious editor and gracious correspondent, White sent along detailed comments on the poems she and her colleagues wanted Rich to revise. Among these was "Living in Sin," destined to become one of Rich's best-known early poems. Poet and editor went back and forth about the title, which White considered too colloquial and familiar an expression. White proposed "Illicit" as an alternative title for this poem about a young woman's oppressive domestic life with her boyfriend. In response, Rich stood firm, arguing on behalf of the original title's "moral irony." As a concession, she suggested putting the title in quotation marks. White replied that she and her colleagues were persuaded by Rich's argument and now preferred the original title, without quotation marks around it.[7]

After the magazine had published five of her poems in rapid succession, White offered her a first-reading agreement. For the privilege of considering her poems before she submitted them anywhere else, *The New Yorker* would pay her a hundred dollars for a one-year contract and boost the rate of payment she received per line of verse.[8] Though she may have mentally leaped for joy, Rich responded with muted thanks.

Her strong sense of self-worth and professionalism told her to assert herself as an equal partner rather than play the grateful supplicant.

During the early months of the first-reading agreement, Rich mailed her poems from Oxford and eagerly awaited the response, which sometimes came from White and sometimes from Moss. To Hall, who had not yet published a poem in *The New Yorker,* she wrote with increasing bravado of her dealings with these editors. In May 1953, she told him the magazine had accepted "Love in the Museum" but rejected "Second Honeymoon" and "The Middle-Aged": "They never do take the ones I think of as being most NYkerish but maybe that's good for my soul."[9]

By the mid-1950s, White was working from her home in Maine, which she shared with her husband, E. B. White, the famed author and *New Yorker* writer. Though she still had a say in what was accepted or rejected, Moss was poetry editor. Rich didn't feel any rapport with him and noted with annoyance that his secretary signed his letters to her.[10]

Her writing of publishable poems while in Oxford speaks well of her ability to follow through on her plans, despite the distraction of her long-distance relationship with Alfred Conrad. During the fall and winter of her fellowship year, she was busy with her tutorial and weekly lectures; in the spring of 1953, she ended her academic studies without a backward glance so she could travel around Europe. True to her word in her Guggenheim application, she was in Oxford to learn and write, not to earn a degree. Her spring travels fulfilled the other objective of her fellowship plan. She loved Italy and made a point of going back before returning to the States. Throughout this period, she was writing steadily with an eye toward completing the manuscript that would become her second volume, *The Diamond Cutters and Other Poems.*

The strangest episode of her Oxford sojourn involved an elaborate act of surveillance that would have sickened and infuriated her if she had known what was going on. The person surreptitiously seeking intelligence on her was none other than her erstwhile fiancé. Traumatized by their aborted engagement and suffering from what appears to have been a bout of mania, Sumner Powell sought out Bernard Crick, a twenty-three-year-old English wunderkind and Harvard faculty member in political science. To Crick he poured out the tale of his love affair with Rich. Now twenty-eight years old, Powell wanted Crick to help him find someone in England who could go to Oxford and pump Rich for information and report on her appearance. In the weeks leading up to Christmas of 1952, the two young men orchestrated their scheme from across the Atlantic Ocean.

Crick's friend Francis Celoria, a graduate student in archaeology at the University of London, was the spy of choice. He opened up his mail one day to find a copy of *A Change of World* and a check for twenty dollars from a stranger named Sumner Powell. A day or so later, he received a lengthy typed letter from Crick, playfully laying out the plot. The political scientist and the historian wanted the archaeologist to figure out a way to take Rich on a date and then send them a letter including as many details about her as Celoria could muster. Powell was willing to underwrite the whole thing, as evidenced by the book and the check. Throughout the letter to Celoria, Crick's elaborate literary comparisons and humorously ironic turns of phrase sent a double message: He wanted his friend to know they could have a good laugh at the obsessed American's expense and get the material for a novel in the bargain.[11] Crick fancied he and Powell and Rich were akin to characters in Shakespeare's *Cleopatra*: "I am playing Eno Barbus [*sic*] to his Anthony, that is exactly the set-up, now no bum steer, chum."[12] All of this meant, of course, that Rich had the title role.

The broken engagement of two young Americans thus became the stuff of a droll British drama with a lascivious wink for all involved. Charmed and amused, Celoria was happy to take up his part. The two young Brits wanted to believe what they were doing was all in good fun, nothing more or less than a "sophisticated adventure."[13] There was no malice in their intent, but neither Celoria nor Crick gave serious thought to their exploitation of an unsuspecting young woman. As for Powell's obviously disturbed state of mind, it became a source of concern later on but didn't deter the other two from pursuing the scheme. The "pleasant madman," as Crick called him, had not only poured out his tale of romantic woe in great detail; he also bragged about how smart he was and declared he was going to run for the state senate and later become a U.S. senator. Crick related all of this in his lavishly apostrophizing letter to Celoria, which Powell apparently was permitted to read. In a penciled note at the top of the first page, Crick referred to the letter's contents as "nonsense" and directed Celoria to a private postscript, which read: "This man is a bumptious s—t."[14] Nonetheless, the game was on.

Celoria went to some trouble to obtain Rich's address. He then wrote to her at the Oxenford Private Hotel. In a letter to Crick and Powell, he described the four-page missive he sent to Rich as "a murderous masterpiece of Machiavellianism. I believe it contained 95% truth but 110% dishonesty." Writing from London, he told Rich that his English friend Bernard, lately of an American university, had sent him a copy of *A Change of World,* which Bernard admired. Bernard had suggested Celoria seek out the author, known to be in Oxford on a Guggenheim Fellowship. Since Celoria claimed to share his (made-up) friend's pleasure in her poems, he wanted to exchange letters and arrange a meeting. He knew Rich might be reluctant, but he "felt sure she was not a 'stuffy' person." Although he hadn't made a copy of his letter to her, he provided Crick and Powell with his recollection of the letter's closing appeal: "For surely you are not a stuffy Minerva of Scholarship, nor yet a gawky Artemis who will trot off distantly into the woods, but rather, if I read your poems aright you are a fairly sad Proserpine out of cosmic context." There was further silliness that Celoria found embarrassing to recount, but it was too late now: The letter had been sent.[15]

When Rich didn't reply to this peculiar overture, Celoria gathered his courage and picked up the phone. The beginning of the conversation was awkward on both sides, but Celoria convinced her he was a harmless admirer and potential friend. She was pleased to learn he was studying classical geography at the University of London and told him her father had a large collection of ancient world maps. With this small bridge between them, she agreed to meet him for lunch in Oxford.[16]

Powell wrote frequently to Crick during this time. By the end of November, he was at home in Baltimore in his family's care. In a letter to Crick written on a family member's letterhead, Powell alluded to a difficult meeting with a Harvard dean and a psychiatrist. Undaunted, he remained obsessed with Adrienne. He went so far as to imagine they might marry in Paris at the start of the new year and launch their own personal "Change of World," as he fancied it.[17]

Powell's collapse caused Crick, his Harvard accomplice, to write to Celoria twice in rapid succession. Celoria was alarmed. By now he had met Adrienne. He said the new revelations about Powell's state of mind caused him to rewrite the report he'd originally planned to send. The narrative he enclosed, however, doesn't appear to hold much back. Addressed to both Powell and Crick, his eighteen-page handwritten letter brings Adrienne to life in remarkable, even poignant detail. It was exactly what Powell had wanted.

In the hour or so before their first meeting on November 22, 1952, a nervous Celoria worried that Adrienne might be a physically imposing woman, taller than his five feet, eight inches. To calm his nerves, he shopped for books at Blackwell's. When he emerged from the bookstore at one o'clock, a young woman bundled up in "a bluish-red coat" was approaching him on the sidewalk; it was the outfit his date had said she would wear.

Happily for him, she was "not six feet high." The two walked to a restaurant Celoria knew to be good, but seeing it was crowded, they went to another, smaller place. As they walked along, chatting about Oxford and their studies, Celoria mentally recorded her appearance:

She would be about the height of Joyce [Crick's girlfriend] or perhaps half-an-inch less. Her hair seems brown and not fair, tidy but not overgroomed, since there were a few fringe-like wisps accustomed to lie in undisputed positions. Her face was clearly roundish with slightly (very slightly) plumped cheeks. I must admit that I cannot recall the colour of her eyes or the shape of her nose. Her lower lip, I believe, juts out a little and makes her face incline to the cheekily piquant rather than the very pretty. There may be some freckles here and there. I think there is also a slight stoop in the manner of Susan Shields or Judy Loveday, but it is almost imperceptible. Though she was well wrapped in woolens and tweeds I believe she has a reasonable figure. She prefers medium-heeled and high-heeled shoes to flat heels. Her gloves were green.[18]

In her red coat and green gloves, Rich was festively dressed for the Christmas season. By this time in her life, she had been on many first dates with witty young intellectuals, and Celoria was certainly in that camp. But his roundabout way of seeking her out must have intrigued her. Perhaps, on some level, she saw the date as an audition: If things didn't work out with Alf, here was a potential replacement, a young, single classical archaeologist whom her father might actually approve of.

Over lunch, Rich responded cheerfully to questions about her interests and activities. She was taking driving lessons but had yet to master the English roundabouts; she was planning to spend the holidays with friends in Vienna. (Celoria may have misremembered this, since elsewhere Rich writes of going to Paris for Christmas.) Even the facts Powell already knew must have fired up the synapses in his tortured brain: "She had a sister; her parents had honeymooned in North Africa; A-C-R had herself been there on a family trip and saw places like Casablanca. Spending her holidays in Europe she has garnered quite a knowledge of France and Switzerland. Italy she does not know."[19]

Rich was willing to devote a sizable portion of her weekend to her attentive new acquaintance. After lunch, Celoria bought her a book (*The Quest for Corvo,* by A. J. A. Symons) he had mentioned during the meal, a gift that delighted her, and then took her by bus to Blenheim Palace for a walk around the grounds and tea at a place called the Bear. He had planned this outing on the recommendation of a friend who considered the Blenheim-Bear combination an ideal date. Rich evidently enjoyed herself but had to return to Oxford for an evening engagement. They arranged to meet the next morning.

It was during their second meeting that Celoria tricked her into discussing her father and her broken engagement. Using a newspaper book review as a prompt, he began a conversation about the Victorian poet Elizabeth Barrett, whom Robert Browning had sought out after reading her published poems. Eventually they married, against her father's wishes. Styling himself "a windbag pseudo-Browning," Celoria asked Rich if she had an "Elizabeth Barrett Browning Complex." Rich was quick to assent that she did indeed. He then made up a story about an American girl who fell in love with an excellent Englishman (based on Sumner Powell), only to break up with him inexplicably and go home to the States.

He wrote in his report: "Adrienne questioned me closely on the characters of these lovers and was given data derived from a source that would have startled her if she had discovered it. She suggested that love might be all very well, say at twenty but could its context be slid across the scale of time to apply at the age of thirty? People 'grow'; one has to be sure that there is 'growth' on both sides."

Rich allegedly said she had ended an engagement "for very similar reasons." She went on to say she decided her former fiancé wasn't going to grow along with her, and, no, she didn't think they would ever get back together. She felt bad about the breakup, since he had not taken the news well. When Celoria asked whether she had been in love with the man in question, he quoted her as saying, "'I cannot say, I really don't know what love is.'"[20]

Before leaving for Oxford, she had written in her journal about her love for Alfred, and she told Donald Hall she loved the man she had left behind for a year. But her father's vitriolic reaction to her fiancé had ruined any chance she might've had for a youthful, uncomplicated understanding of this intensely human emotion. Long after her peculiar meeting with Francis Celoria, she would continue to puzzle over the nature of love, in both her life and her writing.

By January 1953, Powell was a patient at a private psychiatric facility. He had received electric shock therapy, which he thought improved his condition. Ever optimistic, he had not given up on his dissertation, and Rich had his heart, as ever. "I gather by implication, that she is still sitting at the Feet of Great Men, (and at those of Papa??)—what I need to know," he wrote to Crick, "is what spins in her dreams & how long will it take to help her form new webs, new patterns, new dreams?"[21] Those were very pertinent questions that Rich would answer in her own time and in her own way, though not in response to Powell.

**P**owell was not the only Harvard man thinking obsessively about Rich. In her absence, Conrad had untangled himself from Annette Strum.* He was now anticipating Adrienne's return to Cambridge so they could marry and begin their life together.

The time had come for them to inform her parents of their plans. While Adrienne held her breath across the ocean, her fiancé traveled

---

* There is no record that Conrad and Strum divorced in Cambridge, Massachu-setts. However, since Strum went on to marry again, it seems evident she and Conrad were legally divorced.

from Harvard to 14 Edgevale Road to announce his intentions. Cynthia was at home when this visit took place, and Arnold asked her, not his wife, to be present for much of the awkward meeting.

According to Cynthia, Alf talked freely about his previous marriage and his name change from Cohen to Conrad. Eventually, Arnold allowed Cynthia to leave the room. He and his prospective son-in-law continued to talk. After Alf left, Arnold sought out Cynthia again. He made it clear he didn't like Conrad and didn't trust him. He was well acquainted, of course, with the anti-Semitism Conrad was trying to escape. He could hardly object to the name change, since his own father had changed his surname from Reich to Rich, a less markedly Jewish name. But perhaps it was the combination of the name change and nose surgery that led him to view Alf as devious or duplicitous in some way. Alf's treatment for TB and his recent divorce also raised questions. Was he healthy enough to remarry? Had he dishonored himself by giving up on his wife, who suffered from mental illness?

Whatever it was that rankled him, Arnold had made up his mind, and his judgment was final. He strongly objected to Alfred and looked down on his parents, since he generally considered Orthodox Jews clannish and lowbrow.[22] Emanuel Cohen's success in business meant nothing to him. No matter that he had not met either Emanuel or Anna Cohen, he held fast to his belief that the Cohens of Brooklyn were not good enough for the Riches of Baltimore.*

In "Sources," the long autobiographical poem she wrote in the early 1980s and mostly addressed to her father, Rich included a prose passage that described Alf as "the other Jew. The one you most feared, the one from the *shtetl*, from Brooklyn, from the wrong part of history, the wrong accent, the wrong class. The one I left you for."[23] In hindsight she saw her marriage to Conrad as a supreme act of rebellion. Choosing a husband should have been her decision alone, but Arnold Rich had called the shots for so long that he didn't see it that way, and it took every drop of courage and rebellion Adrienne had in her to defy his wishes.

---

* There is irony here, since Conrad's first wife, Annette Strum, had not felt welcomed into his family. Now Conrad was the one who didn't have his future father-in-law's approval.

Because Adrienne was still on her Guggenheim Fellowship, they communicated by mail. Arnold's long, hateful missives were laced with anti-Semitism. The letters filled her with grief and outrage. On May 1, 1953, as she prepared to travel to Florence, she wrote in her journal of the matters she needed to attend to and then added, "Over all the weight of Father's most recent letter, the chill of English weather, the soreness in my bones." Her arthritis possibly worsened by stress, she felt deeply alone and in need of someone to take care of her, "and yet I go on nerve, somehow, at the hectic pace required for travel and for pulling up roots."[24]

She had confided in Donald Hall, who said that during their Oxford days, "she talked about Alf all the time. I didn't know a great deal about him but I knew he was an economist and I knew she loved him—and I knew that her father disapproved." Hall said that one day when he dropped by to see her, she was "crying and furious" over a "nasty letter" from her father. "She said he was anti-Semitic, and didn't want her to marry a Jew."[25]

Arnold had essentially gone mad; he wrote her letter after horrible letter. In a later poem, she recalled "my Jewish father writing me / letters of seventeen pages / finely inscribed harangues."[26] Writing to Hall from Florence on May 9, 1953, she said she was exhausted and could do little else besides sleep. She hoped things would improve soon, but in the meantime, she wished she could discuss Theodore Roethke with him "and forget about myself."[27]

While in Rome, she was overcome with loneliness and anxiety. In early June, she wrote in her journal of her longing for Conrad and the guilt that consumed her because she was making her own choices in life. Her complex relationship with her father was at the root of it all: "Father is with me like a nightmare."[28] Two days later, she again wrote about the horrors of standing firm between her father and the man she planned to marry.[29] Despite her pattern of temperamental outbursts, she had always acted the part of the dutiful and loyal daughter; to marry Conrad would destroy that illusion once and for all. But by now she felt it would be unhealthy for her to be anywhere near her father.

She tried to keep her pain at a remove in "The Tourist and the Town," subtitled "San Miniato al Monte." The poem, which she wrote in 1953 and included in *The Diamond Cutters and Other Poems*, explores the difference between the tourist who sees only the beautiful surface of a town and the one who suffers there and becomes truly part of the place. Like Wallace Stevens before her, Rich distilled her strong emotions into a glistening, impersonal revelation. It is only in the third stanza that the poem edges toward her experience:

> Here she goes untouched,
> And this is alienation. Only sometimes
> In certain towns she opens certain letters
> Forwarded on from bitter origins,
> That send her walking, sick and haunted, through
> Mysterious and ordinary streets
> That are no more than streets to walk and walk—
> And then the tourist and the town are one.[30]

Rich originally used masculine pronouns in the poem. "But the tourist was a woman—myself—and I never saw her as anything else. In 1953, when the poem was written, a notion of male experience as universal prevailed which made the feminine pronoun suspect or merely 'personal,'" she wrote in a note included forty years after the fact in her *Collected Early Poems* (1993).[31] To take her gender out of the poem entailed "footwork of imagination," as she later ruefully described her prefeminist approach to writing poetry.[32] It would take many years and a completely new reckoning of her life before she could write in the first person about the hardships of that time.

Likewise oppressed by Arnold, Cynthia Rich had nonetheless chosen to defer her enrollment at Radcliffe for a year so she could live at home and write fiction. For she, too, had an eye on a writing career and wanted to qualify for an advanced fiction-writing course at Harvard. In the fall of 1952, she began her freshman year at Radcliffe and became part of the Cambridge scene that Adrienne had described with ecstatic delight. Strangers pointed her out as the sister of the local literary star, and both Sumner Powell and Alfred Conrad thought of her as a useful conduit. Cynthia didn't want to be drawn into her sister's affairs, especially since she resented her parents' preoccupation with Adrienne's social life—a preoccupation that Adrienne's long, newsy letters home from college had fueled—but the family drama was hard to escape.

When Cynthia saw Powell around Harvard, he spoke of a scheme that would involve a hometown boyfriend of Cynthia's and somehow, in his mind, draw him closer to Adrienne. Alarmed, Cynthia warned her friend to beware of any contact with Powell.

Her conversations with Conrad were also discomfiting. There was nothing she could do to change her father's reaction to the pending marriage, but Conrad seemed to think his fiancée's sister could be of use. On one occasion, Conrad asked her to lunch at the Harvard Faculty Club, an invitation designed to impress. In the midst of their discussion of his vexed engagement, she shared her perspective: "I had made it clear that I was being made truly miserable by my parents' behavior, to the point that I wouldn't go home during vacation."

To her surprise, it appeared her companion was barely listening. "I was struck by Alf saying to me in a breathless kind of way, 'You are just so beautiful when you're unhappy.' I don't think I felt like trusting somebody who could say that." While the remark could be read as flirtatious, she didn't think he was coming on to her. Instead, she felt he was changing the subject because he was uninterested in her feelings.[33]

Meanwhile, Adrienne continued to date, as seen by her leisurely weekend of activities with Francis Celoria. In her journal she wrote about an unidentified man who confessed his love for her. She did not return his feelings, but they had spent enough time together for him to feel strongly attracted to her. She became close to another man, who later became the subject of her poem "For L.G.: Unseen for Twenty Years." According to the poem, they walked around Paris together, talking at length, and felt a mutual attraction they both knew would go nowhere: "Your words have drifted back for twenty years: / / *I have to tell you—maybe I'm not a man—/ I can't do it with women—but I'd like / to hold you, to know what it's like / to sleep and wake together—*" Written in 1974, the poem imagines the man going on to a life of cruising bars and cocktail parties, or "maybe you live out your double life / in the Berkeley hills, with a wife / who stuns her mind into indifference / with Scotch and saunas / while you arrange your own humiliations / downtown." It was possible he had a much better life than what she envisioned for him, but Rich knew they shared "the fear of being cripples in a world / of perfect women and men." Their choices at the time seemed predestined: "[D]ear heart, I know, had a lover gestured / you'd have left me / for a man, as I left you, / as we left each other, seeking the love of men."[34]

॰॰

During her year abroad, Rich accomplished all she set out to do. She wrote steadily, published in high-profile magazines, studied at her leisure, made new friends and literary contacts, and adventurously traveled around Europe. On the surface, it was an enviable sojourn, yet in 1968 she remembered it as the worst year of her life.[35] Her desire to marry Alfred had exposed her father's very worst qualities. He was obsessive, controlling, and completely lacking in empathy. His expressions of anti-Semitism were staggering. But that actually may have made it easier for Adrienne to go ahead with her plans. There was no reason to obey him now that he had lost all sense of reason and proportion. Even so, the resulting break with her father, her lifelong tutor and tormentor, caused her pain beyond reckoning.

In returning to Cambridge, Massachusetts, she would begin a new phase of her life. At times she felt real joy, as evidenced by her letter to Katharine White of *The New Yorker* excitedly announcing her upcoming marriage (while arranging a time she could meet the editor regularly publishing her poems).[36] But her father's refusal to bless the nuptials, and her mother's unwavering loyalty to her father in all things, made for a hard journey. More than twenty-five years earlier, Helen Jones Rich had sailed alone, from New York to Paris, carrying a long letter from her new husband—the infuriating missive spelling out his demands of her that she had thrown overboard. Now Adrienne Rich sailed home, angered by his controlling ways.[37] He would not make her decisions for her any longer, but his judgments were not easily dismissed.

After Adrienne's return to the States, she went to Cambridge for her wedding. The service took place on Friday, June 26, 1953, at Harvard's Hillel House "under a portrait of Albert Einstein." Rabbi Maurice L. Zigmond conducted the ceremony uniting an assimilated Jew, who had changed his name and nose, to the daughter of an assimilated Jew full of anti-Semitic self-loathing. No family members from either side were present. "My parents refused to come. I was marrying a Jew of the 'wrong kind' from an Orthodox eastern European background," Rich wrote years later. "My father saw the marriage as my having fallen prey to the Jewish family, eastern European division."[38]

The marriage certificate gives the bare facts of the day. The groom, Alfred Haskell Conrad, was twenty-nine years old and his bride, Adrienne Cecile Rich, was twenty-four. He listed his occupation as economist. The author of *A Change of World* listed no employment; she was merely "At Home." The economist lived at 17 Gray Street in Cambridge; the bride gave her home address as 14 Edgevale Road, Baltimore, Maryland.[39] She had no identity or means of support beyond the family home she was leaving and the husband's home she was about to join. Stepping out of Hillel House on that June day, emancipated at last from her father's control but still in the firm grip of the patriarchy she didn't yet object to, the poet Adrienne Cecile Rich was now Mrs. Alfred H. Conrad, wife.

CHAPTER 8

# THE UNBORN SELF

*1953–1957*

L ike most woman of her generation, Adrienne Rich had wanted
to marry young, and Alfred Conrad was in many ways an ideal
husband for her. He was smart, well read, ambitious, humorous, and
handsome. He even had green eyes—her favorite eye color. He wanted
her to succeed in her career as much as she wanted him to succeed in
his. They loved each other and had a strong sexual connection. But
she became his wife thinking she had a script to follow. If everything
about that script had been at odds with her goals and objectives, she
would have known right away. As it was, the intermittent dissatisfaction
confused her and blocked her as a writer. Beginning in 1953, the year
she married, she had no idea how to reconcile the genuine pleasures of
marriage and domesticity with the uncanny feeling she was performing
a tedious bit part in a play that would never end.

During the first several years, her letters to Donald Hall portray
a busy young newlywed attending faculty parties with her husband,
learning to cook, and finding humor in situations that struck her as
inherently foolish. Four months into her marriage, she wrote Hall, "I
have been playing the Young Faculty Wife and going to Ladies' Teas in
hats, where one shakes hands with Mrs. Pusey and gets a cup of coffee
poured by Mrs. Levin."[1]

Mrs. Pusey was the wife of Harvard's new president, Nathan Marsh
Pusey, and Mrs. Levin was the wife of Harry Levin, an English profes-

sor and Joyce scholar whom Rich later angrily claimed did not allow women to take his classes. These women derived their status from their husbands' standing at Harvard. The same was now true of Adrienne Conrad. It didn't matter whether she was the author of *A Change of World* or a Guggenheim recipient; what mattered were her husband and her hat.

Alfred faced no such bifurcation of his identity, but the pressure on him to succeed was enormous. He did not publish a book based on his dissertation, "The Redistribution of Incomes and the Matrix Multiplier: The Impact of Fiscal Policy on the Distribution of Income in 1950." Eventually he made his mark in a new subfield called "cliometrics," defined as "the application of economic theory and quantitative methods to the study of history,"[2] and sometimes called the "new economic history." It is categorized within econometrics, "the application of statistical and mathematical theories in economics for the purpose of testing hypotheses and forecasting future trends."[3]

Throughout their years in Cambridge, Adrienne and Alfred socialized with his economics department colleagues and their wives. Prominent among them were John R. Meyer and his wife, Lee. Meyer and Conrad were graduate school friends who later collaborated on an important article and subsequent book. In the period before either couple had children, the Conrads and Meyers got together regularly. The Meyers' son, Robert, heard about their camping trips when he was a child. His parents were very fond of the Conrads: "Adrienne was the writer, my mother the aching to write, and [the] men were the social thinkers." Robert Meyer recalled that his mother treasured a poem Adrienne wrote just for her.[4]

The Conrads also were close friends with Alf's dissertation director, Wassily Leontief, and his wife, Estelle, who introduced them to the bucolic pleasures of Vermont's Lake Willoughby. In a letter to Hall, written in August of 1955 from Lake Willoughby, Adrienne called Alfred "the Beard," a joking reference to the beard he had grown during their vacation. They were spending much of their time with the Leontiefs, who had a summer home near the lake. She said the two men had gone trout fishing that day, and Alf returned with no fish and reported that he and his friend had talked about "marginal productivity." In the same letter she enclosed a draft of a poem about a dead or dying fisherman.[5] If the poem is based on Alf, it implies Adrienne perceived deep feelings of isolation and sorrow lurking beneath her husband's genial exterior. Far worse, it anticipated an early death for him.

The untitled draft stands in stark contrast to the favorable impression Conrad made on most people he met through his wife. Peggy Webb Patterson, her childhood friend from Roland Park, said, "I was very much impressed by him. To me, he was good-looking and strong and very male. He reminded me of the sort of person you could see in another age. Dashing."[6] Boston poet and editor Peter Davison thought of him as "charming and outgoing."[7] The poet Kathleen Spivack, who got to know Rich in the early 1960s, considered Conrad the "perfect" foil for his intense wife.[8] Smiling, cordial, and gently humorous, he made a pleasant impression without revealing much about his inner life.

Cynthia Rich saw more of Alfred than many of Adrienne's friends did. She was aware of his surface charms and his devotion to her sister but didn't feel she ever got to know him. On the occasions when the newlyweds visited her in her Radcliffe dormitory, she was uncomfortable: "They wouldn't look at me, or ask me about myself. They looked at each other and talked about people I didn't know, agreeing on their contempt for those people. It felt like judgments on others was their great bond." She thought both Alf and Adrienne were "self-dramatizing."[9]

Donald Hall wanted to be friends with Alfred but didn't feel his interest was returned. After he finished his degree at Oxford, he spent a year at Stanford as a creative writing fellow and then returned to Harvard. As a member of Harvard's Society of Fellows, he had a flexible schedule: "[I]n my first year back in Cambridge I took care of my baby Andrew while my first wife Kirby went back to Radcliffe and took her B.A. So I did breakfast and the morning bath and so forth with Andrew, and once a week Adrienne came over at eight a.m. and we talked poetry until midday." His rapport with her didn't extend to her husband. "I never felt close to Alf. I felt that he did not want to be close to me. There was something stiff about him. I wondered if it was because I was also a poet and a male? I have no reasons for this speculation. Maybe he was shy of new people, and a bit off to others?"[10] In her letters to Hall, Rich appears oblivious to the emotional distance between the two men. She quoted Alfred's response upon hearing Kirby Hall was pregnant: "Great day in the morning!"[11] She seemed to think Hall would appreciate her husband's spontaneous remark, though his choice of expression conveys surprise, perhaps, more than delight.

Conrad may have felt threatened by his wife's close friendship with Hall, in whom she had confided when she was receiving her father's terrible letters before her marriage, but he was willing to socialize with him and his wife's other poet friends. When Robert Bly visited their household in October 1953, Alf joined their tipsy shouting match. According to Rich's letter describing the occasion to Hall, Bly "told me I should write in the American tradition and I said I was a woman and could only write about immediate subjective things and Alf said I'd insulted myself as a poet, and Bly kept invoking Napoleon and Jesus Christ, not defining anything."[12]

At another party, Adrienne and Alf sparred with fellow guests, including a man they didn't know, about the creative merit of academic criticism. Just to be contrary, they insisted that literary scholarship could not be creative, only to find out the stranger with whom they were butting heads was Bill Phillips, editor of the *Partisan Review*. To Hall, Rich wrote cavalierly that she expected harsh reviews from the journal from now on.[13]

Around the time Conrad completed his Ph.D. in 1954, he began job hunting while continuing to teach and conduct research at Harvard. The possibility of a job at UCLA caught his attention and Rich's, though they weren't eager to leave Cambridge. In the meantime, they were planning to start a family. If Adrienne wanted to publish a new book of poems, now was the time to get on with it. She had plenty of poems to choose from. With her characteristic care, she organized the best of the poems she had written since the publication of *A Change of World* into a cohesive collection and began looking for a worthy publisher. Though contractually obligated to allow Yale University Press to consider her new manuscript, she aspired to greater prominence than she thought her first publisher could offer her. Yale rejected her collection in late April 1954, with editor Eugene Davidson citing the press's limited budget for poetry books. He praised Rich's writing and suggested what she already knew: A trade publisher would help her reach a larger audience. He said Yale was going to devote its poetry resources to W. S. Merwin's second book, which he promised to send her. Rich responded graciously. She admired Merwin's poems and would soon become friends with him. More to the point, Davidson's decision freed her to shop elsewhere, as she wanted to do.

The top two presses on her list were Knopf and Harcourt Brace, but neither was interested in her submission. Suddenly worried, she turned to Katharine White. Her calculatingly humble letter to this important editor was a rare instance of Rich's asking a literary elder for help.

The ever warm and gracious White wrote back with the names of several publishers with which she had connections. The best of the lot was Harper & Brothers, which had published *Charlotte's Web*, her husband's masterpiece. Rich was quick to take the suggestion and soon had a book contract from Harper. Her editor was Elizabeth Lawrence. Although Rich later complained she had been made a token in the male literary establishment, she could have pointed out that the publication of her second book was largely a women's project. Without White's name providing Rich with an entrée, who knows but that Harper might have rejected the book, just as Harcourt Brace, Knopf, and Yale had done.

The forthcoming volume was now called *The Diamond Cutters and Other Poems*.[14] Rich had a knack for elegant book titles, and this one was much better than two possibilities she had discarded: *Talk of Earth* and *The Celebration in the Plaza*. Publication was set for 1955, four years after her debut volume—a much longer gap than she would have liked. Though her poems still appeared regularly in *The New Yorker* and elsewhere, she wasn't writing as prolifically as she once had. The fallow periods disturbed her, and even the prospect of her new collection didn't set her mind at ease. She was beginning to feel fissures in her identity as it became harder to compartmentalize her roles as writer, wife, and soon-to-be mother.

On March 28, 1955, Rich gave birth to David Ephraim Conrad. The page proofs for *The Diamond Cutters* arrived the same day. On April 1, Conrad wrote to Elizabeth Lawrence, reporting that mother and son were doing well. He promised her Adrienne would begin correcting proofs as soon as she could, though she might miss her deadline by a few days.[15] His ebullient letter radiates a new father's joy and love for his wife and newborn son.

Rich's emotions were much more complicated. Her mother had not come to stay with her during the final days of her pregnancy, when she could have used the help and emotional support. As she wrote in *Of*

*Woman Born,* things got much worse when she became ill shortly before giving birth:

> Two days before my first son was born, I broke out in a rash which was tentatively diagnosed as measles, and was admitted to a hospital for contagious diseases to await the onset of labor. I felt for the first time a great deal of conscious fear, and guilt toward my unborn child, for having "failed" him with my body in this way. In rooms near mine were patients with polio; no one was allowed to enter my room except in a hospital gown and mask. If during pregnancy I had felt in any vague command of my situation, I felt now totally dependent on my obstetrician, a huge, vigorous, paternal man, abounding with optimism and assurance, and given to pinching my cheek. I had gone through a healthy pregnancy, but as if tranquilized or sleep-walking. I had taken a sewing class in which I produced an unsightly and ill-cut maternity jacket which I never wore; I had made curtains for the baby's room, collected baby clothes, blotted out as much as possible the woman I had been a few months earlier. My second book of poems was in press, but I had stopped writing poetry, and read little except household magazines and books on child-care. I felt myself perceived by the world simply as a pregnant woman, and it seemed easier, less disturbing, to perceive myself so. After my child was born the "measles" were diagnosed as an allergic reaction to pregnancy.[16]

Helen did visit her in the hospital, but there was no meaningful reconciliation. Rich was left to figure out motherhood on her own. The books she read on the subject were of little help. She tried mightily to tend her child, her living creation, and still write poems, the artistic creations she lived for. The balancing act proved treacherous for her. With the benefit of hindsight, she began to understand how unformed she was, how much she craved an identity for herself that went beyond disparate fragments. In *Of Woman Born,* her narrative of pregnancy and childbirth emerges as her own creation story:

> I still identified more with men than with women; the men I knew seemed less held back by self-doubt and ambivalence, more

choices seemed open to them. I wanted to give birth, at twenty-five, to my unborn self, the self that our father-centered family had suppressed in me, someone independent, actively willing, original—those possibilities I had felt in myself in flashes as a young student and writer, and from which, during pregnancy, I was to close myself off. If I wanted to give birth to myself as a male, it was because males seemed to inherit those qualities by right of gender. And I wanted a son because my husband spoke hopefully of "a little boy." Probably he, too, wanted to give birth to himself, to start afresh. A man, he wanted a male child. A Jew, and a first-born, he wanted a first-born son. An adult male, he wanted "a little boy."

I wanted a son, also, in order to do what my mother had not done: bring forth a man-child. I wanted him as a defiance to my father, who had begotten "only" daughters. My eldest son was born, as it happened, on my father's birthday.[17]

Gazing back at the early years of her marriage, Rich rubbed her eyes in disbelief. How could she have been so naïve? How could she have ignored her "unborn self" for so long? Her husband and in-laws had happily anticipated the children she would bear, but, she emphasized in *Of Woman Born,* "I had no idea what *I* wanted, what *I* could or could not choose. I only knew that to have a child was to assume adult womanhood to the full, to prove myself, to be 'like other women.' "[18]

But the author of *The Diamond Cutters* was not like other women. She was still young, in her mid-twenties, and she had made the leap from a university press to a prominent New York trade publisher. There was no mistaking the fact that she was a professional poet. In the circles that mattered to her, she was a name to be reckoned with. She may have privately bowed under the weight of societal expectations, but her public persona was one of great self-confidence. Her identity as a poet was never in doubt, not to her or to anyone who knew her outside the confines of Harvard tea parties.

Despite her later criticism of the volume, *The Diamond Cutters* was a solid, if not dazzling, sophomore effort, as major reviews attested. In *The New York Times Book Review,* John Holmes praised "her extraordinary skill, her tuned ear, her sure control of language"—compliments she'd received after the publication of her first book. Recalling Auden's comment that Yeats and Frost were obvious influences on her debut volume, however, he said Auden's influence was now present, as well: "It is unfortunate that in an otherwise fortunate book that his face should peer from the boughs more than once, and in the very first poem, 'The Roadway.'"[19] The transparency of her influences in *The Diamond Cutters* was one reason Rich later came close to disowning the volume. But Holmes's memorable image of wizened male elders parting the branches of her poems made her seem like more of an apprentice than she actually was.[20]

It took a while for critics to perceive what was going on in the new book. Years later, in a review of Rich's early volumes, Helen Vendler aptly identified "homelessness, with its accompanying ache of filial nostalgia," as the key theme in *The Diamond Cutters*.[21] Rich had been living in Oxford or traveling in Europe when she wrote many of the book's poems, but it was very likely her estrangement from her parents that threaded the book with its feelings of pain, loss, and displacement. And as a new wife weighing her individual needs against society's expectations of conformity, she was beginning to ache in new ways she barely had words for.

In "The Middle-Aged," she writes of visiting the beautiful home of an older couple whose faces mirror the understated elegance of their possessions and surroundings. The narrator, seeming to speak for a young married couple, knows the elders "would share anything they had but could not transfer their experience," replete with the silences accompanying the stains and cracks and locked-up letters that characterize their seemingly tranquil life together. The understanding would come later, Rich writes, when the younger couple has lived a long time together and become inured to the compromises and silences underlying a peaceful union.[22] These closing lines make a poignant leap in logic. Whatever grace and wisdom a couple might attain in middle age, a price has been paid in suffering and conflict. The only way to really understand that is to live it for oneself. Given the exigencies of her early married life to a man her parents had rejected, Rich had a head start in comprehending that truth.

"Living in Sin," one of the book's many poems that first appeared in *The New Yorker,* is another highlight. For the woman in the poem, domestic cohabitation is mundane, messy, the opposite of carefree. She is stuck with workaday chores while her lackadaisical lover slips out to enjoy his freedom. In the evening, presumably when they are in each other's arms, "she was back in love again, / though not so wholly but throughout the night / she woke sometimes to feel the daylight coming / like a relentless milkman up the stairs."[23] The woman has come into a new kind of loneliness. Romance in the night does not blot out the gray tedium of the endless days ahead.

For anyone interested in how she approached writing poems in the mid-1950s, the title poem is invaluable. In "The Diamond Cutters," she portrays the making of art as a momentous task requiring respect for the raw materials and complete, selfless devotion to the task. No time was to be spent playing around or foolishly admiring one's own labors. As the poem puts it, "Be serious, because / The stone may have contempt / For too-familiar hands," and "Love only what you do, / And not what you have done." In the final stanza, Rich advises that the diamond cutter capable of singular focus will realize "that Africa / Will yield you more to do."[24]

The poem later became a source of intense regret. In a note appearing in her *Collected Early Poems: 1950–1970*, Rich took herself to task for her metaphor: "I was trying, in my twenties, to write about the craft of poetry. But I was drawing, quite ignorantly, on the long tradition of domination, according to which the precious resource is yielded up into the hands of the dominator as if by a natural event." Because she was unaware at the time of the way African laborers in "actual" diamond mines were exploited, the poem "does not take responsibility for its own metaphor. I note this here because this kind of metaphor is still widely accepted, and I still have to struggle against it in my work."[25] Rather than remove the poem from her collected works, she decided to make a lesson of it—or rather, add a corollary lesson. For the truth of the metaphor still holds. A poet or any other artist really is a dominating force, a willed shaper of the materials at hand. What she came to associate with her own unexamined racism and imperialism was an entirely apt metaphor.

It was not the title poem alone but the whole book that troubled her in later years. In the foreword to her *Collected Early Poems,* she declared that "many of the poems were, at best, facile and ungrounded imitations of other poets—Elinor Wylie, Robert Frost, Elizabeth Bishop, Dylan Thomas, Wallace Stevens, Yeats, even English Georgian poets— exercises in style." Even as she criticized her own efforts, she wanted her readers to know she had read and admired women poets early in her career. There is scant evidence, however, that she was ever deeply indebted to Wylie or Bishop. Before the 1960s, her chief role models were the male poets she considered true masters of the form. In any case, she came to see *The Diamond Cutters* as "a last-ditch effort to block, with assimilation and technique, the undervoice of my own poetry."[26]

W hen the book came out in 1955, Rich could not yet hear the plaintive notes of that "undervoice" stirring in her unconscious mind, but she sensed she had hit a plateau of sorts in her poetry and was eager for constructive criticism that would help her do better the next time she published a book. In the small, incestuous world of mid-twentieth-century poetry reviewing, when close friends often wrote about one another's books, criticism was doled out with delicacy. Such was the case when Donald Hall reviewed *The Diamond Cutters* for *Poetry* magazine. He considered her new book better than *A Change of World*, which he pronounced "sometimes tame, and even a little smug about its ability to keep experience away from the door," but he thought Rich fell in the category of young poets "who are gifted with easy competence and are plagued by not always sounding quite like themselves. [. . .] Miss Rich's problem is to find things she cannot with all her skill do, and then try to do them. If she should become satisfied with the poems she is writing, she could repeat them until doomsday, but growth will require a diet of dissatisfaction."[27]

The review came as no surprise, since Hall had read it to her over the phone before it was published. After it appeared, Rich wrote to thank him, even though she knew it was in poor taste to do so. She reassured him and herself that she wouldn't have bothered if he had only complimented her. His insights were what mattered, and she said she'd feel lucky if other criticism proved equally valuable.[28]

In fact, she received a similar review from Randall Jarrell. No one took more delight in damning bad poetry or exalting the good than this severely principled poet-scourge; a Jarrell review was intended to illuminate and amuse, often at the poet's expense. He was not above sexism tricked out in hilarity, as readers of *Poetry and the Age* (1953) were well aware. In that celebrated volume of taste making, he gleefully damned

Muriel Rukeyser (whose poetry Rich would later champion) as "the Common Woman of our century, a siren photographed in a sequin bathing-suit, on rocks like boiled potatoes, for the weekend edition of *PM,* in order to bring sex to the deserving poor."[29]

Jarrell was quite taken with Rich. Writing in *The Yale Review,* he saw exactly what other benevolently condescending critics saw in her and then imagined what else, and what more, she could be:

> Adrienne Cecile Rich is an enchanting poet; everybody seems to admit it: and this seems only right. Everybody thinks young things young, Sleeping Beauty beautiful—and the poet whom we see behind the clarity and gravity of Miss Rich's poems cannot help seeming to us a sort of princess in a fairy tale. Her scansion, even, is easy and limpid, close to water, close to air; she lives nearer to perfection (an all-too-easy perfection, sometimes—there are a few of Schubert's pieces that are better the first time than they are ever again, and some of Miss Rich's poems are like this) than ordinary poets do, and her imperfections themselves are touching as the awkwardness of anything young and natural is touching. The reader feels that she has only begun to change; thinks, "This young thing, who knows what it may be, old?" Some of her poems are very different from the others, some of her nature is very far from the rest of it, so that one feels that she has room to live in and to grow out into; liking her for what she is is a way of liking her even better for what she may become.

Jarrell did not believe Rich's youthfully feminine, metrically correct charms were an end in themselves, and his review was clearly meant to provoke and challenge her. He had dared to imagine Rich as a "thing" grown old, a poet stripped of youth and corporeal beauty, capable—perhaps—of real and lasting vision. After offering his thoughts on specific poems, including "Pictures by Vuillard," "Living in Sin," and "Autumn Equinox" (which he called "almost the best Frost-influenced poem I've ever read"), he pointed her toward her destiny with an encouraging smile and a pinch on the cheek: "It seems to me that she herself is, often, a good poet who is all too good—one who can afford to be wild tomorrow; meanwhile, today, she is also an endearing and delightful poet, one who deserves Shakespeare's favorite adjective, *sweet.*"[30]

After Jarrell's death a decade later, Rich said in a memorial tribute, "Reading that review was like getting a letter from Randall, a letter of love and exhortation, drenched, like all his criticism, with concern for unfulfilled possibilities, for the life of those poems and all future poems by the same hand. One felt that this brilliant, caustic, affectionate stranger had suddenly involved himself in one's fate—not for his own reputation, or for the sake of purveying a personal influence, but because he was a kind of conscience of poetry." The combination of his critical acumen and staggering knowledge of poetry enabled her to engage in a kind of call-and-response with him for years to come. Having worked so hard to please her taskmaster of a father, she turned her hungering attention toward Jarrell, who commended her youthful Shakespearean sweetness while daring her to grow old and wild. She would go so far as to say that, for many of her generation of poets, if "asked, 'To what or whom do you address your poems?' the truthful answer would be: 'To the mind of Randall Jarrell.' "[31]

What she knew of Jarrell's mind appealed to her because it seemed much like her own: broadly knowledgeable of the Western literary canon of white male poets, rigorous, reflective, and searingly judgmental. His was, of course, a male mind, and in those years Rich wrote primarily for male arbiters of taste. To accomplish what Jarrell said he wanted from her, she would have to recast her whole way of seeing, thinking, and writing. In the process, she would embrace what was womanly about her mind and let go of the patterns of thought she associated primarily with men.

By January of 1956, the Conrads had moved away from Cambridge. The anticipated job offer from UCLA hadn't materialized, and the couple had ended up, rather less glamorously, at Northwestern University in Evanston, Illinois. Rich tried to appreciate Evanston's suburban charms, but she was restless and unhappy from the beginning. Not long after her arrival, she wrote to her friend Jack Sweeney, curator of Harvard's Woodberry Poetry Room, that she and Alf missed Cambridge. No matter how appealing their new acquaintances might be, they were not the same as old, close friends.[32] She was less circumspect with Donald Hall. Evanston was the America she had heard of but never experienced before, and she found it extraordinarily dull. While allowing that the city wasn't entirely lacking in culture, the characteristic niceness of the Midwest irritated her no end. She was appalled by what she perceived as a lack of tension and an absence of substantive history.[33]

Eventually she and Alf settled in a town between Chicago and Evanston, a compromise that offered her the worst of both worlds. She couldn't create a niche in the university community, nor could she explore Chicago at her leisure. Instead, she was an anonymous suburban housewife, alone much of the time with her young son and deprived of the intellectual camaraderie that was her lifeblood. During her lonely days at home, she read Martin Buber's *I and Thou,* as little David looked on. Many years later, she shared this bit of information with her friend Barbara Charlesworth Gelpi before a poetry reading at Stanford. Gelpi included it in her introduction and said Rich's reading of Buber in the company of a "speechless baby" was "a kind of paradigm of the modern condition, but that condition is what her poetry is helping to change."[34] At the time, Rich was merely trying to stay intellectually alive under isolating circumstances, though the poignancy of her "I and Thou" relationship with her baby son wasn't lost on her.

Conrad's scholarly career enabled him to return to Harvard periodically to work on a research project. It was during one of these visits that he and his friend John Meyer began collaborating on a widely publicized and hotly debated paper about the economics of the antebellum slave trade; it would make their names in the subfield of cliometrics. Alf's innovative work in cliometrics very likely raised his stature among his Cambridge colleagues. When he was invited to join the faculty of Harvard's economics department as an assistant professor, he and Adrienne hurried back to their old stomping grounds. Their midwestern sojourn had lasted for only the winter and spring quarters of 1956.

Casting about for a new home, they settled on 20 Whittier Street, a duplex about a mile from Harvard and half a mile from their old address on Gray Street. Rich later described Whittier Street as a crowded tenement neighborhood, but at the time it must have offered a refreshing contrast to what she considered the numbing niceness of the Chicago suburbs.

Back in Cambridge, with Alf employed in a tenure-track position, they prepared to have their second child. On July 17, 1957, Rich gave birth to Paul Gershon Conrad, nicknamed "Pablo."

During these intense years of childbearing and rearing young children, she discovered, to her chagrin and supreme irritation, that her writing was falling by the wayside. She had the husband and children she wanted. What she hadn't wanted was to sacrifice her life as an artist, just as her mother had done. Her frustration spilled over in her dealings with others. Though fully capable of warm affection, she had no qualms about alienating professional contacts who had helped her in the past.

In October 1957, she asked Howard Moss why *The New Yorker* hadn't published a couple of her poems more than a year after their acceptance. Moss responded, "You are right, of course, and I do sympathize."[35] He explained that the eleventh-hour layout of the weekly magazine meant poems sometimes got bumped to later issues. Unappeased, Rich weighed her options. She didn't like Moss, and she had begun to feel constricted by the thought of trying to write poems he would accept. When the time came to re-up her first-reading contract in February 1958, she mailed back the unsigned document apparently without a word of explanation. A shocked Moss tried to bring her back into the fold. Assuming she was upset because he had rejected her recent poems, he told her not to take it personally. The contract, he added, was still hers for the asking.

Rich's papers at Harvard include a heavily marked-up reply to Moss, but it is unclear whether she mailed him a version of it. So icy in its tone that merely touching the page would seem to invite frostbite, the draft implies she had grown in wisdom and scope, while *The New Yorker* had not. She claimed not to be bothered by the recent rejections. Perhaps she would still submit the occasional poem without being hamstrung by a lucrative contract, but even that seemed unlikely: "On the whole, my decision is as much a severance with a part of myself as with the New Yorker."[36]

Two years later, when an editor at Yale University Press invited her to submit a few comments in support of the Yale Series of Younger Poets, she made a similar point. She wrote back to say she was grateful to Auden mainly for telling her which poems to exclude from her first volume. Further, only a handful of poems in *A Change of World* still pleased her, and as much as she had enjoyed being published at a young age, she didn't recommend it for every poet. Reading between the lines, one could infer that Auden's faint praise of her "neatly dressed" poems still rankled.[37] And even if she didn't think much of *The Diamond Cutters* anymore, Yale's rejection of it didn't help the cause. She wasn't inclined to do the editors in New Haven a favor, because she didn't feel she owed them one.

The mid- to late 1950s were shaping up to be very hard on her, and for her, in ways she hadn't anticipated. She was well aware that many women of her generation, including her fellow Radcliffe alumnae, were housewives. So was she, but she continued to work at being a poet of serious intent, not just a housewife who dashed off the occasional rhyme. What a shock and letdown, then, when she realized she was mortal and couldn't easily do the work of two people at once.

No matter how frustrated and exhausted she got, she kept trying, and few noticed a gap in her string of professional accomplishments. Because she had worked so hard for so long, she was able to coast for a while, at least in the public eye, on her past successes. Her poems were beginning to be anthologized, most significantly in *The New Poets of England and America* (1957), which Hall had coedited. Although she had once joked with him that the *Partisan Review* would probably pan her after she had accidentally insulted its editor, the influential journal's review of *New Poets* singled out her poems for qualified praise while disparaging the anthology as a whole. Reviewer F. W. Dupee of Columbia University wrote that Rich's "language is neither systematically colloquial, as Frost's language tends to be, nor alternately colloquial and conceptual, as Eliot's was in his early poems; nor does it burst into a fine spray of fantastication as Stevens's was apt to do. Miss Rich seems to have access to some common style, a language which she and her contemporaries all tend to speak easily, with a minimum of individual inflection." Like Auden before him, he couldn't compliment Rich without keeping expectations low: "A woman in a non-feminist age, an artist in a time that is not conspicuously creative, she makes poetry out of a sense of limitations, is equable without the accusing calm of the self-accepting, wise without being a young owl."[38] She was the very best, Dupee implied, of a stunted lot.

For Sylvia Plath, three years her junior, Rich was in an enviable position. Plath had closely followed her career ever since the publication of *A Change of World*. In a letter to a college boyfriend, she wrote, "I keep reading about this damn adrienne cecile rich," "a yale younger poet and regularly in all the top mags. . . . Occasionally, I retch quietly in the wastebasket."[39]

Blissfully unaware of Plath's retching, figurative or otherwise, Rich marched on. She may not have been writing the great new poems she longed for, but she continued to publish poems in national magazines and attract an increasing number of enthusiastic readers. Happily for her and her publisher, *The Diamond Cutters* went into a second printing after the initial print run of a thousand copies sold out.[40]

In keeping with her pattern of harsh reassessment, however, Rich soon looked back on her second book as a largely failed effort. She thought she could do much better. When she published a selected volume in England in 1967, she included only two poems from *A Change of World* and three from *The Diamond Cutters*.[41] The remaining thirty-five poems came from later books.

A couple of years after the publication of *The Diamond Cutters*, Harcourt Brace editor Peter Davison invited Rich to lunch in Harvard Square to discuss her work. The woman he encountered and got to know over the next several years was "pixyish and charming, witty in person as her written work seldom is, though her conversation never lacked a slight sharpness of edge." He was later surprised to read her essays describing the anguish she had endured as the daughter of Arnold Rich and as a young married woman. Yet he glimpsed something of her complexity when he complimented her writing during that first meeting. "[S]he was clearly as glad as anyone to be admired, but she was holding something back, not only her own consent to the work she had finished, but her commitment to the work she was yet to create. When I praised her work she looked at me quizzically, as though there were something she (or I) did not understand."[42] No longer at ease with the persona she had created in her second volume, she wasn't yet able to imagine the poet she would become, the as-yet-unimagined poet Randall Jarrell wanted her to be. Her undervoice was still dormant.

In their reviews, Holmes, Hall, Jarrell, and perhaps especially Dupee had pointed out the shortcomings that she herself belatedly recognized. From a professional standpoint, it had been time to publish a second book, and *The Diamond Cutters* had done what it was supposed to do: It sold respectably for a poetry collection and won the Poetry Society of

America's Ridgley Torrence Memorial Award. It was even a finalist for the National Book Award (losing out to Auden's *The Shield of Achilles*). Despite these measures of success, Rich knew she had fallen short of her artistic standards. Her mocking reference to the book as "the Gold Diggers" said as much.[43] She wanted to believe she could do better; she just didn't know what "better" would look like.

The quizzical expression that lingered in Davison's memory reflected her desire to be accurately judged, not given a drop more than her due. She had achieved an enviable station in life, personally and professionally. But she was not satisfied with herself or her art, and she was torn between her desire to write and her responsibilities to her family. At times she felt her divided loyalties would drive her mad.

Despite the success of *The Diamond Cutters,* she was losing herself and had no idea of the way forward. She had been motivated her whole life by her desire to *become,* a word Jarrell used in his motivational review of *The Diamond Cutters.* Jarrell had compared her to Sleeping Beauty, and Rich retrospectively called herself a sleepwalker. Restless, angry, still determinedly writing for male minds, she knew it was time to wake up and make something new of herself, but rousing herself from what Robert Lowell called "the tranquilized *Fifties*" would not be easy.[44]

# CHAPTER 9

# BURSTING WITH BENZEDRINE AND EMANCIPATION

*1958–1963*

O n a tenaciously wintry day in April 1958, Sylvia Plath and Ted Hughes drove from Northampton to Cambridge, Massachusetts. Plath begged her husband to slow down. The windshield wiper on her side was broken, and they were traveling through "a horizontal whirl-wind of sleet," as she described it in her journal. "I saw only the vast looming shapes of approaching trucks through the semi-opaque lid of sleet and each shape seemed, coming, looming, a menace, a possible death."[1] In this fraught state of mind, she was accompanying Ted to Harvard, where he would read from his debut collection of poems, *The Hawk in the Rain*. The invitation from Jack Sweeney, curator of Harvard's Woodberry Poetry Room, was a significant early coup for the future poet laureate of England. The occasion would also give her the opportunity to meet the woman she thought of as her chief rival in poetry, Adrienne Rich.

The ferociously competitive Plath had graduated summa cum laude from Smith College and continued her studies at Cambridge University. Like Rich, she treasured writing and reading above all else. But Rich had two books of poetry to her name, while Plath as yet had none, and Rich had privileges at Harvard that Plath did not. Although the univer-sity continued to exclude women from Lamont Library, home of the Poetry Room, Sweeney made an exception for Rich, whom he held in great esteem. All she had to do was go to the circulation desk in Lamont and ask for him, and she would be escorted to the Poetry Room and allowed to use it as long as she wanted.[2] She was the rare woman of her era, perhaps the only one, with regular access to Harvard's vast collection of books and audio recordings of modern and contemporary verse.

Plath, meanwhile, had spent much of the academic year teaching undergraduate literature courses and grading papers. While Rich deeply resented the maternal duties that took her away from writing and studying poetry, Plath felt the same way about teaching in Smith's English department. Neither woman was happy at the time.

Because Ted was the star on this cold and wet April day, Sylvia had the chance to observe Adrienne and the rest of the Cambridge crowd without the burden of performing for them. That is not to say she didn't feel self-conscious as she entered the sophisticated, if rather stifling, literary milieu in which Adrienne moved with apparent ease. With Sweeney leading them across the Harvard campus, the guests set out for the afternoon reading:

> We slogged in ice mud & rivulets. Fell into a taxi & rode to Radcliffe's Longfellow hall. Sepulchral. Deserted. I imagined no one would come. Followed a white-dressed attendant down echoing marble-speckled & polished halls to a lavatory where a thick horse-bodied Radcliffe girl was combing her hair. [. . .] Back to the hall to shake hands with Harry Levin's dark, vigorous small Russian wife. "Harry is onder ze wedder. I bring a good ear." We went in, after greeting Mrs. Cantor, Marty & Mike, & Carol Pierson, and the room blurred before my eyes. Very big room, very sparsely peopled—listeners scattered. I followed Mrs. Levin & saw [Mairé Sweeney's] luminous pallor, gold hair done in a low chignon, and a quaint small hat of black and russet feathers like a bird-down cloche. Ted began [. . .] to read. I felt cold, felt the audience thin & cold. The poems, which I knew by heart, sent the inevitable chill of awe & wonder over me: the foolish tears jumped to my eyes. Mrs. Levin squirmed, reached for her pocketbook & scribbled something in pencil on a rattling envelope, asked me to repeat the title of "The Thought-fox." Afar off, somewhere, a clock struck five. Ted spoke of out-Tennysoning Tennyson—the audience laughed, a pleasant muted burble. Laughed & warmed. I began to relax [. . .].[3]

Afterward, Plath chatted with her mother and greeted old friends who had traversed the sleet and slush for the special occasion. And then, at last, she faced the woman whose career she had followed for years: "Adrienne Cecile Rich: little, round & stumpy, all vibrant short black hair, great sparkling black eyes and a tulip-red umbrella: honest, frank forthright & even opinionated."[4]

Plath's brief sketch captures Rich at a time when she was taking steroids to control her arthritis. The medication made Rich rounder than she would have been otherwise. On a miserably cold and wet day, she was very likely in some pain, but she had shown up in full vibrancy, ready to engage with Plath and Hughes and spend the remainder of the day with them.

Alfred Conrad joined his wife and the guests of honor for a cocktail party the Sweeneys hosted at their apartment, which was decorated with stunning modern art. There among the original Picassos and the Juan Gris Plath spied "the doe-eyed tan Al Conrad, an economist at Harvard, whom I felt cold & awkward with at first." Seated next to him at dinner, however, she loosened up: "I talked to Al about trudo, tuberculosis, deep, deeper, enjoying him."[5] "Trudo" was Plath's rendering of the Trudeau Sanitarium, where both Alfred and one of her college boyfriends (the basis for Buddy Willard in The Bell Jar) had recuperated from tuberculosis. Conrad's often-cited charm and good humor, combined with wine, helped her relax.

Jack Sweeney, seated on her other side, was patiently waiting to invite her to record a selection of her poems for the Poetry Room's collection.[6] When Plath finally turned away from Conrad to talk to him, she got the good news. The pleasing invitation must have helped convince her she would do well if she and her husband followed through on their plans to move to Boston.

Sylvia and Adrienne weren't destined to become close friends, but they did have further contact. Later that month, they saw each other at Mount Holyoke College, apparently at another poetry event,[7] and after Ted and Sylvia moved to Boston, the Conrads and the Hugheses socialized. Writing to Jack Sweeney in February 1959, Adrienne said she and Alf were going to visit Sylvia and Ted the next evening. She hoped to read Ted's new poems.[8] He was the one, not Sylvia, with whom she already was forming a mutually edifying poets' friendship.

Plath had not dropped the rivalry. About a week after her first meeting with Rich, she wrote in her journal, "I have the joyous feeling of leashed power—also the feeling that within a year or two I should be 'recognized'—as I am not at all now, though I sit on poems richer than any Adrienne Cecile Rich."[9]

At some point, Rich gave Plath advice relevant to her career as a writer. According to W. S. Merwin, she "advised Sylvia very strongly not to have children." Merwin had learned of this conversation from his wife, Dido, one of Sylvia's confidantes. Rich herself confirmed it thirty years later.[10] If Plath had heeded Rich's advice, it might well have made a saving difference in her life. But by the time she and Hughes separated in 1962, they had two young children. When the clinical depression that precipitated an earlier suicide attempt returned with a vengeance, her responsibilities to her daughter and son added to her feelings of despair and helplessness.

Rich was very likely pregnant when she told Plath not to have children. There had been a time not so many years ago when she wanted four children, three boys and a girl. Now, with David a busy toddler and the baby, Pablo, requiring much of her attention, she was increasingly on edge. She loved her children but hadn't planned for another baby and couldn't imagine why Plath or any other woman writer would conceive the first. With hired help (though never enough to suit her) and leisurely summer vacations at Lake Willoughby, she wanted to feel grateful for her bountiful life, but she wasn't writing as much as she thought she should, and what she did write, she didn't particularly like. She promised herself the day would soon come when both children were in school and some semblance of a normal writing routine could resume.

But that day was pushed back when fate granted her old wish of three sons. In "Anger and Tenderness," the lead essay in *Of Woman Born*, Rich wrote in detail about this time in her life and quoted from the journal she kept during her third pregnancy:

By July of 1958 I was again pregnant. The new life of my third—and, I determined, my last—child, was a kind of turning for me.

I had learned that my body was not under my control; I had not intended to bear a third child. I knew now better than I had ever known what another pregnancy, another new infant, meant for my body and spirit. Yet, I did not think of having an abortion. In a sense, my third son was more actively chosen than either of his brothers; by the time I knew I was pregnant with him, I was not sleepwalking any more.

*August 1958 (Vermont)*

I write this as the early rays of the sun light up our hillside and eastern windows. Rose with [the baby] at 5:30 a.m. and have fed him and breakfasted. This is one of the few mornings on which I haven't felt terrible mental depression and physical exhaustion.

. . . I have to acknowledge to myself that I would not have chosen to have more children, that I was beginning to look to a time, not too far off, when I should again be free, no longer so physically tired, pursuing a more or less intellectual and creative life. . . . The *only* way I can develop now is through much harder, more continuous, connected work than my present life makes possible. Another child means postponing this for some years longer—and years at my age are significant, not to be tossed lightly away.

And yet, somehow, something, call it Nature or that affirming fatalism of the human creature, makes me aware of the inevitable as already part of me, not to be contended against so much as brought to bear as an additional weapon against drift, stagnation and spiritual death. (For it is really death that I have been fearing—the crumbling to death of that scarcely-born physiognomy which my whole life has been a battle to give birth to—a recognizable, autonomous self, a creation in poetry and in life.)

If more effort has to be made then I will make it. If more despair has to be lived through, I think I can anticipate it correctly and live through it.

Meanwhile, in a curious and unanticipated way, we really do welcome the birth of our child.[11]

Rich admitted her fear of "drift" and "spiritual death." She knew she had within her an autonomous and artistic being who had yet to speak or cry. Her certainty that such a self deserved to exist is testimony to her bedrock resolve. She wouldn't abort her baby or her own nascent self, "a creation in poetry and in life." No, she would have the child and somehow find a way to do her work in the world and give birth to the woman, the artist, she knew she had within her.

She was increasingly self-aware. It would take years, however, for her to fully articulate what bothered her about her life and why her objections mattered. In "Anger and Tenderness," she used her younger self as an exemplar for all women who experienced similarly gradual awakenings:

The life of a Cambridge tenement backyard swarming with children, the repetitious cycles of laundry, the night wakings, the interrupted moments of peace or of engagement with ideas, the ludicrous dinner parties at which young wives, some with advanced degrees, all seriously and intelligently dedicated to their children's welfare and their husbands' careers, attempted to reproduce the amenities of Brahmin Boston, amid French recipes and the pretense of effortlessness—above all, the ultimate lack of seriousness with which women were regarded in that world—all of this defied analysis at that time, but I *knew* I had to remake my own life. I did not then understand that we—the women of that academic community—as in so many middle-class communities of the period—were expected to fill both the part of the Victorian Lady of Leisure, the Angel in the House, and also of the Victorian cook, scullery maid, laundress, governess, and nurse. I only sensed that there were false distractions sucking at me, and I wanted desperately to strip my life down to what was essential.[12]

But she had little in common with her old favorite, Henry David Thoreau, who had done exactly what she wanted to do. An unencumbered life of writing and reading was not an option for her. Given the dire circumstances, another artist might have prayed. Rather than petition the heavens, Rich presented her dilemma to the secular entity she once playfully called "St. Gugg."

In the fall of 1958, both she and Alfred applied for Guggenheim Fellowships. Her application laid bare her abundant frustration: "In erratic starts and flashes I have begun to see how I must work, and that the technical equipment with which I felt so secure in my early twenties will be worth no more than clockwork to me in the thirties and forties. At the same time, my discoveries and conclusions have been made at a painfully, to me a shamefully, slow rate." Although she allowed that any progression had its moments of trial and error, she said her greatest frustration was "directly attributable to my situation during the past five years. Increasingly I have been forced to work, even to think, in fragments of time, never absolutely to be counted on, and snatched with varying degrees of difficulty from the responsibilities of raising two—soon three—young children, with only intermittent outside help."[13]

Rich was beginning to see how the world worked against virtually all women, the privileged and the unprivileged, and her increasing awareness of all the ways she was being held back fueled her righteous indignation. It wasn't just a hunch or her hope. She knew her work was too important to relegate to stolen hours when her husband and young children didn't demand her attention.

As it happened, one of the Guggenheim judges during that period was a woman predisposed in Rich's favor. The poet and critic Louise Bogan, who had evaluated poetry applications since 1944, had praised *A Change of World* in *The New Yorker* in 1951 and very likely signed off on Rich's first Guggenheim award the following year. Commenting in 1963 on her duties as judge, Bogan dismissed the quality of recent poetry applicants: "Academics and beats; beats and academics. Pretty poor stuff."[14] Rich fell into neither category. With Bogan in her corner, she was well positioned to win the coveted award yet again.

While she waited on word of the fellowship, Rich turned to her friends for solace and encouragement. Her most important new friend in the late 1950s was Robert Lowell. She had first heard about him from her old college friend Robert Bly, who had recited long passages of Lowell's poetry to her during a walk around Cambridge her freshman year at Radcliffe.[15] A tall satyrlike man with a knowing smile, Lowell was a dozen years her senior and shared her absolute commitment to the art of poetry. His recurring mental breakdowns interrupted his life but didn't significantly slow his career. *Lord Weary's Castle,* his second book, won the Pulitzer Prize for Poetry in 1947. When he and Rich met in 1958, he was soon to publish *Life Studies,* the book that would seal his reputation. Rich's early poetry greatly impressed him, and they got to know each other while he was teaching at Boston University.

Rich held her own with Lowell and his second wife, the writer Elizabeth Hardwick. Hardwick was formidable in her own right and went on to help found *The New York Review of Books.* During the early days of her friendship with the literary power couple, Rich made a strong impression on Lowell. In a typically arch and gossipy letter to Elizabeth Bishop on October 16, 1958, he wrote, "Adrienne Rich is having a third baby—one that defied all preventative science—and is reading Simone de Beauvoir and bursting with [B]enzedrine and emancipation. She and Lizzie [Hardwick] had a forty-five minute argument, carried on in [the] dining-room, pantry and library about two people neither liked or really knew. We like her very much."[16]

Though Lowell may have been indulging in hyperbole, the image of Rich on speed is an indelible one. In the 1950s, Benzedrine was sometimes prescribed for depression; others took it in hopes of losing weight. It was also a writer's drug: The Beat movement writers Jack Kerouac and Allen Ginsberg were among those who used it so they could concentrate for hours on end. If she actually experimented with speed, improved concentration may well have been Rich's objective. She was on record as confessing that her third pregnancy had taken away her usual vitality. She wrote to Jack Sweeney that after she had her baby she expected she would shake off the "physical lassitude and a kind of mental paralysis" she was currently suffering.[17]

Just days before Rich argued with Elizabeth Hardwick, she had returned to Roland Park Country School to speak during her alma mater's fiftieth anniversary celebration on October 11, 1958. Her impassioned lecture drew inspiration from Beauvoir's *The Second Sex* and prefigured much of what she would argue in later years about the education of women. For anyone assuming that she metamorphosed into a feminist in early middle age, her talk offers a clear corrective. Her remarks indicate she was not ready to claim feminism, but it was obviously beginning to claim her.

Most women, she told her audience, struggle to balance family commitments with a desire to hold a job, make art, engage in politics, or otherwise step outside the domestic realm. Society tells them to suppress those desires:

> It is, and will continue to be, an individual struggle which each individual woman will wage in her own way and to her own degree. But I believe that a school for girls should recognize that every one of its graduates is going to face the problem in some form and to some extent. And, therefore, that it should consider itself as preparing its girls, not *for* marriage and child-rearing, but *against* the pressures which that future time may exert on their thinking, percipient selves. This is a less feminist plea than it sounds. I do not mean that a school for girls ought to view each of its students as a future career woman. But the school should be and I believe this school is, above all concerned with the future life of her mind, in spite of all the things with which schools are told they *ought* to be concerned.[18]

Anticipating Betty Friedan's *The Feminine Mystique* by five years, Rich spoke bluntly about the problems many homemakers endured in the name of being good wives and mothers. "The life of a woman restricted to her situation in the home is, at different times and to different degrees, prone to several major liabilities. Chief among these are fatigue, physical confinement, the fragmentary nature of her daily activities, and the constant, tedious demand of physical objects for her attention." The housewife, in short, was at risk of terminal stultification. "In the course of her day, in the park, at the grocery counter, in the back-yard, she encounters for the most part women like herself, equally fatigued, equally frustrated, and who offer her no great stimulus to transcend the routines which they all share, or to reflect critically upon the values which they all accept."[19]

Rich was beginning to think deeply about what it meant to be a woman in a world controlled by men. As her thirtieth birthday approached, she didn't want to stop being a wife and mother, and she was a long way from becoming a radical feminist, but she realized the difference it would have made in her life if she had been taught early on to challenge and even reject societal expectations that sapped her strength and wasted her time. She wanted future generations of women to be better prepared to think for themselves than her generation had been—and from now on, she would make a point of saying so whenever the opportunity presented itself. Her lecture to her former teachers was a very early rehearsal for many a feminist jeremiad yet to come.

On March 4, 1959, Rich gave birth to Jacob Franz Conrad. The sequence of events around that time only increased her awareness of the obstacles women face on a routine basis. As she wrote in *Of Woman Born*, she wanted to be sterilized after her baby's birth, but it was not her decision alone:

> My husband, although he supported my decision, asked whether I was sure it would not leave me feeling "less feminine." In order to have the operation at all, I had to present a letter, countersigned by my husband, assuring the committee of physicians who approved such operations that I had already produced three children, and stating my reasons for having no more. Since I had had rheumatoid arthritis for some years, I could give a reason acceptable to the male panel who sat on my case; my own judgment would not have been acceptable. When I awoke from the operation, twenty-four hours after my child's birth, a young nurse looked at my chart and remarked coldly: "Had yourself spayed, did you?"[20]

Rich was not used to being demeaned. Her strong sense of self-worth came from Arnold Rich, who taught her to believe in herself and stand up for herself when she was a young girl. One of the great paradoxes of her life was that so much that was steely and strong in her character came from her despotic father. In the words of Cynthia Rich, he "was the patriarch of patriarchs who created a woman confident enough to later rip away at patriarchy."[21]

Rather than merely stewing in anger after she came home from the hospital, Adrienne pushed herself to think ever more deeply about the female condition and her own life as a mother. In a candid letter to Margareta Faissler, her history teacher at Roland Park, who had become a dear friend, Rich confessed she was not "a born mother." In the years since her first child was born, she had come to recognize the source of her seemingly endless frustration: "A degree of arrogance and restless impatience is altogether necessary for the creative thinker but ruinous to the maternal state—at least where very young children are involved."[22] She went on to say that adjusting to a child's needs and demands was not easy or always done gladly. Writing mostly without recourse to the first person, Rich nevertheless made it clear she had reached a personal turning point: The myths of idealized motherhood meant little to her now. She was restless for a future that would contain more poems and less mothering.

In the crucial weeks right after giving birth, Adrienne had help with her three young children. In another letter to Faissler, Rich lavished praise on the nurse who worked a ten-hour shift and did everything, including baking brownies for the older children. With the children in good hands, Adrienne was able to sleep in peace. She called it a "ruinously decadent existence" that eased the hard weeks after childbirth.[23] She would eventually speak out on behalf of poor and working-class women who had little or no help with child care. For now, even with the provident help of a good nurse, she was still struggling. Her innate love for her children could not change who she was. She didn't have the patience or forbearance to be a good mother to very young children, and she said as much to Donald Hall.[24]

On this occasion, it was St. Gugg to the rescue. When both she and Alfred were awarded Guggenheims, foundation secretary Henry Moe began his letter to her on a jolly note: "I shall write to you as—as far as I am concerned!—the senior member of your wife-husband fellow-Fellow team." The patronizing patron knew this would be Conrad's first Guggenheim and Rich's second. Still, the senior member of the team identified herself as Alf's dependent and wanted only a stipend for child care. Her husband's proposed budget would cover her other needs. In the end, she received more than she asked for: $3,600 instead of $2,500, while Alf, who intended to spend a year working at an economics institute in Rotterdam, was granted a bit less: $5,500 instead of his requested $6,850. Their total award of $9,100 would translate to approximately $75,000 today, with Adrienne's share for child care being equivalent to a generous $30,000.[25]

The foundation allowed the couple to postpone their joint fellowships until 1961–1962. Having left Harvard's economics department for Harvard Business School, Alf was required to teach for a couple of years in his new position before taking a sabbatical. In the meantime, he and Adrienne bought a house on Brewster Street, a step up from Whittier Street, and committed themselves to Cambridge yet again. According to Rich, the house located at 17 Brewster Street was "restrainedly Victorian, large enough for our family without being manorial, and very much the sort of house we've always wanted."[26] One of the best things about it was the room on the third floor that she made into her study. Here, at last, was a place where she could work in relative peace.

In mid-June of 1959, just a few months after Jacob's birth, Rich and Conrad attended a party at the Boston home of Lowell and Hardwick. The occasion came shortly after the release of *Life Studies,* the volume marking Lowell's crucial turn toward the stylized, achingly personal verse that secured his reputation as one of the great poets of his time. The party also, not coincidentally, celebrated Lowell's release from McLean hospital, the expensive private mental institution where both Sylvia Plath and Alfred's first wife had convalesced. Among the other party guests was Anne Sexton, who had also been treated for depression at McLean. A psychiatrist had recommended that Sexton try writing, an activity she had enjoyed in her youth. Her interest and keen imagination coincided serendipitously with her viewing of a Boston TV program featuring I. A. Richards, a Harvard professor and friend of Rich's. With Richards as her televised instructor, Sexton began writing sonnets.[27]

Glamorous, amusing, and gifted, the emotionally fragile Sexton was a female counterpart to Lowell, though she lacked his long years of formal education and scholarly immersion in poetry. Lowell thought she was terrific and said so to Rich and his other friends. "I remember feeling that suddenly there was this *woman* whom Lowell and people around Cambridge were talking about, this woman who was going to publish a book called *To Bedlam and Part Way Back,*" Rich wrote many years later. "I would never have acknowledged it at the time, but I felt threatened, very competitive with her. There was little support for the idea that another woman poet could be a source of strength or mutual engagement. I think I suspected—and not because of some profound character defect in me—that if she was going to take up more space, then I was not going to have that space."[28]

Rich wasn't the only woman poet of the era who took a dim view of Sexton. In 1960, Elizabeth Bishop told Lowell she thought Sexton's poems "had a bit too much romanticism and what I think of as the 'our beautiful old silver' school of female writing. . . . They have to make quite sure that the reader is not going to mis-place them socially, first."[29] Although Bishop considered Sexton's class markers characteristic of a certain kind of "female writing," her friend Lowell also made sure his readers knew his social status; there was a sideboard's worth of "our beautiful old silver" in his poems eviscerating his Boston Brahmin ancestors.

By 1960, Rich had spent the better part of thirteen years in her adopted hometown and had fallen into a predictable and sometimes meaningless swirl of activities. But it wasn't just Cambridge she was tired of; it was the whole country. The Cold War mind-set—the air-raid drills, the construction of bomb shelters—irritated her no end. The combination of the political climate and her personal circumstances put her in an existential funk.

Kathleen Spivack, a college student completing a poetry tutorial with Robert Lowell, witnessed Rich in her funk during visits to the Conrad home around this time. She first visited 17 Brewster Street at Lowell's urging and later returned on a number of occasions to babysit the Conrad children. On her first visit, she closely observed Rich and her environs: "Opening the door and leading me in, Adrienne Rich inclined her chiseled head toward me with intensity. Her sleek feathered hair and focused glint created an impression of a proud young eagle. [. . .] She had a suppressed impatience about her being, a hardly tamed striving that showed itself only in fine strain marks about the eyes. They warned one." Once inside, Spivack thought the house was "dark and too cold and depressing, with kitchen windows giving off to sad shrubbery in winter. I kept my sweater on and a coat around me." Adrienne, too, was bundled in layers against the cold.

While her hostess ironed clothes, Spivack heard the Conrad children playing upstairs. The occasional "loud bump on the floor" or quarrel distracted Rich's attention and drew her upstairs. Once she returned, she resumed speaking so eloquently and with such forceful intelligence that Spivack felt intimidated. It was only after she got to know her well and read her later poetry and prose that Spivack realized how hard Rich worked to maintain her habitual "grace and control."[30]

Meanwhile, Rich's reputation continued to rise. In May 1960 she won a grant from the National Institute of Arts and Letters, an honor announced at a formal occasion in New York. Of the seven writers receiving grants of fifteen hundred dollars, Rich and May Swenson were the only women; other recipients included Norman Mailer and Philip Roth. Hilda Doolittle, better known by her pen name, H.D., was feted with a medal and a prize of a thousand dollars. To Denise Levertov, she downplayed her and Alf's attendance at the "National Institute thing" and said the seventy-three-year-old H.D. "looked haggard and seemed violently moved to the point of being unnerved—she blurted out her acceptance of the gold medal before Mark Van Doren was able to read the citation, then looked distraught and staggered back to her chair." The whole occasion left her feeling "everyone there must have had some reservations about finding himself in the company of some of the others!"[31]

Even if she refused to be in awe of her latest accolade, there was one person deeply moved by it: Arnold Rich. Adrienne had told her parents about the honor, and her father had made three photostat copies of her commendation from Glenway Westcott, president of the National Institute. In a one-sentence letter to his daughter preserved in her papers at Harvard, Arnold said he thought she might like each of her children to have a copy of the commendation when they were grown. He had addressed the note to "Dearest Adrienne" and signed it "Love, Father."[32] Here was tangible proof that he wanted a relationship, however formal and removed, with the daughter he had very nearly disowned when she announced her plans to marry Alf. His pride in her achievement, the achievement he always believed would be hers, had overridden his old anger and disappointment. Rich was willing to be in touch with him, and her inclusion in her papers of his note and the fragile photostats (not distributed among her sons) seems designed to illustrate the continuing thread of contact between daughter and father.

In December 1960, Rich gave the Phi Beta Kappa poetry reading at the College of William and Mary. By now she had been giving public readings for a decade. She had a natural command of the stage and read with a crisp, clear enunciation that grew out of her musical training and showed a deep respect for her audience. Since she was herself a Phi Beta Kappa member as well as the author of two well-received books of verse, she was a logical choice for this occasion. But more to the point, at age thirty-one she was already in demand as a public speaker outside the Boston area. At a time when she felt she was falling short in productivity, she actually was gaining in professional momentum. And rather than play it safe and read poems she knew would go over well, she read new, as yet unpublished work. In a letter to Denise Levertov, she enclosed a copy of "A Marriage in the 'Sixties," which she planned to read at William and Mary.[33] With references to Fidel Castro and scientific advancements of the era, the poem describes a new age and a marriage in flux. As the 1960s take shape around them, wife and husband are acutely aware of time's passage. The wife voices anxious questions: "Will nothing ever be the same, / even our quarrels take a different key, / our dreams exhume new metaphors?" But no matter what the future holds, she promises her "fellow-particle" that in the whirling chaos she will "hang / beside you like your twin."[34]

The poem captured the strain on her marriage even as Rich professed her continuing devotion to her husband. Though she had no intention of leaving him, it was as if they were on parallel tracks rather than the same one. Typical of an ambitious scholar and professor—and much like her father—Alf spent many hours engrossed in his research. Adrienne's letters from the 1960s often mention how hard he was working. He went away for long periods to the Middle East and Africa to consult on monetary policy. His absences left her in charge of the household and the rearing of their three sons. He was traveling the world in pursuit of the work he loved, while she stayed home in Cambridge to mind the children and maybe work at her desk for an hour or two when the house finally went still late at night.

The best of times came when she and Alf broke away from the routines that gripped both of them. She enjoyed weekends when they took the boys to a nearby land preserve, and wrote happily to Denise Levertov of a family day trip to the whaling museum in New Bedford.[35] Her spirits rose whenever she explored a new place and saw her love of history and nature mirrored in her husband and children.

To keep the quotidian nature of her life at bay, she indulged in small extravagances. On one occasion, Cynthia Rich visited her sister at 17 Brewster Street and came upon a vase overflowing with fragrant peonies. At a time when neither sister had money to spare, Adrienne still bought flowers to adorn her home. In Cynthia's recollection, "I couldn't bring myself to splurge like that, and that was part of my sense of our difference—what we deserved."[36]

But Adrienne felt she deserved more than a bouquet of peonies. It was her Guggenheim year in the Netherlands that truly revived her spirits and made her feel whole. The family arrived in Rotterdam in the summer of 1961 and moved into a comfortable rental house. Alf began his residency at the Econometric Institute while she organized the household. She told Denise Levertov how much she liked their house on the outskirts of Rotterdam, where grazing cows and goats and a windmill added picturesque touches. Adding to her satisfaction was a park, complete with tree-lined avenues, canals dotted with swans, "and a gorgeous privet labyrinth with a distorted mirror in the center as if it had been invented by Chirico."[37]

The Guggenheim grant paid for a housekeeper who stayed home with the children while the economist and the poet traveled at their leisure. Adrienne loved Leiden and Haarlem and savored Amsterdam, where "one could walk forever, like Rome or Paris." In her letter to Levertov, she marveled over Rembrandt paintings completely new to her and raved over Rembrandt's contemporary Frans Hals, whom she and Alf now loved: "I've never felt very strongly about him and after seeing three of his paintings at the Haarlem museum I feel they themselves were worth the fare to Europe."[38] This was the kind of discovery that made Adrienne feel vibrantly alive and awake, her synapses joyfully firing. As she shook off the yoke of resentful homemaker, she began to see a way forward at last.

Free to travel around Europe, sometimes alone, she successfully staged an intervention in her own writing life. Untethered from the duties at home that had stifled and stymied her, she wrote the poems that would complete her next book. She also studied Dutch (which she could still speak years later, when the opportunity to converse presented itself) and began translating Dutch poems into English. Working steadily and socializing when the spirit moved her, she relished her emancipation, temporary though it was. In a letter to Jack Sweeney late in her stay in Rotterdam, she wrote, "It's been a lovely year. Very productive, happy and full of discoveries and rediscoveries. We feel very much settled in Holland and that in future travels coming here will be a real homecoming. Good acquaintances, good neighbors, a pair of real friends. But also much time for ourselves and each other and work." Once again, she was prolific; once again she was writing poems she genuinely liked. She told Sweeney her new book of poems would come out from Harper early in 1963.[39]

During their stay in the Netherlands, Rich and Conrad did not make a side trip to England to see Sylvia Plath and Ted Hughes. But both Sylvia and Ted were still thinking of Adrienne. By now, Plath had tamped down her envy of Rich. In 1961, she had chosen three of Rich's poems—"The Evil Eye" (an excerpt from "Readings of History"), "Living in Sin," and "Moving in Winter"—for a small anthology she was editing called *American Poetry Now*, a supplement to the Oxford journal *Critical Quarterly*. The other poets she chose were Merwin, Sexton, Starbuck, and Levertov.

It was Hughes, not Plath, who actively corresponded with Rich. He wanted to include her in an anthology of young American poets he was compiling for Faber & Faber—a much bigger deal than the pamphlet Plath edited. In particular, he was interested in reading Rich's recent poems written in free verse.[40] Hughes's invitation had led Rich to inquire whether Faber might publish a complete book of her poems rather than merely including her in an anthology. Writing from his and Sylvia's home at 3 Chalcot Square in London, Hughes didn't think the distinguished publishing house would go along with that. Being in the anthology, he argued, would earn her more money up front than traditional royalties and serve as a stepping-stone toward book publication. He made a persuasive case.

In September 1962, he again wrote. By now, he and Plath and their young daughter and baby son were living at Court Green, North Tawton, in Devon, England. The Faber anthology of young American poets had gone to press without any poems by Rich. Hughes regretted that he hadn't seen any of her new work in time to include it in the anthology. Rather than linger over this unexplained gap in communication (possibly related to Rich's time away in Rotterdam), he said he also regretted not seeing any of Sexton's new poems in time for his deadline. Suspicious of his attraction to Sexton's seemingly artless style, he nevertheless realized there was a lesson in it for him, one he rather pointedly shared with Rich: "I think it's a means of acquiring speed by dumping cargo. Speed and cargo together, that would be it."[41] Rich took heed.

When she and Plath first met, both were carrying literal cargo they couldn't easily dump. There weren't enough hours in the day to do all that they wanted to do. Things didn't ease up for either one of them over the next five years, and both of them grappled with frustration, anger, and depression. But on February 11, 1963, it was Plath, not Rich, who couldn't hang on long enough to see what the next day, let alone the next era, would hold. By gassing herself to death, she simultaneously performed the roles of Holocaust victim ("I think I may well be a Jew"[42]) and patriarchal executioner—"Herr Enemy."[43] Little did she know that her final act, combined with the best of the poems she wrote in the last few months of her life, would bring her the fame she had long craved. After her death, it became almost impossible to discuss her signature poems, "Daddy" and "Lady Lazarus" (to say nothing of her novel, The Bell Jar), without recourse to her biography. Plath had unwittingly driven a stake in the heart of New Criticism, the coolly methodical approach to literary analysis championed by T. S. Eliot. With its tight focus on metaphor, symbolism, word choice, meter, and form, New Criticism had no use for biographical interpretation. Although she was hardly the only poet to blur the lines between her art and life, Plath's suicide exposed the limitations of New Criticism in ways that a lesser poet's could not, for what she had written really was art. Her death forced conscientious readers to reckon with her as a writer whose genius and suffering had everything to do with her gender.

It was in some ways the fault of the times themselves, Rich knew, that Plath could not imagine a world, or a situation, different from the cold and lonely one in which she lived and died. In the early 1970s, Rich observed, "What I find particularly painful, as a woman, in reading Plath, is the sense of all she saw and all she could not see; how close she came to recognitions and resources which ten years after her death would have been available to her; how great her powers were, how dark and aborted her vision."[44] Rich's tenacity—what she would later call her "wild patience"[45]—meant she was willing to wait and see what would happen next. Though she suffered from periodic depressions during the late 1950s and early 1960s, along with arthritic pain, she didn't want to miss a minute of her life. In 1963, the year that Plath died, Rich published *Snapshots of a Daughter-in-Law*, a book in which her newer poems picked up speed without losing substance.

Rich was too curious about the world, and the next day, to ever kill herself. No matter how angry and depressed she felt, she would push forward with extraordinary determination and resolve. She would find a powerful new direction for her life, first in the civil rights movement and then in the emerging women's liberation movement. Plath was the author of the iconic poem that has raised gooseflesh on many an arm, but it was Rich who rightly could be called "Lady Lazarus." She was the real "walking miracle" who emerged from the ashes of the 1950s determined to survive, thrive, and—if need be—"eat men like air."[46]

# PESSIMISTIC OPTIMIST

## *1963–1966*

*S*napshots of a Daughter-in-Law grew out of a strained, hectic, and ultimately fruitful time in Adrienne Rich's life. As she prepared the book for its publication in the spring of 1963, she included the year of composition after each poem. She had begun dating drafts of her poems in 1954, but this was her first book to include dates. She later wrote, "I had come to the end of the poetry I had collected in *The Diamond Cutters* and felt embarked on a process that was precarious and exploratory; I needed to allow the poems to acknowledge their moment."[1]

The poems in *Snapshots* span eight years, from 1954 to 1962. One of the few people who fully appreciated what she was doing in the book when it first appeared was a Harvard Ph.D. student named David Kalstone. The two enjoyed each other's company in Cambridge and later socialized in New York when they both lived there. Kalstone, who was gay, was one of the first critics to write about Rich in depth. When he interviewed her a decade after *Snapshots* came out, she told him what was going on in her life at the time she wrote the poems:

> I felt I was changing so much, and it was like trying to keep my finger on the pulse of that change; I very much wanted [the poems] to be in chronological order. I remember I dated the poems in that book because I was saying to myself and maybe saying to the reader, "In these years this is what I've been able to do." I was very conscious of the fact that when I was first having

children I wrote maybe only one or two poems a year that I could even remotely think of as finished. But as time went on, I began to write more again. I'd always been very prolific, so there *was* some conflict there; the dates were stating that.[2]

She wanted readers to see how motherhood had hampered her creative productivity. What they would take away from that insight was up to them. For her, the point was that the roles of mother and poet were in direct conflict: It was a cold, hard truth she had known for years, but in *Snapshots* that truth entered her public record.

Also for the first time, in *Snapshots,* she included notes explaining some of her sources,[3] and she insisted on writing her own jacket copy rather than leaving the task to an editorial assistant at Harper & Row, who would surely come up with what she called "one of those awful adjectival things."[4] In a brief paragraph of introduction, she put readers on notice that poems in *Snapshots* "move into neighborhoods usually zoned for prose: e.g., the situations of some women of our time, the meaning of written history for us today."[5]

By providing these guideposts, Rich shaped her story for future readers and critics. As a young girl she had dreamed of being the subject of a biographical study, and in an unpublished essay from the early 1950s called "Pages from a Memoir of the Forties," she wrote of herself and her undergraduate peers, "We all saw in our mind's eye the criticisms that might be written of us, the beautiful format of the little reviews which we read as studiously as we did the original works themselves. When we had written a paragraph or stanza that particularly pleased us, we would immediately see it inset in smaller print on a page devoted to an analysis of its complex merits."[6] Now in her early thirties and keenly aware she had reached a bend in the road of her development, she was intent on curating her work in ways few writers bother to do. She wasn't just attempting to guide reviewers and critics of her own time; she was placing herself in the historical continuum of poetry and looking to ensure her standing as a poet for the ages. Doing so revealed the degree of self-confidence she had in her own work and her evolving stature as an artist.

As for the poems in *Snapshots,* they represent a logical progression when viewed in the larger context of her life and later work. The first nine poems, beginning with "At Majority" (1954) and ending with "After a Sentence in 'Malta Laurids Brigge'" (1958), reflect an agile and inventive mind capable of taking calculated risks. Then, suddenly, these self-assured lyrics from her *New Yorker* period give way to "Snapshots of a Daughter-in-Law" (1958–60), a ten-part sequence poem of jagged edges and harsh insights. The composition dates reveal a long gestation period, a poem that could not be easily finished. An inspired choice for the title poem, "Snapshots" put Rich on the map of feminist thought at an opportune moment, though it didn't seem that way to her at the time.

"Snapshots" chronicles the considerable thought she had given to the limitations placed on women throughout history and in her own era. Beginning with the seemingly artless title, the poem concerns women's inability to act or be seen as individuals of depth and consequence. Going further, it shows how women have effectively deformed themselves in a world where nothing much is expected of them other than compliance.

Based on the poet's perceptions of her mother and their difficult relationship, the opening section addresses the mother still "in the prime of life," who was "once a belle in Shreveport." In a blistering indictment, Rich says the older woman's mind is now "mouldering like wedding-cake, / heavy with useless experience, rich / with suspicion, rumor, fantasy, / crumbling to pieces under the knife-edge / of mere fact." Appearing to describe herself in the third person, Rich then introduces the "glowering" daughter who "grows another way." The second part of the poem describes a woman, perhaps also based on Rich, who hears voices urging her on with her life while she is trapped in a domestic world that she loathes. She says the voices are "probably angels" telling her *"Have no patience," "Be insatiable,"* and *"Save yourself."* So distraught that she can hardly feel pain anymore, the woman doesn't seem capable of accepting guidance.

In the third part, Rich implies there is no rest or peace for any woman who dares to think about her plight in a male-dominated world. Her lines sharply answer Yeats's "Leda and the Swan." Rachel Blau DuPlessis writes, "When Yeats asks, 'Did she put on his knowledge with his power / before the indifferent beak could let her drop?' Rich responds, 'A thinking woman sleeps with monsters. / The beak that grips her, she becomes,' turning the question back, and showing an ambivalent judgment about the possession of phallic power and knowledge."[7]

Nor is there peace for women in each other's company. From the thinking woman alone with her demons, Rich shifts her attention to two "proud, acute, subtle" women verbally wounding each other, "The argument *ad feminam,* all the old knives / that have rusted in my back, I drive in yours, / *ma semblable, ma soeur!*" There is no unity, as yet, in sisterhood; women who might have helped each other instead vie for dominance and co-opt themselves to a destructive patriarchy. The next section turns to Emily Dickinson, who in the midst of a lifetime of homemaking wrote, *"My Life had stood—a Loaded Gun—."* The brief portrait or "snapshot" gives us the unmarried and childless Dickinson, "iron-eyed and beaked and purposed as a bird," whose expansive genius pulsates within a cramped domestic world. DuPlessis has pointed out that Dickinson appears to be a stand-in for Rich herself, who likewise knew her gifts but remained trapped in a life that suppressed her at every turn.[8]

In the next four parts, Rich builds her case against the societal forces that have warped women's lives. Thick with allusions to sources as disparate as Mary Wollstonecraft, Thomas Campion, and Denis Diderot, these bitingly worded sections express her anger at the unending abuse and hypocrisy that men and patriarchal institutions visit on women. As in the opening section, she has no patience with passive women, who settle for memories of "all that we might have been, / all that we were." While she acknowledges that women who dare "to cast too bold a shadow / or smash the mould straight off" can expect violent silencing, she refuses to traffic in collective self-pity.

The final part doesn't offer resolution to the enormous issues the poem raises, but it does suggest that women could define themselves and make their way in the world, if only they would find the inner strength and courage. Her vision of evolved womanhood takes the form of metaphor:

> Well,
> she's long about her coming, who must be
> more merciless to herself than history.
> Her mind full to the wind, I see her plunge
> breasted and glancing through the currents,
> taking the light upon her
> at least as beautiful as any boy
> or helicopter,

> poised, still coming,
> her fine blades making the air wince
> but her cargo
> no promise then:
> delivered
> palpable
> ours.[9]

Consciously or otherwise, Rich had taken Ted Hughes at his word when he mused that the best new poetry would combine "speed and cargo," the latter actually named in the poem. Her complex metaphor for womanhood was another in a lifetime of presentiments. She was no longer a glowering daughter but not yet the luminous force capable of writing the wholly new poems in *Diving into the Wreck* and *The Will to Change*. But the change would happen; she would get there, and in some innate way she could already see her new self cresting the horizon.

Although *Snapshots* was widely reviewed in newspapers large and small and received many positive notices, an aggrieved Rich later remembered it as a book entirely misunderstood by the men whose opinions mattered to her. In 1975, she remarked that this collection, "in which I was changing my forms, changing my structures, writing about women's lives, writing about my own life very directly and nakedly for that time and for me at that time—this book was ignored, was written off as being too bitter and personal. Yet I *knew* I had gone out beyond in that book. I was also very conscious of male critics then, and it was like flunking a course. It was as though they were telling me, 'You did so well in book two, but you flunked book three.' But I *knew* I was stronger as a poet, I knew I was stronger in my connection with myself."[10]

When Rich said the book was ignored, she was very likely thinking of its absence from the pages of *The New York Times*, which had reviewed her first two collections. Though there were circumstances that could justify the exclusion, it's easy to see why she felt she had been deliberately slighted. *Snapshots* was released early in 1963, in the midst of a printers' strike that affected all the major newspapers in New York City. On April 7, the *Times* published encapsulated reviews of books that would have received full treatment had the strike not intervened. Already on its way to becoming a blockbuster, Betty Friedan's *The Feminine Mystique* earned a thumbs-down from Lucy Freeman, a *Times* reporter.[11] But even a brief, critical review was better than nothing. And in Friedan's case, a sucker punch from a female reviewer hardly mattered, since her blunt, well-reported book about the ways women had been silenced and shut down in the past decade was designed to spark debate, and it accomplished that goal and sold extremely well.

*Snapshots* didn't make it into the digest of reviews. Perhaps her publisher, Harper, didn't push hard enough on the book's behalf, or maybe it was merely a space issue in the wake of the printers' strike. But given the condescending assessment *Snapshots* received in the inaugural issue of *The New York Review of Books,* a publication founded to fill the void in book reviewing during the strike, Rich had reason to wonder whether putting women front and center had cost her a review in the pages of the newspaper that mattered most to her.

The job of reviewing Rich in *The New York Review of Books* fell to R. W. Flint, a translator, book critic, and fellow Cambridge resident. Given the small and clubby world of literary Cambridge, it's hard to imagine they weren't acquainted, but Flint wasn't a close friend who habitually reviewed her work. Since the earliest days of her career, she had enjoyed positive notices from fellow poets who had no qualms about reviewing a friend's book. Reviews of her books by Donald Hall, Philip Booth, and later Robert Lowell and Hayden Carruth were not puff pieces, but because these men were fond of her, their critical objectivity was in doubt. There was always either a hint of brotherly affection or a whiff of Eros in their evaluations of her work. Randall Jarrell was no different. Though he had yet to meet Rich when he reviewed *The Diamond Cutters,* he was already wildly enthusiastic about her, not just her poetry.

She was, therefore, blindsided by Flint's commentary, a textbook example of encoded sexism. It warrants quoting at length because it shows the resistance she faced outside her circle of male poet friends:

Adrienne Rich's new book, *Snapshots of a Daughter-in-Law,* moves in predictable ways to escape the epithet "enchanting" once hung on her by a sympathetic Randall Jarrell, who wrote that she "... lives nearer to perfection than ordinary poets do." This book is unmistakably middle-aged, middle-period, in intention at least, spare and hard with experience, trying as hard as possible, against her taste for melodrama, to be ordinary. Modern poetry supplies a ready set of conventions for this change of key: the emotional or domestic crisis defined in a sort of imagistic shorthand that gives only a mood or state of mind away, not much of the crisis itself; the short, dour, columnar, unrhymed poem ending with a swat—"you are their king"; "Your glory was here."; "That is your true element."; "It is only a door."—all last lines from this book. And a rather relentless mention of missed opportunities, friends lost or gone wrong, dryness, acedia, hopeless suffering, stiffening mental joints—"Today we stalk / in the raging desert of our thought / whose single drop of mercy is /each knows the other there."

Because I liked a half-dozen poems in this book, it may be worth carping at Audenisms like the above, Empsonisms like "It is the grass that cuts the mower down / It is the cloud that swallows up the sky" or Lowellisms and Audenisms mixed, like "Baudelaire, I think of you! Nothing changes / rude and self-absorbed the current /dashes past, asking nothing, poetry / extends its unsought amnesty, / autumn saws the great grove down." Well, we all think of Baudelaire now and then, it's a pardonable luxury, but Miss Rich is a fair distance in many of these poems from substantiating her luxuries of imagery and tone. They are elegant notes, suggesting wide reading and devotion to the best, most anguished models.

What more than saves the title poem, "A Marriage in the Sixties," some of "Readings of History," "Antinous: the Diaries," "The Afterwake" or "The Loser," is the presence of having something to say beyond the need to write a certain kind of poem in a certain year at a certain age. Once a poet has slipped off her coming-out dress and donned the homely, melodramatic smock, we are as much on guard against an over-neat house as once we feared the party manners. But in her best poems here, Miss Rich puts us at ease with some graceful nuggets of truth. "Sometimes, unwittingly even, we have been truthful. / In a random universe, what more / exact and starry consolation?" Her skill and taste are beyond question.[12]

Flint saw what Rich wanted to do, and he had every right to point out what he did and didn't like about the way she went about doing it.

But his disparagement revealed the misogynist at his core. Well aware of Auden's comments about her neat and tidily dressed poems, he picked up the metaphor and dressed her in a "homely, melodramatic smock." This was a way to mark her as a woman whose poems could never match those of Auden, Lowell, or even the dolorous William Empson. While careful to say he admired a few of her new poems—a strategic hedge, central to the misogynist's playbook—he condemned her as middle-aged, boringly ordinary, and hopelessly derivative of male models to which she had no rightful claim. The best he could say of her was that sometimes her "nuggets of truth" put readers at ease, as if any serious poet would care to do that. Praising her skill and taste was his final, backhanded salvo, the kind of thing one would say about a very fine cook.

Flint was not the harshest assessor of *Snapshots*. That distinction belonged to none other than Arnold Rich. His furious poem-by-poem review of the book is a radioactive jewel of damnation tucked among Adrienne Rich's papers at Harvard. A cryptic note at the top of the first page reveals that the document was "copied in the hand of HJR"—that is, Helen Jones Rich. Since neither Helen nor Arnold knew how to type,[13] they did not keep carbon copies of their personal correspondence. Instead, Helen was in the habit of copying her letters and her husband's by hand. Perhaps that was her intent in this instance and she had sent her copy to her daughter, or perhaps Arnold had dictated the commentary to her, and Adrienne preserved the only extant copy. The archives don't indicate whether Adrienne received the document shortly after *Snapshots* came out or at some later date. It is clear from its inclusion in her papers, however, that she wanted future generations to see what her father was capable of and to know Helen literally had a hand in his savage response.

Arnold Rich disliked everything about *Snapshots of a Daughter-in-Law*, beginning with the title. He believed the poems were preoccupied with all things ugly and nasty, and he recoiled from what he perceived to be his daughter's bleak worldview. The title poem made no sense to him; "A Marriage in the 'Sixties" he deemed "Too private and personal for public consumption." He condemned several poems as self-centered and neurotic and questioned why Adrienne could no longer see beauty in the world. As for "Rustication," which briefly mentions Martin Luther King, Jr., he argued that topical references had no place in poetry intended to last beyond its historical moment: He was convinced no one would remember King in a few years' time. Summing up, he wrote, "I wouldn't want to present these 'beat,' sordid, irritable and often nasty poems of unrelieved despair to the world as representative of the quality of my mind, heart, character and life."[14] Though Adrienne liked the poetry of John Wieners and was intrigued by Ginsberg's "Howl," she was not part of the Beat poetry crowd.[15] Her father is probably the only person on record who ever thought she strayed into their territory.

Most of Rich's poet friends in the early 1960s were men, but she enjoyed a mutually supportive relationship with Denise Levertov. When Levertov expressed her admiration for "The Roofwalker" in draft form, Rich decided to dedicate it to her in *Snapshots,* even though she rarely dedicated poems at that point in her career. The two had met in 1959 through their husbands, who had been Harvard classmates, and quickly developed the sort of literary friendship Rich cherished. Like Rich, the English-born Levertov knew from an early age that she wanted to be a writer. Her father was a Russian Jew who converted to Christianity and became a priest in the Church of England. Her Welsh mother was a former schoolteacher who frequently read the Bible and poetry to the whole family. Both parents encouraged Denise and her older sister, Olga, to pursue their love of the arts.

Growing up in the countryside outside London, Denise was educated at home and enjoyed a profound spiritual connection to the natural world. Though she was blessed with creative talent, her parents didn't hound her to make something of her gift. She chose not to attend college, opting instead to serve as a nurse during World War II. When she arrived in the States as a young woman with one book in print, poet and critic Kenneth Rexroth helped make sure she gained an American following.[16] Later on, she became deeply involved in the antiwar movement of the 1960s and took a strong political stance in her poems.

Levertov was much closer in spirit to the Beats and Black Mountain poets than Rich was. Each was praised and elevated by prominent male poets—"Levertov by Kenneth Rexroth, William Carlos Williams, and Robert Duncan, and Rich by W. H. Auden and Robert Lowell."[17]

Levertov had an intuitive grasp of poetry that complemented Rich's more scholarly approach. Their many letters from the early 1960s show them learning from each other and influencing each other's views on individual poets and poetic techniques. After the publication of Don Allen's Beat-centric anthology, *The New American Poetry: 1945–1960,* which included Levertov but not Rich, they had a lengthy and spirited exchange about the strengths and shortcomings of the poets in the volume.[18]

In time, their circles of friends began to overlap. Rich introduced Levertov to Robert Lowell after Levertov read at Harvard in the spring of 1960, and Levertov made sure that Rich became acquainted with Robert Duncan, whom Levertov revered as a mentor and close friend.

Rich's meeting with Duncan did not go well. Although Duncan was probably no more egotistical than Lowell was, he didn't have Lowell's flair for spirited repartee or his deep interest in what Rich had to say. She was at home with an ailing son when Duncan took a seat in her kitchen. "It was clear he inhabited a world where poetry and poetry only took precedence, a world where that was possible," she wrote in her recollection of the visit,[19] her remarks echoing a long-ago criticism of Robert Bly, whose endless talk of poetry also wearied her.[20] "My sharpest memory is of feeling curiously negated between my sick child, for whom I was, simply, comfort, and the continuously speaking poet with the strange unbalanced eyes, for whom I was simply an ear."[21] Cross-eyed as the result of a childhood accident, Duncan was the object of Rich's cold scrutiny as he held forth without cease. It irritated her no end that he refused to acknowledge he had picked a bad day to visit her. The circumstances of their one-sided conversation lingered in her mind, as evidenced by a comment she made during a panel discussion with Lowell. When Lowell described Coleridge as a monologist who "could talk forever," Rich shot back, "Yes, imagine Hannah Arendt trying to cook with Coleridge in her kitchen."[22]

On November 21, 1963, the Academy of American Poets hosted a poetry reading by Rich and William Stafford at New York's Guggenheim Museum. Introduced by May Swenson, Rich was in her glory as an important poet commanding a sophisticated New York audience. Other events advertised in *The New York Times* alongside an announcement of Rich's reading attest to New York's vibrant mix of high culture and spirited fun in the early 1960s. One could go see the movie *Cleopatra* at the Rivoli; attend a performance in Sheridan Square of Genet's *The Maids;* drop in at the Five Spot Café to hear Thelonious Monk; catch a comedy act by Stiller and Meara at the Blue Angel; listen to Walter Kaufmann lecture on "Tragedy and Philosophy" at the YM-YWHA— and reserve tickets for a Christmas show at Carnegie Hall starring Mel Tormé and Count Basie, with the "Extra Added Attraction" of Woody Allen.[23]

On this occasion, Rich and Conrad were staying with Levertov and her husband, Mitchell Goodman, in their Greenwich Village loft apartment. The day after the reading, Adrienne and Alf went to a daytime rehearsal of Lowell's play *The Old Glory*. Little suspecting that they and the whole nation would soon be consumed by the horrifying news of President Kennedy's assassination, they took their seats in St. Clement's Episcopal Church, an Off-Broadway theater located in Hell's Kitchen, near the Theater District.

When the terrible news broke early in the afternoon, the people inside the theater knew nothing about it until they dispersed after the rehearsal. In a letter of February 1964 to Rich, Lowell recounted the cab ride he took immediately after leaving St. Clement's:

> The radio was going in a confused way [. . .] and the driver was grinning and giggling in a compulsive way, and saying, "The President has been shot." The death hadn't been announced but seemed probable. I asked the driver why he was smiling, and he said "Because it hurts so, it just hurts." . . . I must have been very wrought up anyway, because I lay for a long time on my bed listening to the reports and weeping. One felt as if a civil war were beginning. No rational daylight law seemed to hold, and it's easy to see how Johnson rushing to his plane feared lest an atomic war might be beginning.[24]

In a later letter to Lowell, Rich recalled how the two of them had been perched in "that crazy theatre-church" while a national tragedy was unfolding.[25]

Levertov heard about the shooting when she ventured out from her apartment to buy groceries for the party celebrating Rich's new book and her Guggenheim reading. Mitch Goodman found out while shopping for wine. By the time they all converged back at the apartment, everyone knew Kennedy was dead. People on the street were clustered around radios, listening to the latest bulletins. As Rich approached the apartment, she saw Levertov rushing downstairs to meet her and the others. Levertov threw out her hands in a silent gesture of shock and grief.[26]

In the aftermath of the assassination, Lowell suffered another breakdown, and Randall Jarrell sank into a debilitating depression. For Levertov, the revelation that the assassin, Lee Harvey Oswald, "had left-wing connections" magnified the horror of the occasion.[27] Because she hadn't admired Kennedy, Rich wasn't at risk of romanticizing him or his legacy. But she was not immune to the collective sense of devastation, and, in a way, the national mood of grief and mourning validated the bitter notes in *Snapshots of a Daughter-in-Law.*

With much to ponder in her life and art, Rich was hardly sitting around wondering whatever happened to Sumner Chilton Powell. One can only imagine her surprise when her former fiancé's name made headlines. Lo and behold, Powell had risen from the depths of his mental suffering and won the 1964 Pulitzer Prize for History. His winning book, *Puritan Village: The Formation of a New England Town,* was a detailed, genealogically precise study of the English settlers who founded Sudbury, Massachusetts. It grew out of the Ph.D. dissertation Powell had begun during his engagement to Rich.

*The New York Times* reported that Powell had "worked himself into ill health and was forced to abandon a teaching career during a 14-year struggle to explore the theme of his book and to get it published." Powell told the reporter he hoped the award would help him land an editing job.[28] It turned out that he had completed his doctorate and worked successfully as an educator for a number of years. Following in his mother's footsteps as a prep school teacher, he had taught at the Choate School in Connecticut and later at the Barnard School for Boys in New York City.

He also did some college teaching, but his unstable health stood in the way of a longtime career at any one place. When the Pulitzer was announced, he was unemployed and living with his mother. In later years he lived in group homes and was in and out of VA hospitals. Yet the rare honor of the Pulitzer confirmed the early promise his Harvard professors and Rich herself had seen in him. He had made an important contribution to the study of Colonial American history and earned the acclaim he always assumed would come his way.

✻

During this period, Rich's friendship with Lowell was intense, though they didn't necessarily see each other often. In an intimate letter dated June 3, 1964, he praised several of her poems and then wrote, "I was thinking of something more personal though yesterday as we sat at coffee, chatting about various people, Berryman, Susan Sontag, the Dutch paper on the table, and near you, all around you, your house, your children at school, Alf in Pakistan, and somewhere throwing shadows, your recurrent images of the doomed elms. I think you are saying that this last image is not what we are, it's rather some vein of decay, fatigue, tearing imperfection, and impatience that we carry about in us."[29] Rich would eventually turn against Lowell, but for now his insights into her personality and art must have been thrilling. He understood her in ways few others did.

Lowell's bouts of mental illness were well known to his friends even before he put the illness front and center in his poetry. Rich visited him at the hospital when he was recuperating and distracted him from his bleak circumstances with lively conversation. She saw how much he suffered, yet he still summoned the courage to take principled, public stands—there was a lesson here for her. When he was invited to the White House in 1965 to read his poetry as part of a daylong arts festival, he initially accepted and then reneged. In a letter to President Johnson, he wrote, "I thought of such an occasion as a purely artistic flourish, even though every serious artist knows that he cannot enjoy public celebration without making subtle public commitments." Even though he was "very enthusiastic" about much of Johnson's domestic policy, he continued, "I nevertheless can only follow our present foreign policy with the greatest dismay and distrust. What we will do and what we ought to do as a sovereign nation facing other sovereign nations seems to hang in the balance between the better and worse possibilities."

Not satisfied with a private exchange, he distributed copies of his eloquently worded letter to newspapers. His rebuke of Johnson was considered so noteworthy that *The New York Times* published a front-page story about it. Lowell was not the only poet speaking out against the Vietnam War—the *Times* referred to antiwar remarks Archibald MacLeish had made the previous week—but Lowell's pedigree seems to have been a factor. When the Pulitzer Prize–winning descendant of Boston Brahmins publicly rebuffed the president, it qualified as news.[30] Decades later, in response to a similar invitation to the White House, Rich would follow his lead.

She was not yet a consciously political poet, but she was moving in that direction, and not solely because of Lowell's example. In her sister and in Levertov, she had significant female models of public political engagement. Cynthia Rich became involved in antiwar activism starting in 1960 and soon took on the cause of racial equality as well,[31] long before Adrienne did. As for Levertov, the war in Vietnam consumed her; she would march in many demonstrations and protest in her poems, as well. But Levertov brought a subtlety to her understanding of political poetry. She was moved and inspired by the life and death of her sister, Olga, an unconventional woman and human rights advocate. Levertov biographer Donna Krolik Hollenberg has written, "She gradually came to view her identification with her sister as instrumental in her commitment to the ideology of the New Left." And in trading poems back and forth with Rich, she found inspiration for her sequence titled "The Olga Poems."[32]

Rich and Levertov might have drawn even closer, and learned even more from each other, given their overlapping political and artistic concerns. Their friendship flagged early in 1966, however, when Rich exploded in anger in Levertov's presence. They wrote to each other shortly after the incident. Addressing a brief letter of March 10, 1966, to "Dearest Den," Adrienne thanked her for her recent note and then said her flare of temper reflected pent-up thoughts and feelings she was just now able to express. She assured Levertov she hadn't turned into "a Golden Notebook woman, or a heartless woman, or an intellectual Emma Bovary,"[33] but she was neither apologizing nor recanting.

In her allusion to Doris Lessing's novel, *The Golden Notebook* (1962), in which the notebook author Anna Wulf suffers a breakdown, Rich hinted that she was in a terrible, dark state of mind. Although it is unknown what provoked her outburst, it clearly startled Levertov. Levertov's journal indicates that she took care of the Conrad boys for a week that fall, around the time Rich needed knee replacement sur-gery[34]—a significant and generous gift of her time and energy. But even if Rich's fit of pique didn't end the friendship, it exposed an emerging rift.

Levertov began distancing herself from Rich. They had continuing, intermittent contact, and more than two decades later, there would be some friendly exchanges, yet they would never again be as close as they once had been. Rich's side of their correspondence shows her repeatedly trying to mend the relationship, without much success. She had better luck with Goodman, whom Levertov eventually divorced. After her falling-out with Levertov, Rich and Goodman continued to communicate and occasionally visit.

In May 1966, Rich helped organize a reading at Harvard, the first in a national series protesting the war. Attracting about eight hundred people to Sanders Theatre, the occasion was her debut as an antiwar activist. In addition to Rich and Allen Grossman, a poet and Brandeis professor who helped her plan the event, the list of participating writ-ers included Anne Sexton, Rich's friends Robert Bly and I. A. Richards, and Susan Sontag.[35] The reading may have been the first time Rich encountered Sontag, who was fast becoming an intellectual celebrity, thanks to her newly published essay collection, *Against Interpretation*.

By 1966, Rich and Conrad began preparing for the second time to leave Cambridge, the city where they had fallen in love, married, and had their children. The impetus for their move had to do with Conrad's status at Harvard. He had taught there for a decade, first in Harvard College's economics department and later at Harvard Business School, a move considered downwardly mobile in the rarefied world of Harvard economists. He did not earn tenure from either his home department or the business school. Rich's correspondence indicates he hadn't expected to get it, but that wouldn't have softened the blow of the denial.

Once he began looking for positions, he had a tantalizing array of options. He was considering the University of Rochester, a position in Sussex, England, and two offers in New York City. There also was the exotic but less likely possibility of a year and a half in Bogotá. But Conrad was interested in moving back to New York, where he had grown up, even though he was unsure it would be a good place to rear the children and wondered whether he could afford a large-enough apartment for a family of five.[36]

In the end, Conrad nixed Rochester, Sussex, and Bogotá. With high hopes, he accepted an offer from City College of New York, where he would be a tenured professor of economics and lead City University of New York's new Ph.D. program in economics. Although the move to CCNY was a step down in prestige, the working-class public school was known at the time as the proletarian Harvard. It paid its faculty well and offered a first-rate education and free tuition to top graduates of New York City's high schools. Many of the students and faculty were Jewish, but by the time Conrad arrived, black and Puerto Rican students were pressuring the CCNY administration to expand and diversify the student body and develop a more racially and ethnically inclusive curriculum. He would soon join sides with these activists and become heavily involved in campus politics.

Before taking up residence in a spacious rent-controlled apartment on the Upper West Side, Alf and Adrienne and their sons, now ages eleven, nine, and seven, traveled to Jerusalem for the summer. It was a work trip for Conrad, who gave lectures and consulted with government officials, but Rich and the children had ample time to explore the ancient city. In July 1966, she wrote enthusiastically to Lowell and Hardwick about the enormous stars shining overhead, the Dead Sea, and the rocky hills that reminded her the Earth was a planet. The people of myriad nationalities fascinated her; she expressed her admiration for the city's handsome young people. The children were likewise relishing the trip, and she wrote with particular pride of the adventures David was having. Her eldest boy had climbed Mount Zion, crawled through tombs with only a candle to guide him, and seen the site where the Last Supper purportedly took place. Rich shared in his excitement. She had yet to embrace her Jewish heritage, but her delight in Jerusalem was palpable.[37]

In her 1966 conversation with a *Sunday Sun Magazine* reporter, shortly before her departure for Jerusalem, Rich talked matter-of-factly about global concerns. She said the prospect of individual death was a burden on everybody, but the possibility of world-ending destruction was a burden of a different order. Still, she said, "I don't think [global destruction] is inevitable. As Robert Lowell says, we are at a time in history when we can go either way. We can create a world more wonderful or more horrible than anything we have dreamed of. I think of myself as a pessimistic optimist."[38]

It was an apt description. Hard on the world and on herself, she always believed she could do better, that everybody could. Nothing engaged her more than her interwoven pursuits of knowledge and improvement. The troubles ahead would test and ultimately strengthen her resolve. Though she would drink from a deep cup of sorrow, she would find ways to fulfill the enormous promise she limned in the final lines of "Snapshots of a Daughter-in-Law," her mind sailing—flying!—into a future she could almost but not quite see.

# CHAPTER II

# LIKE THIS TOGETHER

## *1966–1968*

Just as she had once embraced Cambridge, Adrienne now set about falling in love with New York and making it her hometown. Over the next several years, she would walk the sidewalks in a private reverie, gaze meditatively at urban snows and sunsets, inhale deeply on the rare days when the city air smelled pure and fresh, and savor the neighborhood scenes she and her family were now part of. She would begin a teaching career that led her to City College, where both she and Alf immersed themselves in civil rights causes. The city would give her the raw materials for her storied middle years, yet living there during an era of national chaos would set her and her husband on a ruinous path.

In the first few months after the move, coming on the heels of the summer in Jerusalem, she told her friends how well things were going. The whole family was having new adventures that sounded idyllic when Adrienne described them in letters. Alf escorted David, Pablo, and Jacob to Marx Brothers films on Saturday afternoons and then walked them across the Brooklyn Bridge. The boys rode their bicycles in Central Park on mild days and sledded there when it snowed. Writing to Hayden and Rose Marie Carruth in December of 1966, Adrienne talked about going to the Thalia, a pleasingly quirky little theater on the Upper West Side, to see a double feature of *Potemkin* and *Alexander Nevsky:* "Coming out into the bitter cold, after-dark brightness of upper Broadway and buying coffeecake to take home and pushing against the wind all along 93ᵈ

Street was a curious urban kind of happiness."[1] It was as if she were in a movie of her own making. She wanted to believe her life would be better in Manhattan than in Cambridge, where she had felt increasingly cramped intellectually and socially.

In 1966, she published her fourth book of poetry, *Necessities of Life*. The gap of eight years between her second and third collections had worried her, but the new book was coming out just three years after *Snapshots of a Daughter-in-Law*. The new volume had a stylistic cohesion and wholly contemporary flavor. The ghostly imprint of Frost and Yeats no longer clung to her typewriter ribbon. She was done with sitting at one great knee or another.

*Necessities of Life* contains a series of her original poems and a selection of poems she'd translated from the work of Dutch poets, the fruits of the project she took on during her year in the Netherlands. The original poems include "After Dark," a preemptive elegy for her difficult relationship with her father, now in failing health and unable to manipulate her as he once had; and "Like This Together," a bleakly revelatory poem rooted in her marriage to Alfred. The translations are of poems by Martinus Nijhoff, Hendrik de Vries, Gerrit Achterberg, Leo Vroman, and Chr. J. van Geel. Most notable in this group is the Achterberg poem "Eben Haëzer," about a solitary man growing old as he tends to his farm. Rather than translate the title as she had for the other Dutch poems, Rich included a parenthetical note explaining that "Eben Haëzer" is "Hebrew for 'Stone of Help'; a common old name for farmhouses in Holland."[2] The title would soon take on significance in her personal life.

In later years, she often commented on what she considered the underlying theme of *Necessities of Life*. It was important to her that critics and other readers understand what she herself hadn't fully grasped at the time of composition. In rereading the collection, she said, "I was struck by the awareness that it's almost entirely about death, something I never noted when I was writing the poems. In some ways, I thought I was dying then—essential portions of me were dying and I wanted to explore this. That was a period of my life, too, when I really saw for the first time that we all die ultimately, that we are dying all along, while we're living."[3]

Her bold new poems in *Necessities of Life* were hard won, many of them exposing a deep sorrowfulness not present in her earlier collections. Her ruminations on death are hard to miss in unambiguously titled poems such as "The Corpse-Plant" and "Mourning Picture." The book's overarching theme is also evident in "Halfway," an elegy conflating her life with that of her deceased maternal grandmother, Mary Gravely Jones, and "Autumn Sequence," which ends with an image of the narrator's "hero" passing out, his tongue coated with old gossip.[4]

"After Dark" was provoked by Rich's feelings upon watching her father fall asleep at home in his sickbed. In his infirmity, he was no longer the despot she had known in her younger years. From the opening lines, in which she describes him as "old tree of life / old man whose death I wanted / I can't stir you up now," she doesn't hide her animosity toward him, but with the foreknowledge of his death comes a pained nostalgia for the battles now ended:

Alive now, root to crown, I'd give

—oh, something—not to know
our struggles now are ended.
I seem to hold you, cupped
in my hands, and disappearing.

When your memory fails—
no more to scourge my inconsistencies—
the sashcords of the world fly loose.
A window crashes

suddenly down. I go to the woodbox
and take a stick of kindling
to prop the sash again.
I grow protective toward the world.[5]

A small masterpiece of chilly candor, the poem shows just how much Rich loathed her father and just how hard it would be for her to live in a world without him.

"Like This Together" is not precisely about death, but it portrays a troubled marriage that contained the seeds of its dissolution. Given that Rich wrote the poem in 1963, before she and her family began their new life in New York, she probably hoped it captured what could be benignly labeled a rough patch. In fact, it was a grim predictor of worse things to come. The poem begins:

Wind rocks the car.
We sit parked by the river,
silence between our teeth.
Birds scatter across islands
of broken ice. Another time
I'd have said "Canada geese,"
knowing you love them.
A year, ten years from now
I'll remember this—
this sitting liked drugged birds
in a glass case—
not why, only that we
were here like this together.[6]

From the poem's time of publication in *Necessities of Life* in 1966, Rich and Conrad would have just four more years together. She would grow increasingly frustrated by her inability to get him to talk to her about what was wrong between them. But in 1963, and in 1966, she had no intention of leaving him or any fear he would leave her. The poem assumes a durability that ultimately wasn't there.

The new book's positive notices puffed Rich's sails as she entered New York's literary society as a resident member. As usual, her friends cast favorable votes. "There is not a glib word in it, nor a wasted breath," Hayden Carruth wrote in *Poetry*. "What gives [her materials] their originality is, first, her diction, pared to words of extreme force, and second, her syntax, driven into quick, bright spurts of feeling. Behind diction lies her gift, greatly and expressly human, which we call, although again the word is narrower than the thing itself, intelligence."[7] In the *Christian Science Monitor*, Albert J. Gelpi heralded Rich's volume as "the most important book of new poems since Randall Jarrell's 'The Lost World.' It places her, clearly and unmistakably, in the forefront of the generation after Robert Lowell, John Berryman, and Jarrell, and that ranks her among the most interesting poets writing in English today."[8] Gelpi and his wife, Barbara Charlesworth Gelpi, had known Rich at Harvard and were to be lifelong friends and champions of her work.

Of all the reviews she received, the most significant to her was Robert Lowell's in *The New York Times Book Review.* Incisive and quotable as ever, Lowell managed to sum up his deep knowledge of her and her work in a single sentence: "Adrienne Rich has grown steadily more interesting from book to book and now in her fourth work, *Necessities of Life,* this advance, tortuous and sometimes tortured as it has been, is an arrival, a poised and intact completion." He could have stuck with "interesting," the way Gelpi did, but the imp in Lowell, the friend who wasn't quite a friend, couldn't resist a retrospective jab at *Snapshots of a Daughter-in-Law:* "Sometimes we seemed to be watching the terrible and only abstractly imaginable struggle of a beetle to get out of its beetle shell and yet remain a beetle."[9] In her letter thanking Lowell for the review, she made no mention of this unkind metaphor.

There were other readers whose interest in the book went beyond the poems. Back in Baltimore, Helen Rich added a postscript to a letter she and Arnold had jointly written to a friend of theirs: "I agree with you completely that Adrienne's photograph in the N.Y. Times and in her book (!) was 'unflattering.' It was too bad that she permitted anyone to publish it, or that she accepted such a photograph at all."[10] Needless to say, this wasn't the kind of critique Adrienne wanted or needed from anyone, especially her mother, but it was typical of the mutually tone-deaf relationship they had.

The author's photo notwithstanding, the success of *Necessities of Life* redounded to her new publisher's credit. For this latest volume, Rich had ended her relationship with Harper & Row in favor of W. W. Norton, where Denise Levertov had recently become the acquisitions editor for a new poetry series. Her defection from her old publishing house had been in the works for several years. Harper had not paid her an advance for *Snapshots,* nor had it kept the book in print. The 1963 volume, which was dear to her, had sold about a thousand copies, with approximately two hundred of those remaindered. Since she had anecdotal evidence the book was still in demand, she felt her publisher's decision not to do a paperback edition was a mistake. In its publicity materials, further, Harper referred to her as Adrienne Cecile Rich, when she had long ago dropped her middle name from her published works.

Causing her still more irritation, she found out indirectly and belatedly that her editor, Elizabeth Lawrence, had retired.

Casting about for a better option, Rich pondered the advantages of going to a smaller publisher, a counterintuitive move. She thought a small press might promote her books more vigorously than Harper had done, and she said so. Various people at Harper, including publisher Cass Canfield and her new editor, Frances Monson McCullough, tried to convince her to stay. Especially noteworthy is a flattering missive from Canfield in which he said that if Rich ever wrote a novel, he would want Harper to have the option of publishing it.[11] This was a tacit acknowledgment that a promising novel could earn her a sizable advance. Canfield may have been aware that she had devoted a great deal of time to writing fiction in her youth.

In the end, she stuck with poetry and landed happily at Norton, thanks to Levertov. In the years ahead, as Rich generously assisted women whose writing she believed in, she chose not to laud the women in publishing who helped advance her own career. It was a curious omission, but to credit Levertov and Katharine White (and Elizabeth Lawrence, had she felt especially generous) would have complicated the story she told about herself later on. There were elements of tokenism in her career, as she insisted, and she was right to decry the virulent sexism in publishing, but both women and men provided her with the sort of inside assistance found in almost every commercially successful writer's career.

The actual editing of *Necessities of Life* had fallen not to Levertov but to George Brockway, the president of the publishing house, a seasoned editor whom Rich considered "decent" and "receptive," though not brilliant.[12] Brockway had published Betty Friedan's *The Feminine Mystique*, the blast of truth that helped launch the second wave of feminism in the United States.

In taking Rich on, Brockway acquired another feminist powerhouse in the making. Norton reprinted *Snapshots* in both hardback and paper, and everybody at the publishing house treated her with the deference she found lacking at Harper. The new relationship quickly paid off. The following year, *Necessities of Life* was named a finalist for the National Book Award for Poetry, an honor for author and publisher alike. By 1968, she had a new editor at Norton, John Benedict, the editorial genius behind the famed Norton anthologies. Benedict won Rich's trust and provided her with valuable counsel for the next two decades.

$\gtrsim$

A drienne had grown up in an academic household, and her husband was a professor. Many of her poet friends earned a sizable portion of their income by teaching creative writing. It was natural, then, that she would turn to teaching as a supplemental career. In the spring of 1965, she had served as Swarthmore College's Phi Beta Kappa poet; the following spring, she returned to give a reading with her friend Philip Booth. By the summer of 1966, while in Jerusalem, she had agreed to teach a noncredit poetry-writing workshop at Swarthmore, a small liberal arts college near Philadelphia.

Shortly after her first day on the job, she wrote to Carruth that she had trembled on the train all the way from New York to Philadelphia and felt like "a woman going to her first assignation with a new lover." Once she was in the classroom, she enjoyed the attention of admiring students. She told Carruth that teaching poetry would bring new focus to her own study of poetry—an unexpected boon.[13] The academic year was off to a very good start.

Not far into the semester, however, Rich learned she needed surgery on her severely arthritic right knee. She had known a prosthetic knee was in her future but had planned to put off the operation until summer. Now her doctor and consulting surgeons advised that she have it as soon as possible to ensure a full recovery. Rich informed her department chair, George Becker, that she would be hospitalized for a month after surgery and on crutches for nearly a month after that. She had no choice but to endure the long and arduous ordeal if she wanted to walk normally again. Becker accommodated her absence but reduced her salary. They agreed she would return to her teaching as soon as she was able.[14]

During her recovery at New York University's hospital, she corresponded regularly with the Carruths, who showered her with get-well gifts of flowers, books, and cakes. Although she alluded to pain and depression, she was determined to emerge revivified on the other side of her lengthy hospital stay. In December, she wrote to Hayden and

Rose Marie, "Captivity, passivity, are the worst of it—pain the least—and I hate this weakness which makes even reading and writing still uphill work." Her cast would soon be removed and her leg put in traction. Then, a grueling exercise regimen would begin.[15]

In the meantime, she passed her days and evenings gazing out the hospital window at the East River. The tugboats and barges, the "most poetic and soothing of industrial scenery," held her interest. "At night the tugs move downstream, all yellow and green lights, silently, like little lantern hung boats in a dream, a procession. But the hours are very slow here."[16] A few days later, Rich welcomed a "terror of a physiotherapist" who taught her exercises designed to strengthen her muscles and increase her flexibility. "It is all pain and tears and uphill work at first, but there's a curious element of pride in forcing oneself to endure a good deal of physical discomfort, driving on through it."[17] Soon, she was walking with crutches and anticipating her return home on Christmas Eve.[18]

At home, her convalescence continued. While she rested in bed with the family cat as her constant companion, the children went sledding in Central Park and Alf wrote at his desk. At night the couple lay in bed, chatting idly. She was grateful for the quiet time as she realized they had made it through a year of major changes.[19] By New Year's Eve, she was forcing herself to exercise a staggering six hours a day, in hopes she would achieve the full recovery her doctors had promised her. She wrote to Carruth that she would push through her daily labor for the next couple of months as if she were cramming for a doctoral exam or something else equally awful and important.[20] Along with her strength and energy, her mood was improving. Denise Levertov had brought her a batch of Carruth's poems to read, and she rejoiced she could again concentrate on something other than her body.[21]

In late March, in a surprising coda to her surgery, Rich was required by NYU's hospital to participate in a surgical conference on the treatment of rheumatic joints. The conference took place at Bellevue, a historic public hospital whose name was synonymous for many with psychiatric care. Once she arrived at Bellevue, she had to traverse cavernous wards full of male patients in varying conditions. Unattended by doctors or nurses, most lay in bed, staring into space. Rich's further descriptions of guffawing patients and snickering aides suggest her path took her through a psychiatric ward. Unfazed, she noted the pale sunlight barely penetrating dirty windows high above the patients in their beds. After the conference, while she waited for a cab to take her home, a paddy wagon filled with drug addicts arrived at the emergency room's entrance. From behind the vehicle's barred windows came whisperings and loud laughter that reminded her of a radio suspense drama.[22] This, too, was New York. With her knee rehabilitated and her day at Bellevue completed, a stoic Rich listened and learned.

Upon her return to Swarthmore, her students welcomed her back with cookies and heroic couplets written in her honor.[23] Still on crutches for the first part of the spring term, she was glad to be with them again, though the first bloom of her teaching career was over. She had begun to feel she wasn't particularly good at it.[24] Nevertheless, when Columbia University invited her to teach in its new MFA program in creative writing, she accepted.[25] She stayed a second year at Swarthmore and then resigned, telling Samuel Hynes, George Becker's successor as department chair, that as much as she liked the students, she was ready to concentrate her teaching energies on "the excellent, and more committed, students at Columbia."[26] She recommended her close friend Jean Valentine as her successor and was pleased to learn some months later that Valentine had been selected for the position.[27]

For a long time, Adrienne and Alf had wanted to own a vacation home in Vermont. They enjoyed their friends in Willoughby, where they had rented a house in the summer for many years. They also liked the idea of being near Hayden and Rose Marie Carruth, who lived in Johnson. The Carruths' way of living, close to the earth and without pretension, fascinated Adrienne. Although Alf's occasional letters and postcards to Hayden reveal his affection for the couple, the primary bond was between Adrienne and Hayden. By the time she had moved to New York, she considered him her dearest, wisest, and most poetically gifted friend. She had sought him out after reading drafts of his poems that Denise Levertov had showed her several years earlier, and they had corresponded ever since, each sending the other drafts of poems and essays in progress.

With his shaggy beard and penetrating green eyes, Carruth was a mesmerizing blend of manly sturdiness and crystalline fragility. He had majored in journalism at the University of North Carolina, served in the military during World War II, and earned a master's degree from the University of Chicago on the G.I. Bill. He was on his way to early prominence as editor of *Poetry* magazine before mental-health problems interrupted his career. Plagued by depression and agoraphobia, he retreated to a mental institution in White Plains, New York, near where his parents lived. Eventually, thanks to a psychiatrist determined to rehabilitate him, he was able to live on his own again. He chose a penurious and physically difficult existence in rural New England in the company of his third wife, Rose Marie. (She said his psychiatrist insisted on interviewing her before she and Hayden married and exacted a promise from her never to leave her husband.[28]) With temperatures dropping far below zero during the punishing Vermont winters, he chopped firewood, tended the chickens and other animals, and then went inside to write poems, reviews, and countless letters, many of them to Adrienne. Their correspondence was a lifeline for both of them.

His hardscrabble life caught and held her attention. Solicitous to a fault, she urged him to take teaching jobs to boost his income and fill a social void, offered to shop for him if he needed stationery supplies from the Manhattan stores she frequented, and eagerly loaned him books, in hopes he would enjoy them as much as she had. She would do virtually anything for him, so long as he kept writing to her, critiquing her poems, and giving her an outlet for a version of herself she especially liked. That version, that persona, was warmhearted, kind, and generous—a far cry from the austere, off-putting, and frosty persona that had pleased her so much around the time she published *Snapshots of a Daughter-in-Law.*

She soon began writing to him at length every couple of weeks, often every week or even twice a week. Sprinkled in between her typed letters were handwritten notes and postcards. Though her early letters were often addressed to both him and Rose Marie, by 1968 she usually wrote directly to Hayden, and it was clear all letters were for him, just as in her college days her letters home were written for her father even if addressed to her whole family. Given her love of literary correspondence, Hayden was a dream: a poet she considered her equal, a critic whose knowledge of poetry matched and in some areas exceeded her own, and a judicious reader of her poems. It didn't hurt that he was a man. Her letters are effusive in her praise of him, a sign that she still hadn't overcome her desire and need for male approval.

While she clearly wanted to believe their love for each other was beyond reproach, the intimate, almost entirely epistolary friendship became a source of concern for Rose Marie. Hayden had a history of infidelity, and she worried that the poets' friendship would spill over into a love affair. Hayden made a point of collecting the mail from the mailbox, so Rose Marie didn't realize how many letters Adrienne was writing to him. When Adrienne later professed shock and displeasure that he had kept many of her letters a secret from his wife, that still left open the question as to why she felt compelled to write to him so frequently and with such intensity. No matter the heavily intellectual content or the friendly allusions to Rose Marie, the flood of letters laid bare her deep investment in another woman's husband. As for Alfred, he was used to Adrienne's need for poet friends who could match her letter for long letter. He liked both Hayden and Rose Marie and bought them gifts when he traveled abroad; he occasionally wrote his own letters to them. There is no indication he viewed Hayden as a threat to his marriage, but whether either spouse acknowledged it or not, her heavy correspondence with Carruth was evidence of her divided attentions.

When Alf found a farmhouse for sale in West Barnet, Vermont, about an hour's drive from the Carruth home in Johnson, it seemed like an omen. Alf saw the property in October 1966 and reported back to Adrienne, who wrote the Carruths that the house was "plain" but "nice," with a bay window in the kitchen and an impressive barn. The property had a pleasing view and sugar maples that would yield syrup.[29] The owner was initially reluctant to sell his field across the road, which the couple wanted as a buffer zone. Negotiations were painstakingly slow, but by the spring of 1967, the house was theirs. In time, they were able to purchase the additional acreage.

Their vacation home was located a few miles from the small town of Peacham, and it was just what Rich had wanted. She and Alf eagerly learned the history of the whole area. They found out the house had been owned and probably constructed by early Scottish immigrants, members of a Reformed Presbyterian sect, who were buried in a nearby graveyard. Alf named the house "Eben Haëzer," after the poem by Gerrit Achterberg that Adrienne had translated and included in *Necessities of Life*. Their new home's stone foundation and prominent doorstones had called the poem to his mind.[30] The unusual name, more familiar to most people as Ebenezer, reflected their hope and belief that the house would be a true Stone of Help, a refuge whenever they needed one.[*]

In the fall of 1967, Rich began teaching in Columbia's new MFA program. In addition to writing poems, her students were assigned a significant amount of reading. A syllabus preserved in her papers at Harvard lists the following as required reading: Ezra Pound's *ABC of Reading*, Louis Zukofsky's *A Test of Poetry*, an anthology called *The Structure of Verse*, and numerous essays by D. H. Lawrence, A. E. Housman, Paul Valéry, Gottfried Benn, and Randall Jarrell. Without her supervision, students also were expected to read Shakespeare, Dante, Blake, Hardy, Lawrence, Frost, Heidegger, Wittgenstein, Thomas Traherne, William Carlos Williams, Theodore Roethke, and the *Oxford Book of Nursery Rhymes*. The assigned readings, Rich wrote in the syllabus, "represent a few attempts, by poets or men who took poetry seriously, to see where poetry intersects with life, and what kinds of poetry stand the best chance of doing so."[31]

There were no women listed on Rich's syllabus—no Levertov, Plath, Sexton, or Sarton. The glaring absence, combined with her unselfconscious reference to "men who took poetry seriously," shows how far and fast she would have to travel in the next several years to become one of the nation's premiere feminists. She assigned poems by an African-American man, LeRoi Jones, later known as Amiri Baraka, whose work she distributed on mimeographed sheets, but if her students wanted to read books of poetry by women, it appears that they were on their own.

Rich held her MFA class in her living room. During the first of her two years teaching in the program, a student named Hugh Seidman was in her class. He later recalled his first impressions of her and Conrad:

---

[*] It's unclear whether the name stuck. Rich rarely referred to the property as "Eben Haëzer" in her later correspondence with friends.

"She was only eleven years my senior—I was somewhat older than the others, having already been to grad school in math and theoretical physics—but she had by that time been a celebrated poet for almost two decades since winning the Yale prize at twenty-one. 'Alf,' her husband, was unobtrusive. He appeared from time to time with a word for her or to offer a cigar or a drink. He seemed to like to play the host—to make people feel at ease."[32]

While in her class, Seidman worked on the poems that would appear in his first book, *Collecting Evidence*. Rich liked him and his poetry, and hosted a party in his honor a few years later when his book was published in the Yale Series of Younger Poets. She also became close friends with Jack Litewka and Elise Young, also students in her class. There was still another student, however, who would go on to have a career as distinguished as Rich's own, and the two of them didn't hit it off at all.

Louise Glück was twenty-four years old when she audited Rich's class at Columbia in the fall of 1967. Her background was unusual. As a teenager she had suffered from anorexia and withdrawn from high school so she could get well. Later, the illness recurred and she was forced to withdraw from college. In the meantime, she was studying and writing poetry with serious intent. By the time she attended Rich's class, she already had a collection of poetry in print, *Firstborn*. She wanted exacting criticism that would help her learn how to revise her new poems. That was not what she got from Rich. In her memory of the class, her awestruck classmates waited for their professor to pass a quick judgment on their drafts.

Glück said the other students loved sitting on the floor with their professor, calling her by her first name (as Rich instructed them to do), and getting a quick, hip reaction to their submissions. If she liked a poem, Rich would say, "I dig it." If not: "I don't dig it." Glück didn't dig the class or her professor. She wanted to talk poetry in depth; she didn't feel comfortable in the artificially relaxed setting, nor did she share her professor's interest in the unrest afflicting Columbia. Thinking back on the course, she didn't recall the long list of books on Rich's syllabus; it's possible that as an auditor, she wasn't expected to do the reading. In any case, she said she learned more from Seidman's revisions of the poems that would appear in his first book than she did from Rich.

Glück recalled showing her professor a poem that Rich obviously didn't like, yet there were no suggestions for revision. Unwilling to scrap the draft, Glück took it to the poet Stanley Moss and asked him for guidance. Moss gave her the detailed response she was looking for. After revising the poem, she took it back to Rich. In Glück's recollection, Rich said, "Oh, you made it better." The younger poet came away feeling angry that her professor could have helped her but chose not to. She assumed Rich viewed her as "irredeemably bourgeois, a person of no interest."[33]

Rich spent hours writing to her poet friends and offering close readings of their drafts; she backed up her opinions with incisive comments on word choice, imagery, symbolism, diction, and meter. She generously poured her complete attention into helping them improve their work. Her contrasting, and surprisingly lenient, approach to the MFA class that Glück audited was in all likelihood a by-product of the times. She didn't feel comfortable asserting authority over graduate students, whom she viewed as allies in the antiwar movement. She would get them and herself through the semester; if she developed lasting friendships with those she especially liked, they could talk about line breaks and caesuras later—much later.

In Baltimore, a world away from Rich's life in Manhattan, Arnold Rich's condition grew worse. He spent his days and nights in bed at the Wrennery, as he had long ago named the elegant home where birds sang outside his windows. Retired from Johns Hopkins since 1958, he had suffered a heart attack in April 1964 and now suffered from dementia as well as heart and prostate problems.[34] His occasional periods of lucidity were excruciating for him, for it was then he realized just how sick he was. Fearing he would be scorned by anyone who came to his home and saw him in his frailty, he refused all visitors except for family and his physician. Helen Rich tended her husband with the help of Pearline, the black housekeeper, whom she thought of as her "Rock of Gibraltar."[35] The bedridden Arnold was barely recognizable as the overbearing genius who had once discoursed on all manner of subjects to a young Adrienne while she perched at the foot of his bed.

As his death neared, he remained tragically ambivalent about his

Jewish heritage. In "Sources," Adrienne wrote that he closely followed radio reports on the Six-Day War in 1967, during which Israel triumphed over its Arab neighbors. Perhaps he had felt kinship with other Jews all along; he never told her if he did. He was like the title character in her poem "The Roofwalker"—vulnerable, exposed, in an untenable situation of his own making. Helen bore the brunt of his anguish and confusion. Not long before he died, he wanted to speak with a rabbi, but they decided not to summon one in the middle of the night, when he felt the urge to talk. During his last days, he insinuated to her that he had let people think *she* was anti-Semitic as a means of distancing himself from other Jews. Helen was justifiably furious, though perhaps, so close to death, he was no longer speaking rationally.[36]

Although both daughters paid visits to Baltimore, they were too far away to help with day-to-day care on a regular basis. Cynthia and her husband, Roy Glauber, lived near Boston with their young son. Although Glauber was Jewish, Cynthia believed Arnold had not objected to the Harvard physicist because he was a professor, not a mere graduate student (like Conrad was when he and Adrienne married), and he came from a solidly established middle-class Jewish family (rather than one with more recent immigrant origins like Conrad's now-affluent parents). Or maybe Arnold simply wasn't as invested in Cynthia's choice of a mate as he was in Adrienne's: Adrienne was always the apple of his censorious eye.

As "After Dark" makes clear, Adrienne's visits with her ailing father were difficult. At some point after David's birth, she had begun seeing both of her parents again, but according to Cynthia, Adrienne and Arnold never truly reconciled. Cynthia suggested there was little for them to reconcile, since Adrienne and her father had only a superficially meaningful relationship to begin with. After his death, Adrienne said she had hated him for a long time.[37] A prod and a scourge, a man whose love of knowledge far exceeded his knowledge of love, Arnold had propelled her into literature before she could even write. She had spent her life becoming the accomplished poet he wanted her to be. Like a champion tennis player who excels at the game while chafing against the controlling coach who never lets up, she could not stop being his creation no matter how much she resented his influence. Out of filial duty, she made her way to Baltimore and visited him.

⁂

On April 4, 1968, Martin Luther King, Jr., was assassinated in Memphis. In a sign he wasn't as brilliant at predicting the future as he was at so many other things, Arnold had once said King would be so soon forgotten that Adrienne should not have mentioned his name in a poem in *Snapshots of a Daughter-in-Law*.[38] The riots in Baltimore after the world-famous civil rights leader's assassination suggested otherwise, and the chaos meant Helen Rich couldn't get to Johns Hopkins Hospital, where her husband was now a patient. In a letter to Dr. David C. Sabiston, a Duke University heart surgeon who had previously worked at Hopkins, Helen Rich described the pandemonium: "By now you must have heard that the Hospital is surrounded by Federal troops and the interns' families have had to be evacuated from '550' because of very near and numerous fires and looting." While trying to visit Arnold, she got caught in the middle of a race riot. "Sunday I innocently attempted to drive to the Hospital but was turned back by a gathering mob on Harford Road and escorted part way home by a police car. I am now staying in the house until further notice."[39]

As fires raged in the black neighborhood surrounding the hospital, Arnold Rich faded in and out of consciousness. He had spent his career making important discoveries and teaching generations of medical students at this very hospital where he now lay dying. A decade had passed since he talked art and philosophy with his colleagues and then conducted research late into the evening before summoning Helen to drive him home. Now, although the doctors on staff knew who he was, they saw him as a dying patient rather than a formidable scientist and mentor.

As head pathologist, he had foreseen the numbing impersonality of sprawling medical complexes. Though it seemed counterproductive to his colleagues, he resisted pressure to pursue lucrative government grants. What he wanted to preserve was a collegial hierarchy in which doctors and medical students solved problems, made discoveries, and treated patients in the service of philosophical inquiry much greater than the sum of its clinical parts. Once, when Dr. Ivan Bennett, a friend and Hopkins colleague, proudly showed him a sophisticated new laboratory funded by a federal grant, Arnold had remarked, "You know, Bennett, I'd trade it all for one good idea."[40] He couldn't stop progress, but he could deflate its pretensions with a well-placed jab.

Dr. Arnold Rice Rich died on April 17, 1968, at age seventy-five. Obituaries in the Baltimore newspapers, *The Washington Post,* and *The New York Times* were picked up by wire services and published across the country. These articles and later biographical portraits left no doubt that Arnold Rich was a monumental figure in mid-twentieth-century medicine. His thousand-page magnum opus, *The Pathogenesis of Tuberculosis* (1944), was translated into French and Japanese, and a second edition was published in 1951. The French government had named him a chevalier of the Legion of Honor, and the University of Toronto honored him in 1956 as the individual who had made the most important contribution "toward practical knowledge in medical arts and science" in the past decade. An honorary fellow in the British Royal Society of Medicine, he had received top honors from the National Tuberculosis Association and the Association of American Physicians. Other honors had come from the Association of Military Surgeons, the American College of Physicians, and the Japanese Society of Tuberculosis.[41]

In 1993, twenty-five years after her father died, Adrienne Rich received a letter from Dr. James Shaka, who served as a medical resident under her father. Shaka had loved Dr. Rich, whom he viewed as a stand-in for his own father. He wanted a closer, warmer relationship than the older doctor was willing to have. On one occasion when Dr. Rich dismissed his ideas as foolish, Shaka was deeply hurt.

But Shaka, observant and empathetic, saw beneath Arnold Rich's seemingly impervious exterior. He was aware that one of the most magnificent minds to pass through the medical school had been held at the rank of associate professor of pathology for twenty-one years before finally being promoted to full professor. Even then, Dr. Rich had to wait another three years before getting the top post in the pathology department, a job he had been doing for those three years in an acting capacity. Shaka thought anti-Semitism was to blame. He told Rich that her father "chose to overcome all obstacles and was ultimately successful, but it is a tough, lonely road. I think he wanted all of us to be equally tough."[42]

Adrienne's innate drive could hardly be separated from the work ethic her father had instilled in her since toddlerhood. His death freed her from his earthly domination, but her relationship with him would continue for the rest of her life. He was an influence on her like no other. A bully, a bane, a father whose genuine love for her was tangled up with a myriad of demands and unreasonable expectations, he nonetheless had inspired her unwavering devotion to learning and guided her toward the career that meant the world to her. She knew these were not inconsiderable gifts.

In his last months, his continued suffering had penetrated the sheet of ice around her heart. When he died sooner than she expected, she was glad his pain had ended: "So it's a relief—and, more than I could have believed—a blow."[43] The graveside service at Baltimore National Cemetery was private. Adrienne and Alf took David to the funeral, but not their younger sons. That morning at 14 Edgevale Road, in the company of her mother and sister, she chose the Twenty-third Psalm and a chapter from Ecclesiastes for the rabbi to read during the service. The rabbi had never met Dr. Rich and knew nothing of him other than what the family told him to say.[44] Adrienne told Carruth the rabbi read Ecclesiastes 12, known to many for the line "Vanity of vanities, saith the preacher, vanity of vanities; all is vanity," whereas in Cynthia Rich's recollection, it was Ecclesiastes 3, which begins, "To every thing there is a season, and a time to every purpose under the heaven: / A time to be born, and a time to die; a time to plant, and a time to pluck up that which is planted." Cynthia said Arnold was fond of quoting this chapter, one of countless passages of verse he knew by heart and one that would be more appropriate for a funeral than the chapter Adrienne cited.

Given the competing recollections, this may be a rare instance of Adrienne misremembering an important detail. Perhaps in reading the Bible the morning of the service, the darker of the two chapters lingered in her mind even though she chose the other for the service. Chapter 12, verse 12, may have spoken to her personally: "And further, by these, my son, be admonished: of making many books there is no end; and much study is a weariness of the flesh." In any case, she came away feeling the author of Ecclesiastes was an existentialist,[45] a provocative remark her father would have appreciated.

At the end of the service, she and Cynthia and Helen each threw a pachysandra into the grave.[46] The green plants covered the hill in front of 14 Edgevale Road; their gesture was a way to acknowledge Arnold Rich's love of his cherished Wrennery, where he had lived for nearly three decades.

In the years ahead, Adrienne and her mother had the opportunity to get to know each other anew. They never formed a close bond, and at times, an angry and frustrated Adrienne wanted to disavow all familial connection to Helen. However, in the months after Arnold's death, they both made an effort. Adrienne invited her mother for a summertime visit in Vermont while Alf was traveling in Ghana. In a letter to a friend, Helen said she was writing from "the cool Vermont mountains with Adrienne and I feel much stronger both mentally and physically. She is such a stimulating person to be with so very energetic, writes almost every night until after midnight, and busy all day with her three boys."[47] Helen regarded her daughter as if she were a new acquaintance—and in some ways she was, since they had spent little time together in the fifteen years since Adrienne's marriage.

Helen's letter portrays her as more of an observer than a participant in her daughter's life. All signs indicate that's how Adrienne wanted it. Tightly wound and preoccupied, she was deep into writing a sequence of ghazals, a poetic form she adapted to English after reading translations of the nineteenth-century Indian poet Ghalib. The translations were by a Pakistani scholar named Aijaz Ahmad, with whom she was corresponding and soon would meet. Helen watched her sequester herself late at night so she could write in peace. To relax before bedtime, Adrienne might have a glass or two of vodka to go along with her cigarettes. The next morning, if she'd drunk too much, she dosed her hangover with quinine water and aspirin.[48] One wonders what Helen privately thought about this woman who happened to be her daughter: vigilant mom by day, chain-smoking, hard-drinking poet by night.

In her letter, Helen asked her friend in Baltimore to accompany her to Arnold's grave, now that the tombstone was in place. Surely this was a topic she and Adrienne had discussed, but the tenor of her letter, by turns bravely upbeat and sorrowfully vulnerable, suggests her elder daughter wasn't available to go back to the cemetery with her. Adrienne had her children to tend to while Alf was away, but it wasn't just that. As the survivor of a peculiar form of childhood abuse—her father's insistence that she apply herself to her writing as if nothing else mattered, and her mother's complicity in it—Adrienne felt the need to keep her distance. She had taken on the mission he assigned her and made it her own, but that didn't mean she appreciated his extreme measures or that she'd forgotten his unconscionable reaction to her husband. It would take her a long time to excavate the love buried beneath the myriad of other emotions she felt in regard to Arnold Rich. Together in Vermont, she and her mother grieved in their separate ways.

# CHAPTER 12

# WHAT THE AUTUMN KNEW WOULD HAPPEN

## *1968–1970*

After the assassination of Martin Luther King, Jr., and the death of her father, Adrienne decided she could no longer stand by while black people and other minority citizens suffered from institutionalized racism. During the summer of 1968, she began acting on her new-found principles. The Reverend David Lee Johnson, a black minister, had moved with his family from California to the previously all-white community of Irasburg, Vermont, about an hour's drive north of West Barnet. In a tale that combined elements of the gothic with blatant racism, the Johnsons were initially welcomed to the community and then violently harassed by other local residents claiming Johnson had committed adultery with a young white woman in his living room. Hoodlums shot up the Johnson home, and suddenly northeast Vermont was beginning to look a lot like the Jim Crow South.

Rather than doing what they could to protect a victim, the local police began investigating Johnson for adultery. Adrienne was among many people outraged by the situation. She helped keep a vigil on the Johnsons' porch to protect the family from further violence. The so-called Irasburg affair was written up in *Life* magazine in 1969, after the Johnsons had left town; it had crossed the threshold from a local contre-temps to national news. Although Hayden Carruth cautioned Adrienne not to assume the case was purely a matter of racism, she couldn't see it any other way. Alluding to her life in New York, she acknowledged that living "9 months of the year in a racial pressure-cooker" had shaped her views.[1]

She could not escape the social and political turmoil of the times, nor did she want to. The outrages of war and institutionalized bias were an obsession she shared with her husband, whose politics aligned him with the New Left. Both she and Alf now thought of themselves as radicals. When she returned to New York at the end of the summer, she prepared to begin her second year at Columbia and her first as a part-time lecturer at City College. She had turned down an offer to be City College's poet in residence so she could teach in the SEEK (Search for Education, Elevation, and Knowledge) program. SEEK offered remedial coursework, stipends, and housing to students coming out of the city's poorest high schools. Mostly black and Puerto Rican, SEEK students who successfully completed their coursework were eligible to enroll in one of City University's four-year colleges.

A mutual acquaintance once told Rich's childhood friend Peggy Webb Patterson that Rich was someone who needed a cause.[2] In SEEK she found one that laid the groundwork for all her future causes. Her prominence as a poet gave her a greater voice on campus than she otherwise might have had, and her activism on behalf of SEEK aligned with that of her husband, one of City College's most outspoken advocates for the rights of minority students.

In keeping with her girlhood faith in noblesse oblige, she wanted to draw on her privileged background and education and make a difference in the lives of others. But there was more to it than that. In retrospect, she wrote that her "motivation was complex. It had to do with white liberal guilt, of course; and a political decision to use my energies in work with 'disadvantaged' (black and Puerto Rican) students. But it also had to do with a need to involve myself with the real life of the city, which had arrested me from the first weeks I began living there."[3] Thus spoke the author of "The Tourist and the Town," her poem from the 1950s describing how a tourist must suffer and struggle in a place to become truly one with it. As much as she enjoyed Manhattan's high culture, she sensed she would miss out on the "real" New York boiling over in the streets, and be a mere tourist, if she didn't immerse herself in the city's racial politics.

Her students at City College were nothing like the undergraduates at Swarthmore or her Columbia MFA students, who were well on their way to becoming professional writers. She quickly realized the SEEK students' technical deficiencies in grammar and syntax didn't mean they were unintelligent or uninterested in learning. Paired during her first year with an instructor who taught them grammar and sentence structure in a separate class, Rich was free to concentrate on expansive, topical writing assignments. This approach was greatly encouraged by Mina P. Shaughnessy, who directed the Basic Writing Program. Rich felt liberated by Shaughnessy's creative approach to the teaching of writing.

During her second year, budget cuts eliminated the separate instruction in grammar. Rich then began teaching grammar in her class and doing what she could to hold the attention of students often preoccupied with family and work responsibilities and distracted by the political controversies roiling their campus. Nevertheless, they came to learn, and a determined Rich made her purposeful way from the Upper West Side to Harlem, where she eyed her young charges with at least as much curiosity as they eyed her.

During her several years of teaching at CCNY, Rich got to know some prominent or soon-to-be-prominent black colleagues in the City University system, including Audre Lorde, June Jordan, Toni Cade Bambara, Addison Gayle, and David Henderson. For a time, she shared an office with Gwendolyn Brooks, a towering presence in American poetry and quite tall in stature. Brooks memorably recalled Rich as "an interesting little person."[4] They did not become close. However, Rich became lifelong friends with Lorde and Jordan.

Both Columbia and City College were simmering cauldrons of racial tension in the years Rich taught at the two schools. She and Conrad became vocal supporters of radical students. Much of their energy was directed at City College, where overlapping conflicts between students, faculty, and the administration began coming to a head around the time they arrived in New York. By 1968, it seems they were equally committed to civil rights, but of the two of them, Conrad was by far the more active and visible presence on campus.

His involvement in radical student politics required courage. Although Harvard hadn't granted him tenure, City College considered him a catch. His pioneering success in cliometrics and the demand for his professional expertise enhanced the school's reputation, and as head of the newly created graduate program in economics, he provided the star power it needed to attract Ph.D. students. In 1967, he was elected chair of the economics department, an additional and important administrative duty that he wanted to take on. He had the makings of a terrific career on his hands, but rather than turn away from long-haired, raggedly attired students protesting the Vietnam War and racial injustice, he walked into their midst and did all he could to support them.

During his time at City College, waves of increasingly volatile students protested the Vietnam War, the inequity of opportunity for minority students, and the ROTC program. There was further outcry over on-campus recruiting by Dow Chemical and other companies profiting from the war effort. Students and faculty alike objected to proposed hikes to student fees and college-wide budget cuts.

Judging by student newspaper accounts of protests and marches, Conrad rarely missed a battle. Like Rich, he ramped up his political activity after King's assassination. In late April 1968, he was among nearly eighty faculty members who signed "A Declaration of Conscience" in support of draft resisters. He and many of his colleagues canceled classes for a day in solidarity with students boycotting classes in protest of the war, the draft, and racism. He was a marquee speaker at a campus rally.

A short distance away, Columbia also was in turmoil. In late April 1968, a student strike started out as a nonviolent protest against the war in Vietnam and the university's plans to build a gymnasium in Morningside Park. The police intervened; more than seven hundred people were arrested; in the aftermath, the Columbia campus temporarily closed.[5] Rich discussed the crisis with her MFA students. Rather than canceling the semester's remaining meetings, she set aside the syllabus she had labored over. She and the students met as equals over wine and cheese at her apartment. If someone brought in a poem, it was discussed. Otherwise, there was no set agenda, though politics always came up. "Because of severe arthritis she could not march in the streets with us, but after a march," her former student Jack Litewka recalled, "we would meet at her house and she would ask us about what had happened, what exactly was said, what was the atmosphere like, and she just had a thirst for finding out what was happening out there."[6]

By November 1968, Adrienne and Alf were thoroughly preoccupied with political concerns. Alf spent much of his time vociferously defending a nineteen-year-old army private, Bill Brakefield, who had deserted his unit and arrived at City College seeking sanctuary from further military service. After taking up residence in the student center, Brakefield became a cause célèbre. A crowd of sympathetic students joined him in a vigil and closed ranks around him when the police arrived. With Adrienne sometimes accompanying him, Alf paid frequent visits to Finley Center in solidarity with the young man and his student defenders. On one occasion, Brakefield and the students temporarily left Finley to mount a protest against Dow Chemical, which was holding interviews at a nearby campus building. In spontaneous comments that reveal his emotional involvement in the proceedings, Conrad rebuked bystanders for making fun of their activist classmates: "It's very funny when you think about 1933. It's very funny when you think about 1945, it's very funny when you think about the crummy job you can get from Dow."[7]

The sanctuary movement, as it was known at the time, continued for a week, until the college's president, Buell Gallagher, called in police to shut it down. The *Observation Post,* a student newspaper, reported that six hundred uniformed police officers descended on the student center in the middle of the night and arrested Brakefield and 170 others, mostly students, on charges of criminal trespass. Large numbers of students and faculty were furious that Gallagher had broken a perceived promise not to bring in police without the faculty's permission. Amid the upheaval, Conrad helped raise bail money for the students and stayed in touch as best he could with Brakefield, who was eventually sent to a military prison and placed in solitary confinement. In the November 8, 1968, edition of the *Observation Post,* below an editorial denouncing the college administration, a brief tribute appeared: "Kisses on You, Prof Conrad—Those of us you helped will never forget."

Fifty years later, the sentiment still held true. Ronald B. McGuire, a white man expelled from City College for his radical activism in support of black and Puerto Rican students' demands for equal educational opportunity, remembered Conrad as "an extraordinary man" and "very special professor." He said that Conrad tried to help the student activists without imposing an agenda of his own. "He wasn't just giving us his money, his support; he was giving us his genius, giving us his soul. He empowered the students." A lawyer who devoted his career to bringing student suits against the City University of New York, McGuire had nothing but praise for the man he still thought of as Professor Conrad. "He was the most honest and most steadfast white tenured faculty ally that we had. We gloried in having him around," McGuire said. "He wanted to listen; he wanted to learn; he wanted to help. We believed that he understood."[8]

Not all of Conrad's colleagues shared his political convictions, but Jay Schulman, a sociology professor and fellow activist, thought highly of him. When Schulman was denied tenure, Conrad was among those on the faculty who rallied on his behalf. The two didn't become close friends, however. To the contrary, it seems Conrad kept his distance from the people he went out of his way to help. Schulman thought of his defender as a glamorous and inscrutable hero. He first glimpsed Conrad hurrying out of the hearing room at the Tombs, the old municipal jail where many of Private Brakefield's supporters were being held. "[A]n angular man with shades and longish hair," Conrad paused to announce that bail had been posted for all of the students arraigned so far. "With this assurance, and taking no notice of me, Alf pushed his way through the crowd in the hall to insure that bail was made for the rest of the students busted in Bill Brakefield's sanctuary."[9]

Conrad was the one who repeatedly put his name and reputation on the line, but Rich did what she could. Since she, too, was teaching at City College, she had a personal interest in the students' fate. Like Alf, she agreed with the stand the sanctuary participants had taken. Along with Allen Ginsberg, Paul Blackburn, and Diane Wakoski, she gave a poetry reading for the young resisters a couple of nights before the police put an abrupt end to their sit-in. As she read, she watched her audience out of the corner of her eye and liked what she saw. Lounging around the room, some of them sprawled on the floor, the students listened closely to her poems. At a time when she had decided to cast her ballot in the presidential election for black civil rights activist Dick Gregory rather than vote for either Richard Nixon or Hubert Humphrey,[10] she took heart from the students' antiwar fervor and interest in poetry.

Conrad's reputation as an activist began to spread beyond his home campus. Early in 1969, he was a guest on *Firing Line*, the weekly TV program hosted by William F. Buckley, Jr. Titled "Restructuring the University," the episode also featured Allen Grossman, a politically liberal poet and Brandeis English professor, and Jeffrey Hart, a philosophy professor at Dartmouth and staunch conservative. Dressed in a blue suit and tie, Conrad sat between the two other guests. When someone else was speaking, he typically kept his arms folded across his chest. His voice rarely rising, he regarded Hart with impatience and Grossman with gentle indulgence. As for Buckley, he looked at him with a steady smile, as if he recognized him as his only equal on the stage.

In making introductions, the irrepressibly droll Buckley said Conrad had earned his undergraduate and graduate degrees in economics at Harvard, "where he learned to love the national debt." The host then orchestrated a sharp exchange between Hart and Grossman, the latter of whom ponderously argued that the cause of violence on college campuses was "the inability of universities to speak to the desirable self-realization of individuals." Invited to weigh in on the bickering, Conrad put both of his fellow panelists in their place and then reframed the debate:

CONRAD: It sounds to me like a faculty meeting. I'm struck by the fact that the students are aware that most of the time the universities are engaged in a colossal lie. And that we provoke action of increasingly bad manners and, as the manners escalate, we become more, we, I'm including myself, all those who fit in the front of the catalog, we become more self-righteous, and eventually, it's almost inexorably reached the point where some one of the crazies, as we call them, commits arson or some act of overt destruction.

BUCKLEY: What is the nature of this lie that you're engaged in?

CONRAD: The nature of this lie is that we talk one kind of democracy and practice another kind.

BUCKLEY: Who? You? I thought you were talking about the academic—I thought you were talking about the university.

CONRAD: Yes.

BUCKLEY: The university talks one kind of democracy?

CONRAD: The university talks about democracy; it does not practice it.[11]

Throughout the show, Conrad came off as impassioned, earnest, and above the fray. He refused to exonerate himself from blame or responsibility, yet in his words and manner, he distanced himself from both Grossman and Hart. Buckley was the only one onstage who interested him. Alf's remarks show how philosophical he was—an inclination no doubt honed by years of intellectual conversation with his wife. He obviously believed students deserved a strong say in their own education. He and Adrienne were of like minds on this topic. Their discussions probably influenced what he said on *Firing Line,* and his comments presage some of what she said later on about education. Neither of them was afraid of accusing universities of lying to their students. Though they were different in crucial ways—he was a street-smart New Yorker and her roots were in segregated Baltimore—both came from families that wanted the best of education for their prog-eny. Querulous and skeptical, earnest and at times poignantly naïve, husband and wife shared a deeply ingrained, idealistic faith in what a university could and should be.

Their shared values and political interests notwithstanding, the Rich-Conrad marriage was in trouble. For years, Alf's frequent travel abroad had left Adrienne alone with the children. The trips continued after they moved to New York, and he was often away for weeks at a time. At times, she found it liberating to let the children do as they pleased while their father was absent. But other times, her energy flagged and depression set in as she awaited Alf's return from Pakistan or Ghana or some other impossibly faraway place. When he finally came back, it was a relief, but she was not getting the meaningful communication she craved from him.

Because Adrienne was so busy caring for her young children dur-ing the family's years in Cambridge, she and Alf probably waited until they moved to New York to have an open marriage.[12] Evidently, she no longer thought marriage a "heavenly thing" as she had during her engagement to Sumner Powell. Perhaps she had come to believe something like what Susan Sontag once wrote in her journal: "Who-ever invented marriage was an ingenious tormentor. It is an institution *committed* to the dulling of the feelings. The whole point of marriage is repetition. The best it aims for is the creation of strong, mutual depen-dencies."[13] In an open relationship, Adrienne and Alf could experiment without forfeiting their mutual dependencies. They were attractive, passionate people. If they were available, there would be takers.

One of Rich's takers was none other than Robert Lowell. Teasing, witty, and always admiring, the nation's most prominent male poet had been circling around her for a long time. Their affair, probably brief, was a noteworthy literary coupling. In a letter to Rich in August 1967, Lowell had written, "Dear Adrienne, I hope you are not too lonely, off by yourself, with no Mary McCarthy,* with no Alf. I couldn't have had a better time with you, and have been thinking back on it all summer."[14] In the heady afterglow of the affair, Rich told a confidante about her fling with Lowell, one of twenty or so she talked about with this individual. The confidante reports that a tipsy Rich would call late at night to discuss an affair just ended. Other times, at parties she and Conrad hosted, she would breathlessly whisper, "I had an affair with him!" while the paramour in question chatted with other guests. The confidante pointed out that in the socially liberal circles in which Rich traveled, an extramarital affair was often viewed merely as a mutual expression of affection.[15] With guilt removed from the equation, why not indulge? But no matter what she or Alf wanted to believe, their open marriage was like a house built on sand, the opposite of a Stone of Help.

Adrienne's feelings for her husband remained strong, and her poems and correspondence indicate they had an active sex life. The problem, to which she alluded in "Like This Together," was that she couldn't get him to talk to her with the emotional honesty she felt they owed each other. There were times when she knew he was depressed, even anguished. Her attempts at provoking meaningful conversation went nowhere, and she ended up a bystander in her own marriage, baffled and increasingly alarmed. They were headed in opposite directions.

The year 1968 saw the assassination of Robert F. Kennedy as well as that of Martin Luther King, Jr. The police assaulted protesters at the Democratic National Convention in Chicago. The violence of

---

* Lowell and Rich enjoyed trading derisive witticisms about McCarthy, a mutual acquaintance and author of the bestselling *The Group*.

the Vietnam War and racial discord on the home front lit up the TV news every night. With all of that as the backdrop, Alf and Adrienne continued to advocate for minority students and draft dodgers. While they tried to help the vulnerable and dispossessed, they also suffered. Adrienne's poem "November 1968" isn't dedicated to Alf or necessarily about him or him alone. In hindsight, however, it's hard not to read it as an anticipatory elegy about the man becoming ever more mysterious as he effectively disintegrated before her eyes:

> Stripped
> you're beginning to float free
> up through the smoke of brushfires
> and incinerators
> the unleafed branches won't hold you
> nor the radar aerials
>
> You're what the autumn knew would happen
> after the last collapse
> of primary color
> once the last absolutes were torn to pieces
> you could begin
>
> How you broke open, what sheathed you
> until this moment
> I know nothing about it
> my ignorance of you amazes me
> now that I watch you
> starting to give yourself away
> to the wind[16]

Adrienne was a volatile woman who experienced deep depressions and sometimes indulged in screaming fury. She nevertheless came down solidly on the side of life. Alf was gradually losing the capacity to do that. Read as if addressed to him, the austere and awestruck "November 1968" implies he was slipping away from the world. She would later say she realized in the mid-1960s that "we are dying all along, while we're living."[17] The metaphors in "November 1968" take that viewpoint to its extreme.

This was the stuff of her poetry and private musings, not the sort of thing she wanted to dwell on all the time. On January 2, 1969, when Alf turned forty-five, she cheerfully wrote to Hayden Carruth about the family's celebratory plans for the day: cake and ice cream and gifts in the afternoon, a dinner and movie date for husband and wife that night. They were going to an Indian restaurant on Broadway and then to see *La Chinoise,* a Godard film. In passing she mentioned that Alf had said "by the standards of his family he has lived precisely half his life."[18] Longevity was indeed a family hallmark: His father would live to be a hundred and his mother lived into her nineties. But in retrospect, his statement applied not to him but to Adrienne. She was the one who would live into her eighties, more than twice her age at that time.

His birthday may have been lovely, but the year 1969 turned out to be a draining and ultimately terrible one for Alf. As a faculty leader in the black and Puerto Rican students' fight against the City College administration, he stood up for them even when their strikes and demands disrupted daily life on campus. In his work on behalf of the Black and Puerto Rican Student Committee, he spent several onerous weeks preparing a report for the faculty senate on the incendiary topic of open admissions. Though there were other faculty members involved, Conrad took on the bulk of the research project. The time he put into studying New York public schools and interviewing high school students, teachers, and local black residents could have gone into his teaching, scholarship, or family life, but Conrad was by now a thoroughly driven activist. According to his colleague Jay Schulman, the purpose of Conrad's statistically based report was to construct "a 1970 freshman class in which black and Puerto Rican high school graduates would have no less than 35% of the places, without violating the 1964 Civil Rights Law barring racial quotas."[19]

Alf became depressed because he feared his colleagues would ostracize him for insisting on open admissions, but in fact the faculty senate, of which he was an officer, voted overwhelmingly in favor of his proposal. It was a thrilling validation for both him and Adrienne, who wanted so much for him to succeed.[20] Alf was the campus hero who successfully unraveled the knotty problem of inequitable admissions. But the state board of higher education did not like his solution one bit, and suddenly the university-wide quarrel blew up again, angrier and louder than ever and with no end in sight. Near the end of the spring semester of 1969, enraged black and Puerto Rican students and their white allies shut down City College's South Campus.

In too deep to get out, Conrad fought on, while many of his colleagues stepped away. Jay Schulman, though always sympathetic to the man whose principles he deeply admired, watched him become "an even more lonely and haughty figure as he rose over and over again to elucidate a point, but most of all to lecture the faculty on what he considered to be its moral and social responsibility to the city's victimized high school graduates. Alf's orchestrated efforts to reach and to arouse the conscience of his fellow faculty members had little effect. But his remarks seldom failed to sting faculty consciences."[21] He had become a scold.

During this period of extreme unrest, he was still furthering his career as an economist. He continued to travel abroad to consult and conduct research, and he was charged with launching CUNY's new Ph.D. program in economics. He had the respect of his peers, but two retrospective commentaries indicate what a competitive profession he was in and how hard it was to rise to the very top. Stanford health economist Victor Fuchs, who knew Conrad slightly when they were colleagues at the CUNY Graduate Center, remembered him as "absolutely first-class." However, he said economic history, the area in which Alf made his mark, was not considered "one of the star fields" in their discipline.[22] Robert Solow, a Nobel Prize winner who knew Alf when they were both in graduate school at Harvard, offered this telling assessment: "He was a good economist. He aspired to be better than he was."[23]

His old friend and collaborator John Meyer, the creator of transportation economics, was on his way to becoming one of the nation's most prominent economists. He believed in Conrad's potential.[*] As president of the National Bureau of Economic Research, based in Manhattan at the time, Meyer recruited Conrad to the organization. Located in that era in a tenth-floor suite at 261 Madison Avenue, the office was a hive of activity that put Conrad in the company of many stellar economists.

He made a favorable impression at NBER on Christine Nagorski, a

---

[*] The paper that Meyer and Conrad coauthored in 1958 laid groundwork for research on the economics of slavery by Robert W. Fogel and Douglass C. North, who shared the Nobel Prize in Economics in 1993.

research assistant. Like virtually everyone who recalled meeting Conrad, she thought he was good-looking. She knew he was caught up in the campaign for open admissions at City College but saw no signs of trouble in his demeanor or his interactions with colleagues. On one occasion that lingered in her mind, he and another economist, Ishaq Nadiri, stood in her office doorway and excitedly relayed some news to her: "They were very upbeat and cheerful." She also remembered two of his sons, probably Pablo and Jacob, coming to the office with him. The rambunctious boys ran up and down the halls while their father attended to business. Her overall impression of Alf was of a "humorous and lively" man who had everything to live for.[24]

Adrienne saw him when his collegial mask was off. She supported the causes that consumed so much of his time and energy, rejoiced in his successes, and suffered with him when he clashed with colleagues. The pandemonium at City College consumed her, too, but she didn't spend as much time on campus as he did. She was still first and foremost an artist, and her compass needle always returned to poetry, her true north. The affirmation of her peers and her audiences reminded her, if she needed reminding, that poetry was her calling. Some of her friends had the impression that her rising fame as a poet was a sticking point in the marriage. It was she, not Alf, who had the star power, even if he was the one providing the bulk of the household income and traveling all over the world doing consulting work.

For a while Adrienne busied herself with the art of translation, a subtle form of political activism she knew would outlast faculty meetings and ink-smudged headlines. Her translations from the Dutch were an integral part of *Necessities of Life,* and she was among the poets whose translations appeared in a new book called *Poets on Street Corners: Portraits of Fifteen Russian Poets,* edited by Olga Carlisle.

Working with literal translations of the poems, some contributors— Richard Wilbur, Theodore Weiss, Denise Levertov, and W. S. Merwin— adhered as strictly as they could to the original form and content of the Russian poems. Rich opted for more fluid renditions, as did Stanley Kunitz, Jean Valentine, and Robert Lowell. According to a *New York Times* article marking the book's publication, the contrasting approaches were central to "a lively debate in the literary community" about the art of translation. When it came to literary debates, Rich was always an eager participant. The *Times* photo of Olga Carlisle with five of the contributors to *Poets on Street Corners* shows a relaxed and smiling Rich in a milieu she loved. The occasion was a New York reading, during which she and her fellow contributors discussed the challenges of translation.

Like many distinguished American poets of her generation, Rich saw translation as an important part of her work. It was a way to play with the boundaries of her native language and relate on an intellectual, creative, and almost cellular level with poets whose cultural backgrounds and life experiences were vastly different from hers. As Nadezhda Mandelstam, widow of the Russian poet Osip Mandelstam, wrote to Robert Lowell in regard to his loose adaptations of her late husband's work, "There are two different kinds of poetic translations. One kind is the rendering of verse with great skill but rather mechanically. The other is a great moment, the meeting of two poets writing in two different languages. There is sudden recognition between them, as if the poet and his translator had struck up a close friendship."[25] Like Lowell, Rich was seeking that sudden recognition, a melding of spirits that transcends the literal and potentially mundane translation. Translating also kept her engaged with the act of writing poetry when original poems weren't flowing easily. Sooner or later, both the art and physical act of translation would stimulate poems of her own.

It was natural, then, that Adrienne was interested in Aijaz Ahmad, whose literal translations of Ghalib's ghazals provided models for her adaptation of the form in *Leaflets,* her 1969 collection of poems. After meeting Ahmad for the first time in September 1968, her new acquaintance's charming personality and direct manner immediately won her over. By the spring of 1969, Ahmad was teaching English classes in City University's SEEK program (though not at City College); it is unknown whether this was coincidental or if Rich encouraged him to apply for the job. In any case, he was an important new friend with whom she could discuss poetry.

Ahmad also was a distraction from her marriage to a man who was himself distracted. He had helped spur her feverish burst of ghazal writing in the summer of 1968, when Helen visited her in West Barnet after Arnold Rich's death. A future Marxist theorist, Ahmad had read widely in American poetry—a decided bonus for Rich, who, like Lowell, loved few things more than debating the merits of contemporary American poets and poems. After *Leaflets* came out early in 1969, they began giving readings together, Ahmad from his translations of Ghalib and Rich from her adaptations of the ghazal form. They had become a team. When John Berryman invited her to dinner, he merrily told her to bring along her "Pakistani friend."[26]

The title of *Leaflets* alludes to the political pamphlets so common around the city and the fresh beginnings of young leaves; the title also conjures up Whitman's *Leaves of Grass*. Among the poems in the opening section, titled "Night Watch," are several adaptations or loose translations of poems originally written in Dutch, Yiddish, or Russian. The second part, "Leaflets," contains poems reflecting Rich's desire to write about war without limiting herself to contemporary events in Vietnam. The final section, "Ghazals (Homage to Ghalib)," unveils seventeen ghazals Rich wrote between July 12 and August 8 of 1968 and titled by the date of composition. There are a handful of days when she wrote more than one ghazal; Roman numerals are appended to the dates in these instances. Written in unrhymed couplets of five or six stanzas, the poems are impressionistic and often hover on the edge of despair. The ideas in one tend to blur with those in others. If not totally successful as individual poems, the sequence powerfully suggests a cornered mind seeking release from a host of violations and outrages.

Her ghazals repeatedly circle around to sex, a topic evidently much on Rich's mind. In "7/23/68," she writes, "When your sperm enters me, it is altered; / when my thought absorbs yours, a world begins." The poem titled "7/24/68: I" describes feelings of pained remoteness and asks whether "When we fuck," the experience is more remote than it was for "fucking bodies" of the past. The poem ends, "How many men have touched me with their eyes / more hotly than they later touched me with their lips."[27] What begins as a question ends with a bitter revelation.

The anguished ghazal titled "8/4/68" is dedicated to Aijaz Ahmad. In the penultimate stanza, Rich asks, "How is it, Ghalib, that your grief, resurrected in pieces, / has found its way to this room from your dark house in Delhi?"[28] This was the sort of luminous question that kept her from yielding to despair. Sorting through the rough diamonds of her partial insights in the politically chaotic months following the assassinations of Martin Luther King, Jr., and Robert F. Kennedy, she remained steadfast in her faith in the human connection. Though the whole sequence throbs with loneliness and anger, it is also life-affirming. The final poem, "8/8/68: II," dedicated to "A.H.C.," asks an unanswerable question of the poet's husband: "How did we get caught up fighting this forest fire, / we, who were only looking for a still place in the woods?" The poem, and the sequence, ends with an image of the hairs curling on the man's bare chest, "while the strong heart goes on pounding in its sleep."[29]

In the wake of her father's death and at a time when her frayed marriage was entangled with her politics, Rich's poems were growing ever darker and more intense. They were far less orderly than the lyrics she once wrote with *The New Yorker* in mind. Her early tendency toward primness had given way to an unapologetic, even flagrant, raggedness—a move toward fulfilling her long-ago desire to write poems that were "messily passionate and grand."[30] Even though the epiphanies in her ghazals didn't add up to clearly discernible patterns of meaning, she pushed on: fearful, exhilarated, on fire with a jumble of emotions and insights that came to rest, uneasily, in a poetic form that accommodated lacunae and fragmentation.

With the aid of Ahmad's literal renderings, she had begun translating Ghalib's poems. In March 1969, they shared the stage in New York at a gala event marking the centenary of the revered poet's death and hosted by the Consulate General of India. In a letter to Carruth, Rich said Ahmad showed a typescript of her translations to the Indian ambassador to the United States, who remarked, "In this couplet she's got all the elegance, the finesse, the delicacy of the original—but she hasn't caught the eroticism." Unoffended by the criticism, she said she didn't think any American politician would be able to offer the same sort of insight.[31] Of course, few American politicians would have known who Ghalib was. There was a larger truth to the ambassador's insight, however. Although Rich wasn't shy about mentioning sex in her poems, eroticism was not yet in her repertoire. That would come along some years later, when she wrote "Twenty-One Love Poems," an intricate sequence poem.

The fragmented form of the ghazal freed her to write about her volatile emotional state and explore her evolving interest in black activism. The ghazals in *Leaflets* refer to LeRoi Jones and Eldridge Cleaver, and the title poem in her next collection, *The Will to Change* (1971), alludes to Bobby Seale and Lloyd Delany. She was preoccupied to the point of obsession with black male revolutionaries. Their drama, endangerment, and righteous anger fed her appetite for social change.

The least prominent of these men, Lloyd Delany, was a Queens College psychology professor with whom Alf worked on the open admissions project. Rich met him only once, when she and Alf had dinner with him. Two days later, on November 9, 1969, the forty-six-year-old man whom Adrienne had mentally cataloged as a "Black militant" died of a heart attack. Horrified, she wrote to Carruth that after her dinner with Delany she had dreamed of him, "gagged and shackled like Bobby Seale, in a courtroom where I was a witness. But he wasn't only gagged and shackled, he was standing up enclosed in a coffin." She had told Conrad about the nightmare and worked the image into a poem. Something of Delany's essence stayed with her until she heard about his death. That in itself was bad enough, but Rich confessed to Carruth that what felt like a premonition was the latest in a frightening yearlong pattern of prescient dreams. She wondered whether she had gotten "some vibration of the death in him" when she met Delany.[32]

Caught up in the shock of her new acquaintance's death coming so soon after her nightmare, Rich overlooked the fact that Delany wasn't murdered. Perhaps in her dreams she indeed tapped into a spiritual energy encircling the visible world, but her premonitions of terror didn't necessarily have to do with him. Her deep sense of foreboding was like an internal solar eclipse that frightened and exhilarated her at the same time.

By the spring of 1969, Alfred was nothing if not a driven man. For two weeks in late April and early May, when activist students shut down City College's South Campus, he stayed in the thick of contentious negotiations between them and the college administration, while Adrienne conducted her SEEK class by mail. In late May, he stepped down from his position as chair of the economics department. A later account indicated "he was accused by his colleagues of having publicly distorted statements made by some of them in a departmental faculty meeting."[33] He had wanted to quit the administrative post a year earlier, but the college's president had refused to accept his resignation.

Now he belatedly had his wish, but it came at the price of his good name in the department. A day before what was essentially an ouster, Rich wrote to Carruth denouncing her husband's colleagues, many of whom she believed were jealous of his professional accomplishments and upset by his activism.[34] And who else in the department had gotten so much attention from the press? The media requests kept coming after he appeared on *Firing Line*. Conrad was among a handful of City College faculty interviewed for a *New York Times* article about open admissions,[35] and the night before he lost his post as department chair, Conrad was scheduled to debate open admissions on a CBS television program.*

Adrienne and Alf shared a sense of being under siege. "The political forces are now all howling around us," she told Carruth. A seemingly biased press, the candidates for mayor of New York, Jewish organizations opposed to open admissions, and "the paranoid ignorant middle-class"—all were lined up against her and Alf, or so she felt.[36] Conrad had received obscene phone calls and hate mail ever since he began appearing on TV. Rich had seen profane letters calling him "'You ugly Commie Jew'" and threatening "vague awful reprisals" based on racist assumptions. Handwritten and anonymous, these toxic missives alarmed her more than the vituperative phone calls.[37]

Rich tried to find reasons for hope. On May 16, her fortieth birthday, she and Conrad attended a rally organized by black and Puerto Rican students. The event as she described it was a celebration of Harlem rather than a denigration of City College's administration. In her account of the evening to Carruth, she marveled over the physical beauty of the students in their African garb and said she had looked on in bemused fascination as a black preacher "gave a kind of Black Power gospel sermon." Not exactly of Harlem even though she was definitely in it, she and Alf "paraded" partway to campus before ducking out to a restaurant for a dinner of barbecued ribs. Yet she felt involved and wanted to believe in a new, enlivening energy: "In all the violence and trouble of this country, I feel we are groping and stirring toward something. Much of the energy is young, most of it is black. I feel great hope at this moment, long-term hope, with a sense that the short-term scene is likely to be very rough indeed."[38]

---

* It is unclear whether he kept this engagement.

About a week later, the Conrads attended a "pot party" on Lower Broadway. Adrienne had tried marijuana before, but this was the first time she registered the effects of the drug. As she and Alf walked through Washington Square Park afterward, she felt fully connected to her surroundings. Like a seasoned pothead, she gazed at the lit-up park's bright green squares of grass and marveled at a sight many would have found disgusting: "[T]hree sailors on a dark path, one peeing under a tree, filled me with pleasure as if they were commedia dell'arte characters, in their white uniforms, the sound of the one who was urinating fell deliciously on the concrete, but all of this was extremely lucid, not blurred as under alcohol, I felt wholly competent, not all loosened up but rather integrated, intellectually alive, and very happy." In keeping with her lifelong habit of denouncing places she had once praised, she added that Washington Square was far better than Boston Common.[39] Savoring her late-breaking bohemianism, perversely charmed by the urinating sailor, she considered herself a real New Yorker now.

In the fall of 1969, the political temperature at City College remained at the boiling point, and Rich was again lame. The good results of her surgery and intensive rehabilitation a few years earlier hadn't lasted. This setback compounded her mounting sadness and anxiety, the flip side of her resurgent feelings of hope and pot-induced pleasure. When Alf went to Washington, D.C., to participate in a huge antiwar march on November 15, she had no choice but to stay home. To Carruth, she wrote that as much as she wanted to go, she knew her infirmity would hold back anyone she was with and she didn't feel safe going by herself. She added that she felt like she was always on the verge of tears: "For so many reasons. Not depression but simply the nature of things."[40] A couple of years later, she would tell Carruth that this period in her marriage had been terrible. For now, admitting she was vulnerable and upset was as far as she would go.

She and Alf were of like minds politically, and she never wavered in her support of his activities at City College. Sometimes she accompanied him to meetings with student rebels. On one such occasion, she watched an argument unfold between two black women and the headstrong leader of the black radical students. It was a crystalizing moment as she suddenly realized the women were doing most of the work, while the male leaders took all the credit.[41]

One wonders what that meant for Rich personally during this time of marital discord. While she loyally attended meetings alongside her husband and helped him prepare for a press conference on open admissions, he was not the only man in her life. She and Hayden Carruth maintained their blizzard of correspondence, even after she felt compelled to scold him for attempting to flirt with her.[42] When she gave a reading at the Guggenheim Museum, an occasion showing how highly regarded she was, she devoted much of her time to reading Carruth's poetry instead of her own. Although he wasn't in the audience, members of his family were. She was a slavishly loyal friend to him. And she continued to travel with Ahmad, whose youthful company offered a respite from her workaday problems. On the bus ride back to New York after a joint reading she and Ahmad gave in Philadelphia, she thrilled to the sight of the crimson sky above the Hudson River and felt "like one of those 20-year-old provincials entering the metropolis for the first time, full of hope and terror and joy."[43] Those were the powerful emotions that animated her, along with a rising tide of fury that would soon crest and flow through her life and writings for years afterward.

# CHAPTER 13

# BRILLIANT, MAD, HUMAN, AND IRREPLACEABLE

## *1970*

By early 1970, the black and Puerto Rican student activists had essentially won their long, bitterly fought battle. Conrad feared it would be a pyrrhic victory. Starting in the fall, the administration planned to enroll all interested New York City high school graduates into one or another four-year or two-year college in the City University system. The wholesale admission of underprepared applicants would radically alter the profile of City College, the academic gem of the City University of New York. Remedial coursework would no longer be the province of SEEK students alone, and a much larger enrollment would lead to crowded classes and scheduling problems. Although it appeared the radical students whom Conrad aided and abetted got more than they asked for, they now faced the possibility that the new plan, rushed into place, would collapse on itself and undermine their original goals of inclusion and equal opportunity.

In February 1970, Alfred publicly debated open admissions with City College's new acting president, Joseph Copeland, in Finley Center's ballroom. According to his colleague Jay Schulman, Conrad had grave doubts about the new plan. In the debate with Copeland, he excoriated the university for not having the students' best interests at heart. Schulman knew Conrad "worried that most of the black [students] and Puerto Ricans coming into the university under open admissions would be shunted into community colleges. He doubted that many victimized high school graduates could stay in college for long without stipends and a coherent counseling and remediation program. Most of all, Alf thought they would need stimulation and support from more seasoned students and an identity to rally around. He was concerned that an artificial barrier would keep apart SEEK and high-risk open admissions students." These were reasonable concerns, but Conrad's rhetoric during the debate had an incendiary edge. According to Schulman, "A black student blurted out to Alf, 'You tell us it's all a trick. What do you want us to do?' Alf told the student to do anything and everything to fight this program. This was the closest I ever heard Alf come to calling for militant action."[1]

The prospect of open admissions, which he'd spent two years fighting for, now infuriated him. He would not back down, and his activism on other fronts continued at a dizzying pace. In the spring of 1970, he was arrested for illegally entering a draft board meeting.[2] He joined with other faculty members who went on strike in defense of Schulman, who was denied tenure. In his capacity as vice-chair of the CUNY Faculty Senate, he likewise defended a group of ten SEEK lecturers who had been fired. He spoke at a rally protesting a hike in student fees.

In early May 1970, as another tumultuous academic year staggered toward its close, he again sided publicly with rebellious City College students. The occasion was the chaotic aftermath of the Kent State massacre. When radical students vandalized the campus ROTC building and once again forced the temporary closure of City College, Conrad stepped in as a negotiator and offered the occupiers of Finley Center his encouragement and reassurance. He never stopped fighting, and new battles kept coming.

Perhaps inevitably, students began to chafe against his feverish interventions. He could come off at times as bureaucratic and controlling. In the wake of the latest protest and occupation of Finley Center, some students no longer wanted either Conrad or Schulman playing a parental role. In retrospect, Schulman wrote, "That point was illustrated for us a couple of days later in Night Court. Alf was there to make bail for the three students charged with trashing ROTC. As Alf was about to reach for his wallet, one of the students took several large bills from his pocket and put up bail for himself and the two others. Alf was nonplussed."[3]

Conrad had invested so much of himself in his activism that it is hard to know who he was without his political causes as protective coloration. Something similar could be said of Rich, but she stood apart from her husband in her determination to adapt and keep going even in the face of infuriating local dilemmas and ongoing national and international crises. Just as she had as a teenager, she looked ahead with stubborn and quite genuine enthusiasm to what she might contribute and who she might someday become. She savored equally the grit and sunlight and water droplets of the everyday world and the promise of the days and years ahead. She would never stop, but she was willing to pause, and she knew when to go home and rest. As a poet, she was aware that her difficulties, whatever their scale or scope, were a gold mine of material—that was a benefit she tried hard not to exploit. But it wasn't just this tantalizing possibility that pulled at her. Like Thoreau, whose writings had moved and inspired her for decades, she wanted always to "live deep and suck out all the marrow of life."[4] That desire— that intention—helped define who she was.

The couple's obsession with the war and a myriad of racial and educational injustices made them seem, at times, more compatible than they actually were. According to Cynthia Rich, "I can remember visiting them in their Vermont home and at night waking to hear the two of them drinking or smoking pot and passionately discussing whether it was getting to be a time for gun violence—such discussions not being unusual in those heady days. I didn't stay awake long enough to find out the answer. However, later I concluded the answer was probably not."[5] They could talk politics all day and all night, but the unhappiness in their marriage was much harder to broach.

Late in 1969, Rich wrote an anguished poem called "Tear Gas," in which her marital discord becomes the jumping-off point for a new, politicized understanding of herself. She didn't include it in her 1971 volume, *The Will to Change,* where it would have fit chronologically, but instead saved it for her *Collected Early Poems,* published many years later. Unusual for Rich in its raw emotion, "Tear Gas" shows how fiercely determined she was to survive when her marriage was at its nadir.

The poem's epigraph reads, "October 12, 1969: reports of the tear-gassing of demonstrators protesting the treatment of G.I. prisoners in the stockade at Fort Dix, New Jersey." The opening stanzas imagine what it would be like "to feel the full volume of tears in you," and release a flood of grief in sorrow, fear, and pity "for the rest of time."

The lines imply crying is a viable response to the multiple outrages of the era. The poem then moves into more intimate territory as Rich describes being alone and afraid in Vermont and crying wildly. She quotes the line *"our words misunderstand us,"* which appears in her earlier poem for her husband, "Like This Together."

Her frustration is evident as she admits she has no adequate language for all she feels. The poem then slips into a fragmented stream of consciousness as she struggles to articulate a rush of insights about herself and her failing relationship. Later in the poem, having rejected images that "are not what I mean," Rich writes, "I mean that I want you to answer me / when I speak badly / that I love you, that we are in danger / that she wants to have your child, that I want us to have mercy on each other / that I want to take her hand." These jarring lines suggest her open marriage had gone haywire. Though she wants to communicate frankly with her husband, she knows the marriage is essentially over. Her desire for mercy extends to the woman who wants to bear her husband's baby.

As "Tear Gas" moves toward its denouement, she acknowledges "these repetitions are beating their way / toward a place where we can no longer be together." Then, in a closing couplet, she pulls back from her agony and declares, "(I am afraid.) / It's not the worst way to live."[6] This was the pessimistic optimist acknowledging her despair but refusing to give in to it.

But being afraid *is* a terrible way to live, and one day in December 1969 Adrienne's fears took on a new and horrifying form. Standing at the top of a subway staircase, she realized she was afraid to take the first step. Walking was hard for her anyway, but this was something new. She realized the phobia had been gradually building in recent weeks and months. It had become real a week earlier when she hesitated to descend a steep flight of stairs at Cynthia's home near Boston. When her sister extended a hand, her fears dissipated. Now, however, it took all her willpower to descend into the subway station. She wrote to Carruth that she was possessed by "this awful double fear—the fear of the stairs, and the fear of the fear itself and what it implied." Making matters worse, once she arrived in the subway station, she was overcome by a "terrifying vision of something coming on very fast, capable of paralyzing my life."[7] Here again was a premonition, surely the worst she'd had about herself. She confessed to Carruth she'd often forced herself to do things that frightened her, because deep down she knew she could prevail. But now her fears had the upper hand. She knew she needed help.[8]

To help her through the crisis, she turned to Dr. Leslie H. Farber, a prominent psychiatrist newly arrived in Manhattan. He had previously worked at the Washington School of Psychiatry and the Washington Psychoanalytic Institute, both in Washington, D.C., and at the Austin Riggs Center, a psychiatric hospital in Stockbridge, Massachusetts. A learned, literary man whose Upper West Side practice attracted writers and other artists, he was well known in professional circles for his existential approach to analysis and his enthusiasm for Martin Buber's philosophy. Going beyond a scholar's conference papers and journal essays, he published two books for general audiences, *The Ways of the Will* (1966) and *Lying, Despair, Jealousy, Envy, Sex, Suicide, Drugs, and the Good Life* (1976).* His knowledge and erudition thoroughly engaged Rich as she plunged gratefully into analysis.

Breaking with professional convention, Farber didn't believe in taking a cool, dispassionate view of his patients and their problems. He told them exactly what he thought of what they said and did, and he expected them to develop and maintain moral standards. According to one summation of his views, he believed "that what lies beyond theory and training is the ability of the therapist *to know* the patient, not just *know about* the person. This provides the possibility of meeting, the mutual encounter, which Buber calls the *I-Thou* relationship."[9] A fellow therapist wrote that Farber disliked the way most psychological approaches to therapy "tend to collapse the person into historical antecedents and component drives. [Farber] saw how easily this kind of knowledge could be used to rationalize and excuse, what a self-serving relief it could be to view oneself, no matter how reprehensible, as the inevitable consequence of impersonal forces and historical accidents." A therapist's morally neutral stance freed the patient to divulge painful personal secrets without fear of judgment. "But the price of this safety was to marginalize the relevance of the patient's assessment of his moral responsibility. For Farber, this was comparable to including everything in a study of Shakespeare, but the plays and the sonnets."[10]

---

* Echoes of Farber's book titles can be heard in Rich's *The Will to Change* (1971) and *On Lies, Secrets, and Silence: Selected Prose 1966–1978* (1979).

Always hungering for insight and connection, Rich had met her intellectual match in Farber, whom she liked and trusted right away. With his guidance, she quickly conquered her phobia of staircases. The next order of business was to probe its origins and figure out what was truly disturbing her. Rich approached that difficult assignment with her characteristic gusto.

During the time she was meeting regularly with Farber, she began seeking out independent-minded New York women who were creating the women's liberation movement. She began to enjoy the company of women who identified as feminists; they provided a haven from her imploding marriage. Her most important new acquaintance during that time was Robin Morgan, a poet and former child actress who became a civil rights and antiwar activist in the early 1960s. By the time Rich met her, Morgan already was deeply involved in the women's movement. She had launched a large-scale protest against the Miss America pageant in 1968, helped found two organizations, New York Radical Women and W.I.T.C.H. (Women's International Terrorist Conspiracy from Hell), and would publish, in 1970, a wildly popular feminist anthology, *Sisterhood Is Powerful.*

In a few years, they would be close friends, and she would introduce Rich to feminists and women's audiences craving what an eloquent, soon-to-be lesbian poet had to offer them.

Sharing the stage with Morgan would help make her a star of the women's movement, but for now, they were attending some of the same meetings and getting to know each other. At these meetings of radical feminists and radical lesbian feminists, Adrienne listened and observed. It had been a long time since she first read Simone de Beauvoir's *The Second Sex,* a book that might have changed her life in the 1950s if she'd had a community of like-minded women to discuss it with. Here, finally, were those women and that community. Listening to Morgan and other women rant, weep, and confess, she felt the tectonic plates of her interior life shifting.

In Morgan's eyes, Rich was "a well-meaning, liberal white lady" gradually coming into a new understanding of herself. "She was obviously a fine poet. She was not a feminist, and she was the last person to call herself a feminist at that point. She was one of those people who take great pains to say, 'I'm no feminist, but—' and they drive you crazy when what comes out of their mouth after that is feminist. But they don't want to own the word."

Rich believed fighting racism and class divisions was more important than women's issues. She supported "the Movement," which typically referred to the New Left men such as Conrad who opposed the Vietnam War and fought for social justice. When Morgan pointed out that women made up more than half the population on the planet, she still balked. And in conversations about poetry, she confided to Morgan that she didn't want to renounce the male poets who had welcomed her into their circle. "She said she felt that being one of the few permitted on Mount Olympus was a very good thing to be. And so she was torn, she was conflicted." Morgan considered Rich's dilemma characteristic of token women who enjoy the power they've been granted. "They're being asked seemingly to operate against their own self-interests."[11]

Despite her ambivalence, Rich's sense of fairness and justice quickly kicked in. She began letting go of long-ingrained prejudices against early feminists such as Susan B. Anthony and Carrie Nation, whom she had grown up believing were "funny creatures" deserving mockery.[12] She also let go of the 1950s mind-set that put the needs of her husband ahead of her own.

An avowal of sorts came one summer day in Vermont when she and Alf and the Carruths went on a picnic near the Conrads' vacation home. Sitting near a flowering tree humming with bees, she announced to the group that she planned to give away her pots and pans and do a lot less cooking. It was a surprising announcement from someone who liked to cook. Perhaps she overstated her plans for dramatic effect, but Rose Marie Carruth took her at her word.[13]

If the only problem on the home front had been a question of who would cook and clean up after meals, she and Alf could have figured it out. The trouble went far deeper. Adrienne's correspondence with Hayden gives an intimate account of the next several months as she moved inexorably toward unspeakable grief. In June 1970, after six months of seeing Farber regularly, she told Carruth her personal life was in turmoil and had been for some time. She felt bad that she had let their correspondence lapse when a depressed Hayden needed attention she wasn't able to give. She wanted to be more responsive to him and resolved to be a better friend.[14]

Later that month, she chastised him for not sharing all her letters with his wife and thereby stoking Rose Marie's suspicions of an affair. Then the emerging feminist in Rich unveiled herself. The problem was bigger than the two of them, she argued: "I am sure that much sexual jealousy on the part of women is really a bourgeois mislabeling of a much deeper but unconfessable jealousy of the autonomy of men."[15]

That wasn't all. She saw it now, very clearly: Men subjugated women. It had to stop, and Hayden had to agree with her. Armoring herself with the slang of the day, she wrote him, "If this sounds like a Women's Lib rap, baby, it is."[16]

On July 3, she wrote him again with astonishing news: She was going to move out and take an apartment of her own. The children would stay with Alf. Buoyed by her conversations with Farber, she felt certain she was doing the right thing, no matter what other people might say or think. She was hopeful again. After a very difficult period, she was looking forward to reshaping her life and felt she had to do it.[17]

In late July, she reported to Carruth that she and Conrad had told the children about their plans to separate. She said her sons, the youngest of whom was eleven years old, were "used to changes, to unconventional arrangements." As she prepared to move away from them, she pronounced them "one of the best things Alf and I have done together." She was certain she and Conrad would continue to be good and mutually supportive parents.[18]

The following week, possibly in response to questions from Carruth, she told him she didn't plan to cohabit with someone else or initiate a divorce.[19] No, she just needed her own space and time to herself. She would go on sharing some meals at Central Park West with Alf and the boys, and they would come visit her. Some people would likely say she had abandoned her children, but she wouldn't let that prevent her from doing what felt right to her. She said she was much better off than she had been when she had stood paralyzed at the top of the subway stairs and insisted she was not acting out of anger at her husband. In fact, she believed her decision to move out was "an act for both of us, in the long run."[20]

Her decision to move out startled and angered Conrad, who now decided he, too, would confide in Hayden Carruth. Driving from West Barnet to the Carruth home in Johnson, he joined his wife's close friend in the small cowshed that Hayden had converted into a writing studio. There, Hayden listened for a couple of hours to Alf's complaints about his wife and her bombshell decision to get a place of her own. After he left, Hayden went into the house and hugged his wife long and tenderly. He didn't tell her what Alf had said.[21]

More than three decades later, however, he told a reporter for *The Guardian* that Conrad was deeply frustrated because his wife " 'was becoming a very pronounced, very militant feminist.' " He continued, " 'I don't know what went on between them, except that Alf came to me and complained bitterly that Adrienne had lost her mind.' "[22]

It was a familiar charge by men shocked when their wives stood up for their own beliefs and needs: The woman *had* to be crazy if she tore up the script of her marriage and insisted on something more to her liking. But sometimes women walked out because they felt they would go mad if they stayed. That was one of the points Robin Morgan made in her essay "Goodbye to All That," published in 1970. Aimed squarely at the hypocritical men of the New Left who asserted their liberal beliefs while mistreating their wives and girlfriends, she wrote:

> There is something every woman wears around her neck on a thin chain of fear—an amulet of madness. For each of us, there exists somewhere a moment of insult so intense that she will reach up and rip the amulet off, even if the chain tears the flesh of her neck. And the last protection from seeing the truth will be gone. Do you think, tugging furtively every day at the chain and going nicely insane as I am, that I can be concerned with the puerile squabbles of a counterfeit Left that laughs at my pain? Do you think such a concern is noticeable when set alongside the suffering of more than half the human species for the past 5,000 years—due to a whim of the other half? No, no, no, goodbye to all that.[23]

Still, Alf had a different take on madness than did most people. Because his first wife suffered from mental illness, the charge carried an extra layer of meaning.* If Adrienne's behavior was in any way reminiscent of Annette's, he may have been sincerely worried.

By early August, Adrienne was looking for an apartment a short distance from the family home. Even as her surgeon recommended putting her on crutches and encasing her leg in a cast from hip to ankle to ease the pressure on her arthritic knee, she rode the bus around Manhattan and braved the crowded sidewalks in order to check out apartments.[24] An accidental jostle could have knocked her down and landed her in the emergency room, but she was willing to take the risk.

The terms of her separation from her family were in flux. Later in that month of profound transition, she went to Vermont to spend time with her husband and sons. She was therefore at a remove from the Women's Strike for Equality, a gathering of some ten thousand women who marched down Fifth Avenue on the night of August 26. Organized by Betty Friedan, the strike, and related marches and rallies in cities across the country, was front-page news in the next day's *New York Times*. The occasion marked the fiftieth anniversary of American women's suffrage and mobilized women and men who supported the Equal Rights Amendment. Friedan was quoted as saying, "This is not a bedroom war, this is a political movement."[25]

In Rich's case, it was both. She wrote years later, "I had been looking for the Women's Liberation movement since the 1950s. I came into it in 1970." At the time of the New York women's march, she distributed women's rights pamphlets around rural Vermont "in small public libraries and clinics and bookstores. Even at the time, I wondered a bit about their impact then and there, aimed as they were at young urban political women, yet it was an action of a kind, a statement to myself, that I wanted and needed what this movement was affirming: the solidarity and empowering of women."[26] No longer a distaff member of the New Left, she was staging a lonely strike in rural Vermont while thousands of women in big cities, many of them soon to be her ardent fans, gathered en masse and stood up for their rights.

By September, she had moved out of 333 Central Park West. Her small furnished place at 65 West 106th Street, apartment 2B, was less

---

* In addition, his mother suffered from clinical depression and was treated with shock therapy, according to Rich in a December 28, 1996, letter to Helen Margolis Smelser Daube.

than a mile from her old home but a world away from her old life. Four years after she had moved to New York full of energy and anticipation, she had left her husband and sons. She would go back to make dinner for them, but the break felt definitive nonetheless. It was her first time on her own since her days as a young Oxford student anxiously awaiting letters from her fiancé and weeping over letters from her father, and she relished her freedom. On the last day of August, she wrote to Hayden Carruth to say how hopeful she was: "Today the air is absolutely clear and unpolluted in the city, it is fresh, cool, golden, the way it might always be, like the first day of the world."[27]

As she rejoiced in her first days of liberation, her husband was living out his last days on Earth. At some point later that summer, they again spent time together in Vermont. He told her he had been fantasizing about killing himself. This, then, was the impasse they had come to. While she envisioned for herself new beginnings dappled with golden light and enlivened with cool, clean air, he stumbled ever deeper into wretched darkness. There would be no reconciliation, no meeting of the minds.

The new academic year began, and classrooms were crowded now that open admissions was a reality. The SEEK writing classes were crammed into partitioned spaces in Finley Center's Great Hall. Rich wrote serenely to Carruth that the new arrangement suited her better, because she preferred sitting around a table with her students. In a jab at his isolated life far from big-city politics, she added that he had no idea how bad things had been at City College in recent months.[28]

The whole Conrad family spent a rainy weekend in West Barnet in early October. She and Alf talked late at night by the woodstove and in the car along roads covered with yellow and red leaves. Back in her New York apartment, she allowed herself to cry and reveled in the relief that weeping brought to her. On Sunday, October 4, she wrote to Carruth that she would be staying most of the week with the children at Central Park West while Alf attended a professional conference in Vienna. Although her personal life was in limbo, she was trying to settle into a routine and create stability for herself. She told herself that her simple little apartment felt like home.[29]

The following week, Conrad returned from his European travels; he had brought home a box of fancy cigars he intended to give to Carruth. He was so distraught that Rich became frightened. On Tuesday, October 13, he rented a car and told the children, and perhaps Adrienne as well, he was going on a short trip. It was oddly timed, a week before classes were to be canceled so students could participate in campaigns for national midterm elections. Why was he leaving now, while classes were in session? And why was he renting a car, when he and Adrienne had a car of their own in a nearby garage?

She assumed, correctly as it turned out, that he was going to Vermont. But if his purpose was to close up the house for the winter, that task wasn't urgent. For the days ahead, Vermont's *Caledonian-Record* reported, "Zinnias and marigolds will be allowed to continue growing 'on borrowed time' as extended summer weather prevails in the area."[30]

Alf probably arrived in West Barnet in the evening, when rain was expected.[31] Perhaps he stayed at the beloved home he and Adrienne had purchased when they were still full of hope for their life together, but she didn't think he had. In her reconstruction of events, he spent the night in the rental car or at a motel.[32]

In a letter dated October 13, the day Alf left, she turned to Carruth in an agony of fear. Trying to normalize a horrifying situation, she paused in her narrative to praise her friend's new book. She told him it had "arrived at the end of one of the worst nights of my life [. . .]. I've been struggling in a dark passageway full of cobwebs—last night in extreme pain I began to see some light. The book, your face, the lines of poems glanced at through the book, came as a kind of early glimmering." Then she admitted she was terrified for her husband and felt she could no longer do anything for him. Her hope was that he would turn again to Carruth for support and friendship.[33]

She also was in touch with Hayden by phone. On Wednesday, she asked him to go to the house in West Barnet and look for her missing husband. He complied and left a note asking Alf to call him. On Friday, he drove back and continued searching. Meanwhile, a state trooper visited the Carruth home and spoke with Rose Marie Carruth. Eight-year-old David Carruth participated in the conversation, as well.

Hayden found no evidence Alf had been to the house. The missing New York economics professor now became a news item. The local radio station broadcast an appeal for volunteers to help search the area around his vacation home. Then a break came: The state police found the rental car abandoned on Martin Pond Road, a remote road near Peacham, a few miles from West Barnet. There was still no sign of Conrad. The next morning, a search party consisting of police, game wardens, Carruth, and local residents scoured the area. According to Carruth, some members of the group exhibited a distressing lack of respect for the task at hand. In a letter to his mother, he described how they joked around and approached the search as a kind of lark.[34]

By now, Conrad had been missing nearly a week. In Cynthia's recollection, Adrienne had little doubt Alf had killed himself. Around this time, Adrienne called Cynthia and asked her to come to New York. By then, their mother had sold the family home in Baltimore and moved to Cambridge to be near Cynthia and her family. But it was Cynthia, not Helen, whom Adrienne wanted by her side. Helen went instead to Cynthia's house to help look after her two young children.

On the morning of Sunday, October 18, after a search of the area near the car, police found Alfred's body in a meadow where he and his family had once picnicked, possibly the same place where, according to Rose Marie Curruth, Adrienne had announced she wanted to give away her pots and pans. He had shot himself in the mouth with a .22 rifle. Adrienne later received the canceled check showing he had bought the gun in New York the day he left town.[35] The gun and suicide notes for her and the children lay nearby. The gruesome job of identifying the body fell to Hayden, who then called Adrienne. "She wasn't unprepared," he said thirty-two years later.[36]

He described the suicide notes to Adrienne over the phone, and the day after he identified Conrad's body, he elaborated on the topic in a letter. He said writers (meaning the best of them) aimed to express themselves originally, but there were times of extremity when that was not possible. At those times, instinct kicked in and gave way to convention, and that was what he saw in Conrad's notes.[37]

Their exchange on this delicate topic recalled Robert Frost's words to Rich many years earlier. Alluding to F. O. Matthiessen's death, Frost had said, essentially, not even suicide notes are immune from literary judgment. On some level, Carruth and Rich felt the same way. But he was trying to understand Conrad's final words, not pass judgment on them. His eye was not quite as cold as Robert Frost's.

On the same day that Carruth wrote to her, Rich wrote at least one letter of her own, to the poet X. J. Kennedy, who had succeeded Donald Hall as poetry editor of *The Paris Review.* Hall had left a backlog of accepted poems not yet scheduled for publication. Rich wrote Kennedy that her husband had committed suicide the previous day. "She did not say how or why," Kennedy noted. Swerving away from the tragedy that would consume her for years to come, she wanted to know when Kennedy would be publishing a poem of hers that Hall had accepted. "I guess she was just dissipating her pain by turning to poetry business," Kennedy recalled, adding that eventually he did publish the poem in question, though it took at least a year or two because the backlog of accepted material was so large.[38]

Rich also told her friend John Berryman about Conrad's suicide soon after it happened. She knew Berryman was an alcoholic who suffered from depression, but perhaps she thought he could offer her insight that few others could. In a letter dated only "Monday," Berryman responded from St. Mary's Hospital in Minneapolis, where he was being treated for alcoholism. He said he could more readily imagine the agony that drove Conrad to his death than the pain Rich felt in the aftermath. He urged her not to blame herself and to realize that in the face of the taboo against it, the person who commits suicide is insane.[39*]

On October 20, *The New York Times* ran a substantial news story about Conrad and his death and included a photo of him.[40] With word of her husband's suicide ricocheting across the land, Adrienne soldiered on. After his body was returned to New York, she sat shiva with her in-laws at a Jewish funeral home. Then the man they all had loved was buried in an Orthodox Jewish cemetery on Long Island. Though unified in their harrowing grief, there was tension between her and the Cohens. They were reportedly upset with her, the woman who had left their son just weeks before his death. It would take the gentle interceding of Alf's brother, Morris Cohen, before they decided Adrienne was not to blame.

While Adrienne participated in the Jewish rites of grief and loss, she carried a knowledge that added to her private devastation. Shortly after she learned Alf had died, she found some letters among his things. They indicated he was romantically involved with a close friend of hers,

---

* Less than two years later, Berryman jumped from a bridge in Minneapolis and ended his life.

a woman she had known and liked ever since they were both students at Radcliffe.[41] She told Cynthia and some of her most intimate friends about her discovery. Although she, too, had indulged in affairs, this particular breach added a new layer of pain to her turmoil.

By now, Adrienne had moved back to 333 Central Park West to be with her children. In the days and weeks after Alf's death, she was roiled by emotions, but her powers of analysis were in high gear. She wrote to Carruth that she was realizing just how "totally out of contact—manic in a very un-obvious way, suicidal, terror-stricken" Alf had been in his last months. "Unable to forgive himself," he seemed unhinged by their unhappy relationship. Though she didn't say so, perhaps she wondered whether he felt guilty about his affair with her close friend.

She was beginning to believe "all his relationships were screwed-up and desperate." With laserlike perception, she told Carruth, "The suicide seems to me a choice which he made in order not to have to make other, living choices. They were there, needing to be made, and I'd hoped by giving him some elbow room to make them easier. I don't feel in the least responsible for his death, but I felt extremely responsible toward him while he lived."[42]

In addition to his wife, sons, parents, brother, and extended family, the forty-six-year-old Conrad left behind a large number of colleagues and students who had been in close contact with him up until days before his death. They, too, were shocked, and on a purely practical level, his suicide created administrative and public-relations problems. At the CUNY Graduate Center, the nascent Ph.D. program in economics teetered on the verge of collapse with no one at the helm and word of Conrad's suicide spreading. Mina Rees, president of CUNY's Graduate School, took the situation in hand. She directed Victor Fuchs to recruit a new director and hired additional faculty. The program was able to weather the crisis.[43]

Christine Nagorski, the research assistant at the National Bureau of Economic Research, was stunned by the news of Conrad's suicide. She had chatted with him the previous week and nothing seemed amiss. To her fell the task of cleaning out his desk and saving personal items for his children. There was no mention of Adrienne. Nagorski learned that Alf had marital problems, an insight into his personal life not previously mentioned by NBER colleagues, whom she recalled as being very circumspect. Since he worked mostly out of other offices, his desk contained little for her to go through. Nevertheless, a singular treasure awaited her: one of Alf's notebooks from a Harvard economics class. Nagorski marveled over the beautiful handwriting that filled page after page and then set the notebook aside for her colleagues to give to Alf's sons.[44]

In mid-November, a memorial service at City College attracted a crowd of about 150 faculty and students. The group gathered in Finley Center's Grand Ballroom, where Alf had so often spoken up during faculty meetings and protest rallies. The occasion also commemorated the late Betty Rawls, an African-American counselor in the SEEK program, who had died in a small-plane crash. The Reverend Frederick Douglass Kirkpatrick sang, and a group called Theater of the Black Experience performed. According to Steve Marcus, a student reporter for the *Observation Post*, "Students read from their writings, played music and recited poetry as a tribute to the teachers, who befriended student activists while working for adoption of the open admissions policy."[45] Rich had been scheduled to read from Conrad's journal, but the *Observation Post* article makes no mention of her presence.

Another *Observation Post* reporter, Jonathan Neumann, described Conrad vividly in a eulogy published alongside sociology professor Jay Schulman's remembrance of his colleague. Newmann recalled the prominent faculty member as "an overwhelmingly intense, sharp, and gentle man" who was hard to know but appealing all the same. "Conrad was a razor blade and a fist," Neumann wrote. "I remember riding the subway with Conrad once, not saying very much, just staring at his eyes, and he staring at mine. I have never at the same time felt so afraid and so secure, and so totally confused and ignorant. I could only sense that there was something brilliant, mad, human and irreplaceable within Alfred Conrad."[46]

A razor blade, a fist, a sharp and gentle man—the mass of paradoxes that was Alfred Conrad had driven north, away from one home and toward another, his last night on Earth. He found the "still place in the woods" his wife believed was all they truly wanted. But he was there by himself, with no one to hold his hand or listen to what was bothering him. Decades later, Adrienne wanted to address him directly in "Sources": "To say: no person, trying to take responsibility for her or his identity, should have to be so alone."[47]

With both her husband and her father gone, Adrienne Rich was suddenly, finally, emancipated from the control of men. Given her history of premonitions, perhaps she had known this time was coming. In "The Days: Spring," a poem she didn't include in any of her books until the 1993 publication of *Collected Early Poems: 1950–1970,* she presents an oblique exchange with a man, likely based on her husband, who was still alive at the time she wrote it. In the final lines, she envisions herself walking on her own. The constellation above her head calls to mind Andromeda, the Woman in Chains, a tantalizingly ambiguous image that speaks to the poet's dual sense of freedom and entrapment. Her acknowledgment of the duality was in itself liberating.

However connected she was to a mythical and historical past, however well acquainted she was with individual and collective pain and subjugation, Rich was not stuck in one time or place. Though in "Tear Gas" she admitted to being afraid, she would never turn back. Giving in to fears and phobias was not her style, as "The Days: Spring" makes clear. Each pained step inspiring the next, she kept walking:

> This early summer weekend.
> The chance of beginning again.
> From always fewer chances
> the future plots itself.
> I walk Third Avenue,
> bare-armed with flowing hair.
> Later the stars come out like facts,
> my constellation streams at my head,
> a woman's body nailed with stars.[48]

# CHAPTER 14

# A WOMAN OF THE 1970S

## *1970–1972*

In the several years immediately after her husband's suicide, Adrienne Rich moved swiftly into radical feminism. She was preoccupied with what she saw as the inability of men and women to communicate honestly and directly with one another, a perception that grew out of her relationship with Conrad and her emerging feminist consciousness. Books coming out in the early 1970s, such as Kate Millett's *Sexual Politics* and Shulamith Firestone's *The Dialectic of Sex: The Case for Feminist Revolution*, influenced her thinking. At meetings of radical feminists, she encountered lesbians, some of whom had forsworn "sleeping with the enemy" and taken female lovers, in part as an expression of their politics. Rich searched her past for evidence of lesbian attraction and came up with her prep school friendship with Ellen Carter Speers, whom she knew to be a lesbian, and her undergraduate crush on Eleanor Pearre (married with children). Other than that, she had little material to work with. Women's lives and history had her full attention, and she occasionally felt attracted to members of her own sex. But it would be nearly four years before she began a love affair with a woman and still another year before she came out publicly as a lesbian.

Much of her time was consumed with practical concerns. There were bills to pay and her husband's estate to settle. Contrary to what some people assumed, she was not a Baltimore heiress with family money to fall back on. She knew she would have to work hard to maintain the comfortable way of life she and her children were used to.

Closing up the Vermont house for the winter was an early order of business. Unable to do it herself so soon after her husband's death, she enlisted Hayden to drive over from Johnson and strip the beds, pack up the blankets, empty out the refrigerator, and strategically place rat poison in the kitchen.[1] He spent a day in early November following her long list of typed instructions.[2] At home in New York, Adrienne promised herself she would someday go back to the idyllic meadow where her husband had recently killed himself, but a darker part of her, furious at Alf for what he had done and where he had done it, would have sold the West Barnet property without a second thought. In a letter to Audre Lorde recalling her tumultuous emotions in the weeks after his death, she confided that she felt her husband had stolen a beloved refuge away from his family. She was grateful that he hadn't killed himself on their property, but just the thought of Vermont left her reeling in agony.[3]

Overruling her emotions, just as she had when she forced herself to descend the subway stairs that terrified her, she drove to the University of Vermont to give a poetry reading a month after Conrad's death. When she visited the Carruths in Johnson, her grief was palpable. Rose Marie, who later said she had no memory of Alf's name being mentioned then or on any future occasion when she saw Adrienne, watched her young son approach their guest and drape his baby blanket over her head and shoulders. She told Rich that "the Bo," as he was known in the family, liked to bestow his soiled but beloved blanket on anyone he thought was sad. He had once placed the blanket on Denise Levertov, who shook it off with a shudder and a groan. Rich calmly accepted it as the source of consolation the little boy meant it to be.[4]

She took a leave of absence from City College in the spring of 1971. Time off gave her privacy when the whole campus was feeling the loss of her husband, but she had to keep working. Because speaking engagements were a quick and relatively easy way to boost her income, she gave numerous poetry readings before and after the publication of *The Will to Change,* which came out early in 1971. And in a development that showed her versatility and willingness to take an assignment some might have thought beneath a highly decorated poet, she ghostwrote a book about horror movies, a project that thoroughly absorbed her.

The freelance job paid $150 per week when she worked on it nearly full-time.* She loved film and said that if she'd had to choose a different career path, she might have written film criticism.

To all appearances, she was coping well. She kept up her involvement with the Elizabeth Cleaners Street School, the alternative school that Pablo and Jacob were attending and that she had helped get up and running in the last months of her husband's life. She saw a lot of Elise Young and Jack Litewka, her former MFA students. They helped her with the children and the Vermont house, and Adrienne thought of them like family.[5] She also was in touch with Estelle Leontief, the wife of Alf's dissertation director. Their relationship was a source of mutual aggravation,[6] but Adrienne was reluctant to drop someone she'd known since her earliest days with Alf.

She had begun seeking out female friends who had never known her husband. In January 1971, she had lunch with Audre Lorde, whom she decided was "a real, genuine, authentic, living human woman." Long before, she had read Lorde's poetry and sensed they would hit it off, but this evidently was the first time they talked at length. Rich was quick to decide she "loved her."[7] A graduate of Hunter College with a graduate degree in library science, Lorde taught at John Jay College of Criminal Justice. She had married and had children by her gay white husband, but her sexual relationships were primarily with women, both black and white. Witty, extremely outspoken, and possessed of a blazing intelligence, she was very likely the first black person Rich had met whom she considered her intellectual equal. Lorde represented her future, while Estelle Leontief and Hayden Carruth were beginning to look like the past.

Rich was going through the motions of a normal life, but in private, she was a mass of vulnerability as the shock waves of Conrad's suicide rolled over her. During the day, she had to work and tend to her children, but at night, she numbed her pain with alcohol and lay awake for hours. There were times she thought she was going mad. Devastated, angry, full of guilt and grief, she had gone back to Dr. Farber and was seeing him several times a week. On winter days, she sat in Farber's

---

* Rich wrote the manuscript for Joseph Goldberg, a film professor at The New School, who supplied her with his notes and some partially written sections for the study, which took a psychological approach to horror films.

office on the twenty-fourth floor of a building on Riverside Drive and watched seabirds pausing to rest on icy patches of the Hudson River.[8] She could likewise rest and let down her guard in her doctor's presence. She credited him with helping her stay sane.[9]

At Farber's urging,* she made herself look to the future. Less than two weeks after her husband killed himself, she wrote to Hayden Carruth that she was constantly thinking about what Alf had done and what it meant. "But I also have to go on with my life, which seems endlessly strange and curious and amazing."[10] To survive, she knew she had to step through door after door leading to her new world, and she was not blind to the excitement of it. Five years later, looking back on this period, she wrote to her friend Susan Griffin, "Apart from all the pain & grief & anger that followed [Alf's death], there was a real exhilaration in being separate, autonomous, making all the decisions for myself."[11]

As much as she wanted to be at peace and get on with her life, she could not shake the feeling she was somehow responsible for Alf's suicide. Robin Morgan tried to talk her out of this misperception: "[S]he was feeling consumed with guilt over Alf's death and also very angry. And I was taking the feminist approach: It was not her fault. She was trying to live a different kind of life, trying to come out of her own cocoon. He had been depressed and suicidal for some time. It was not her fault. Her response to this was, interestingly enough, you must think it was my fault because you think it was Ted Hughes's fault that Plath killed herself. And I said—I think it was one of the first times that I ever used the phrase 'false equivalence.' This was all 101, but not to her in 1971. At this point in history, in a patriarchal culture, any relationship between a man and a woman, a man has more power, whether it's emotional power, financial power, whatever."[12]

Morgan had published a poem called "Arraignment," which blamed Hughes for Plath's suicide. She didn't see parallels in the relationship

---

* Rich likely heard a version of Farber's stern words: "Repeatedly, [the suicidal person] announces to himself that his state is unbearable. But, should he be challenged on this score—that is, how is he to know what is and what is not bearable for himself; in other words, what gives him this godlike certainty?—his answer, to himself at least, is that it must be unbearable, otherwise he would not be thinking of suicide." Leslie H. Farber, *The Ways of the Will* (New York: Harper & Row, 1966), 94.

Rich had with Conrad. "'You are not responsible in the same way that Hughes is responsible for what Plath did,'" Morgan told Rich. "I went down the whole list of differences, and she didn't see and didn't see and didn't see and didn't see."[13]

It wasn't for lack of trying. In a conversation with Kathleen Spivack a few years after Alf's death, a distraught Adrienne said again and again that she did *not* feel responsible for her husband's suicide. In those raw moments, as Spivack stroked her hand to calm her down, it was obvious Adrienne didn't believe what she was saying.[14]

In 1971, just a few months after Conrad's suicide, she published *The Will to Change: Poems 1968–1970*. Dedicated to David, Pablo, and Jacob, and heralded by a sublime cover photo showing the foamy residue of a crested wave,* the collection is both more intimate and more abstract than any of her previous volumes. The title comes from the beginning of a poem by Charles Olson, "The Kingfishers," a line that also serves as her book's epigraph: "What does not change / is the will to change." The formulation so aptly suited Rich's life in the 1970s that it now seems more hers than Olson's.

Even though she had written all the poems in the collection before Conrad killed himself,[15] the timing of the publication made it feel like a response to his death—and in a way, it was. But just as *Leaflets* transcends its historical moment during the Vietnam era, *The Will to Change* rises above her tormented marriage. In poems such as "The Photograph of the Unmade Bed," which alludes ironically to a luxuriant 1957 photo by Imogen Cunningham, and "Planetarium," which pays tribute to the astronomer Caroline Herschel, she threaded truths of her life into poems that went beyond her personal experience. Throughout the book she drew on the imagery of dreams, films, and photographs as she wrote about pain, loss, and survival. In a vexed time, she called her readers' attention to the interconnectedness of all lives and things, as evidenced in the often-quoted lines from the book's title poem: "We're living through a time / that needs to be lived through us."[16] And in

---

* The photographer was John Benedict, the poetry editor at Norton, who by now was Rich's close friend.

"Images for Godard," she stated with blithe certainty that "the notes for the poem are the only poem" and "the mind of the poet is the only poem." And finally, "the moment of change is the only poem."[17] She would live through the poems that needed to live through her.

Like the great works of Eliot, Yeats, and Stevens, the poems in her new book resist biographical readings, yet also in the tradition of her modernist forebears, Rich is unmistakably present in every one of them. She is present as a woman, a feminist, a furiously engaged mind determined to fashion her own truths out of what she called "the oppressor's language."[18] *The Will to Change* emerges as literary feminism; one might even call it high feminism (akin to the high modernism of *The Waste Land*) in its rendering of a stance at once startling, recognizable, strange, and new.

In his review of Godard's *Pierrot le Fou*, Roger Ebert described how "a Godard movie becomes a montage of pure technique; the parts don't fit together—but they add up to an attitude."[19] The same could be said of *The Will to Change*. Although the volume contains disparate moments of resolution and revelation, it adds up to an attitude more than anything else—an attitude of severe cynicism dappled with intellectual extravagance and resurgent hopefulness. Having forsworn the tidy poem that easily could be dropped into an anthology or dissected in a senior thesis, Rich was like the barely limned craft she imagined in the closing lines of "Snapshots of a Daughter-in-Law," a womanly force moving beyond the scope of ordinary vision. One would have to follow her closely to get a glimpse of what she saw.

In mid-February 1971, Rich experienced a bad flare of pain in her right knee. Her doctor outfitted her with the splint and crutches recommended months earlier. The physical discomfort exacerbated her old problem of insomnia; it seemed her private life could hardly get any harder than it was. Despite her precarious condition, she traveled to a poetry festival at Northwestern University just a day after her doctor said she could remove the splint. A couple of weeks later, in March, she flew to Ohio to give ten readings across the state in nine days—a grueling itinerary she knew would involve "pure gritting of the teeth & hanging on."[20]

Her host at Ohio University, Stanley Plumly, saw her at her most daz-zling and most fragile. Walking with a cane, she gave her usual excellent performance and dined afterward with Plumly, Wayne Dodd, and Wal-ter Tevis. She had agreed to a postdinner interview with poets Plumly and Dodd for the *Ohio Review*, a new literary magazine, and Tevis, a novelist, was allowed to join in. Rich and the three men went to her room at the Ohio University Inn, where they talked for several hours about poetry and the politics of sex and sexuality. "She was luminous," Plumly recalled. "The interview atmosphere was intense, I remember that: dark and smoky (Walter smoked), but Adrienne seemed to really enjoy the company and the chance to really talk."

During the interview, Rich announced she was no longer in thrall to the poetic masters of her youth. In response to Tevis's praise of Yeats, whose greatness he implied contemporary poets could not attain, she said she still loved Yeats, who was "absolutely" her master when she was twenty-one, "but *I* don't want to deal with language the way Yeats dealt with language. I want to be eloquent in my way, and I am a woman of the 1970s, and I am not an Irish male of the beginning of the century. I don't sound like that table-rapping—you'll forgive me now—but that table-rapping fascist."[21]

The interview reached a crescendo in the closing exchange as Rich refused to allow the men to speak for her. As they discussed the future of poetry, Plumly asked, "I think this is the question, where is *your* work going?"

DODD: The answer probably is that you don't know.
RICH: I have some ideas.
PLUMLY: I think you intuit that, yes, sure.
RICH: I have some clues as to where I think I would like to be going at this point, where I am at this moment in time. This whole subject of sexuality in its broadest sense, and I mean really the full sense of it—I mean, what it means to be a man, what it means to be a woman, I think, is perhaps the major subject of poetry from here on. Because I think it's the ultimately political question, and it is going to affect all the other questions. When we were talking, you know—with that guy at lunch who had the brother who went to Vietnam? I was thinking this and it's almost as if every man is taught from the cradle that this is what he's

for. Ultimately our task as a male is to be able to go out and kill
some enemy. And this is an incredibly primitive notion.

TEVIS: Oh horse shit!

RICH: It IS true, and it's true in the education. I'm saying that it's not
true necessarily in any given family, or any given cultural situation, but in an overall political sense, it's true.

PLUMLY: Yes, the John Wayne syndrome.

RICH: Yes, right. And, in another sense, women are brought up to
feel they're going to bind up the wounds of the wounded from
this carnage. I mean it's almost as if Western Civilization had
come to view the world as a battlefield, as a struggle for power,
in which men are going to kill each other and be killed and then
they're going to drag off the bodies and eat off the meat from
them, or something. And that's got to change, you know, or
we're *all* going to die. It's very simple, and this is the ultimate
political thing, you know, about sexuality, and I think is, to me,
a major concern for poetry because it's a major concern for my
life; I cannot . . .

PLUMLY: What exactly has to change? The role-playing?

RICH: The role-playing, the kinds of acculturation, the kinds of
assigned sensibility that we get. And then as far as writing poetry
is concerned, I would just think: you know, how do you deal with
that inward person who you are—whether a male or a female?
How do you look at that? How much of it do you accept as
being intrinsically you? How much do you sort of reject as being
something you've been told about yourself?

When Plumly pressed her to say whether she thought there was "an
actual and realizable difference, between male and female," Rich said
she did but that no one seemed able to define it. She then began talking about ideas informing poems she would include in her next book,
*Diving into the Wreck*:

RICH: In the most physical sense [sexuality] is the metaphor for
a great deal else. And, you know, today, any kind of physical
relationship, activity, is O.K. . . . you're free for that. But you're
actually unfree for something more. I mean *we* have *never* been
free for anything beyond that, really. And now there's this sort

of hard-won sexual, in a limited sense, freedom. What really fascinates me is, once we've been through that, you know, we've seen that—O.K., then what?

TEVIS: You seem to edge around this in a way that's uncharacteristic of free-spoken, modern-poetry-type people.

RICH: Free-spoken modern? I'm Emily Dickinson!

TEVIS: But, when you talk about sexuality, do you mean dirty movies that we all run in our minds, or are you talking about male and female role-playing in public, how we are dressed and behave?

RICH: Yes, all those things are part of it. I mean, it's who you fuck with and how you fuck, and it's your wet dreams, and it's your masturbatory fantasies, and it's the definitions of self that you have at any point. And it's also how you see other males and other females, and it's how you bring up children. I mean, I can't think of anything that it isn't. And finally it's what people do to each other.[22]

With Rich facing three men in her hotel room at night, the interview had a sexual dimension. If the antagonistic Tevis wanted her to spell things out, she would see his "horse shit" and raise him "fucking." Talking like this was one way to bring sex and violence out in the open and put all three men on notice she was no Emily Dickinson, nor was she a tease, sexual or otherwise.

Rich was scheduled to read at Ohio State University the next afternoon, and Plumly offered to take her there in his aging Volkswagen Beetle. Looking back nearly fifty years, he recalled the snowstorm that imperiled their journey. "I know she was worried that we might not survive the trip, considering the circumstances—that is, the combination of the driver, the car, and the weather. Yet in the course of the drive she seemed to have come to trust me and asked me to stay through the time of the reading." Taking his arm, she was able to navigate the sprawling campus in the snow. Plumly saw how vulnerable she was: "Wetness and chill were her enemy; the damp seemed to curse her very bones."

There was nevertheless a vitality, a sexual charge, evident in her that Plumly also noticed. She had wanted to talk sex with him and his friends, and he interpreted the title The Will to Change as a commentary on her evolving sexuality. He thought she was probably bisexual even if she hadn't yet begun having relationships with women. "The problem," he said, recalling his long-ago impressions of her, "is that what's in the heart and what's in the act can be separated in time, the former, of course, ahead of the latter."[23]

Plumly had read Rich's heart correctly. She was no longer ruling out the possibility of a relationship with a woman. Women on a similar path recognized something of themselves in her. At Ohio Wesleyan University, another stop on her Ohio tour, future attorney and lesbian activist Mary Dorman was in the audience when Rich gave her poetry reading. Dorman had grown up in the Middle East, the daughter of an American diplomat; she felt out of place and isolated at a rural American college. At the time, she was still dating men.

"I trekked through the bitter cold and snowy weather to hear her read. It was a very small room as very few people showed up because of the weather," Dorman recalled. "Her poems resonated with me, and I was very moved and realized there were others on earth like me." Back in her dorm room, she wrote a "kind of love letter" to Rich and then went to the hotel where she assumed the visiting poet was staying. The desk clerk gave her Rich's room number: "I knocked on the door, she answered, I gave her my letter and thanked her and walked away. Later, we both came out as lesbians and activists."[24]

By the time Rich traveled to Ohio, she was writing poems again.[25] In December, she looked back on her brief period of writer's block as a matter of artistic restraint. When she started writing poems again, they were about the broken male-female bond in her own life and in relationships all around her, she told her West Coast poet friend Kathleen Fraser.[26] With her letter to Fraser, she enclosed a handful of poems destined to appear in *Diving into the Wreck:* "Waking in the Dark," "Song," "Incipience," and "The Mirror in Which Two Are Seen as One."

During the hardest, most emotionally taxing years of her life, she was working on these poems and others, such as "Trying to Talk to a Man," "Diving into the Wreck," and "Rape," that went beyond the stark feminist emanations in *The Will to Change.* In the terrible months right after Alf's death, she had viewed her inability to write poems as a horror unto itself. But perhaps her stilled hand had worked in her favor and given her time to get where she needed to go, for her new poems exuded a stunning certitude and cohesiveness: She really *was* changing, not just willing herself to do so. And though a lifetime of preparation lay behind *Diving into the Wreck,* the actual writing of the book happened stunningly fast.

She was not the only one in her family who was changing. Her sister, Cynthia, was in the process of divorcing Roy Glauber, who would go on to win the 2005 Nobel Prize in Physics. The divorce promised to be an exceedingly difficult one. During a visit with her, Adrienne sized up her sister, who had graduated summa cum laude from Radcliffe, completed postgraduate work in English at Harvard, created Harvard's writing center, and taught at Harvard. In Adrienne's eyes, Cynthia looked beautiful and had an admirably firm grasp of her situation.[27] Following a pattern begun long ago, she paid lip service to her sister's strengths and talents but didn't seem deeply moved by her plight. She had turned to her in desperation when Alf went missing, but now she had resumed her authority as a dispassionate observer of Cynthia's choices in life.

In the summer of 1971, Adrienne and her children went to San Francisco on a vacation they had been planning for months. While the boys went off on their own adventures—two of them took the opportunity to smoke hashish—she wished Alf were there to experience the times and places she knew he would have loved. She delighted in all the different plants she saw in Golden Gate Park; she relished a drive into the hills, where she took in the foggy headlands of Marin County and glimpsed the very top of Golden Gate Bridge, otherwise lost in fog. Walking the beach, she basked in the presence of seals and pelicans and happily inhaled the scent of eucalyptus trees. At these times, she missed Alf. But, as she wrote to Carruth, that was different from thinking they should have stayed together. She had begun to think of her late husband as if he were split into two parts, with all that was good and passionate about him stamped out by all that was miserable and desperate.[28] What she didn't say was that a similar split existed in her. Though she didn't think of herself as a sinner, as she suggested Alf did, she zigzagged back and forth between feeling her life was on the right track and nearly giving in to a terrible despair.

During this trip, Rich continued working on poems that would appear in *Diving into the Wreck*. From San Francisco and Vermont, she and Carruth wrote back and forth about "Waking in the Dark" and other poems she sent him in draft form. Given that *Diving into the Wreck* would make her name as a radical feminist poet, it is interesting to see her still turning to Carruth for constructive criticism. She wanted a man's opinion; she wanted *his* opinion. Time and again, even as she took an increasingly dim view of contemporary men's poetry (which she found tiresome and unimaginative in its persistent despair[29]) and men in general, she continued to seek out Carruth's poetic counsel. She had other close male poet friends, such as Hugh Seidman and Jack Litewka, but Carruth's vast knowledge of poetry and his skills as a critic could not be discounted. She wanted him to weigh in on poems that she knew represented a new benchmark in her poetic growth.

Writing to him in anticipation of his fiftieth birthday, she also wanted him to know "what joy, serious joy, your existence gives me."[30] She said she placed him second only to Alf in the range, depth, and continuity of her conversations with men. This high praise was characteristic of the way she had always written to Carruth. But in linking him with her late husband, she inadvertently hinted at the trouble their friendship was in. She wanted more from Hayden than he was prepared or able to give. Though she believed in "serious joy"—a wonderfully evocative expression—it was hardly a primary or frequent emotion in the years immediately following her husband's death. And it didn't account for the impatience she increasingly felt in her dealings with Hayden. Her habitual good manners faltered as she demanded he talk sexual politics on her terms.

When the new academic year began in 1971, she immersed herself in her teaching at CCNY and worked on behalf of open admissions, the endeavor that had meant so much to Alf. As a newly appointed assistant professor of English, she was teaching freshman English and a poetry-writing workshop in City College's new MFA program. The work was satisfying, and evidence of her professional success—her tenure-track job and the popularity of *The Will to Change*—was all around her. There were times the optimist in her reemerged; she exulted in the new life she had made for herself and felt more capable of loving others.[31]

Other times, loneliness was inescapable. She was close to her sons but didn't expect them to fill the void in her life, and she knew they were reeling from the loss of their father. As the first anniversary of Alf's suicide approached, she could barely face her time alone. She confessed to Carruth that she was drinking herself into a stupor so she could get a few hours of sleep. Hungover and despairing, she awoke while it was still dark outside. In early October 1971, she wrote to him that she felt "at the root of things, in spite of work, children, the love of friends, a hunger that seems almost to be myself, not an experience or a quality but to be who I am."[32] She had tried to tamp down her need and desire for companionship, but those feelings—that hunger—could not be suppressed forever. She ached with a loneliness that threatened to topple her precariously balanced life.

Despite her private sorrows, the year 1972 got off to a good start. Her arthritis was responding so well to gold injections that she had stopped taking other medication for the affliction. In the early, unseasonably mild days of January, she walked around Manhattan for hours, free of the pain that usually accompanied her every step. Although the deaths in rapid succession of John Berryman, Kenneth Patchen, and Padraic Colum registered on her as "a bad weekend for poets,"[33] she thought she might escape the depression she often felt in January.

By March, however, her mood had darkened. Her frustration and rage had begun to consume her. She was working on a new poem, "The Phenomenology of Anger," that articulated her growing fury not just with men but the patriarchal order that assured women of second-class status no matter who they were. She would later tell an interviewer that the poem, published in *Diving into the Wreck,* grew out of "feelings of rage at being a woman in a patriarchal society; being powerless at wanting a relationship between man and woman to be possible and feeling all the ways in which it becomes impossible; feelings of all the ways in which the old consciousness sits on you when you're trying to break through to a new consciousness; the difficulty of becoming oneself."[34]

She continued to use alcohol to mute her sorrow and fury. She was drinking so heavily that Robin Morgan became concerned and suggested she see a therapist. As gently as she could, Morgan told her, "I'm worried about the drinking." She had feared Rich would fly into a rage, but instead, her eyes filled with tears as she replied, " 'I'm worried about the drinking, too.' "[35]

Continuing to write and revise "The Phenomenology of Anger," she returned once again to Dr. Farber's care. She had stopped seeing him due to their philosophical disagreements, but now her anger was so intense, she again feared for her sanity. Because he had helped her survive the worst of times in the recent past, she wanted to believe he could see her through her current crisis. In hopes that he would understand, she intended to talk freely and furiously about sex and power—the topics that beat inside her skull.

She hadn't stopped trying to have that conversation with Hayden Carruth. After a decade of letters in which she lavished him with praise and repeatedly turned the discussion away from herself and on him, she now insisted her old friend and admirer answer for his weaknesses and respond meaningfully to her searing rage and pain. Although she found it hard to talk to men, she badly wanted to. In April 1972, she wrote to Carruth that she didn't want a lover, but, instead, men with whom she could have real conversations: "It's the only way I can imagine transcending this time of terrible sexual aridity, cold-hearted fucking as Lawrence called it."[36]

Although the correspondence continued, it was no longer a source of mutual comfort. Carruth was willing to hear her out so long as she didn't attack him personally. Rich insisted she was commenting on patriarchal society at large, but her volleys of criticism made it clear she could no longer tolerate his serial philandering or his litany of personal complaints. He wrote that he could no longer bear her anger—but then decided to keep the letter in his files rather than mail it to her. Though neither wanted to let go of the other, Adrienne had changed the terms of their relationship. She was no longer in thrall to him, and she expected him to keep pace with her enlightenment. The cold winds blowing through her letters caught him off guard and hurt his feelings. He was beginning to see Rich's temper as ungovernable.

With this important friendship falling apart and her drinking attracting the worried attention of Robin Morgan, Rich met with Farber in early April 1972. It seems he, too, was at an impasse with her. Promising they could continue as friends outside the confines of their doctor-patient relationship, he suggested a female psychiatrist might be able to help her more than he could. The proposed transition made her uneasy. She wanted to hash things out with a man and therefore felt seeking help from a woman was pointless, but she took his advice anyway.

Shortly thereafter, her relationship with Farber imploded. He and Rich had some kind of friendly interaction that his wife objected to. When Mrs. Farber insisted he never see Rich again, Rich erupted in fury. She should have known better than to think her psychiatrist's wife would welcome her into their social circle, but she had naïvely believed she and Farber could meet as equals and as friends. Enraged and humiliated, she poured out her story to her new doctor, Lilly Engler, who told her to go back to Farber and confront him.[37]

It is unknown whether Rich did that, but just as she had immediately trusted Farber, now she felt safe and at ease with Engler. Whatever doubts she had about seeing a female psychoanalyst melted in the face of the Jewish, Viennese-born Engler's abundant warmth and acute insight into the artistic temperament. Eleven years Rich's senior, tall, green-eyed, and big-bosomed, Engler was the analyst of choice among opera stars at the Met, and though she probably didn't talk about her personal life right away, Rich eventually learned Engler had made a dramatic escape from Nazi Germany and was a lesbian, whose past lovers included Susan Sontag. After their first meeting, Adrienne saw Engler on a regular basis. She was enormously pleased with her new psychoanalyst and no longer thought a male doctor would better serve her needs. There was excitement ahead for the two of them, but neither of them knew that yet.

In the fall of 1972, Rich was named the Fannie Hurst Visiting Professor of Creative Writing at Brandeis University. The lucrative one-year position offered her leverage for future academic positions but took her away from New York, the city she thought of as her true home, and the therapist she had grown to depend on. They would maintain contact, however, and Rich very likely saw Engler on return visits to New York during the academic year.

Before moving back to Cambridge, the city she had left so gladly six years earlier, she bought a co-op apartment on the Upper West Side: 670 West End Avenue, apartment 10D. The purchase gave her a solid stake in the city she loved. Rather than leaving the apartment vacant during her absence, she rented it to Anthony Burgess, author of *A Clockwork Orange*, who would be teaching at City College while she was at Brandeis. In a letter to him, she described a spacious apartment "with a very large bedroom-study, two baths, two smaller bedrooms and maid's room."[38] Burgess and his wife and son moved in shortly after she moved out. It seemed like an ideal arrangement for both writers, but Burgess would prove to be a ludicrously awful tenant.

Robin Morgan had coined the phrase "The personal is political," and there was no one for whom that was more true than Rich. She took the notion a step further in "The Blue Ghazals," in which she wrote, *"The moment when a feeling enters the body* / is political."[39] Full of unresolved feelings of loss and longing, she had pronounced herself a woman of the 1970s in her interview with the *Ohio Review*. She was determined to distance herself from male poetic precursors, like Yeats, whose lives and artistic experiences had little in common with her own, and find meaning and inspiration in her identity as a woman and feminist. Perhaps doing so would help fill the existential void that felt like insatiable hunger.

In these years immediately after her husband's death, she saw her marriage's combustible mix of silence, desire, rage, and infidelity writ large in the history of relationships between man and woman. Conrad's violent death transmogrified into a dark gift, for in the absolute failure of her marriage she could no longer pretend she understood how men thought. Bolstered by her reading and the like-minded women she was meeting, she believed the mutuality of understanding and respect that she craved was tragically lacking in the history of the male-female bond. It became her mission to point out that pervasive absence, and her objective as a poet to record her observations about the problems she witnessed and knew firsthand. What, she wondered, was on the other side of the void? She wanted very much to converse with men who shared her interest in finding answers, and she was constantly assessing their ability, or lack thereof, to meet her halfway in the discussions she craved.

But now that she saw herself as a radical feminist, she found it difficult to be around men. She reportedly insisted on negotiating her contract at Brandeis with a female faculty member rather than dealing with the male chair of the English department. In time, she would try to keep men out of her poetry readings. This hard-line political persona accommodated feelings of pain and rejection she attributed to the men in her life and the patriarchal nature of the world. She wouldn't keep it up forever, but for a while it allowed her to give her full attention to her life as a woman, the subject that the times and her circumstances told her she could no longer afford to ignore. For guidance and comfort, she had Lilly Engler. It was Engler, her trusted psychiatrist, who would lead her by the hand into a whole new world of love and desire and give her the raw material for "Twenty-One Love Poems."

# CHAPTER 15

# THE BOOK OF MYTHS

## *1972–1973*

Adrienne returned to Cambridge in the fall of 1972 because her visiting appointment at Brandeis was too good to turn down. She taught undergraduate creative writing two days a week and was required to give several public lectures. This latter duty gave her the chance to research Emily Dickinson and other subjects of her choosing—an ideal assignment. Never one to squander an opportunity, she told Elizabeth Hardwick she was working extremely hard and Cambridge's social life held no allure for her. She had chosen to live there rather than some neighboring town because her sons wanted to be back in their old neighborhood. She happily described to Hardwick the prose project that would become *Of Woman Born*, which she knew would require prodigious research.[1] In the meantime, she was finishing up *Diving into the Wreck: Poems 1971–1972*, which would come out in the summer of 1973.

During this crucial year away from New York, Rich lived at 65 Sacramento Street, in the upper levels of a two-family house in Cambridge. Seventeen-year-old David was performing with Boston-area bands, while Pablo and Jacob were enrolled in alternative schools. Pablo spent some of his time living in a group house with several other teenagers.[2] She encouraged her sons' independence and was pleased when they pursued education in ways that made sense to them. With the boys often out of the house, she luxuriated in the privacy she had craved for years, and wrote and read for hours on end.

She had become a voracious reader of literature and journalism by women. Like many literary feminists of her generation, she was a passionate devotee of Virginia Woolf and Emily Dickinson.* They were the high priestesses of women's literature, but there were countless contemporary authors and feminist journals Rich turned to with excitement and gratitude. She wrote her friend Kathleen Fraser about her discovery of Barbara Deming's essay about anger in *Liberation* and an article by Linda Thurston, "On Male and Female Principle," in *The Second Wave*. She thrilled to the increasingly sophisticated arguments appearing in feminist journals, especially the "real analyses of the pass to which a split in sex-roles has brought us, and attempts to locate a real femaleness amid all the masks and roles and stereotypes—or rather, beyond them."[3] And she loved the feminist journals and newsletters themselves. Produced by self-taught printers on their own presses or simply typed and mimeographed, these grassroots efforts allowed women to circumvent the staid journals, both large and small, that rarely published work by women. Inventive, homespun, at times stunningly original, they were, for Rich, a source of instruction and delight.

Once *Diving into the Wreck* was in print, she sent Deming a letter and a copy of the book. She was determined to build alliances with prominent feminists, many of them lesbians, whom she saw as her intellectual peers. In addition to Deming, she wanted to know the radical lesbian theologian Mary Daly. Praising Daly's *Beyond God the Father: Toward a Philosophy of Women's Liberation*, Rich wrote to her friend Elaine Hedges in November 1973 that she thought Daly's new book was the greatest feminist treatise since *The Second Sex*.[4] Soon she would be in direct contact with Daly.

Though not a lesbian, the fiction writer and memoirist Tillie Olsen was a feminist of an older generation, and her woman-centered vision in *Tell Me a Riddle* (1961) helped convince Rich she was not alone in her new understanding of the world. She cultivated a deep and tender correspondence with Olsen, and they shared an appreciation of the way one's domestic life weaves its way into everything. In one letter from

---

* Taking a dizzyingly contrarian view, Levertov referred to Dickinson in a letter to Robert Duncan as "cold and perversely smug" and "a bitchy little spinster." In quoting that letter, Rich asserted that Levertov later changed her assessment. *HE*, 78.

this time period, Rich told Olsen she had intended to send her the *New York Times* review of Quentin Bell's biography of Woolf, but the page had ended up in the cat's litter box.[5]

When Rich wrote to Kathleen Fraser about "a real femaleness," she was alluding to her own search for something of utmost importance to her. Her alliance with the women's movement gave her not just reason to hope but also reason to be. In the first couple of years after Alf's suicide, she desperately needed both. In "From a Survivor," in *Diving into the Wreck,* she wrote:

> Next year it would have been 20 years
> and you are wastefully dead
> who might have made the leap
> we talked, too late, of making
>
> which I live now
> not as a leap
> but a succession of brief, amazing movements
>
> each one making possible the next[6]

It was as if she had pulled still frames from a film about her life after her husband's death and made those frames into poems. Whereas the strength of *The Will to Change* lay in her willingness to write, however obliquely, about the dire extremity of her condition and imply that it was not the end of her story, the power of her new poems came from her unfiltered portrayal of the world opening before her. It wasn't all good, but it was full of possibilities, as was she.

Her metamorphosis was exhilarating but often lonely. In "Song," another poem in *Diving into the Wreck,* she accepts the burden of loneliness with equanimity and makes of it something sublime:

> If I'm lonely
> it must be the loneliness
> of waking first, of breathing

dawn's first cold breath on the city
of being the one awake
in a house wrapped in sleep

If I'm lonely
it's with the rowboat ice-fast on the shore
in the last red light of the year
that knows what it is, that knows it's neither
ice nor mud nor winter light
but wood, with a gift for burning[7]

Rich wrote some of the best poems of her career while she was in limbo between her past as a married heterosexual woman and her future as a partnered lesbian. Whenever she had time to herself, her ideas proliferated and the writing flowed. Intellectually and creatively, she had once again reached the condition for which she was made. She didn't want to be alone for much longer, however, and desire was stirring within her.

Two years after her husband's suicide, she remained deeply preoccupied with sex and sexuality, subjects that inevitably found their way into her poems. In the explanatory note she wrote to accompany the hardback edition of Diving into the Wreck, she said her new poems represented "a coming-home to the darkest and richest source of my poetry: sex, sexuality, sexual wounds, sexual identity, sexual politics: many names for pieces of one whole." Direct though that statement is, Diving into the Wreck is a book of searching, not finding. While she was writing the poems in this volume and going deep into feminist politics, lesbianism began to feel more possible for her, but she was still not a lesbian. She was waiting, it seems, for the right woman to lead her out of her liminal state of half-articulated desire.

Cheryl Walker was not that woman, but she was nonetheless an important friend to Rich during her time at Brandeis. In her mid-twenties and married, Walker was writing her Ph.D. dissertation on women poets under the direction of the poet J. V. Cunningham. Her project was well under way when Rich arrived on campus and Walker asked her to be a second reader on her dissertation committee. Rich agreed, and they began meeting regularly at Rich's home.

Dr. Arnold Rich,
Adrienne Rich's father,
in his office at Johns
Hopkins Hospital,
in the early 1960s.
*Schlesinger Library,
Radcliffe Institute,
Harvard University*

In this passport
photo with
her mother,
Adrienne is about
three years old.
*Schlesinger Library,
Radcliffe Institute,
Harvard University*

Adrienne on vacation with her family in Easthampton, Long Island, circa 1935. *Schlesinger Library, Radcliffe Institute, Harvard University.*

Helen Rich with Adrienne's sister, Cynthia, in front of the family home in Roland Park, an upscale neighborhood in Baltimore, circa 1940. *Schlesinger Library, Radcliffe Institute, Harvard University*

Adrienne in 1947, upon graduation from Roland Park Country School. *Courtesy of the Roland Park Country School Archives*

Cynthia Rich and Helen Jones Rich, around 1947, on a family vacation in Hudson Bay, Canada. *Schlesinger Library, Radcliffe Institute, Harvard University*

Rich posing at Radcliffe College during her senior year. She graduated in 1951.
© *Peter Solmssen*

Rich (front row, second from left) in 1966, at the Yale University memorial for Randall Jarrell, the poet and critic whose early review of her poetry spurred her to greater experimentation. Back row (left to right), Stanley Kunitz, Richard Eberhart, Robert Lowell, Richard Wilbur, John Hollander, William Meredith, and Robert Penn Warren. Front row, John Berryman, Mary Jarrell, and Peter Taylor. *Getty Images*

Alfred Conrad, Rich's husband and a professor of economics at The City College of New York, appearing on a 1969 episode of William F. Buckley's *Firing Line. Hoover Institution Archives*

Rich in 1973, photographed on Broadway. © *Nancy Crampton*

Rich at her apartment on West End Avenue in 1973. © *Nancy Crampton*

Michelle Cliff in the early 1980s. Rich and Cliff lived in this house (shown in 2019) in Montague, Massachusetts, from 1979 to 1984. *Photo of Michelle Cliff © Noel Furie / Photo of the Montague house © Paul Mariani*

Rich speaking at the Women Against Violence in Pornography and Media conference in San Francisco in November 1978. © *Lynda Koolish*

Rich gave countless poetry readings for nearly sixty years. Here, she talks with her audience at Modern Times Bookstore in San Francisco in the mid 1980s. © *Lynda Koolish*

Rich speaking at Stanford in 2001. © *Linda A. Cicero / Stanford News Service*

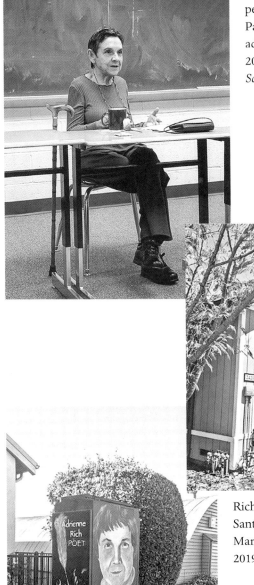

Throughout her long career, Rich periodically returned to visit Roland Park Country School. Here, Rich addresses a class at the all-girls school in 2004. *Courtesy of the Roland Park Country School Archives*

Rich lived at 2420 Paul Minnie Avenue in Santa Cruz from 1986 until her death on March 27, 2012. The house is shown here in 2019. © *Hilary Holladay*

As part of a public art project designed to brighten up utility boxes around Santa Cruz County, Santa Cruz artist Peter Bartczak painted Rich's image on the box at the intersection of Soquel and 7th avenues in 2014. © *Hilary Holladay*

Their conversations were long and spirited and gave both of them the opportunity to hone their arguments. Rich was quick to challenge the condescending attitude toward women poets that infiltrated Walker's writing and reflected Cunningham's influence. "She would tear my chapters apart," Walker said. "I became a feminist because of the things she asked me about." What could have stayed a formal relationship between professor and graduate student evolved into a close and mutually supportive friendship. Rich introduced Walker to her sons and sometimes invited her to stay for dinner. Despite the relaxed nature of their meetings, Walker never lost sight of her mentor's status. She recalled a time Rich was cleaning the kitchen, "rag in hand, talking away, wiping down the counter and the stove." Walker blurted out that she hadn't realized Rich did such ordinary things. "Of course I do those things," Rich shot back.

In retrospect, Walker was struck by "the incredible amount of time and love and generosity" Rich poured into their relationship. She felt no one today in a position equivalent to Rich's would give of herself so freely to a graduate student. But Rich was benefiting, too. With her open heart and youthful intelligence, Walker arrived on her doorstep like a gift. "She was a well-established poet at that time, my senior certainly," Walker said. "She saw in me the daughter that she didn't have. And I saw in her the mother I didn't have. But there was also a kind of flirtatiousness, also love, that kind of equalized us."[8]

The warmth and good humor that Walker brought into Rich's life provided an antidote to the projects that consumed so much of her private time: It was as if Rich had turned into a graduate student herself as she read endlessly and wrote in an analytical style new to her. She worried that writing prose about the same political concerns that animated her poetry might be a mistake for her art, but she was relieved to find she could still write poems. She compared her poems to dreams, and her critical writing to dream analysis.[9]

Two prominently placed book reviews she published that year were a testing ground for ideas that would find their way into *Of Woman Born* and influence her thinking for years to come. In her review of Midge Decter's *The New Chastity and Other Arguments Against Women's Liberation* in *The New York Review of Books,* she wrote at length about "the notion of a matriarchal origin of civilization," a topic that would consume many pages in *Of Woman Born*. It came as no surprise that she disliked Decter's antifeminist screed, which she dismissed as "harmless, predictable, and sad." Decter's writing was "lifeless," she argued, "because she attempts to stand outside something which, like it or not, is about and within her; and in so doing she manages to sound not like a woman but like a priest lecturing his flock on the newest temptation." Rich would not make that mistake in *Of Woman Born*. She would later remark that being a mother had radicalized her,[10] and that personal truth would be evident throughout her first prose book.

For all that Rich had to say about the dismal realities of patriarchal culture and the hopeful possibilities of matriarchal alternatives, the most memorable lines in her review of Decter's book have nothing to do with either one. She declared, "I believe that feminism must imply an imaginative identification with all women (and with the ghostly woman in all men) and that the feminist must, because she can, extend this act of the imagination as far as possible."[11] These were words to live by. They were also a succinct statement of the philosophy underlying *Diving into the Wreck* and her 1978 collection, *The Dream of a Common Language*.

Rich's other important review that year appeared in *The New York Times Book Review*. She had met Phyllis Chesler at a party in New York and learned that the psychotherapist's groundbreaking feminist study, *Women and Madness*, had gone virtually unnoticed by the mainstream press. Rich hinted she would take action. Her affirming, copiously researched review appeared on the front page of the *Times* book review section on December 31, 1972, and, in Chesler's opinion, made *Women and Madness* a bestseller.[12]

As a former psychiatric patient of Leslie Farber and a current patient of Lilly Engler, Rich had a vested interest in Chesler's book, which concerns the patriarchal bias underlying psychology and psychiatry and the resulting harm done to female patients. What she found in *Women and Madness* illuminated everything she had read in Jung, R. D. Laing, Karen Horney, and other texts on psychology and psychiatry, no doubt including Farber's writings.*

---

* Rich wanted nothing more to do with Farber, but she could not escape him in print. In the December 1972 issue of the *Partisan Review*, her poem "Waking in

Where is a woman to seek confirmation of her existence, support and nurture in the struggle to love herself better, care for herself more intelligently, desist from self-destructive gestures? How is she to act on Otto Rank's admission that "since modern psychology is not only masculine but derived from our neurotic type of man, a great deal of its terminology originated from misinterpretation of woman in terms of man's sexual ideology" and that "woman had to be made over by man in order to become acceptable to him"? ("Beyond Psychology") She may trust her therapist's good faith and good intentions; how is she to deal with his training, his acculturation, his unconscious?[13]

These were not just rhetorical questions for her. She had trusted Farber and believed, with his encouragement, that he was her friend. During the time when she was beset with the staircase phobia and in the months immediately after Alf's death, she was in no condition to guard against whatever biases and yearnings, unconscious or otherwise, that he brought to their sessions. She was likewise vulnerable when she turned to Lilly Engler. Bereft and emotionally wounded by the way things had ended with Farber, she saw Engler as the ally and friend she desperately needed.

She taught at Brandeis, but Rich spent most of her time in the enveloping shadow of Harvard, the institution she once claimed had made her who she was. When Harvard's Signet Club, a formerly all-male literary society, invited her to read at its Christmas banquet in December 1972, she accepted. The occasion gave her a fresh opportunity to engage with her alma mater, the object of her comingled love and scorn. She was planning to read from the soon-to-be-published *Diving into the Wreck* after a playwright and Harvard alumnus named Timothy S. Mayer made his remarks. But his ribald toast so incensed her that when it was her turn to speak, she told the audience of 150 people that "the Signet had shown itself still to be a male-dominated institu-

---

the Dark" follows "Questions of Guilt," a transcribed conversation by the doctor and several of his colleagues.

tion, and thus an inappropriate forum for her poetry."[14] With that, she walked out into the night and left a crowd of students and their faculty friends gaping in disbelief.

Mayer told a student reporter for *The Harvard Crimson* that the contretemps wasn't worth covering, and Rich couldn't be reached for comment. Her abrupt departure nevertheless garnered a story in that paper. In a letter to the editor a few weeks later, an angry Rich wrote, "I had expected to find at the Signet a liberalized, though not radicalized attitude toward women. I found a group of token women, myself included, expected to enjoy the sexist humor of a traditional stag club. I was deeply disturbed by the fact that Mr. Mayer's monologue was received with hilarity and applause by those present, including both men and women who I am sure, if asked, would say that they had found it offensive. I felt the atmosphere of the dinner to be so decadent that I lost all desire to read poetry in such a situation or to collaborate with it further."

She might have left it at that. But Rich had advanced so far from her Radcliffe days, when (as she confessed in her journal at the time) she "pitied old maids" and "damned sterile feminism,"[15] that she couldn't resist making a larger point: "Until those men who think of themselves as civilized liberals examine the fear and hatred of women underlying their jokes and amusements, they will go on perpetuating a puerile and false virility in themselves and their sons. Until elite women begin to protest the reification and devaluation of women in general, their influence and dignity in male institutions will always be at the mercy of a misogyny which can break through even the most cultivated and civilized veneer."[16] In severe, sophisticated language showing she, too, was a member of the ruling class, she socked it to the conceited male standard-bearers of the New Left and the young women in the audience whose attitudes were not so different from her own twenty years earlier. She was showing all of them what happens when a token stops laughing and starts lecturing.

By now, Rich's intimate epistolary friendship with Hayden Carruth was fraying badly. He didn't appreciate her politicized reactions to his personal problems, and she was relentless. The previous spring, she had written him that she'd been furious with all the men in recent months with whom she'd attempted to have honest conversations, so it was inevitable that she would blow up at him, too. She told him she would be devastated if their friendship ended, while warning that many of the younger women she knew "have simply given up on men," and often she was tempted to do the same thing.[17]

Still, they stayed in touch. In February 1973, she responded to a letter in which he had evidently asked a blunt question about her sex life. Her candid reply illustrates how willing she was to trust him with her innermost thoughts. It also reveals how torn she was between heterosexual and lesbian desire: "No, I haven't been into a lesbian experience; in fact I've recently been very turned-on sexually by a man, but a man in kinds of trouble that I don't need. Actually, I have found for a couple of years that my erotic feelings for women are quite strong, especially women whose minds interest me. [. . .] Women attract me very much; but I feel that a man as open, developing, exploratory and risk-taking as so many women are today can attract me as much." She had begun contemplating androgyny—a concept gaining in popularity in the 1970s and which she would have encountered in reading Virginia Woolf. She told Carruth that androgyny "would relieve each sex of its burden of being all to the other—the idea of it as a social condition appeals to me enormously."[18]

Her interest in androgyny became public in "The Stranger," a poem in *Diving into the Wreck:*

I am the androgyne
I am the living mind you fail to describe
in your dead language
the lost noun, the verb surviving
only in the infinitive
the letters of my name are written under the lids
of the newborn child[19]

Here was a "living mind" that refused to be defined by a static sexual identity. The "newborn child" is the emerging self whom she does not yet know. This was in some ways the most telling frame taken from her evolution in progress. As it happened, she was not cut out for androgyny. Sexual fluidity in mind and body was a passing fancy that appealed to her at a time when she wanted to throw her lot with women but still felt "very turned-on" by a man whose identity remains a mystery.

By the end of the academic year, Rich was ready to leave Cambridge and get back to her life in New York. She had secured a full professorship in the English department at City College, quite a step up from the untenured assistant professorship she had held when she left town. Even better, her advance from Norton for *Of Woman Born* would allow her to write full-time and postpone teaching for a year. Before settling back into the apartment where she hadn't lived long before her year at Brandeis, she would take some vacation time.

The transition did not go as smoothly as she had hoped. She told Elaine Hedges, who had recently founded the women's studies program at Towson State College, that she had enjoyed two weeks of travel with Jacob in the Southwest, but otherwise devoted much of her time to moving back to New York and helping her sons get settled in their own abodes.[20] What she didn't say was that subleasing her apartment to Anthony Burgess had been a disaster.

Her tenant had cut a tornado's path of destruction through her home. She came back to West End Avenue to discover a mattress missing; a box spring ripped; bedroom tables dotted with cigarette burns; kitchen utensils missing, burned, or broken; a lamp broken; and a sofa and rug stained with spilled food. To top it off, Burgess had not paid the utility bills. When Rich demanded that he reimburse her for all he owed, a haughty and defensive Burgess expressed his objections to Rich's lawyer. He considered her complaints "petty" and felt certain the security deposit of $475 would more than cover the supposed damages to her property. He implied that Rich should have been grateful that he had the apartment wired for cable TV and had replaced burnt-out lightbulbs; he said he couldn't do any more.[21]

The new lightbulbs helped Rich see his destructive and careless treatment of her property. And, in fact, he did do more: Burgess set a misogynistic novel, *The Clockwork Testament, or Enderby's End* (1974), in a fictionalized version of her apartment. The protagonist, Enderby, sublets the place from a scholar-writer clearly based on Rich. He took the slight precaution of turning her into a novelist on leave in England—a humorless, man-hating novelist, whose bookshelves bulge with treatises on race, gender, and revolution that Enderby views with distaste.

*The Clockwork Testament* was not part of the thoughtful conversation with men that Rich wanted, but it still said a lot, none of it good. Like her old nemeses John Simon, the Harvard graduate student turned reviewer who never missed a chance to mock her, and R. W. Flint, the reviewer who disliked her poetry on (sexist) principle, Burgess objected to her because she didn't bow down in obeisance to men. Royally perturbed whenever a woman challenged the authority they took as their birthright, he and his brethren wanted Rich to vanish into thin air and take everything ever uttered about female empowerment with her.

She wasn't vanishing and her utterances were drawing more attention by the day. While she wrangled with Burgess, *Diving into the Wreck* was propelling her into ever higher reaches of fame. The book came out in the summer of 1973, the year of *Roe v. Wade* and a year after Title IX was signed into law. In the arc of these historic events, at a time when women's music festivals and women's bookstores were filling a previously untapped need, especially among lesbians, her seventh volume of poetry took its place as a cultural milestone. In "Trying to Talk with a Man," "When We Dead Awaken," "Waking in the Dark," "Translations," "The Phenomenology of Anger," "For a Survivor," and "August," she exposed the raw pain of her life as a heterosexual woman who tried and failed to connect with men. In "Song," "Dialogue," "The Mirror in Which Two Are Seen as One," "After Twenty Years," and "Diving into the Wreck," she scissored men out of the picture. What remained was uncompromised, noble, and whole. Anthony Burgess and his ilk would never see that; they would not care to read her new book or anything else she wrote. But many people were reading her with enormous interest, and *Diving into the Wreck* attracted her largest audience yet.

The collection reveals Rich on a hard journey requiring honesty and courage. Whereas some of the poems in her past several volumes, especially the ghazals, feel like one side of a stylized conversation, artful and compelling but ultimately baffling, the best poems in *Diving into the Wreck* are clear and complete without sacrificing metaphor or nuance; they glide from the personal to the archetypal and back again. Nowhere is that more true than in the title poem, which many people consider the signature poem of her career.

In her previous volumes, Rich revealed her vexed relationship with written history. Poems like "Readings of History" in *Snapshots of a Daughter-in-Law* and "Study of History" in *The Will to Change* show her trying to reconcile all she was able to find in books with all that wasn't there and perhaps never would be. Books were her gods, and if she couldn't find answers in their pages, where would she have to go? She effectively answers that question in "Diving into the Wreck."[22] History as she had previously conceived it gives way to "a book of myths," a term that conjures not only archetypal truths but also lies and omissions. Whatever it may say, true or untrue, the book of myths matters: Along with her other tools of exploration, she takes it with her as she pursues a new understanding of the world and her place in it. Perhaps she will check her discoveries against its contents or look for ways to incorporate its lessons into a more inclusive vision of the past—or perhaps she will leave it behind as part of the "wreck" she came to see.

From now on, this poem implies, Rich would risk everything in pursuit of the wreck that in its magnificence and grotesquerie proves the existence of all that is missing from the published record. As she prepares to go down into the vast depths of the ocean (perhaps symbolizing Jung's collective unconscious), the ladder is a recognizable talisman, the logical way to descend into the underworld. For Rich, whose phobic fear of descending a staircase had required psychiatric aid, the thought of a staggeringly long ladder would have been unpleasant at best. Given the limited mobility she frequently suffered and her long experience with physical therapy, the crippling flippers and the prospect of learning to move one's body "without force / in the deep element" also draw on her life experience. But thanks to her powerful mask—the mask of the poet, the chosen identity that was more real to her than any other—she expects to survive. The poem is evidence that she has done so.

If one aim of the poet's descent is to uncover more about herself, then what she finds is that she is at one with the wreck and all that lives in its strange and watery world. Once she has arrived ("This is the place"), she metamorphoses into both a mermaid and merman. In subsequent lines, she is "the thing itself"—the ruined tools of direction and record, the drowned travelers. She belongs in the underworld, like all who seek it out. The line "by cowardice or courage" implies some of her fellow searchers arrive by default, unable to handle the realm of "human air." One wonders whether Rich counted Conrad, a suicide, among the cowards plunging into the unknown to escape the hazards and cruelties of the known.

Her interest in androgyny comes into play late in the poem. The line

"I am she: I am he" may be read as a way of including men who share her desire to upend the old myths and falsehoods, but it may also mean that this singular explorer is not solely female or male. (Both Rich's note of introduction specifying the book is about sexuality and "The Stranger" point toward this latter interpretation.) In either case, the line infuses the poem with a tender inclusiveness reminiscent of Walt Whitman's "Crossing Brooklyn Ferry." In "Diving into the Wreck," Rich had written a poem for the ages, one that rewards readers willing to explore its translucent depths of meaning.

Once *Diving into the Wreck* was in print, the reviews began pouring in immediately. Among the first was Erica Jong's lengthy and complimentary assessment in *Ms.*, the mainstream feminist magazine in its second year of publication.[23] That was a coup, but Rich waited as always for *The New York Times* to weigh in. The poet Harvey Shapiro, clearly not among her many dutiful friends who always gave her positive reviews, had little good to say about her in the review he published in the weekday "Books of the Times" in late August. His chin figuratively resting on his hand in studied skepticism, Shapiro found *Diving into the Wreck* "patronizing," "off-putting," "self-congratulatory," and "ideologically chic." In regard to the closing passage of "The Stranger," he asked, "Is that language finally any more alive than the dead counters of language we push toward each other every day of our lives?"[24] The answer to his question was yes, but having struck the pose of a skeptic, Shapiro would not budge.

Better news would be coming soon from the *Times*, but for a few more months, Rich had to settle for mixed verdicts. The English poet Rosemary Tonks wrote a long, enigmatic critique in *The New York Review of Books* that implied Rich had traded art for politics and come out on the losing end of the bargain. Rich's young protégée, Cheryl Walker, wrote an admiring review for *The Nation*. "Some, I'm sure, will object to the use of the self in these poems," Walker observed of her mentor's new collection. Then, in an obvious rebuke to Shapiro, she wrote that anyone who found "self-aggrandizement and self-congratulation" in "The Stranger" would not grasp "that the process women are undergoing today requires coming into new relation with the self, requires a self-love which is not narcissism."

In an instructive aside, she said, "I remember particularly two things Adrienne Rich has said: one, that she would like to write poetry which could be useful to women, and two, the only real maturity is one in which the self is so small it disappears and so large it encompasses a great many more than one. Thus, the figure, the 'I,' which recurs in these poems, is and is not Adrienne Rich." These are valuable insights into Rich's thinking at the time she was writing *Diving into the Wreck,* especially the title poem, which Walker considered "surely one of the most beautiful poems to come out of the women's movement." To her mind, "The poem is utterly personal but there is nothing in it which draws away into private life."[25]

Walker's perceptive understanding of the book reflects a deep familiarity with Rich and her poetry. She was among several of Rich's friends who published highly favorable reviews of *Diving into the Wreck* in national publications. Kathleen Fraser lauded it in *The Washington Post's Book World,* and Richard Howard's words of incantatory praise very nearly elevated Rich to sainthood in *Harper's.* Surely a book of the caliber of *Diving into the Wreck* didn't need a thumb on the scale, but Rich had never seen a conflict of interest when friends reviewed her books, nor did she discourage them from sharing drafts of their reviews with her before publication. In return, she routinely sent gracious acknowledgments. She told Walker, for instance, "Your review of <u>Diving</u> seems to have been a turning-point in its career."[26]

Her friends' well-reasoned arguments helped counter hostile criticism by Harvey Shapiro in the *Times* and William Pritchard in *The Hudson Review.* Pritchard regarded Rich's "Rape" as a mere exercise in propaganda that, "with a little polish added, could have been written by a small committee composed of Germaine Greer, Susan Brownmiller and Ti-Grace Atkinson."[27] He was irritated by Rich's many awards, which he considered proof she knew nothing of the suffering that permeates *Diving into the Wreck.* And even if she had suffered, he still expected her poems to bring a smile to his lips: "I am aware that very different, certainly more favorable accounts of her volume will have been given by the time this one is published. But I would hold that whatever else poetry gives us it must, in Stevens' terms, give Pleasure. These poems do not give pleasure."[28]

In its December 30, 1973, issue, *The New York Times Book Review* published a front-page review by Margaret Atwood that was exactly what Pritchard had anticipated. Rich was aware of the young Canadian writer on the rise and had begun reading her with interest, but Atwood was neither a close friend paying tribute nor a tweedy mugger jumping out from the patriarchal bushes. As Rich wrote to Walker, Atwood's review was "utterly unexpected."[29] Beginning with her very first lines, Atwood met her subject head-on, her gaze as sharp and steady as Rich's own:

> When I first heard the author read from it, I felt as though the top of my head was being attacked, sometimes with an ice pick, sometimes with a blunter instrument: a hatchet or a hammer. The predominant emotions seemed to be anger and hatred, and these are certainly present; but when I read the poems later, they evoked a far more subtle reaction. *Diving Into the Wreck* is one of those rare books that forces you to decide not just what you think about it; but what you think about yourself. It is a book that takes risks, and it forces the reader to take them also.[30]

Atwood's bold and interesting assertions were like stardust, and they took their inevitable place above Richard Howard's encomium on the back of the paperback edition. The future author of *The Handmaid's Tale* had done for Rich what Rich had done for Phyllis Chesler. No matter what any other reviewer said, Atwood had officially launched the *Wreck*.

# CHAPTER 16

# IN THE NAME OF ALL WOMEN

## *1974–1975*

By the time *Diving into the Wreck* was published, Rich had been giving poetry readings for more than two decades. She was an excellent reader who knew how to pace a performance and hold everyone's attention. Now, with the poems from *The Will to Change* and *Diving into the Wreck* in her repertoire, she was inspiring women who soon would join her in the vanguard of the feminist movement. Among them was the literary scholar Elaine Showalter, who went on to coin the term *gynocriticism* and dramatically influenced the study of British and American women writers. She recalled, "Adrienne's books were the edge of where the women's movement was going, where I saw my life going."[1] Catharine MacKinnon had a similar response the first time she attended one of Rich's readings. After the future activist and leading attorney for women's equality heard Rich read at Yale, she noted the occasion in her journal with three exclamation points. Looking back four decades, she said, "She was an extraordinary poet, speaking of and to women in a voice I hadn't heard before. It was very moving."[2]

With the women's movement swelling the ranks of her readers, Rich vaulted from the sturdy literary prominence she had enjoyed in the 1960s to a new kind of fame and influence. *Newsweek* featured her in a sidebar accompanying an article about the state of contemporary literature and described her as "one of our most affecting and committed poets."[3] Dozens of newspapers and magazines reviewed *Diving into the Wreck,* and her readings attracted awestruck young women who followed her around when she arrived on their campuses. For some of her groupies, her alliance with Robin Morgan burnished her appeal. In the spring of 1974, when she and Morgan shared the stage at the National Women's Poetry Festival in Amherst, Massachusetts, nearly a thousand fans cheered them on.[4]

Joan Nestle, a lesbian activist who would later shape Rich's political views in crucial ways, attended a reading she gave during this era. It was at Womanbooks, a newly established women's bookstore on Ninety-second Street between Amsterdam and West End Avenue. Rich was welcomed as a sort of messiah. "Crowds came to the dark street," Nestle recalled, and lined up to see "a star giving her support to a new feminist venture in a depressed area of New York."[5] The bookstore was a short ride from Rich's apartment, but most of her new acolytes didn't know that. The woman they came to see and hear might as well have descended from the urban sky to instruct them and convert those not yet fully convinced of her grace and power.

At this juncture in her career, Rich's age worked in her favor. In her mid-forties, she possessed mature gravitas but was still young enough to captivate the yearning imaginations of women in their teens and twenties. She had an alluring vitality and simmering quality made of her anger and hopefulness, and she gladly accepted the responsibility that came with being the nation's leading feminist poet. She wanted to use her high profile to advance an agenda that would benefit all women. In doing so, she was not renouncing the privileges of her old life so much as repurposing them for her new one. Nowhere is this clearer than in the weeks leading up to the 1974 National Book Awards ceremony, a night of triumph that showed the world the woman she was becoming—and the woman she had always been.

Sponsored by the National Book Committee, the National Book Awards honored writers in ten categories in 1974. In March, the National Book Committee announced the finalists. In poetry, the nominated books were *Diving into the Wreck; From Snow and Rock, from Chaos,* by Hayden Carruth; *Points for a Compass Rose,* by Evan S. Connell, Jr.; *Collecting the Animals,* by Peter Everwine; *The Fall of America: Poems of These States, 1965–1971,* by Allen Ginsberg; *The Lady in Kicking Horse Reservoir,* by Richard Hugo; *Departures,* by Donald Justice; *Armed Love,* by Eleanor

Lerman; *From a Land Where Other People Live,* by Audre Lorde; *Revolutionary Petunias and Other Poems,* by Alice Walker; and *Hard Freight,* by Charles Wright.

Rich must have been pleased when she learned who was judging poetry that year. Two of the judges, David Kalstone and Jean Valentine, were fellow planets in her Manhattan literary orbit. Kalstone was the old friend from her Cambridge days who had quickly grasped the significance of *Snapshots of a Daughter-in-Law.* Now a professor at Rutgers, he had praised her and her books in the pages of *The New York Times* and the *Saturday Review,* and later he would publish a book of poetry criticism, *Five Temperaments,* in which Rich was one of the contemporary poets whose writing he analyzed. Valentine was a dear friend and an Upper West Side neighbor. As a fledgling poet, she first heard about Rich soon after she arrived at Radcliffe and struck up a conversation with a Cambridge resident who recommended she read *A Change of World.* Adrienne had written her a complimentary letter after Valentine's first book was published in the mid-1960s, and they had been friends ever since.[6] The judge Rich knew least well was Philip Levine, a Detroit-born poet of working-class origins who lived in California and taught at Fresno State. They were friends who liked each other's poetry but didn't have the long history she had with the other two judges.

In a letter to the Carruths, Rich said she thought this was the first time either she or Hayden had been nominated for the National Book Award. She was right about him but mistaken about herself: Two of her previous volumes—*The Diamond Cutters* in 1956 and *Necessities of Life* in 1967—had been finalists. Maybe she had forgotten because being a finalist meant little to a poet of her stature; it was only winning that mattered. But it was a new decade and *Diving into the Wreck* was an unusually strong and timely book. Surely the less-than-objective judges would see its merits. She had reason to be hopeful.

Rich, however, had decided the National Book Awards were a patriarchal sham. She wanted the prize because she wanted the platform it would give her. If she won, she planned to decline the honor as an individual but accept it in the name of the feminist cause she had taken on as her own. Her decision could potentially damage her reputation in the rarefied world of arts and letters, the world that had welcomed her as one of its own when she was still an undergraduate, but she was determined to speak up anyway.

What she set out to do had significant precedents. In 1964, Robert Lowell turned down an invitation to an arts festival at the White House because he was troubled by the direction in which the country was moving under President Johnson. In his 1968 acceptance of the National Book Award for poetry, Robert Bly spoke against the Vietnam War and the American legacy of racial oppression; he donated his thousand-dollar prize to organizations promoting draft resistance. In 1971, W. S. Merwin asked that his Pulitzer Prize winnings be divided between draft-resistance efforts and a man named Alan Blanchard, a painter "blinded by a police weapon in California while he was watching American events from a roof."[7] All of these men, whom Rich knew well, took a stand against warmongering and national policies they found objectionable. They did not want to be perceived as allies of the establishment.

Neither did Rich. She intended to expose what she considered a virulently patriarchal culture that predated the Vietnam War by many centuries. Because she saw the National Book Awards as a microcosm of that culture, she would voice her objections to the awards, as well. First, she had to win—and she fully expected she would. Second, to achieve maximum effect, she needed to get the other female nominees to go along with her.

In her conversations with Walker and Lorde, Rich proposed a pact: If one of them was awarded the prize, the winner would read a statement that rebuked the male-dominated awards hierarchy while championing the cause of all women. She implied or perhaps stated outright that of the three of them, she was the most likely to win because she was white. On the chance that one of the others did win, she was asking Walker and Lorde to spurn the honor and the one-thousand-dollar prize—income they may have wanted to keep. Even if she won, as expected, and they merely stood in solidarity with her, they had little to gain and much they might lose. Who knew but that prospective publishers and employers might reject them for their lack of respect for a literary institution? Although their later books secured their status, at the time they could not be sure that would happen. As black women, they were even more vulnerable to discrimination than Rich was. Seen in this light, her high-minded proposal carried with it a large dose of presumption: first, that she would win; second, that a joint statement from all of them was necessary; and third, that they should imperil their professional standing to validate a point she wanted to make.

Lorde was not happy with the pact, in Robin Morgan's recollection: "In public, Audre said how wonderful, and privately Audre fumed!" Lorde told Morgan she thought she would have kept the prize if she'd won it, but she wasn't going to get into a public dispute with Rich. Morgan said, "Guys can disagree all the time and it's considered healthy individuation or a lively exchange. Particularly at that time and somewhat still today, women disagreeing is a catfight. Some of us were very, very conscious of that, being public feminists."[8]

Walker heard from both Rich and Lorde by phone. Recalling the conversations many years later, she said, "We understood that we were living under apartheid and segregation and all of that. And under such a system, which favored white people, [Rich] would get the award; we knew that. And so we decided, before anything was announced, that we would not accept being ranked." Walker added, "You know, she was a great poet, but it would go to her also because she was a white person. And to her immense credit, she had no desire to be honored as we would be dishonored."[9]*

As it happened, there was another white woman lurking at the edge of these conversations: twenty-two-year-old Eleanor Lerman, a native of the Bronx and the true outlier in the group. Unlike the other three, she was poor and lacked a college education; she spent her days making harpsichord kits in the Village and her evenings cruising gay bars. But she was a serious writer; her debut volume, *Armed Love,* had come out from Wesleyan University Press. Like Rich, she had gotten a precociously early start in her career. The National Book Awards were not on her radar, but when *Armed Love* was named a finalist, she began getting lots of phone calls from strangers, including three of her fellow nominees.

Many decades later, Lerman still gets angry thinking about the pressure they put on her. Rich, Walker, and Lorde assumed she would fall in line: "All three of them called me, in order of importance. Either Audre or Alice called me first. Finally Adrienne called me." Their plan made

---

* Rich's friendships with the judges, not her skin color, held the potential to work in her favor. But those friendships had developed because she and the judges traveled in literary circles populated exclusively by white writers and intellectuals. In that respect, her race did give her an edge over Lorde and Walker.

no sense to Lerman. If she had won the one-thousand-dollar prize, she said in retrospect, "I would've taken it and cashed the check."

In response to the escalating insistence that she go along with them, Lerman refused once, twice, and then a third and final time. No matter how much clout the other women had, she felt they had no right to tell her what to do. Women's rights had come up in conversations with her neighbors, privileged women who thought activism was necessary. The discussions irritated her. Contemplating the phone calls she was getting from her fellow nominees, she felt like it was more of the same. She asked herself, "'Who are these elitist, educated, fancy-schmancy women to tell me what my situation is?' Men were not my problem. Money was, work was." Distressed and a little frightened by all the attention the prize nomination had brought her, she decided to skip the ceremony.[10]

The judging committees met in New York a few days before the ceremony to make their decisions in poetry, fiction, biography, and a number of other categories. The publishers and their winner authors then got the word, with enough advance notice for the authors to write acceptance speeches and travel to New York if they weren't there already. That year, the organizers wanted no one else to know who had won until the ceremony, but thanks to "a combination of loose-tongued judges and publishers and assiduous lobbying by *The New York Times*," the *Times* got a mostly accurate list of winners and published it on Wednesday morning.[11]

Adding a new layer of complexity to the unfolding events, Adrienne was not the sole winner in poetry. Even though National Book Committee staff entreated them to pick just one person, the judges did not comply. They granted the prize to both Rich and Allen Ginsberg and thus diminished the honor for both of them. Each would receive five hundred dollars instead of the full one thousand, and in the annals of literary awards, each would be forever encumbered with the other. Poetry wasn't the only category in which the judges couldn't or wouldn't follow instructions. As an exasperated reviewer wrote in *Esquire*, "There were a lot of split awards, which is always undercutting in a dull way."[12]

All signs point to Levine as the spoiler who deprived Rich of a singular victory. In a note to National Book Committee staff member Joan Cunliffe, dated Sunday, April 14, Levine said, "I think the three of us are finally delighted with the choices. I know I am. All the reading and thinking and what have you was worth it to give these two great poets the prize." The wording ("finally delighted" and "what have you") hints at friction followed by compromise and resigned acceptance. His letter included the award citation he had written for Ginsberg. His statement, which an announcer would read during the ceremony, commended Ginsberg "for his brave book The Fall of America and for giving us a poetry that is visionary, humanitarian, anguished, joyful, outraged, and tender enough to be American, and for leading a generation of poets back to the sources of their greatest strength, their lives and their language." Levine told Cunliffe to ask the other two judges to "barber" his statement if it needed editing. But after typing it into his letter, he exuberantly declared, "On 2nd thought don't change it, carve it on the steps of the New York Public Library."[13]

Though Ginsberg was an engaging and popular poet, most critics in the 1970s (and for many years after) regarded him as the louche impresario behind the Beat movement; they saw no reason to take him seriously. Levine wanted to fix that. He knew that behind the bombast and exhibitionism, Ginsberg was an important poet, even if *The Fall of America* wasn't as good as his long-ago masterpieces, *Howl* and *Kaddish*. Levine may have felt he had to grab a distinguished honor for Ginsberg while he had the chance. He liked Rich and her poetry, but he wasn't prepared to carve an encomium to her on the library steps just yet.

A crowd of about twelve hundred flowed into Lincoln Center's Alice Tully Hall for the awards ceremony on April 18. It was the culmination of a week of business and social gatherings for publishers, editors, authors, agents, and book critics, many of them from New York. Some California book people referred derisively to the event as "the Eastern awards," and along the same lines, one observer claimed that three of the winners lived in the same Central Park West apartment building.[14] Even so, the distinguished winners could hardly be labeled provincial. The cowinners in the Fiction category were Thomas Pynchon and Isaac Bashevis Singer; Pauline Kael was the winner in a category called Arts and Letters; the Sciences award went to Nobel Prize–winning biologist S. E. Luria for a book titled *Life: The Unfinished Experiment;* and the translation prize, split three ways, went to translators of Octavio Paz, Paul Valéry, and a medieval Japanese woman known as Lady Nijo.

The program opened predictably with remarks by National Book

Committee chair Roger Stevens and executive chair John Frantz. Husband-and-wife actors Hume Cronyn and Jessica Tandy read excerpts from four of the winning books, including Rich's and Ginsberg's. They might have read from more, but they were due onstage in a Broadway play and left in a hurry. This was an early indication the night wasn't going to go as planned.

When the time came for the poetry winners to be announced, Ginsberg's name was called first. His boyfriend, Peter Orlovsky, appeared in his stead, and since he wasn't introduced, some people assumed he was Ginsberg. According to *Publishers Weekly:*

> [Orlovsky] strode onstage in a T-shirt bearing the figures of Vietnam war casualties and roared into the microphone, in a loud and unstressed shout, Ginsberg's diatribe about his native land. It proclaimed his foreboding that the U.S. "is now the fabled 'damned of nations' foretold by Walt Whitman" and declared that America's alleged defense of the free world was in fact "an aggressive hypocrisy that has damaged the very planet's chances of survival." Impeachment of a President would not remove "the hundred billion power of the military or the secret police apparatus." "There is no longer any hope for the salvation of America," roared Orlovsky and ended, as directed by Ginsberg, with a thrice-repeated howl of lamentation.[15]

Rich endured Orlovsky's performance and waited for her turn. As she readied herself to rise from her seat and go onstage, she listened to the award citation written by Kalstone, her loyal friend. He knew she would like to hear her own verse quoted: "Adrienne Rich has understood that 'we are living through a time that needs to be lived through us.' Her poetry is open to politics at the deepest level—where commitment meets private feelings and dreams. In her work she makes courageous discoveries which question, to their roots, the lives of men and women alike. She has helped us in a new way to experience our own honest anger and honest mercy."[16]

Because Kalstone's words captured the very things Rich wanted people to find in her poetry, she risked sounding ungrateful and obtuse in going ahead with her prepared remarks, which Norton had provided in advance to the National Book Committee. But going ahead was what she always did. Dressed in fashionable bell-bottoms, her dark hair hanging to her shoulders, she made her way to the stage. Lorde accompanied her, but Walker did not attend the ceremony. Rich's clear, cultured voice rang out as she gave a speech that perfectly encapsulated her feminist beliefs at that time:

> We, Audre Lorde, Adrienne Rich, and Alice Walker, together accept this award in the name of all the women whose voices have gone and still go unheard in a patriarchal world, and in the name of those who, like us, have been tolerated as token women in this culture, often at great cost and in great pain. We believe that we can enrich ourselves more in supporting and giving to each other than by competing against each other; and that poetry—if it *is* poetry—exists in a realm beyond ranking and comparison. We symbolically join together here in refusing the terms of patriarchal competition and declaring that we will share this prize among us, to be used as best we can for women. We appreciate the good faith of the judges for this award, but none of us could accept this money for herself, nor could she let go unquestioned the terms on which poets are given or denied honor and livelihood in this world, especially when they are women. We dedicate this occasion to the struggle for self-determination of all women, of every color, identification, or derived class: the poet, the housewife, the lesbian, the mathematician, the mother, the dishwasher, the pregnant teenager, the teacher, the grandmother, the prostitute, the philosopher, the waitress, the women who will understand what we are doing here and those who will not understand yet; the silent women whose voices have been denied us, the articulate women who have given us strength to do our work.[17]

The cadences and imagery of the statement sound like Rich alone. Lorde and Walker may have suggested an edit or two, but it was Rich's speech and her night, no matter whether she accepted the award or not. In truth, she had done both. *Publishers Weekly* reported that her speech earned the "loudest applause of the evening so far."[18]

Having worked long and assiduously to become a consummate insider in her chosen art, now she positioned herself as a consummate outsider who spoke with an insider's certainty she would be heard and taken seriously. Eloquent and high-minded as always, she spoke to and *for* all women, even those like Eleanor Lerman who resented her presumption and didn't share her views. She may have had Lerman in mind when she referred to women who didn't yet understand the women's movement applied to them.

Rich was also speaking to men. Calling herself a token was tantamount to unmasking all the influential men who had helped her achieve her current position of influence, including her publisher and editor at Norton. If those men really believed she was worth listening to, they would listen now and address the problems she brought to their attention.

When Lorde returned to her seat in the auditorium, Rich took her place onstage alongside Orlovsky. A grainy photo of her in *Publishers Weekly* shows her smiling faintly as she listens to him. She was willing to sit with Ginsberg's proxy and her fellow honorees, but she would insist in the coming weeks that she didn't want to be called a winner because she had "effectively rejected" the prize.[19] *Effectively* was the operative word, since she accepted her half of the thousand-dollar prize and gave it to the Sisterhood of Black Single Mothers in New York.[20]

Rich's solemn speech stood out on a night interrupted by silliness. In the midst of the presentation to the translators, a streaker burst into the hall and ran along the front row, crying out, "Read books! Read books!" The photographer Jill Krementz jumped to her feet and chased after him in hopes of a photo. The man was a publicity rep for the University of California Press; later in the evening, fully dressed, he was spotted socializing at the awards reception.[21]

When the 1974 National Book Awards ceremony was finally over, Rich made sure Lorde and Lorde's publisher, Dudley Randall of Broadside Press, accepted her offer of a limousine ride to a cocktail party at a nearby hotel. Norton had provided the car.[22] She was throwing her lot with the outsiders of the world, but that didn't mean she would give up the privileges that came with her success. On this very interesting night, she was literally a limousine liberal, a woman of importance and influence who intended to keep things that way.

Her publisher had no problem with that. Future editions of her books identified her as a recipient of the National Book Award. There was no accompanying mention of her public renunciation of the prize, and after a while, Norton stopped identifying *Diving into the Wreck* as cowinner and described it simply as the winner. City Lights Publishers did the same for Ginsberg's *The Fall of America*.

In her speech, Rich had hinted at a new facet of her identity. She listed various categories of women struggling for "self-determination"—among them "the lesbian," a label that applied to Audre Lorde, who by now had divorced her husband and was in a relationship with a woman. It also applied to Rich herself. She had at last taken a lesbian lover, with the encouragement of her psychiatrist, Lilly Engler.

As it happened, her lesbian lover *was* Engler. In the weeks leading up to their involvement, Rich told Robin Morgan of the incipient attraction. Morgan warned her to be careful, but Rich was ready to throw herself into a love affair with her doctor. She found in Engler the deeply attentive partner she had craved for so long. No matter that her desire for her therapist was a classic case of transference; no matter that Engler was a mother and father figure wrapped into one. She was Jewish, Viennese, well educated, and well traveled—a reader of literature, a knowledgeable lover of classical music, and a revered psychiatrist with a sophisticated clientele. Adrienne had found a lover who was an idealized version of Arnold Rich contained in a soft, welcoming, maternal body.

By the time she gave her speech at the National Book Awards in April, Rich had already told some of her close friends about her new love affair. On March 21, she wrote to Cheryl Walker about her new relationship, which had begun several weeks earlier. She allowed that there were complications with this woman she had known for a couple of years but wanted Walker to know she was thrilled and deeply moved by the relationship with her lover, whom she described as being about her age or a little older.

In fact, Engler was eleven years older than Rich. Her vagueness on that point suggests there were basic matters the two of them had not yet discussed, despite all their meetings as doctor and patient. Going further, she wrote to Walker, "Intellectually, even emotionally, I think I've wanted a relationship with a woman for some time, but I had begun to feel I was hopelessly heterosexual. Now those names, categories, don't seem to have much meaning—I am astonished at the barriers we put up through language. I don't feel radically changed, just in touch with more of myself than ever in my life."[23]

On an occasion predating her involvement with Engler, a tipsy Rich had pulled Robin Morgan close and given her a sloppy French kiss as they sat in a car and prepared to bid each other good night. Morgan did not yet identify as a lesbian and was not attracted to Rich: "I drew back and she smiled, and I took her by the shoulders and said, 'Adrienne, I really love you—I love you as a friend, as a sister, a poet. We're not going to go there.' And she said, 'Okay, okay.'"[24]

Later on, before she paired off with Engler, the hopelessly heterosexual Adrienne told Morgan she didn't think she could ever be a lesbian. Exasperated with this line of thinking, which Adrienne had voiced many times, Morgan reminded her of the scene in the car. Adrienne said she didn't remember her unsuccessful overture.[25] Perhaps alcohol had wiped out her memory of it.

In a letter to the Carruths two days after she wrote to Cheryl Walker, Adrienne trumpeted her new romance. She adored Lilly's "beautiful, swift, searching mind" and her physicality; she exulted over her lover's generous embrace of life. Though in recent times she had wanted to find a man who possessed the qualities she admired in women, she now realized that Lilly offered her every kind of fulfillment, physical and otherwise. Passionately in love, she swelled with emotion unknown to her since her earliest days of dating Conrad. She felt both grounded and aloft, amazed by the "serious joy"* that buoyed her days.[26]

Still, there was no getting around the fact that dating her own psychiatrist was problematic. The therapeutic relationship that had brought them together soon drove a wedge between them. While Rich wanted to come out as a lesbian, Engler did not and for all practical purposes could not. In 1973, members of the American Psychological Association had voted to remove homosexuality from its list of mental illnesses, but that did little to erase the stigma. Coming out to her professional peers would have compromised Engler's career, and coming out while dating a current patient would have ended it. Discretion was essential. Adrienne told her intimate circle in New York, but in her correspondence with friends, she typically mentioned only Lilly's first name or didn't identify her at all.

Morgan was a trusted confidante. "I learned fairly early on that she

---

* Carruth may have remembered he was once the source of Rich's "serious joy." Clearly, she had moved on.

had gone to bed with Lilly," she recalled. "And I [was] laughing and smiling and praising her and saying, 'Well, okay. How was it?' And she said, 'It was a whole different world, a whole different everything.'"[27]

Morgan was married at the time to Kenneth Pitchford, an openly gay poet and gay rights activist, and they had a son together. Rich had read Pitchford's poetry manuscript a couple of years earlier. At the time, she viewed his work as "out-of-the-closet faggot poetry," not as good as his wife's verse but significant in its daring. She saw his "anguished" and "political" poems as an intriguing alternative to "the usual homosexual mode"—a mode she didn't define—of James Merrill, Richard Howard, Mark Strand, and "even Hart Crane with his complex obscurities." With a life of lesbianism in her near future, she acknowledged her own bias against "male homosexuality" while wondering "what kinds of poetry have been mangled & aborted thru the prevailing attitudes toward homosexuality (in this country particularly)—the deflection from one's primary subject, let's say, suffered by Crane, most dramatically, but also by Moore & Bishop."[28]

It was against that complex backdrop that Rich, a newly minted lesbian, now rejoiced in her friendship with Pitchford. Their camaraderie escalated. She was delighted with him, Robin recalled, "because suddenly he was her gay brother. Overnight they were gay and I was not. You had to roll with the punches. It wasn't hard; it was just amusing." A couple of years later, she included a reference to Pitchford (identified only as "Ken") in "Twenty-One Love Poems," a defining work of lesbian literature and one of the great sequence poems of her career.

Adrienne wanted Robin and Lilly to get to know each other, and Robin dined with the couple on many occasions. Because Adrienne had described her lover in romanticized terms, Robin had expected Lilly to be a "paragon of beauty and sensuality." However, the reality didn't match with her expectations: "I was surprised at my first meeting because she was a classic sort of middle European, slightly older than middle-aged, zaftig, sweet-looking, dumpy woman. She was not this wild erotic creature that Adrienne had immediately cast her as."[29]

The comparative literature scholar Don Levine knew Lilly in the years preceding her relationship with Adrienne. He had met her through his friendship with Susan Sontag, his former professor at Columbia. As Levine put it, speaking generally of the intellectually elite gay and lesbian crowd he was part of in New York, "All these people knew each other. They got involved with each other." Then, after breaking up, "they continued to know each other." It was certainly true of Sontag and her friends. She had a brief affair with Engler, which then became a platonic friendship, aided immensely by Engler's access to free opera tickets. Sontag also had a romance with Eva Kollisch, a New York literary scholar with whom Lilly was involved before she began her affair with Adrienne.

Levine remembered Lilly as a large, feminine woman who wore lipstick and had dyed blond hair. Once, while he was vacationing with her and her lover at the time on Nantucket, he accidentally glimpsed Engler stepping out of an outdoor shower. With no tan lines, an indication she sunbathed in the nude, Engler appeared "all golden," radiant in her corpulence. In Levine's recollection, "She wasn't in the least embarrassed. She knew that she made a fine figure of a woman."

Unlike Morgan, who considered Engler knowledgeable and well read in feminist psychology and other theories of the day, Levine saw her as a "lesbian Jewish mother" who made up in warmth and capability what she lacked in intellect: "We used to say Lilly wasn't very bright, but she was probably a good psychoanalyst," because she made people feel safe and at ease. "Lilly had gemütlichkeit. It felt right to be around her. You felt like you knew this person. I could imagine Lilly being charming for a certain kind of woman to the point of being bewitching."

She cooked big meals, took her lovers and close friends to rehearsals at the Met, and planned road trips for herself and her friends. She did most of the driving on these adventures. For women who liked being taken care of, Levine said, "she'd make it all seem effortless."[30] He and Robin Morgan saw different sides of her personality. Rich knew her much better than either one of them did. Over time, she discovered both sadness and silence beneath Engler's resilient exterior.

Rich and Engler were together for less than a year. They visited with Rich's mother and sister and attended the opera with them in Boston. Cynthia Rich recalled the visit as an awkward occasion, the more so because she and her mother knew they were not supposed to acknowledge Adrienne and Lilly as a lesbian couple.[31] And the topic of how Adrienne had met Lilly was not an easy one to broach.

At one of the dinners the couple shared with Morgan, Engler asked whether Morgan faulted her for continuing to serve as Rich's therapist. Morgan declined to offer an opinion.[32] But evidently the lapse in judgment was on Engler's mind and probably contributed to the collapse of their affair.

To Rich's distress, Engler sank into a deep depression that would not lift. This time, it was the doctor, not the patient, who needed guidance. Adrienne knew the relationship was in trouble and felt powerless to fix things.

Among Rich's friends in that era were Susan Rennie and her partner at the time, Kirsten Grimstad. She met Rennie through a mutual friend at Mother Courage, a feminist-owned restaurant in the Village. Soon she had formed a close bond with both Rennie and Grimstad, who had coedited *The New Woman's Survival Catalog*, and were starting work on a sequel, *The New Woman's Survival Sourcebook*. With the aid of a number of young feminists, they did much of the work on the new book, including the layout and design, in their large loft in the Bowery. Fascinated and eager to help out, Rich frequently came by to advise and visit with her new friends.

When Rich told Rennie and Grimstad about her relationship with Lilly, she was happier than they had ever seen her. Ecstatic with excitement, her face lit with joy, she appeared transformed. Then, six or seven months later, she came for a visit and broke down sobbing. She said Lilly had ended the relationship that she, Adrienne, had expected to last for a lifetime.

"We were literally holding her and she was weeping into our arms," Rennie recalled. In the weeks and months after that, she and Grimstad did what they could to comfort Adrienne. They took her with them to poetry readings and stayed in close touch.[33]

As her first lesbian affair ran aground, Adrienne went through a time of emotional upheaval and sexual experimentation. She invited her friend and fellow poet Susan Griffin to visit her in Vermont. At the West Barnet house that held so much meaning for Rich, the two women made love. In a subsequent letter, Adrienne made it clear they would not be having sex again.

Griffin was disappointed. "Well, I fell in love with her," she said of their time together four decades earlier. Rich was "very, very intense, very honest, and yet very deep and complex at the same time. It's rare to find that. Very outspoken, politically aware. Yet her work had this deep emotional, cultural complexity, and she also confided things she was going through personally that made a bond with me."[34] Adrienne later confessed to Morgan that she regretted the one-night stand, in part because Griffin, in her early thirties, was so much younger than she was.[35] Perhaps Adrienne felt she had taken advantage of a woman just starting out in her career who looked up to her. During this same time period, Griffin learned that Adrienne had an affair with June Jordan. In Griffin's recollection, the relationship ended painfully for Jordan, and Rich paid for Jordan to see a therapist after they parted ways.[36]

The years 1974 and 1975, then, were a time of major transition for Rich. By March of 1975, she was able to write retrospectively to Tillie Olsen of her affair with Engler. She was still hurting but able to see a way forward. In a letter to Olsen, she described the difficulties of the previous fall, when she was teaching at City College, grappling with her failed love affair, and not making any progress on the manuscript that would become *Of Woman Born*. Though still writing poems, she was overwhelmed and unhappy. She told her employer she needed a leave of absence for the spring semester and would not ever come back full-time. "It was a big leap but it was the right instinct. Since January my life coheres again, the book goes, and I'm learning to live again as a separate person."[37] That summer, she told Olsen she was heartbroken because Engler had gone back to her previous partner without telling her.[38] An abandoned Rich was left to conclude that Engler had never completely severed ties with the other woman.

Rich was in the public eye in early 1975 due to a public literary feud she had with Engler's former lover Susan Sontag. In response to an essay Sontag published in *The New York Review of Books* titled "Fascinating Fascism," Rich wrote a letter to the editor chastising Sontag for suggesting contemporary feminists helped promote the Nazi filmmaker Leni Riefenstahl's films. Sounding what was by now a familiar theme for her, Rich wrote, "The feminist movement has been passionately anti-hierarchal and anti-authoritarian. Feminists have also been justly alert to and critical of women who have 'made it' in the patriarchy (and Nazi Germany was patriarchy in its purest, most elemental form). It is impossible not to recognize and mourn the pressures that drive token women to compromise their sisters and to serve misogynist and anti-human values."[39]

Sontag was quick to fire back. She called Rich "a piker compared to some self-styled radical feminists, all too eager to dump the life of reason (along with the idea of authority) into the dustbin of 'patriarchal history.' Still, her well-intentioned letter does illustrate a persistent indiscretion of feminist rhetoric: anti-intellectualism."[40] Sontag implied that Rich (who, like Sontag herself, had spent her entire life cultivating her intellect) had sacrificed her estimable powers of discrimination on the altar of feminist dogma. Perhaps to some degree that was true, but Sontag was so determined to destroy Rich's argument that she ended up bolstering her opponent's claims:

> Suppose, indeed, that "Nazi Germany was patriarchy in its purest, most elemental form." Where do we rate the Kaiser's Germany? Caesarist Rome? Confucian China? Fascist Italy? Victorian England? Ms. Gandhi's India? Macho Latin America? Arab sheikery from Mohammed to Qaddhafi and Faisal? Most of history, alas, is "patriarchal history." So distinctions will have to be made, and it is not possible to keep the feminist thread running through the explanations all the time. Virtually everything deplorable in human history furnishes material for a restatement of the feminist plaint (the ravages of the patriarchy, etc.), just as every story of a life could lead to a reflection on our common mortality and the vanity of human wishes. But if the point is to have meaning some of the time, it can't be made all the time.[41]

Rich would certainly have agreed that most history was "patriarchal history." That was why she wanted to scrutinize the role of Riefenstahl and other token women, including herself and perhaps Sontag as well, in the continuation of it. If women could not recognize their own complicity in events and experiences designed to control and debase them, then who would?

The back-and-forth between Rich and Sontag thoroughly entertained readers who enjoyed intellectual sparring matches. The fact that this one was between two prominent literary women added interest. In a 1977 interview, Rich said she regretted airing her differences with Sontag in print and wished she had contacted her directly. Asked whether she knew Sontag, she replied, "I don't know her well. I got in touch with her after our public exchange, actually, and we got together and talked, not so much about that but really about our lives."[42]

What happened was a little more complicated than that. Rich had indeed contacted Sontag, and in a letter dated March 17, 1975, Sontag said she would be happy to meet with Rich once she returned to New York. She pointed out they were neighbors on the Upper West Side and agreed with Rich that "we have many affections and attachments in common"[43]—she didn't need to say the most significant of those was with Lilly Engler.

At some point thereafter, they met at Sontag's apartment. Rich told a confidante she and Sontag had started out talking and ended up making love.[44] The coupling of these two prominent literary women was the lesbian equivalent of Rich's brief affair with Robert Lowell.

Somehow, Rich still managed to write a great deal during this tumultuous time. She was working on the essays in *Of Woman Born* and "Twenty-One Love Poems," her literary coming-out as a lesbian. Many readers have assumed the sequence is about her relationship with Michelle Cliff, the woman with whom she soon was to fall in love, but these poems grew out of her affair with Engler and trace the arc of the relationship from its early stages through its ending. Thanks to an unnumbered "floating poem," the sequence has twenty-two sections, not the twenty-one specified in the title.

She began the extended project once she was certain of her lesbian identity. As she did with so many of her works over the years, she shared this sequence in draft form with friends, Morgan and Pitchford prominent among them. One night while she was in the midst of working on the poem, the three of them got stoned and lounged on the floor as Rich invited her friends to help her revise. Husband and wife offered their thoughts on the wording at the end of section XVII.[45]

Rich published "Twenty-One Love Poems" with Effie's Press, a small feminist press, in 1976 and included it two years later in *The Dream of a Common Language*. She had composed the sequence over a two-year period beginning in 1974, the year she and Engler became lovers, and ending in 1976, after their love affair was over. It has a precursor in Pablo Neruda's *Twenty Love Poems and a Song of Despair*, a collection of erotically charged poems translated into English in 1969 by Rich's friend W. S. Merwin. The early sections of Rich's sequence show the poet thriving in the presence of a new companion who has thoroughly reinvigorated her: "We want to live like trees, / sycamores blazing through the sulfuric air, / dappled with scars, still exuberantly budding, / our

animal passion rooted in the city."[46] Continuing in this spirit of exulta-
tion, she describes "the desire to show you to everyone I love, / to move
openly together / in the pull of gravity, which is not simple, / which
carries the feathered grass a long way down the upbreathing air." The
lines hint at her desire to come out with Engler, a desire Engler ultimately would not allow her to fulfill.

By section IV, the mood has changed, as Rich reacts to male violence
and cruelty: "And my incurable anger, my unmendable wounds / break
open further with tears, I am crying helplessly, / and they still control the
world, and you are not in my arms."[47] In section IX, her lover's depression has intruded on the love affair, as Rich waits "for a wind that will
gently open this sheeted water" and show her how she can help her
lover, who has "often made the unnameable / nameable for others, even
for me."[48]

In a section titled "(The Floating Poem, Unnumbered)," appearing between the sections marked XIV and XV, Rich writes explicitly
of lesbian sex. For those who recognized Engler as the inspiration, the
lines describing the lover's "traveled, generous thighs" were amusing,
but Rich was completely in earnest as she ventured into new territory,
sexually and poetically, and wrote about "your strong tongue and slen-
der fingers / reaching where I had been waiting years for you / in my
rose-wet cave—whatever happens, this is."[49] This was her way of saying
her identity as a lesbian was permanent.

The literary scholar and photographer Lynda Koolish has written
astutely of "Twenty-One Love Poems" and "The Floating Poem" in
particular:

> Only one of the poems in this collection directly concerns love-
> making. Yet it is sexual passion—all the intimacy, awareness, vul-
> nerability and joy that a love relationship between two women
> engenders—which makes possible the participation of these two
> lovers in the wider realm of their relationship. Rich makes this
> concept a formal metaphor by titling the lovemaking poem "the
> floating poem, unnumbered." Because it is floating free from
> the limitations of a numbered page, like a planet suddenly set
> free from the pull of gravity, the poem allows the sexual aspect
> of the relationship to touch all the other poems in the book,
> without attaching itself to any one of them.[50]

The thinker in Rich, the ruminator, analyzes her affair elsewhere in the sequence. In section XVII, she mentions tape recordings of herself and her lover talking, very likely an allusion to recordings made during therapy sessions with Engler. Wishing the tape recorder could "have caught some ghost of us" so it could teach others coming along later, she imagines the lessons they would impart:

> this we were, this is how we tried to love,
> and these are the forces they had ranged against us,
> and these are the forces we had ranged within us,
> within us and against us, against us and within us.[51]

The last three lines were the ones Morgan and Pitchford helped her revise.

As always, even when her life was at its most difficult, Rich was watching, considering, storing away images and ideas that would find their way into her poems. When she writes near the end of the sequence, "I feel estrangement, yes," this is the observation of a woman speaking to both her therapist-lover and herself. She is becoming "Adrienne alone"[52]—a description alluding to *Alberta Alone,* a novel by the Norwegian novelist Cora Sandel that she loved.[*] Her transcendent joy and hopefulness had melted away, but the core self, the poet self, remained vibrant and strong.

Perhaps on some level Rich knew early on that the relationship with Lilly could not last. In section XII, the approximate midpoint, there is a sense of foreknowledge when she writes, "our bodies, so alike, are yet so different / and the past echoing through our bloodstreams / is freighted with different language, different meanings." Never one for false modesty, she saw her love affair as historically significant and dared to imagine a chronicle in which "it could be written with new meaning / we were two lovers of one gender, / we were two women of one generation."[53]

---

* Jean Valentine writes about visiting Rich around this time: "I remember a warm evening having dinner with David Kalstone at her new apartment; she was reading a book she liked called *Alberta Alone,* and at the end of the evening, as we were leaving, she said, wryly and sadly, that the summer was coming, and she would be Adrienne Alone." Jean Valentine, "A Change of World: A Friendship," *The Virginia Quarterly Review* 82.2 (Spring 2006): 223.

This was a proclamation, a coming-out to the world. It was also something of an epitaph. While Rich may have written these lines after her affair with Engler had ended, their placement in the middle of the sequence shows how aware she was of an inevitable parting, whether it came in life or death. Rich knew the searing pain of losing a spouse, and she was far from done with writing about Alfred Conrad. Now, with Engler, she made sure their relationship would endure in poetry. Writing with remarkable self-assurance of passionate love even as it slipped irretrievably away, she kept her eye on the art she had long believed was her best shot at immortality.

# CHAPTER 17

# I KNOW MY POWER

## *1975–1977*

In the months after her love affair with Lilly Engler ended, Adrienne struggled. Rather than declare the relationship a complete failure, she made a concerted effort to stay friends with her former lover and therapist. Finishing *Of Woman Born* was a preoccupation and welcome distraction that nevertheless could not hold her attention all the time. Her work consumed her, but by day's end, she was lonely in mind and body. She couldn't simply turn off the painful feelings of loss.[1]

By now she was done with City College. Teaching a full load of three classes had exhausted her and left her feeling like a "wage-slave." As she wrote to the Carruths, she was not well suited to a full-time career in academia.[2] In January 1975, after just one semester as a full professor at the school where she had started out in 1968 as a part-time lecturer in the SEEK program, she quit.

A faculty fellowship at Bryn Mawr College suited her better. The one-year position required her to give a series of public talks, one of which was a poetry reading. Her reading at Bryn Mawr in 1975 drew a crowd of between eight hundred and nine hundred people, including students from nearby Haverford College. The president of Bryn Mawr, Harris Wofford, introduced Rich and remained onstage during her reading. After she finished, Adrienne invited questions from the audience.

According to Mary Patterson McPherson, a dean who later became president of the college, "A Haverford student raised his hand to ask a question. Adrienne said, 'I don't take questions from men.'"

Wofford gently informed her that Haverford students were welcome to attend events at Bryn Mawr. In McPherson's recollection, Adrienne said, "'I'm sorry, I don't take questions from men.' So that student sat down. A pall fell over the room. I think people were quite taken aback." McPherson said the occasion had gone smoothly until then. "She read well; she made good selections; she was very animated. I enjoyed it until that moment that was off-putting. She was not very pleasant."[3]

The literary critic Marjorie Perloff attended a dinner for Adrienne at Bryn Mawr during that time. She recalled word going around the room that the guest of honor was not speaking to men.[4] Whether this was strictly true or not, Adrienne was beginning to be known as a separatist even if not everyone knew she was a lesbian.

In a nation, and world, where men routinely decided what women could and could not do with their bodies and their lives, she believed women had a right to take a break from the opposite sex if they chose to. It was a form of turnabout that alienated people who thought she was going too far, but she did it anyway as a matter of principle and politics. Determined to create safe communal spaces for women, she began announcing at college poetry readings she would not read unless the men in the audience left. Not all were willing to obey her wishes, and there were occasions when the debate with the audience threatened to take up more time than her reading.[5] But whether people agreed with her or not, she had a sound rationale. She wanted the women and girls in her audience to know it was not just okay but essential for them to speak bluntly and unconstrainedly about their own lives and experiences; to commiserate and collaborate; and to devise ways to make the social order better for all women, not just themselves. In short, to get moving before they got squashed. She knew her message would come through more definitively in settings where men weren't rolling their eyes, snickering, muttering about "manhaters," and completely dominating the Q&A sessions. In her insistence, she was not asking too much; she was not even asking. She was *teaching*.

Many of her male friends, including close friends, no longer heard from her. Inevitably, there were hurt feelings. One of her former MFA students at Columbia, Hugh Seidman, has written, "[W]hen she eventually cut herself off from most men, I too was one of the men with whom she severed relations."[6] These friends didn't see themselves as sexist or misogynistic, and not all of them were. But all Rich wanted was a break: time to live, think, and write as a woman among women. It was her prerogative—and she was still in the company of men every time she walked down the street. They couldn't be avoided completely.

It was not just her male friends and acquaintances who felt a cold wind blowing their way. Some women also sensed a difference in her behavior. Among them was the poet Kathleen Fraser, who sent a letter pleading for her old friend's attention and compassion. She felt Adrienne (like lesbian writers Fraser knew in the Bay Area) had no interest in hearing what she, a straight woman, had to say. When Adrienne visited San Francisco, Fraser sensed she was avoiding her, and the conversation they had when she drove Adrienne to Berkeley did nothing to restore the ease in their friendship.

In reply to Fraser's heartfelt letter, Rich made a detailed case for herself. She said she had carefully allotted time to see people in San Francisco and Berkeley who wouldn't be on the East Coast anytime soon. In her view, she had done nothing wrong and had not rejected Fraser because she was "straight," one of the labels she considered ridiculous because "I only fully 'came out' to myself in my 'forties." She claimed she had never rejected heterosexual women or men whom she loved and knew to be "in real struggle, fighting for authenticity and faithfulness and honesty in their relationships."

She went on to admonish her friend for idealizing and romanticizing the lesbian community. In her opinion, Fraser failed to recognize the pain and isolation many lesbians tried to overcome by forming communities of their own. Further, she was amazed that Fraser would view her as a separatist, since Fraser knew of her relationships with men, celibate women, heterosexual couples, and her own sons.

As for the awkwardness of their recent visit, she offered a revealing self-assessment. "[A]lthough I may seem like a woman of unremitting strength, I do take a lot of that strength from others. I do have to make choices in my life." This was her way of telling Fraser to back off. She could not be there for everyone all the time; she had to consider her own needs. With pointed references to a male friend and a straight female friend with whom she had visited in California, Adrienne rested her case.[7] She refused to be pigeonholed as a lesbian separatist, even though she sometimes acted the part. Her greater message to Fraser was a thinly veiled warning: Friends who could not accept the way she apportioned her time were in danger of being jettisoned forever.

During her stay in Berkeley, Adrienne had visited with Susan Griffin and met Griffin's friend Kathleen Barry. Adrienne wanted a critique of *Of Woman Born* in draft form. In Barry's recollection, the manuscript needed significant revision. She felt Adrienne had not yet figured out how to convey a cohesive radical feminist message. She supplied a thorough set of comments on the manuscript, for which Adrienne was grateful.[8]

As always, she made good use of constructive criticism, but she finally reached a point where she felt she had to trust her own instincts. As she wrote to Olsen about the book, which Olsen had read shortly before it was published, "What you wish could be different, only makes me trust what you affirm. [. . .] But the shape of this book is the shape my life gave it and I must affirm that."[9]

She was staking a lot on *Of Woman Born*. In the meantime, her renown as a poet continued to grow. Norton published *Adrienne Rich's Poetry*, a selected volume of her verse supplemented by reviews and critical essays, edited by Barbara Charlesworth Gelpi and Albert Gelpi. It was the first Norton critical edition of a living author—a noteworthy coup facilitated by Rich's friendly ties with her publisher and with the Gelpis, one of the few heterosexual couples with whom she was close at the time.

Norton also issued her *Poems: Selected and New, 1950–1974*. Reviewing the book for *The New York Times*, Walter Clemons cited "Stepping Backward"—the poem from her first book based on her complex friendship with Eleanor Pearre—as a harbinger of her "embracement of risk and fallibility" in later volumes. He was reminded of Emily Dickinson's profound clarity of vision when he read Rich's 1968 poem "Planetarium." Her "apprehension of cold, infinite space explored by a lone, competent woman" had made "Planetarium" his favorite of her poems. Upon reading the new poems in her latest volume, however, he declared several of them "as good or better." He saw Rich growing ever stronger in "For L.G.: Unseen for Twenty Years," "White Night," and "From an Old House in America," the long poem she had written from the vantage point of her farmhouse in West Barnet.[10]

She had always written in a self-confident voice, but her sense of herself as an influential entity was new. Clemons was right to draw attention to "From an Old House in America," in which she wrote, "My power is brief and local / but I know my power."[11] This was the mature poet, the unapologetically strong woman, whom she had been slowly, painstakingly birthing for decades. As she entered middle age, she knew her mortal limits. In claiming her power, however brief and local, she made it her birthright. But for those who read themselves into her poems and pronouncements, the implication was that they, too, had power if only they would recognize it in themselves.

For many people in Rich's orbit, her power was a topic of conversation. In a note to the poet Honor Moore, June Jordan wrote about Rich's ability to make a brief comment that would have a profound, long-lasting impact on her friends. "That is power, and I respect her force, particularly because her life cleaves to its implications whether the latter imply agony or happiness."[12] Jordan knew Adrienne as a fellow poet, friend, and ex-lover. She had emerged from their time together, and the ensuing therapy that Adrienne reportedly paid for, capable of seeing her with a loving clarity that eluded some people.

*Of Woman Born* was slated for publication in October 1976. Exacting as always, Rich wanted to be involved in the production process every step of the way. Her editor and friend, John Benedict, made a point of introducing her to every Norton staff member working on her books. The copy editor was a crucial person in that mix. Thus, she began going to the Norton offices on Fifth Avenue to meet with Michelle Cliff, the young woman tasked with going over every line of her heavily researched and at times densely written work of prose.

Although the two women may have previously met in the Norton offices, they began getting to know each other in 1976. In the midst of their discussions of Rich's manuscript, they formed an attraction and by the summer had embarked on a partnership that would last until Adrienne's death, thirty-six years later.

Born in Kingston, Jamaica, in 1946, Michelle was a light-skinned woman who some people assumed was white, though fellow Jamaicans recognized her as one of their own. She had an impish smile, round cheeks, and a headful of curly brown hair. Like Alfred Conrad and Lilly

Engler, she had green eyes—the eye color Adrienne had loved ever since she was a young girl. Of medium height, sturdy of figure and at times plump, she wore pants rather than skirts or dresses and preferred dark or muted colors. One colleague remembered her as "the Katharine Hepburn at Norton" due to her stylish appearance in slacks.[13]

She had grown up mostly in New York City but spent part of her childhood with relatives in Jamaica. In later years, Jamaica filled her dreams. She looked back on her time there with longing, fascination, anger, and sorrow. Asked whether she would someday return, if only for a brief visit, she cited the country's colorism and homophobia and said she would not. She was keenly intelligent and very knowledgeable about popular culture, especially movies. Her salient characteristic was her biting humor, often at the expense of others. Beneath her wit and intelligence, however, there was a very private person fearful of getting hurt. Her friend Opal Palmer Adisa said, "If you observed her, she kept careful boundaries around herself. She was acutely aware she was out in the world and wanted to make sure no one penetrated that boundary around her unless she invited the person to enter that space."[14]

After Cliff had graduated from Wagner College in New York, she began working at Norton. She then left to pursue a master's degree in Renaissance history from the University of London's Warburg Institute. Her old job was waiting for her after she completed her second degree. At Norton, as a production editor, she was a member of a first-rate copyediting team comprised of people who were widely read and capable of editing any book that came their way. Books weren't assigned by a copy editor's areas of specialization, according to one of Cliff's colleagues at the time, so it seems there was no particular reason why Cliff ended up with *Of Woman Born*.

When copy editor and author were getting acquainted, Michelle was not yet thirty and Adrienne was forty-seven. The age difference didn't stand in the way of a passionate mutual bond enhanced by their shared love of women's literature and spirited conversation. Adrienne said they experienced a powerful moment of recognition while discussing the French author Simone Weil.[15] That moment of lesbian recognition opened the door to a lifetime together. Years later, Michelle claimed (possibly in jest) that she'd used her Norton expense account to wine and dine the author she was falling in love with.[16]

Michelle had had previous lesbian lovers, but Adrienne was her first and only long-term partner. As the years passed, their age difference grew more noticeable. Adrienne's body showed the crippling effects of rheumatoid arthritis, while Michelle remained youthful in appearance well into middle age. They experienced tensions resulting from Michelle's feelings of insecurity in the face of Adrienne's fame. In an effort to preserve and strengthen their bond, they would try group therapy and later couples therapy. Their relationship was going to be rocky at times, but it would last.

By August, before the publication of *Of Woman Born,* the two women were a couple.[17] Deeply in love once again, Rich was quick to share her happy news. In a September letter to Olsen, she wrote, "My life is greatly moved and touched and centered because there is day-to-day love in it again—I cut the visit to California short to come back here and assure myself it was so. It is. And it seems a miracle. She sits across from me now, reading Virginia Woolf."[18]

Unlike Lilly Engler, Rich's new lover did not feel the need to be closeted. Donald Lamm, Norton's newly appointed president at the time, recalled a visit Cliff paid to his office. The point of her visit was to inform him that she and Rich were in a relationship. Lamm had not known Cliff was a lesbian or suspected she was involved with Rich. Though surprised, he was not put off by the twin revelations. He liked Cliff. By telling him her personal news, she had defused potential gossip. Lamm appreciated her directness.[19]

By December 1976, Michelle had moved into Adrienne's apartment on the Upper West Side. They soon began thinking about leaving New York. Rich was tired of the noise and crime and generally enervated by the demands of city life. Her farmhouse in West Barnet felt too remote for year-round living,[20] but western Massachusetts interested her because it was home to a thriving lesbian feminist community centered around Smith College and nearby college campuses. It was also a beautiful area that appealed to her love of ripe, vivid landscapes.

With these thoughts in mind, Rich turned to a new friend who lived in Amherst, Janice Raymond. They had a mutual friend in the lesbian feminist scholar Mary Daly, Raymond's dissertation director at Boston College. Daly was denied promotion to full professor around the same time Raymond was denied a job interview at BC, despite evidence she was well qualified for the position she wanted. Feminists rallied around the two women and held a conference that doubled as a protest in the college gym. Robin Morgan moderated and Rich was one of the speakers at the event, attended by about eight hundred people.

In Raymond's words, "I had read *Diving into the Wreck*, and several years earlier had been introduced to Adrienne at a reading of her poetry when she was living in Cambridge and a visiting professor at Brandeis University. But the BC event was the first time I had talked with her. She sought me out after my presentation and said she admired my courage and willingness to speak out, particularly since I was a young scholar, and fighting back openly would probably not help me on the job market."

In fact, Raymond had no trouble finding a job. She accepted a tenure-track position in women's studies and medical ethics at the Five College Consortium in western Massachusetts. Not long after Raymond moved to Amherst, Adrienne called her to ask if she could visit. "She loved the area—the land of Emily Dickinson—and said she wanted me to meet Michelle Cliff, with whom she had recently begun a relationship. She also wanted Michelle to meet her feminist friends. I had just moved in, but I vacated my bedroom since I was aware that Adrienne could never have climbed the ladder to the guest loft in my lovely apartment. We had a wonderful time, and Adrienne signaled that she and Michelle might be interested in moving to the area."[21]

It would be a while before Rich could accomplish this particular goal. Cliff continued to work at Norton and told Rich she was "an intransigent urbanite."[22] In the meantime, Rich had accepted a position at Rutgers University and begun commuting there. Hayden Carruth had written her a recommendation for her job as professor of English at Douglass College, the women's division at Rutgers. Douglass had its own faculty and campus, though the English department's administration was based at Rutgers, on the other side of New Brunswick.

In January 1976, Rich wrote to Olsen about how happy she was to be at Douglass and how well everything was going so far.[23] She was teaching a writing workshop and a large lecture course on American women poets. There were eighty women and one man in the lecture class, which met in the utilitarian and run-down Language Arts building. Joyce Greenberg (now Greenberg Lott), an older student with children, was in the class. In an essay she published several years after studying with Rich, Greenberg noted that the "double classroom" was stuffed with "moveable wooden chairs and no space to move them in." OUT OF

ORDER signs were posted outside the restrooms, and radiators blasted hot air or remained icily cold. The first day of class was snowy, and Rich arrived late. One of her students was a pregnant woman whose young daughter was with her because the child's nursery was closed due to the weather. Greenberg wrote that Rich regarded the crying girl with "a sad smile" and told the mother that her child could draw on the chalkboard. "'It's difficult for women who want to be mothers,'" she remarked to the class at large. In Greenberg's view, Rich spoke "not like a teacher giving a lesson but like a mother who has already learned."[24]

Greenberg also took Rich's advanced creative writing workshop, called "Writing Out of the Female Experience." On the first day, Rich arrived "hurriedly, looking like a lame elf, brushing her gamin-like hair out of her eyes with one hand, carrying a briefcase in the other hand." She had brought nutritious snacks for students who might not have had time to eat before the lengthy seminar. Two weeks later, when she returned papers to the class, Rich spoke with her usual bluntness. Greenberg wrote that Rich told her and her classmates "we were interesting women but that our writing wasn't nearly as interesting." Greenberg felt like she had been slapped. She noticed "[t]wo of the younger women were close to tears; the rest stared angrily at Adrienne."[25]

Unfazed by their emotional reaction, Rich was intent on getting her students to think and see from the female perspective that was their birthright. Reprinted in Greenberg's essay, one of her assignments stated:

> Study your breasts. (Either in the mirror or as you see them when you undress.) Think how you have felt about and perceived them during your life, how they are related to your sense of yourself, to the rest of your body. . . . try to perceive the relationships between your hands/breast/body and the "you" that has been and will be writing, acting, thinking in the world. (1 typewritten page)[26]

Given the foment of the times, Greenberg was exhilarated by the opportunity to study with one of the nation's most prominent and highly regarded feminist writers. She thought the professor she idolized would be pleased with the personal essay she wrote about taking classes with her. But Rich responded angrily to the copy Greenberg sent her.

"Of course I was hurt and didn't know how to continue my relationship with her. I chose to publish it anyway. Being young and inexperienced in the writing world, I didn't realize what a private person Adrienne was. She kept boundaries around herself. I guess she needed to," Greenberg Lott commented many years after the essay appeared in *Parnassus: Poetry in Review,* a journal widely read by poets and poetry critics, and one where Rich herself published.[27] Rich might have congratulated her former student on a significant literary coup, but evidently she felt exploited.

Rich's office at Douglass was next to Elaine Showalter's. Showalter was careful not to overstep the boundaries her colleague drew around herself, but she, too, observed the famous poet and feminist very closely. She noticed that unlike most professors of that era, who did little or nothing to personalize their offices, Rich decorated hers with artful objects she had found or been given. Showalter recalled a Möbius strip, a length of brown paper that could be twisted into various shapes. To her, the artifacts in Rich's office "seemed poetic and said something about a consciousness."

In Showalter's recollection, Adrienne did not attend faculty parties and spent little time on campus beyond what was required of her. They had the occasional conversation, but Showalter didn't expect to become friends with the intimidatingly famous poet, who was "not the sort of person you'd cozy up to."

On one occasion when they might have bonded, Adrienne let the chance slip by. With Showalter at the wheel, they traveled to the University of Massachusetts in Amherst and talked about Emily Dickinson along the way. At one point, the exchange turned personal and Adrienne told her about Alf's suicide. Later in the conversation, Showalter offered a personal disclosure of her own. She mentioned that her marriage to a Gentile had caused her Jewish family to disown her. The revelation was left hanging in the air between them. Showalter said, "Adrienne was really not interested in that at all."

Surely Rich thought of her father's furious response when she announced her plans to marry Alfred and the ensuing rift between her and her parents. She also may have thought about the difficulty Michelle was having with her family, who disapproved of her for being a lesbian. But whatever was on Rich's mind, she was not interested in establishing an intimate rapport with Showalter, a straight woman on her way to becoming a leading scholar of women's literature.[28] With few exceptions, Adrienne's close friends at the time were lesbians.

*O*f *Woman Born* was the stellar achievement that Rich and her publisher had expected it to be. Yet again she rose to an entirely new level of prominence and acclaim. In chapters such as "Anger and Tenderness," "The Kingdom of the Fathers," and "Violence: The Heart of Maternal Darkness," she wrote about what she called "the power and powerlessness embodied in motherhood in patriarchal culture."[29] A brave and at times personal meditation on motherhood, *Of Woman Born* took its place in feminist history alongside the landmark works of Mary Wollstonecraft, Margaret Fuller, Virginia Woolf, Simone de Beauvoir, and her contemporaries Shulamith Firestone, Kate Millett, Andrea Dworkin, and Mary Daly, among others.

At the same time, Rich contributed a woman's clear, uncompromising voice to the American tradition of protest literature. By including parts of her own life story in *Of Woman Born*, she aligned herself not only with her contemporaries Martin Luther King, Jr., and James Baldwin but also with Thoreau, whom she had read with rapt admiration for decades, and Frederick Douglass, whom she had read and taught in the SEEK program.

She would later write movingly of her determination to see the world through a powerful, womanly lens, but in *Of Woman Born* there is no mistaking the influence not only of the brilliant women in her literary genealogy but also the men whose radiant insights and profound hopefulness helped make her the writer and thinker she was. The men included Arnold Rich and Alfred Conrad, the presiding ghosts at her family table, who added their share of steel to the glint in her far-seeing eye.

*Of Woman Born* sold well and came out as a mass-market paperback a year after its initial publication. It generated the widespread debate Rich had hoped for, but she was very protective of the volume she had created during four years of personal tumult. She could not accept criticism of it with equanimity.

Mixed in with the favorable reviews were harsh notices that took aim, sometimes directly and sometimes covertly, at Rich's vision of feminism and the lesbian identity she refused to hide. Two particularly stinging reviews were by women, Helen Vendler and Francine du Plessix Gray, both of whom had the blessing of the male literary elite. Rich thought these two prominent intellectuals should have understood exactly what she was getting at, and she saw their objections to her arguments as evidence of tokenism. She figured they spoke out against her as a way to protect their place in the male power structure.

Writing for *The New York Review of Books,* Vendler found much about *Of Woman Born* to question. She labeled Rich's approach to motherhood as "partisan writing" and took exception to the autobiographical sections:

> The autobiography is retold by a convinced feminist, reinterpreting her past in the light of her present convictions. All autobiographies construct a myth of explanation; some are more complex than others; some authors are conscious of the limitations of their myths (as Yeats was in discussing his "masks"). Though Rich is conscious that she has not always interpreted her life as she now does, her present myth is not offered as provisional; instead, the current interpretation of events of the past forty years, from childhood to liberation, is offered as the definitive one. [. . .]
>
> It is not surprising that a woman who, at this stage in her life, represents her father as seducer, cruel controller, intellectual critic of her first poetic attempts, and angered despot, should find herself protesting the control that a society which she regards as male-dominated, and therefore cruel, exerts over women. It is not suggested in these pages that a woman with a different sort of upbringing—or a woman with the same upbringing who read it differently—might have arrived at different political or cultural feelings.[30]

In the autobiographical passages of *Of Woman Born,* however, Rich was not writing about some other woman: She was writing about herself. Her experiences and perceptions illustrated the way debilitating patriarchal influences played out in her life. For Vendler to criticize her for doing this was to deny Rich the right to frame her argument, and tell her story, as she saw fit.

Vendler's objection nevertheless hit on one salient truth. Rich had a habitual way of looking back on her experiences in life with an angry severity she did not express at the time. The pattern had begun with her perceptions of her childhood and continued through the early years of marriage and life in Cambridge. In retrospect, things typically grew much darker. Even her greatest literary triumphs became the trappings of a token whose early acclaim felt given, not earned. In short, everything was worse than it originally appeared to be. For someone who remained genuinely hopeful about the future, Rich took a startlingly pessimistic view of her past. That was her prerogative and reflected her truth, but it was disconcerting to old friends who had thought she was happy and doing what she wanted.

In a letter otherwise praising *Of Woman Born*, Donald Hall pointed out that while she was pregnant with her first child she had visited him regularly and joined him in lively discussions of poetry; this did not square with the "lethargy about poetry" she recounted in her book. He wrote, "I'm not trying to correct you, but just comparing notes."[31]

Her pessimism appeared rooted, at least in part, in the lesbian feminist politics that Vendler and Rich's other detractors found oppressive and doctrinaire. But it was also just who Rich was. Her judgmental nature informed her every move. Seeing the world anew as a lesbian and, increasingly, as a Jew, she found more to criticize than ever before. Being right about so many things made her a marvel in some people's eyes and a scold in those of others.

Brooding over Vendler's review, which appeared before *Of Woman Born* was actually in print, Rich could not contain her anger and frustration. She blamed the review on institutionalized patriarchy and its female shills. To Tillie Olsen, she wrote that she would turn away from Vendler and other critics whom she expected to serve as hired guns shooting her down and concentrate on what she could learn from Olsen and other feminists she respected. That latter group would help her overcome whatever errors in judgment she had made in her new book and emerge a stronger, more cogent writer and thinker.[32] She craved empathetic readings by women capable of recognizing all that she was aiming for, even if she occasionally missed the mark.

Her prediction of further trouble came true in the person of Gray, who wrote at length about *Of Woman Born* in *The New York Times Book Review*. Gray praised the autobiographical sections that Vendler found problematic but questioned Rich's reliance on sources describing ancient matriarchal societies. Mainly she objected to what she perceived to be Rich's state of mind:

> When Rich draws from her own life to write about daughterhood and "motherhood as experience," she reaches moments of great poignancy and eloquence. When she writes about "motherhood as institution" (which, she asserts, "must be destroyed"), one feels that her considerable intelligence has been momentarily suspended by the intensity of her rage against men. Here she tends to bombard us with unoriginal, muddled polemics against patriarchy, and gushing eulogies of a gynocentric Golden Age, all couched in awkward, vituperative prose that is not worthy of one of our finest poets.

This passage set the tone for the rest of the review, one of the most brutal Rich ever received. A novelist and scholar of Rich's generation, Gray laced her criticism with a few chilly compliments designed to keep the renowned poet, newly out, at a safe remove. She writes elsewhere in the review, for instance, "In its apotheosis of the woman-to-woman relationship, Rich's book is one of the most eloquent Amazonist statements to come out of the American women's movement."[33]

When TV stations canceled interviews with her and some bookstores decided not to stock *Of Woman Born,* Rich blamed the damning early reviews in these two prominent publications. Dozens of other publications published positive notices, and the book was selling extremely well. But Rich could not countenance the broadside attack on her credibility in her home city. Fuming, she set about writing a rebuttal.

In an opinion column published in *The New York Times* on November 20, 1976, a month after Gray's review appeared, she described the pressure on mothers to conform to societal expectations. Facing the reality of "maternal ambivalence," lesbian mothers, and fraught relationships between mothers and their daughters posed a threat to keepers of the status quo, as did the questioning of male domination of women's bodies and lives.

"Such themes anger and terrify, precisely because they touch us at the quick of human existence," Rich wrote. "But to flee them, or trivialize them, to leave the emotions they arouse in us unexamined, is to flee both ourselves and the dawning hope that women *and* men may one day experience forms of love and parenthood, identity and community that will not be drenched in lies, secrets and silence."[34]

On the same day her column was published, Rich participated in a "Motherhood Speakout" sponsored by a feminist publication in Rochester, New York. Like Frederick Douglass, who had lived in that city and was buried there, Rich drew on her superb oratorical skills to win over her audience. Still incensed by Gray's review in the *Times,* Rich could not resist making her rebuttal part of her presentation. The admiring reporter for Rochester's *Democrat and Chronicle* wrote, "Ms. Rich set [Gray] straight on the op-ed page of the *Times.* And Saturday night, at the speakout, Ms. Rich read from both the op-ed article and her book." Her lecture "brought an entire room filled with people—feminists and anti-feminists—to their feet. They were applauding the strength and accuracy of her words."[35]

Rich's defense of her book was still not over. In an interview published in January 1977, she spoke out against Vendler and Gray. The writer Blanche M. Boyd provided her with a forum in *Christopher Street,* a literary magazine for gay men and lesbians, to discuss the reviews *Of Woman Born* had received. Given the specificity of the topic and the fact her book had been out for only a few months, Rich probably arranged the interview as a way of doing damage control and reaching an audience likely to be sympathetic. She began by bringing up Mary Daly's affirming review in the *Real Paper,* an alternative weekly based in Cambridge. By now, Daly was a friend whose ethos and writing Rich greatly admired. It pleased her that the iconoclastic professor at Boston College "challenges me from a position where the major perceptions of the book are not problematic to her."[36]

The discussion of Daly's review was a preface to the main act. When asked to comment on the bad reviews her book had received, Rich spoke with ever-increasing candor.

RICH: Well, I've learned from negative reviews, like the one in the *New York Review of Books* by Helen Vendler and the one in the *Times* by Francine Gray. I can say I've learned from them, but these reviews have not been helpful as criticism of the book, because it seems to me that they are much more about their authors' difficulties with the materials of the book than they are about the book itself. I'm hoping for more substantive discussion of the book as it begins to be reviewed by feminists, or simply by women who are not so unwilling to expose themselves to the book's insights that they have to take refuge in misrepresenting it.

BOYD: What you're saying is that Daly wasn't afraid of the book, but Vendler and Gray seemed to be threatened by it.

RICH: Yes. Exactly.[37]

While Rich seethed over the reviews she got in *The New York Times* and *The New York Review of Books,* they were not the only critical notices her new book received. Andrew Greeley, a Catholic priest and novelist, lit into both Rich and Susan Brownmiller in a column asserting that a "surefire method for writing a bestseller on today's fashionable fads like the women's movement or ecology" involved assigning guilt to "some hated group—men for instance." Aggrieved and myopic, he claimed the recipe for success required the author to "give no consideration at all to the possibility that there might be a nonparanoia, nonconspiracy explanation for that to which you are objecting. If there are no plots and no guilt, you can't write an 'honest and courageous' book."[38]

More so than Vendler or Gray, Greeley was actively campaigning against Rich, but he could not dissuade all the book buyers hungry for what she had to say. *Of Woman Born* was translated into numerous foreign languages; whatever faults some of its reviewers found with it, the book was being bought and read, and it was taught on college campuses. Rich could not single-handedly upend the patriarchy, but she had provided readers all over the world with powerful insights into the exigencies of motherhood. They could learn from her, if they wanted to.

As feminism moved into academia, Rich moved with it. In late December 1976, she presented a controversial essay called "It Is the Lesbian in Us . . ." at the Modern Language Association (MLA) con-

ference in New York. Her panel, titled "Female Self-Definition in Literature and Life," was organized by the Women's Commission and the Gay
Caucus, subgroups within MLA, and drew a crowd of seven hundred
people. The other speakers were June Jordan, Audre Lorde, and Honor
Moore. In a footnote to the published essay, Rich said the panel was
designed "to raise, before a large audience of teachers and scholars,
the question of racism and homophobia in the teaching of literature,
issues with which the Women's Commission had been struggling as a
group for over a year."[39]

Her paper argued that every woman who connects emotionally and
intellectually with other women is tapping into a lesbian ethos. Rich
was not desexualizing lesbianism, as some of her lesbian critics thought,
nor was she implying that one had to be a lesbian to be creative. Instead,
she was doing what she wanted other writers and scholars to do: focus
on women's culture to the exclusion of all else. "I believe it is the lesbian in every woman who is compelled by female energy, who gravi-
tates toward strong women, who seeks a literature that will express
that energy and strength. It is the lesbian in us who drives us to feel
imaginatively, render in language, grasp, the full connection between
woman and woman. It is the lesbian in us who is creative, for the dutiful
daughter of the fathers in us is only a hack."[40]

The literary critic Catharine Stimpson was in the audience that
night. In a later essay about Rich's lesbian-feminist poetry, she described
the moment when Rich read her memorable line about the "dutiful
daughter of the fathers":

> She leaned forward from a dais, where three other poets were
> also sitting: June Jordan, Audre Lorde, Honor Moore. I was on
> a chipped and gilded chair, between two scholar/critics: one a
> divorced mother, heterosexual, who called herself lesbian out
> of political sympathy, a radical feminist act of the late 1960s
> and early 1970s; the second a married mother, about to begin a
> secret love affair with a woman, who rarely (if ever) spoke about
> lesbianism. "Right on," said the first. Enigmatically, the second
> looked at the husband next to her. Grinning, with the casual-
> ness of marriage, he affectionately slapped her thigh. There we
> were—an imperfect, blurry shadow of Rich's continuum.[41]

In the mid- to late 1970s, Rich added the battle against pornography to her portfolio of causes. She was disgusted by the sexually explicit nature of the seedy live shows and movies that saturated Times Square. The national popularity of hard-core magazines like *Hustler* and films like *Deep Throat* made things worse. Motivated by her signature blend of outrage and noblesse oblige, she helped found an organization called the Women's Anti-Defamation League. Created by Susan Brownmiller in the summer of 1977, the group intended to take a vocal stand against pornography. Other founders included Robin Morgan, Gloria Steinem, and Shere Hite, author of *The Hite Report*.[42] Written up in *The New York Times* and the *Chicago Tribune*, it met only a couple of times but proved to be a bellwether for a wave of feminist protests against pornography. A year later, Rich attended a major conference sponsored by Women Against Violence in Pornography and the Media. She would also ally herself with Women Against Pornography (WAP), which Brownmiller organized in 1979.

Her involvement in WAP would end abruptly and dramatically in 1985. For the time being, however, she was a marquee name in the battle against pornography. Less widely known was her censorious view of gay male culture around the same time. She declined a request for a blurb from Karla Jay, who wanted her to endorse an anthology of essays by gay and lesbian writers that Jay had coedited with Allen Young. She didn't like the idea of drawing a parallel between the lives of lesbians and gay men. To her, lesbian-feminist culture offered real potential for societal change because it operated outside the confines of the patriarchy. At that point in her life, she didn't see any hopeful distinctions between gay male culture and male culture writ large.[43]

During these years, Rich had an entrenched lesbian feminist mindset. She saw women's culture, especially lesbian culture, as a potentially utopian world unto itself, not a subset of something else. She refused to attach her name to the anthology Jay and Young had compiled because, she told Jay, she objected to the whole idea of the book. Then, to make her point even clearer, she went on to say she had not liked *The Joy of Lesbian Sex* because she thought lesbianism needed to be understood as the center of women's culture, not something running parallel to heterosexuality or gay male sexuality.[44]

Small and frail, her limp noticeable and her hair beginning to turn gray, Rich was an incongruous presence. She did not appear strong until she spoke and the force of her words rained down on everybody around her. With the power of her convictions sparkling in her eyes, it seemed at times as if she poured all her knowledge of the world into her every utterance. She was becoming legendary for her anger.

In contrast to women like Gray and Vendler who could not hear her in the way she wanted to be heard, many women (and men) rallied around her message. To her believers, including those whose minds and hearts she changed, she spoke a truth equal to that of Frederick Douglass or Susan B. Anthony or Martin Luther King, Jr. "Finally, to hear such poetry from a podium of 'prestige,' before an over-flowing crowd of all ages, both genders, and undoubtedly, all sexual orientations, is an affirmation of how far women have come," wrote a reporter for the *Hartford Advocate* after Rich's reading in honor of a new women's center at Trinity College.

Drawing on ideas that would find their way into her later speeches and essays on higher education for women, Rich spoke "briefly and movingly before her reading about what it means for women in a male university to claim space for themselves. Women are not merely asking for 'rooms of their own in the patriarchal mansion,' but rather creating what they need and building anew. Acknowledging 'the powerful and vicious forces against us,' Ms. Rich explained that feminism is not about women becoming equal in the existing society, but about the destruction of male privilege, out of which will arise new ways to live, work, and relate."[45]

The glowing account in the Hartford paper was part of a large body of reportage that documented her profound impact on audiences for the entire span of her lengthy career. Rich's publisher and her friends faithfully sent her the newspaper clippings, which she preserved in her archives. She knew it was important for future generations to have that record.

As the Hartford reporter made clear, Rich was not one merely to excoriate. She always believed in the possibility of a better world, as *Of Woman Born* amply demonstrates in its closing lines:

> We need to imagine a world in which every woman is the presiding genius of her own body. In such a world women will truly create new life, bringing forth not only children (if and when we choose) but the visions, and the thinking, necessary to sustain, console, and alter human existence—a new relation to the universe. Sexuality, politics, intelligence, power, motherhood, work, community, intimacy will develop new meanings; thinking itself will be transformed.
>     This is where we have to begin.[46]

Her combination of outrage, hope, and strategy put her in line with abolitionists of the nineteenth century, feminist foremothers of the early twentieth century, and civil rights leaders of her own time. She was radical in her earnestness and unflinching in the face of naysayers. Clutching the lectern, her leg aching, she knew her power.

# CHAPTER 18

# HYACINTHS RISING LIKE FLAMES

## *1977–1978*

Rich knew how much her current stature owed to her early publishing successes. Without acceptances when she was still in college from *Virginia Quarterly Review* and *Harper's* and the windfall of the Yale Prize, she might have been consigned to a life on the fringes of the literary world, along with thousands of other women and minority poets of her time. Although no one could say her youthful poems lacked skill or substance, she believed tokenism had vaulted her to prominence. That belief provided the premise for her speech at the National Book Awards in 1974. Even if at times her message came across as subtly self-aggrandizing, she continued to use her prominence to expose societal wrongs and try to right them.

In that regard, she and June Jordan led a charge in 1977 against *The American Poetry Review,* a poetry journal they considered "racist, sexist and anti-youth." With its large photos of the authors and splashy biographical notes, the widely distributed tabloid was about the poets as much as their poems. By 1977, the year of the protest, Rich had published a number of poems in the five-year-old journal, which had featured her photo on the cover of an early issue. Despite her dismay at being turned into a cover model, she wrote columns for *APR,* as did Jordan. Yet most of its contributors were older white men, a sign to Rich that *APR* was not serious about challenging the status quo and was, in fact, in the business of tokenism that she despised.

The fifty authors involved in the protest wanted the magazine to represent the actual range of poets writing in the United States, not just an entitled handful.[1] In time, *APR* did become more inclusive. Her demands met, Rich continued to publish in it, appeared on its cover a second time, and served as the judge of its book prize in 2001.[2]

With Jordan by her side in the front line of the *APR* battle, she conveyed a message of interracial solidarity that had been important to her for a long time. Race relations and racism had concerned her ever since she and Alfred worked at City College and she taught in the SEEK program. Now she was living with the Jamaican-born Michelle, who was deeply preoccupied with questions about race that would inform her writing, including her first book publication, *Claiming an Identity They Taught Me to Despise*. On some level, the two women were always communicating about race even when they were not actively discussing it.

Adrienne told friends about her passionate love for Michelle, but that did not mean all was easy between them. She looked within and without in search of a way forward. As she wrote to Robin Morgan, she was trying to strengthen her relationship with Michelle and connect with lesbian couples who shared their political and personal values.[3]

Although she did not mention Audre Lorde by name, surely Lorde was on her mind. In Lorde, Rich had a dear friend and fellow poet who regularly challenged her views. They gave poetry readings together and publicly discussed race and gender relations in ways that modeled frank dialogue for others. At a joint reading she and Lorde gave at Harvard to draw attention to a series of murders of black women, for instance, Rich said, "I'm here because as a white feminist and a woman-identified woman, I perceive these events in Boston as evidence of the depth of woman-hating." Though she said the horrific crimes would have gained more attention if the victims had been affiliated with powerful white men, she entreated the audience to realize "there is no selective privilege for women."[4]

Despite their moving displays of unity, Rich's and Lorde's love for each other was often complicated by mutual feelings of anger and hurt. When Lorde harshly critiqued a draft of "Disloyal to Civilization," Rich's essay about race relations between white and black women, Rich reeled in shock. But she went back to work on her essay and stayed close to Lorde.[5]

In some respects, Lorde and Cliff were similar. Rich's friends recalled

Cliff as volatile, sharply witty, and often profane in her language. She loved dissecting movies and was quick to disparage people she looked down on.

As for Lorde, Rita Mae Brown said, "God, she was fun. She would say whatever came into her head. She was just a bad girl, and I loved her. I think she liked me. We really did have fun. She wasn't above making fun of other people. She always just hit the nail on the head. She was very aggressive about her lesbianism, which I thought was really funny. She would scare the shit out of the white girl."[6]

Lorde's blend of radicalized intelligence, irreverent wit, blunt sexuality, and surging outrage was indeed intimidating, but Rich was no ordinary white girl. She turned to Audre for a kind of severe truth she could get nowhere else, except perhaps from Michelle. Adrienne's relationship with Michelle, moreover, was an inverse image of Audre's with Frances Clayton, a white sociologist who left her job in academia to be with Lorde and help rear Lorde's two children. According to Lorde's biographer, Alexis De Veaux, "Over the course of their long relationship, Lorde publicly extolled the racial differences between [her and Clayton] as creatively useful. Privately, those differences were a source of deep-rooted tension."[7]

Rich and Cliff were headed in the same direction. By debating race relations with Lorde, Rich was thinking through issues relevant to her relationship with Cliff. In their friendship, at least in theory, Adrienne and Audre could step away from the emotional and sexual pressures that shadowed their every word when racial difference became an issue on the home front. In response to an essay Lorde asked her to critique, Rich said she felt compelled to ask herself questions about her relationships with black women, especially with Cliff and with Lorde.[8]

Lorde, however, was intent on seducing Rich, so their interactions were not purely platonic, at least not on Lorde's side. De Veaux writes, "Lorde needed to feel loved, constantly. She needed to feel respected, recognized, and desired. She equated sex with love—and with intimacy. Lorde believed she didn't really know a person unless she slept with them; she bedded, or attempted to bed, women she knew or was attracted to 'as part of the challenge of friendship.' Her sexual aggressiveness was part of a need to control every aspect of her connection to other women."[9] She unsuccessfully propositioned both Cliff and Rich.[10]

Lorde's aggressiveness was no secret. Blanche Wiesen Cook recalled,

"Audre used to say you don't know anybody until you sleep with them. She couldn't believe Adrienne didn't want to sleep with her."[11]

Rich remained firm in her resistance. Rita Mae Brown remembered Lorde's frustration: "She thought Adrienne was badly informed, making terrible judgments. I said, 'Perhaps not, honey.'"[12]

A current of desire nevertheless lit the circuitry of the intense, dramatic friendship between these two lesbian feminist poets. As late as 1992, more than twenty years after they first met, Rich wrote to Lorde that poetry was the source of their erotic bond. She said they'd never gone to bed together because she was monogamous by nature: "But yes, you have climbed into my poems. And, in less visible ways, I have perhaps climbed into yours."[13]

Complicating things further, Lorde chafed at Rich's greater recognition and clout. After Norton rejected Coal, a collection of Lorde's poetry, Rich wrote to John Benedict, praising the book and practically insisting he accept it.[14] Norton then published the volume with an advertisement listing Rich's books in its back pages. Lorde was pleased to have Norton as her publisher but irritated that Rich's intervention was needed. And she railed against the advertisement, which she had not known about in advance. Taking Lorde's objections to heart, her agent, Charlotte Sheedy, added a clause to her later contracts that required publishers to seek permission before advertising someone else's works in a book by one of her clients.[15]

Lesbian feminism remained at the heart of Rich's politics. In the summer of 1977, at a lesbian pride rally in New York, she gave a speech to a small group of women that had split off from a gay pride march dominated by gay men. In many of those men, Rich saw not kindred spirits but familiar enemies. She criticized their sexualized degradation of Anita Bryant, the figurehead of the antigay movement, for the misogyny that it was. Rather than assume gay men and lesbians were naturally in sympathy with one another, she blasted "homosexual patriarchal culture" as "a culture created by homosexual men, reflecting such male stereotypes as dominance and submission as modes of relationship, and the separation of sex from emotional involvement—a culture tainted by profound hatred for women."[16] For her, Bryant and Phyllis Schlafly were "the masks behind which the system of male dominance is attacking, not just lesbians or 'gay' men, but women, and the feminist movement even in its most moderate form; that the attack is fuelled and fostered by the only people in America with the resources to do so: men."[17]

She was not asking her audience to go to war against male subjugators. Instead, she was telling lesbians to acknowledge what they were up against and find a way to contribute to a "woman-centered vision" that would radically transform society.[18] She wanted them to create a legacy they would be proud of. How, exactly, they would do that she did not say, but the first step would be realizing they had common interests that went beyond sexual identification.

Rich was out of town during New York City's historic blackout in mid-July 1977. When she returned, she recoiled from the heat and smog in "a city still feeling the psychic aftermath of the blackout."[19] The blackout had provoked vandalism, arson, and mass arrests of looters. It seemed like a city completely out of control. Reading the papers and hearing grim stories from friends, Rich recoiled.

More and more, she and Cliff wanted to live peacefully in a safer, quieter place. To accomplish that, they would have to leave their reliable jobs and steady sources of income. They also would have to end their meetings with Bernice Goodman, the lesbian therapist they had seen individually.[20] They would no longer be in close proximity to Audre Lorde and Frances Clayton, Blanche Wiesen Cook and Clare Coss, or other lesbian couples in their intimate circle. Other friends would be left behind, as well. They would no longer be living in the hub of the literary world.

The trade-off left Rich in a stew as she weighed her desire for improved circumstances against her anger at feeling compelled to leave the city she had fallen in love with when she and her husband and sons moved there more than a decade ago. Manhattan held many pieces of who she was. It was there she had left Alfred Conrad and ended her fraught love affair with Lilly Engler. Quitting the city was akin to ending yet another tumultuous romance. Furious and bereft, she mulled over her escape plan.

The blackout was not the only big news coming out of New York that summer. In August, Rich wrote Griffin that serial murderer David Berkowitz, known as the "Son of Sam," had been caught. She was hoping a definitive connection between pornography and violence could be made, if, as she had heard, "piles of pornography" were stashed in his apartment.[21]

In an interview with *The Daily Iowan* at the University of Iowa, Rich spoke about the constant threat of violence against women. She recalled a story she had heard about a college women's group taking action against a man known for claiming women wanted to be raped. A member of the group sent the man a note asking him to meet with her to discuss the issue. When he arrived, she and her fellow feminists pinned him to the floor and pulled down his pants. They told him they would not castrate him, but they wanted him to know what it felt like to be powerless. Rich expressed her approval for this example of what she called "guerrilla theatre."[22]

Although she was not a political activist in the antipornography movement to the degree that Catharine MacKinnon, Andrea Dworkin, and Susan Brownmiller were, she was vocally in their camp and later joined and donated money to Women Against Pornography. Some of the poems she published in her next volume, *A Wild Patience Has Taken Me This Far,* reflected her revulsion at pornography and the harm it inflicted on women. With her eyes on New York, where pornography was a thriving industry, Rich's anger escalated. The city, it seemed, had turned against her and all she believed in.

Her anger was not new, but sometimes it still caught people by surprise. A tempest blew up in September 1977 when Loyola College of Maryland offered her an honorary doctorate and asked her to give the keynote address at its graduation ceremonies. Always looking for a chance to expose what she perceived as hypocrisy, an unflattered Rich copied her letter of refusal to *The Baltimore Sun*. If the Jesuit school had invited her only to lecture on campus, she might well have accepted and given a sidewinder of a feminist speech, but the prospect of the honorary degree irked her no end. True to form, she called "the practice of granting honorary degrees to women a 'ritual of tokenism.'" The *Sun* contacted college officials, who were "'shocked and stunned to get that kind of reply' and said they felt it was 'discourteous' of Ms. Rich to use the 'opportunity' of the invitation to publicize her position on women's rights." As her replacement, school administrators played it safe and chose a male theology professor from Catholic University.[23]

Rich was willing, however, to give the fall convocation address at

Douglass College, where she was in her second year of teaching. As a Radcliffe student, she had loved the ceremonial grandeur and high purpose of convocation. The promise of a new academic year held a different kind of meaning for her now that she was a lesbian feminist, yet she had been thinking about the importance of a rigorous education for girls and women for a long time, as evidenced by her 1958 address to the faculty of Roland Park Country School.

She told the young women in the audience at Douglass College they should actively seek out their education rather than passively receiving whatever was offered to them. To succeed in college, she argued, they needed to take responsibility for themselves, value their minds and bodies, do their own thinking, and demand that the adults around them, including their teachers, take them seriously. She described the implied contract between teachers and female students as "really a pledge of mutual seriousness about women, about language, ideas, methods, and values. It is our shared commitment toward a world in which the inborn potentialities of so many women's minds will no longer be wasted, raveled-away, paralyzed, or denied."[24]

As clear a distillation of feminism as anyone could hope for, these words summed up years of concentrated thinking on Rich's part. By delivering her message at the beginning of the academic year, she put colleagues and students alike on notice that the patriarchal way was not the only way. She was proposing an alternative that would ennoble everyone who gave it a chance.

Later in September, word came that Robert Lowell had died. Rich's old friend had suffered a heart attack on his way to see, and possibly reconcile with, Elizabeth Hardwick. Rich's fondness for him had diminished after he left Hardwick, whom he eventually divorced so he could marry Caroline Blackwood. She objected to his use of Hardwick's letters to him in his poetry. Now, writing to Hayden Carruth on October 5, 1977, she declared, "His death left me feeling virtually nothing at all" because she had stopped caring about him and his poetry long ago.

Lowell's passing still affected her, however, as she looked around and realized she had lost touch with other old friends who were still important to her. To Carruth, she wrote with haughty grandeur, "I want all the pieces of my past, at least to acknowledge them; 'the will to change,' though it often meant rending, was never a will to erase."[25]

Rich knew she had alienated people through her "rending" of old bonds in the name of feminism and equal rights for all. There were no causes more worthy than the ones she had taken on, but perhaps she went too far at times. She was quick to judge when people fell short of her expectations, and her anger and scorn had become defining characteristics. Her ardent admirers as yet unexposed to her wrath saw her as gentle and generous, which she often was; those who accidentally landed in her crosshairs quailed in response to her fury.

Her better instincts fell away as she reacted preemptively to people who displeased her for one reason or another. She ended friendships with both women and men, sometimes explaining why and sometimes not. She was not close to her mother, who lived independently in Cambridge, or her sister, Cynthia, who had come out as a lesbian and also lived in Cambridge. Adrienne's years of therapy and contemplation had not unraveled all the knots in her family relationships. Cynthia and her lover, Barbara Macdonald, were radical lesbian feminist activists and writers, yet Adrienne (and Michelle) seemed incapable of expressing interest in them or their work.[26] As for Carruth, who had occupied her mind and heart for so long, she would not stop caring about him, but he was a touchstone to be remembered in times of nostalgia, not someone whose continuing friendship she depended on as she once had. These days, her emotional life revolved around Cliff and her closest friends, Lorde prominent among them.

Her public crusade rolled on. In November 1977, she voiced her displeasure with the Guggenheim Foundation, whose beneficence had bankrolled her fellowship at Oxford and her year of study and travel with Conrad in Rotterdam, the happiest time in her marriage. Because of her successful track record, poet friends and acquaintances often asked her to write letters of recommendation for them when they applied for fellowships. In a letter to Diane di Prima, Rich wrote that instead of writing recommendation letters requested of her that year, she was going to complain about what she perceived to be the foundation's discriminatory selections of fellowship recipients.

Her previous objections had concerned the foundation's "discrimination against women and against feminist scholarly projects," but she had held fire, for fear of harming the chances of the women whose applications she supported. Now, having freed herself from the task of writing recommendations, she would launch a direct assault, because she was infuriated by the annual spectacle of "some of the most gifted women in America" losing out in the competition to "tokens and non-threatening conservatives."[27]

During this period of her life, Rich was nothing if not a fighter. She poured her energy into exposing the hypocrisy and social injustice animating institutions widely held in high esteem. She did not leaven her message with humor or a conciliatory tone. Skeptical, unyielding, yet always believing in the potential for positive change, she challenged universities, foundations, publications, and individuals to share her high purpose and make a reality out of her vision.

So it went at Douglass College. In addition to teaching, Rich participated in department meetings—which, as a campus star, she could have gotten away with skipping. When her colleagues asked her to weigh in on plans for a writing center, she recommended that it be centrally located in the library, not in the English department. Rather than stigmatizing it as a remediation center, she suggested it be known instead as a place where "writing was honored"—a description her colleagues immediately began using after Rich uttered it. She also wanted the center to offer help to advanced students writing long essays, and she urged her colleagues to make sure the cost of operating the center did not fall to the English department alone. Carol Smith, the chair at the time, said the department followed through on all of Rich's recommendations for the writing center.[28]

According to Smith, faculty members in the Douglass English department did not typically teach in the graduate program in English offered by their counterparts in the men's college. Therefore, when Rich declined a request to serve on dissertation committees, it seems she was not shirking an expected duty but keeping to the job she had been hired to do. Even so, Richard Poirier, the Rutgers English department's director of graduate studies, gently remonstrated with her. Not so gentle in her reply, she told him her involvement in the feminist community came first. She would quit her job if she could not do as she pleased.[29]

Rich had a long train commute from Manhattan, and her increasingly gnarled limbs made it hard for her to walk around campus. Her exchange with Poirier showed how determined she was to conserve her energy for tasks that truly engaged her. Yet there was much about Douglass and the English department that she liked. She was teaching exactly what she wanted to teach, and Douglass was one of the first colleges in the country to offer courses in women's studies. Although Rich's feminist ideology was more "evolved" than that of her colleagues, in her chair's view, she was in a department where women's literature was appreciated and widely taught.[30] It was in many ways just the sort of woman-centered academic environment that she had been calling for.

In a letter to Susan Griffin in the fall of 1977, Rich admitted things were going so well that she might have stayed if she had not already decided to leave. Perhaps in an effort to convince herself she was doing the right thing, she wrote dismissively that most faculty and academic administrators were "totally hopeless as agents for change." She believed "the real action is with students."[31]

In April 1978, after two and a half years at Douglass, she resigned. To Smith, the department chair, she explained that she was "trying to reconcile conflicting elements" in her life and career, including her need to write, her love of teaching, her commitment to feminism, and her appreciation of her professorship's salary and benefits. Rich went on at great length in an often fiery letter. In addition to describing how necessary it was for her to resign and get on with her responsibilities as a writer and radical lesbian feminist leader, she insisted on the primacy of women students and scolded her colleagues for what she considered their shortsighted approach to the academic curriculum.[32]

Around this time, the university was undergoing a reorganization that consolidated departments, including English, across the two campuses. There would no longer be a separate men's or women's college. In response to her resignation, Rich received a courteous response from Tom Edwards, the chair of the newly combined English departments. He wrote, "For me (and many others here) you were never a token but a colleague in the best sense, which I've always assumed meant someone one can disagree with without ceasing to admire and learn from."[33]

Some might conclude she was ungrateful for the chance the university gave her to make a difference in the lives of young women whose education mattered so much to her. But as she approached age fifty, she wanted to step away from the hierarchy of academia. She craved a life of the mind that transcended departmental politics and the routine demands of an academic career. As she wrote to Smith, she was at a point where she could afford that life, and she intended to make the best use of the privilege available to her.[34]

Rich would eventually teach again. She could not go too many years without the regular income and health benefits that a university teaching position offered. And as she made clear, she liked working with young people. Under the best of circumstances, she became a student in her own class, challenged and energized by the material on her syllabus and by earnest students who were as eager to learn as she was. She also depended on academic institutions for much of her income as a public speaker. As a popular visiting poet and lecturer, she commanded a competitive fee, and during these events she expanded her readership and sold a great many books.

But her ambivalent relationship with the academy continued. An institution's veneer of commitment to the educational needs of women and minorities did not placate her. She was an idea person who positioned herself not as a policy maker or educational theorist but as a truth teller. When Smith College, Sylvia Plath's alma mater, offered her an honorary doctorate and invited her to give the graduation speech, she accepted—and made headlines with her blunt criticism of women's colleges.

In 1978, she published *The Dream of a Common Language*. Her latest collection of verse capped off a remarkable decade of poetic achievement. She had surprised her longtime readers and attracted many new ones with *The Will to Change* and *Diving into the Wreck*. With the chapbook edition of *Twenty-One Love Poems*, she had announced herself as a lesbian poet and produced a dazzling sequence that turned out to be the most accomplished long poem of her career. Now, with *The Dream of a Common Language,* she completed the poetic arc of the decade that would define her reputation for the rest of her life.

The book was her first full-length collection concerned exclusively with women's lives and experiences, and Rich knew it was her best yet. To Benedict, her editor, she wrote, "I feel a conviction and excitement about this book that I can't recall having felt before about a book of poems."[35] As usual, she was weighing in on everything, including the number of lines of verse appearing on each page. Somehow the selection of her jacket photo slipped by her. When she received her copies of the book in February 1978, she told Benedict she was "absolutely delighted" with everything except the photo. "It does distress me that I look as if afflicted by petit mal—I don't think this is mere vanity."[36] She did not mind if the photo appeared on paperback editions, since it would be smaller and less noticeable there, but she wanted it removed from future hardback editions.

*

In *The Dream of a Common Language,* Rich explores the lives of accomplished women. The opening poem, "Power," dated 1974, touches on the life of Marie Curie ("she must have known she suffered from radiation sickness") while suggesting she was an archetype, a woman unable to reconcile her strength with her frailty—in that respect, perhaps like Rich herself. Other poems in the first section include "Phantasia for Elvira Shatayev," "Origins and History of Consciousness," "Splittings," "Hunger" (which Rich dedicated to Audre Lorde), "To a Poet," "Cartographies of Silence," and "The Lioness."

"Origins and History of Consciousness"—the title borrowed from Erich Neumann's 1949 Jungian psychological study—introduces the line that serves as the title of the volume. With details drawn from her own life, the opening section appears to describe her bedroom and contains the observation, "No one sleeps in this room without / the dream of a common language." The second section alludes to the relationship with Lilly Engler, which began so promisingly but quickly became rife with complications: "What is not simple," Rich writes, is "to wake from drowning / from where the ocean beat inside us like an afterbirth / into this common, acute particularity / these two selves who walked half a lifetime untouching."

Manhattan's nightmarish dangers seep into the poem as she imagines waking to

[. . .] a scream
of someone beaten up far down in the street
causing each of us to listen to her own inward scream

knowing the mind of the mugger and the mugged
as any woman must who stands to survive this city,
this century, this life . . .[37]

She wants to move beyond the vexed existence she has fallen into with her lover, an existence in which "the night becomes our inner darkness, and sleeps / like a dumb beast, head on her paws, in the corner."[38]

Her desire for communion and mutual understanding remains important in "Splittings." The tension in her relationship with Engler lurks within the poem, dated 1974, but Rich has a new sense of who she is and what she can do, evident in the concluding lines: "I choose to love this time    for once / with all my intelligence."[39]

The sequence, "Twenty-One Love Poems," is the second section, and centerpiece, of *The Dream of a Common Language*. For readers who had not encountered the sequence in its small-press edition, the lyrics tracing a lesbian relationship from beginning to end offered new personal insights into Rich. But the poems are in keeping with the poetic ethos she had embraced for the past decade—that is, her poems would transcend topical occasions and speak to larger human truths. In "Twenty-One Love Poems" the poet consciously chooses to outlive and make art out of a love affair that ultimately proved to be as disastrous as it initially was wondrous. The sequence is, among other things, an extended meditation on the deeply entwined nature of suffering, endurance, and creativity, a mesmerizing expression of the human condition that Rich knew was not hers alone.

The third section of *Dream* shows Rich transitioning away from Engler and beginning a new life with Cliff, to whom the final poem, "Transcendental Etude," is dedicated. Poems preceding this meditation on love and loyalty include "Upper Broadway" ("I look at my face in the glass and see / a halfborn woman"[40]), "Sibling Mysteries," "A Woman Dead in Her Forties," and "Paula Becker to Clara Westhoff," a poem growing out of Rich and Engler's collaborative interest in the two German painters. Rich imagined an intimate friendship between Becker, who died shortly after giving birth to her first child, and Westhoff, who was married to Rainer Maria Rilke. Freed of demanding artist husbands and the expectation they would have children, the poem implies, the two women could have enriched each other's lives, perhaps in a lesbian relationship, and fulfilled their destiny as artists.

Once the volume shifts to Rich's new life, the sorrowful tone gives way to a mature hopefulness that allows for a certain amount of doubt. The lengthy "Transcendental Etude" announces Rich's new love affair in grand terms, but it is the shorter, more understated "Nights and Days" that approaches the sublime. Moving back and forth between the past, dreams, and a dream of the future, the poem has five stanzas, the final one repeating the first. In these repeated lines, Rich wavers between questions and declarations, the ambiguity of the syntax under-scoring her feelings of amazement and anxiety:

> The stars will come out over and over
> the hyacinths rise like flames
> from the windswept turf down the middle of upper Broadway
> where the desolate take the sun
> the days will run together and stream into years
> as the rivers freeze and burn
> and I ask myself and you, which of our visions will claim us
> which will we claim
> how will we go on living
> how will we touch, what will we know
> what will we say to each other[41]

The poem reveals Rich's faith in the new relationship she had em-barked on. She did not expect it to be easy, but she believed it would endure.

*The Dream of a Common Language* placed her deep in the territory she had glimpsed in the title poem of *Snapshots of a Daughter-in-Law* back in 1963. *Dream* was her greatest poetic achievement to date and would remain that until the posthumous publication of her *Collected Poems*.

When *Dream* was not immediately reviewed in *The New York Times*, Rich had reason to think she was being snubbed. In the years between the publication of *Diving into the Wreck* and this new book, Rich had come out as a lesbian and publicly criticized patriarchal institutions that had honored her and helped make her name as a poet. She also had insisted that two prominent female reviewers of her work, Helen Vendler and Francine Gray, were tokens in thrall to male-dominated seats of power.

In a letter to John Benedict, Rich wrote, "We both know that a poet of my reputation would normally have a front-page review for a book like this, with poems excerpted, etc., in the Times Book Review." Frances McCullough of Harper & Row had offered to do "some screaming" on her behalf, but she wanted Norton to make inquiries, as well. "Of course the book will sell (I've been signing copies from New Jersey to Baltimore to Grand Rapids to Minneapolis—praises to the Norton sales people) but to have it totally ignored by The New York Times seems to me a dangerous precedent."[42]

Things were about to get worse. In early June, she heard from a bookseller that Norton's booth at the American Booksellers Association conference in Atlanta did not have copies of her recent books or May Sarton's. Again she complained to Benedict; again she noted the absence of a review in *The New York Times*.[43]

On the positive side, Bantam had published *Of Woman Born* as a mass-market paperback. Her first prose book also was finding its way into foreign markets. An unhappy Rich noted, however, that the Spanish edition's cover art conveyed "a nasty subliminal S&M message." In the future, she told Benedict, she wanted a clause in her foreign-language rights contract to prevent such a thing from happening again.[44]

Finally, on June 11, long after its publication, *Dream* was reviewed in the *Times*. The author was Margaret Atwood, whose praise for *Diving into the Wreck* had given Rich a well-timed boost in the months leading up to the National Book Awards. Atwood wrote that opening a new book by Rich was "an unsettling experience" that required "belief" rather than "the willful suspension of disbelief." In the metaphorical tradition of Robert Lowell, who had once compared Rich's attempts to remake herself to a beetle struggling with its shell, Atwood imagined the author of *Dream* as a physically compromised piano player: "The music is subdued but intense, and it is only after you have been hearing it for some time that you realize the player is half-blind and is missing several fingers. These are poems written *despite,* poems of willed recuperation." Atwood recognized "authority" in Rich's new poems rather than the "immense pounding energy, a raw power," that had awed her in *Diving into the Wreck*.[45]

If not a rave, the review was solid criticism from a woman Rich respected. Once again, Norton harvested Atwood's most complimentary lines to use as jacket copy on future editions, and Rich exhaled. It may have taken "some screaming" to get her book reviewed, but in the end the *Times* had not ignored her.

.  .  .

In the late spring, Rich experienced a bad flair of her rheumatoid arthritis and was diagnosed with hypothyroidism. Instead of going to Paris as they had planned, she and Cliff retreated to West Barnet. Rich arrived at her beloved Vermont house depressed, exhausted, and in severe pain. She canceled most of her speaking engagements and spent time alone with Cliff, who had taken the summer off from her job at Norton.[46] As she began to recover and regain her strength, she attributed her improved health in part to the deep peacefulness of the place and in part to a medicinal drink made of sarsaparilla that Lorde had sent her.[47]

She believed the pain of the arthritis had brought on her depression. To Lorde and Clayton, she confessed, "[I]t is hard to depict how vast a load of fear, despair & self-hatred lifts when the incessant, daily pain lifts & is replaced by only mild mechanical discomfort."[48] Perhaps treatment of the thyroid condition also eased her emotional suffering.

As West Barnet worked its curative magic, her spirits rose. On hot days, she wore her new "striped red running shorts" and enjoyed her freedom from the stultifying conditions of New York in a heat wave. She and Michelle were getting along well, a signal achievement in a place that held so many memories of her life with her late husband. She later said that "mostly because [Michelle] is who she is we were able to remake it together for ourselves; and doing that in part made it plausible to us that we could live in the country, in New England, though for obvious reasons not there."[49] She did not want to live in West Barnet during the wintertime, when the snow, frigid temperatures, and isolation would be more than she could bear. But western Massachusetts, with its thriving lesbian feminist community and the symbolic allure of Emily Dickinson's homestead, continued to call out to her.

That summer, Adrienne and Michelle hosted Janice Raymond and her partner for a visit. Raymond had known for some time that her hosts were interested in moving to the area where she lived. Later, she told the two women about a house for sale in Montague, Massachusetts. The house was in good condition, and the owners were eager to sell.

In short order, Rich and Cliff bought the house and began preparing to move there. In a letter to her friends Catherine Nicholson and

Harriet Ellenberger, the editors of the lesbian feminist journal *Sinister Wisdom,* Rich happily anticipated the transition she and Cliff were about to make: "When I think of living in Montague I think of stillness—not the utter stillness of the woods or plains, but of not hearing sounds that are impinging on me at this moment & which I know I use energy to blot out: a garbage truck groaning as it scoops bulging plastic bags into its rear end; the upstairs neighbor's bath running; and then later, at 3 am, the howls and shrieks of the drunk and the mad 10 stories below." It was time to leave Manhattan. "We are poised for this move, can hardly wait."[50]

Before she moved, Norton released her second prose collection, *On Lies, Secrets, and Silence: Selected Prose 1966–1978,* the final book in her stellar decade of literary achievement.[51] Many of the essays were originally book reviews or lectures. Some focus on specific female authors, such as "The Tensions of Anne Bradstreet," "Jane Eyre: The Temptations of a Motherless Woman," "Anne Sexton: 1928–1974," and "Vesuvius at Home: The Power of Emily Dickinson." Other essays—"It Is the Lesbian in Us . . ." and "The Meaning of Our Love for Women Is What We Have Constantly to Expand"—promote community and mutual acceptance among women. The education of women provides a theme for "Toward a Woman-Centered University," "Claiming an Education," and "Taking Women Students Seriously." The two most personally revealing are "When We Dead Awaken: Writing as Re-Vision," which concerns her development as a poet, and "Women and Honor: Some Notes on Lying," which obliquely comments on the dissolution of her relationship with Engler. "The concluding essay, "Disloyal to Civilization: Feminism, Racism, Gynephobia," is a meditation on race and feminism.

She enjoyed being a public figure when it served as a means to her ideological ends. Woe to those, however, she believed were using her name or her words to advance agendas of their own. Those individuals had to decide what to do when they enraged this famous woman they admired. Ignoring the wrath of her former professor, Joyce Greenberg published her personal essay about Rich in 1979. Around the same time, an undergraduate at Wesleyan University named Jane Cooper also defied Rich. Cooper had read *Of Woman Born* and Rich's poetry with great admiration. With the support of her academic adviser, Gertrude

R. Hughes, she set out to compile an anthology of criticism of Rich's work. To solicit submissions to the book, she placed a query in *The New York Times Book Review.*

When Rich spotted the query, she assumed the student was pretending to be the poet Jane Cooper, a close friend of hers and a faculty member at Sarah Lawrence College, as a way to increase her submission pool. Young Jane Cooper had not known of the elder Cooper's existence. Hughes tried to intervene and explain the coincidence of the names, but Rich was not to be jollied out of her ill humor.

Always hovering in the wings, Rich's old friend Donald Hall accepted Cooper's book for publication in the University of Michigan Press's "Under Discussion" series. Rich was royally displeased and let Hall know it. In his reply, he defended the young anthologist and said he considered her "absolutely sincere, absolutely moral." He didn't think "J. R. Cooper," as he delicately identified her, was trying to make her name off Rich's own.[52]

In Cooper's recollection, Hall was "very reassuring" as the book moved toward publication. Meanwhile, she had to grapple with the knowledge that Rich could not abide her. "I was twenty, and I was devastated."[53] When Rich read at Wesleyan, Cooper introduced herself and they shook hands, but there was no détente in the offing. *Reading Adrienne Rich: Reviews and Re-Visions, 1951–81,* was published a year after Cooper graduated from college. The cover identified her by her full name—Jane Roberta Cooper—to distinguish her from Rich's friend.

By the summer of 1979, Cliff had quit her job at Norton. She and Rich were ensconced in their new home far from the Upper West Side. In those early months, Rich was thoroughly pleased. She told Nicholson and Ellenberger she "felt no shadow of grief, maybe some anger, but no lingering regrets" about leaving New York. "It feels natural to be here, I know I can do my work here, I know I need what this place can give me in order to do that work."[54]

She had a history of anthropomorphizing the places where she lived. She adored Cambridge during her Radcliffe years. She and Alfred had found common ground in their shared love of its cultured, clubby world. Then, feeling they had outgrown the very things about it they most appreciated, they indignantly turned against it. After moving to Manhattan, they looked back on Cambridge, hardly believing they had ever been happy there.

Now, Adrienne and Michelle were repeating that pattern. Michelle was a New Yorker as much as she was a Jamaican, and in their early days as a couple, she didn't want to leave the city. But when she and Adrienne made a brief trip back to New York a few months after their move, she did not enjoy herself at all. Upon her return to western Massachusetts, Cliff wrote, "I don't wonder Emily Dickinson stayed put."[55]

That first summer in Montague, Rich told herself she had done the right thing. Her letters echoed what she had written to Hayden Carruth in the summer of 1970, after she moved to a small furnished apartment of her own. Just as she had done when she wrenched herself away from her husband and children on Central Park West, she was again setting up a new household, a new life, in hopes of revivifying her autonomous spirit and doing the work, the writing, she felt called to do.

It took courage to make the move. But for all her expressions of delight in her new home, the memories that Manhattan held for her could not be forgotten. She did not want to forget. There might be rending and revising, but she was not one for erasing.

# CHAPTER 19

# MY TRUE UNIVERSITY

## *1979–1981*

Adrienne Rich's five years in Montague, Massachusetts, began in joy and ended in resignation. Convinced rural New England would provide the tranquillity she craved, she turned her back on New York as if it were yet another old friend she could no longer stand. She was sick of the crime and noise, the nastiness everywhere. And with so many successful books to her name, being in Manhattan no longer felt crucial to her status as a writer. Surely she could shrug off the cape of the Upper West Side and still fly high in the worlds that mattered to her. She would find out. With Michelle by her side, Adrienne said good-bye to Manhattan with a parting scowl rather than a handkerchief wet with tears.

By July of 1979, the lovers were in residence at 9 Main Street,* in Montague. Their new home was a large brick house built in the 1830s, when the little town was a thriving place with lots of shops and small industries.[1] The house was painted red and the property came with a red barn. In full nesting mode, Rich and Cliff set up their typewriters in separate studies, planted a vegetable garden, stripped the old wallpaper, and painted the walls. Adrienne contemplated her past and the future, and pronounced herself satisfied.[2]

Just as she had predicted, she was able to get work done in her new home. It was there that she wrote many of the poems in *A Wild Patience Has Taken Me This Far: Poems 1978–1981*, and most of the essays in *Blood,*

---

* After the fire department renumbered the houses, the house number became 45.

*Bread, and Poetry: Selected Prose 1979–1985*. *The Fact of a Doorframe: Poems Selected and New, 1950–1984* also grew out of this period. She wrote "Sources," her lengthy autobiographical sequence poem, over a period spanning August 1981 through August 1982; Hayeck Press published it as a chapbook in 1983. Although she had written "Compulsory Heterosexuality and Lesbian Existence" in 1978, it wasn't published in the journal *Signs* until 1980 and therefore became an important topic of academic discussion during her Montague years.

All the while, she continued traveling the country, giving readings and lectures and teaching workshops. Since Boston was less than two hours away, she was once again a vital presence there, and she lectured and participated in conferences at the colleges near her new home. Following the 1979 publication of *On Lies, Secrets, and Silence: Selected Prose 1966–1978*, she went on a lecture tour in England in October 1980. Her participation on the world stage continued with a trip to Nicaragua in 1983. As if all this activity was not enough, from 1981 to 1983, she and Michelle edited and published *Sinister Wisdom*, a lesbian literary journal. They produced eight issues of the journal, a project that consumed much more time than they'd expected.

Rich's complete commitment to feminism propelled her forward, as *The Observer*'s Sara Maitland noted during Rich's tour of England: "Her energy, freed from attention to men, flows towards women in an abundance that is almost overwhelming."[3]

Behind the scenes, however, Rich was struggling. At age fifty in 1979, she had suffered from rheumatoid arthritis for nearly three decades, and her knees were deteriorating. She had both of them replaced, the left in 1980 and the right (for the second time) in 1982. The surgeries helped considerably, but the harsh, snowy climate of her new hometown aggravated the disease and depressed her. She craved warmth and sunshine, and both were in short supply as the nights lengthened. When daylight saving time ended, dusk swept in by the middle of the afternoon. The winter winds raked across her aching limbs; her new home's icy walkway glittered with treacherous intent. One year, there was snow on the ground in May.[4] She had traded the noise and rank odors of the Manhattan sidewalks for a silent town green and an ice-tipped moon. It was a calm, quiet environment, but there were times when she was lonely.

A large lesbian population lived in western Massachusetts, with

Smith College in Northampton as a focal point. Rich was an eminent presence in the region, but she didn't find the utopian community of lesbian sisterhood she seems to have imagined for herself and Cliff. Soon after she settled in, she sniffed change in the lesbian feminist winds and didn't like the sandalwood aroma. She was concerned that women were turning inward, getting distracted by New Age pabulum, and working toward personal fulfillment rather than thinking about the greater good. After Reagan was elected president in 1980, she knew feminists, lesbian and otherwise, needed to stay vigilant, not turn on one another, and do whatever they could to keep the tenuous ground they had gained during the previous decade. If only all the different factions of the women's movement—divided by race, religion, social class, sexual identity, and thoughts on (of all things) sadomasochistic sex—could find a way to work together, the movement could keep moving. It was a very big if. Rich could exhort and proclaim, but she couldn't run the whole show.

That first summer, before she knew what she and the women's movement were in for, Montague felt as cozy and quaint to her as a log-cabin quilt. Her dark eyes gleamed; her mouth curved into the familiar elfin smile. She had a vision in mind of an idyllic life, just as she'd had in her early days in Cambridge and later in Manhattan, and she believed her crush on Montague could grow into something more. In a letter to her old friend and prep school teacher Margareta Faissler, she cheerfully described the "beautiful, backwater village, tiny really," with its post office, church, and the "red-brown stone Victorian building which comprises town hall and library." A sign announcing MONTAGUE in large letters, a relic of the old railroad station, hung on the barn. Looking out the window on her way to the bathroom every morning, she knew "most definitely I am here."[5]

Here, she believed, was a place she could love. Writing to Susan Griffin that fall, she exulted in the sensuous beauty all around her: "The suddenness of cold air after sunset, the mists lit with purple in the valley, torrential rains, great mildness, apple-laden trees, the gardens blazing with pumpkins, diffuse moonlight behind haze, purplish hydrangeas and lavender daisies everywhere. The gold and red leaves on bright-green grass. And the urgencies of winter coming on."[6]

Like Thoreau, whose essays and journals were part of her literary DNA, she craved direct contact with the earth and seasons. Being among those late-blooming hydrangeas and beholding the mist and rain made her feel truly alive and connected to the planet she lived on. That kind of bond had been harder to come by in New York, no matter how closely she watched the weather outside her high windows or took in the elements when she was able to take the long walks she loved. It was in part to preserve her intimate relationship with the rugged countryside that she had kept the family home in West Barnet even after Conrad's death.

Now, in Montague, she dug in and prepared for winter. She and Cliff acquired a Swedish woodstove for their dining room, and she wrote happily to friends about the two and a half cords of wood piled behind their barn. Their next step was to hire a chimney sweep. The man arrived wearing a top hat, an old-fashioned touch in keeping with his trade. When he glimpsed the poster of Virginia Woolf in Michelle's study, he remarked, "I knew someone who used to know her: she drowned, didn't she?"[7] It was that sort of sublime moment of recognition that made Rich feel she had chosen the right place to live.

She and Cliff had been together three years when they moved to New England. They were literary comrades as well as lovers. When they became editors of *Sinister Wisdom,* they shared in all the major decisions related to the magazine. They also talked about their individual projects. Adrienne did much of her writing in her first-floor study looking out on the street, where passersby could see her at her desk, but she and Michelle met throughout the day to trade notes. Rich described this dimension of their relationship in a poem called "Culture and Anarchy" in *A Wild Patience Has Taken Me This Far.* She writes, "Rough drafts we share, each reading / her own page over the other's shoulder / trying to see afresh."[8]

Michelle was just as opinionated as Adrienne was, and she challenged Adrienne on race and a myriad of other topics in ways few others besides Audre Lorde and June Jordan would have dared. Adrienne could take it—she always wanted "to see afresh"—but their deep talks could be wearying. In "The Spirit of Place," a long poem from the Montague years dedicated to Cliff, she wrote of taking a drive in the springtime and noticing the ferns and the sound of spring peepers "while we talk yet again / of dark and light, of blackness, whiteness, numbness / rammed through the heart like a stake."[9] They were both angry at the world.

Their emotional discussions nevertheless felt necessary during these years when Rich was continuing to scrutinize race and sexuality. She praised Michelle for delving into the very subjects that could pitch them into states of fury and numb grief. "She is, for me, an incomparable life-mate and challenge," she wrote to Faissler. "She's so tough-minded and uncompromising, yet so full of generosity and tenderness, spirited ideals and practical earthy instincts."[10]

Michelle gave her endless, heartfelt conversation along with the life-long commitment Lilly had been unwilling to provide. It helped that Michelle's views on how women should relate to one another were similar to hers. In the first issue of *Sinister Wisdom* that they coedited, Cliff's portion of their introduction is revelatory: "We need to allow ourselves complexity in our feelings toward each other. We need to admit our anger as well as our love for each other. But we must avoid endangering our emotions with oversimplification. This is a time for us in which we are beginning to face issues which are complicated but which will bring us, through our efforts, into another place on the lesbian/feminist continuum."[11]

They were a resolutely out couple, and an interracial one. That was important to Adrienne on both counts. After her tormented experience with Lilly, she was not willing to hide her lesbian identity, and her involvement with a woman of color seemed to be a "badge of honor," in the words of one friend.[12]

At times during those years, the lovers appeared to be the picture of domestic bliss. Adrienne's friend Maureen Brady recalled Adrienne sitting in a chair, with Michelle on the floor beside her. With disarming frequency, the two women turned to each other and said, "I love you."[13] Victoria Redel, a young writer who volunteered to help the couple with *Sinister Wisdom*, noticed that Cliff was very gentle with Rich and protective of her health. She saw, further, that the couple shared an irreverent sense of humor and Michelle especially could be "wickedly funny." Redel admired their "incredibly gorgeous" home, which was full of books, art, and cozy places to read. "The vibe in the house was warm, loving, and romantic. They totally dug each other."[14]

Their friend Janice Raymond saw the relationship differently. She had the impression the two women had a good, caring relationship but not one of great passion: "I never felt that Michelle was the love of Adrienne's life. Adrienne's great love was the woman of the 'Twenty-One Love Poems.'"[15]

But if true, Rich was working hard to get past her old feelings for Engler and strengthen her relationship with Cliff. When she traveled, she made a point of calling home frequently, and she not only told her out-of-town friends how much she loved Cliff; she also let them know she was in a physical relationship. Although her disability must have made it uncomfortable at times, sex was important to her and she continued to write about it, just as she had during her marriage to Conrad. In her long sequence, "Contradictions: Tracking Poems"—a Montague-era poem she published in *Your Native Land, Your Life: Poems* (1986)—she wrote explicitly of lesbian lovemaking: "My mouth hovers across your breasts / in the short grey winter afternoon / in this bed," the poem begins. A few lines later, Rich writes of "your fingers / exact" and "my tongue exact at the same moment."[16]

Life in Montague wasn't all candles and afternoon sex. Michelle had a book of prose poems accepted for publication, and she wanted to devote herself to writing, but she needed a steady income. She had taught a short course on women artists at Hampshire College and was teaching freshman rhetoric at the University of Massachusetts Amherst during the spring of 1980.[17] These were temporary, part-time jobs, and Cliff was worried about money. During her first spring in Montague, however, she caught an unusual break: A California research company contacted her and asked if she would measure precipitation at the house. For a tiny amount of work, she would be paid handsomely. She wrote joyfully to Tillie Olsen that she would earn $5,400 merely for gathering rain. In combination with freelance projects, she told Olsen, she would be fine financially and have the time for her writing that she had craved for a long time.[18]

Later in 1980, Persephone Press, a feminist press in Watertown, Massachusetts, published Cliff's first book, *Claiming an Identity They Taught Me to Despise*. The book exposed conflicts within Cliff's family regarding racial passing. It seems more than coincidental that her mother soon disowned her. Living openly as a lesbian, exposing the wounds of her fractured identity, and disavowing the constrictions she had endured well into adulthood, Michelle had unwittingly traded away her family.[19] Her mother and sister disapproved of her for being a lesbian and showed no interest in getting to know Adrienne. Cliff blamed herself for the break with them and bore the burden of what she later called "internalized homophobia."[20] Her desire to identify as a woman of color, even though many people assumed she was white, was a big piece of what her family objected to.

Adrienne admired Michelle for facing her struggles head-on and was pleased when she began seeing a therapist. They were alike in their determination to understand their own lives, but they also had to accept the accompanying loss of connection with those who didn't appreciate what they said.[21] In the quietness of their home, sometimes they turned on each other. Eventually, they began seeing a counselor in Boston for couples therapy.

One of the problems in their relationship defied an easy fix. Ironically, it had everything to do with the qualities that made Adrienne alluring: her brilliance and her prominence in the overlapping areas of literature, feminism, and academia. When the couple went to dinners and awards ceremonies where Adrienne was the guest of honor, Michelle was barely acknowledged. She was a writer, too, but many of their acquaintances saw her only as Adrienne Rich's lover. Even in their own home, Adrienne was the reluctant star of dinner parties.

A resentful Michelle didn't like feeling invisible. She eventually stopped going to most of the functions where Adrienne was honored, but she couldn't bow out of social gatherings at their home, nor did she want to. There were times when the couple's dinner parties went very well, but on occasion, Michelle behaved childishly. Janice Raymond saw how things played out: "I had the sense that it must have been very difficult for Michelle to know that visitors came mostly to see and talk with Adrienne and not with her. This seemed to translate into a psychological tension where one person (Michelle) claimed attention, and where the other (Adrienne) bent over backwards to provide it. There were also times I witnessed in visiting, where Adrienne would make a point in conversation, and Michelle would disparage it."[22]

Adrienne didn't try to police Michelle, at least not when others were present. She was used to her partner's combative style and caustic ways. Since both of them drank heavily, she may not have noticed the degree of discomfort Michelle caused their guests or she may have forgotten it in a tipsy fog. And Michelle didn't always misbehave. When she was happy and at ease, she amused guests with her acerbic wit and won them over with her derisive commentary on movies. She was, as the saying goes, a handful—they both were. Their friends sometimes wondered if Cliff and Rich would last as a couple, but the two took their problems to therapists and teetered onward.

While she tried to maintain a strong relationship with Michelle, Adrienne didn't seem to realize there was another distressed woman who had been standing in her shadow, this one for a lifetime: her sister, Cynthia Rich. After Adrienne moved to Montague, Cynthia came for a visit, which didn't go well. She later wrote to Adrienne that she could no longer bear the burden or expectation of sisterhood. Still, she was open to a friendship based on shared interests and mutual respect. If Adrienne and Michelle wanted to socialize with her and Barbara, perhaps the two couples could start fresh and enjoy one another's company.*

The pronouncement blindsided Adrienne. In a letter to Susan Griffin the spring after Cynthia visited her, she cast herself in the role of the aggrieved one and said she had made an effort to see her sister and work out a truce. She had little idea why Cynthia was unhappy with their relationship but wanted to reach some kind of resolution with her.[23] Many years later, Cynthia didn't recall receiving any response from Adrienne to her letter. Maybe Adrienne had responded—or maybe she just wanted to believe she had. In any case, Cynthia was the one calling the shots, and Adrienne didn't like it one bit.

At that point in her life, Cynthia could not look back on her childhood without getting furious. She deeply resented the years she had been schooled at home and thus denied the company of elementary school teachers and young playmates who might have offered a warm alternative to the weird dynamic she experienced at home. She was aware Adrienne had suffered greatly under their father's unreasonable

---

* In retrospect, Cynthia commented on the notion of starting over as friends with Adrienne: "At a time when women were radically redefining all kinds of relationship, that didn't seem outlandish. However, I think I knew even then that it would never work." Cynthia Rich, email message to author, Dec. 1, 2018.

expectations, but at least the prized firstborn was seen and acknowledged in ways Cynthia felt she never was.

In the past, when Cynthia brought up the inequity with her mother, she had received peculiar answers. Helen said she and Arnold gave their older daughter more attention so Adrienne would not be jealous of Cynthia's greater beauty. Other times, she said World War II was such a distraction that she and Arnold simply lost track of Cynthia—never mind that the favoritism was firmly in place before the war began and did not let up after it ended.[24]

Cynthia had no patience with either of these feeble rationalizations. "To me, family was a disaster in which I bonded with everybody and nobody bonded with me. Nobody was there for me and I barely survived it," she wrote to her mother a few years after trying to get Adrienne to hear her out. "I have great respect for [Adrienne] and wish her nothing but good (as long as it's not at my expense). If we find ourselves together for whatever reason, I'm sure we'd both be considerate and pleasant to each other. My heart has been broken by Adrienne, but not recently."[25]

Adrienne wasn't quite through with her sister. After Cynthia and Barbara Macdonald moved to New Hampshire, she visited them one afternoon. The conversation the sisters had that day didn't feel meaningful to Cynthia. Many years later, she said, "I think I assumed Adrienne wanted to come to address the letter, indicate some shift."[26] By now, Adrienne and Michelle were deep into *Sinister Wisdom,* which required endless correspondence and secretarial work. Not long after her trip to New Hampshire, Adrienne followed up with a brief note to Cynthia, warning her against collaborating on a project with her partner because, as Cynthia recalled the advice, Adrienne "had seen other women do that at the cost of their relationship." In fact, Cynthia and Barbara had written a collection of essays together, *Look Me in the Eye: Old Women, Aging and Ageism,* which would come out in 1983 from Spinsters Ink, a lesbian feminist press run by Maureen Brady and Judith McDaniel, a lesbian couple with whom both Adrienne and Cynthia were friends. Collaborating on the book had not doomed Cynthia's relationship with Barbara.

To her credit, Adrienne had acknowledged Cynthia and Barbara in the first issue of *Sinister Wisdom* that she and Michelle coedited.[27] It was a small but significant way of showing she did, in fact, value them. But the sisters' lives would no longer intersect. Adrienne's visit with Cynthia in New Hampshire in the early 1980s was the last time the sisters saw each other.[28] They traded a couple of notes and had occasional phone conversations, mostly in regard to their mother: That was all. Friends learned not to bring up Adrienne's name with Cynthia or Cynthia's with Adrienne.

Adrienne had to live with the estrangement from her sister and accept the unlikelihood of a meaningful conversation with her mother, who remained impervious to soul-searching. She had been angry with Helen for a long time, and went through periods when she wanted nothing to do with her. (To Griffin she had once confided that as an adult she had only truly lost her temper once with her mother. On that occasion, she was fueled with brandy, which evidently gave Helen an excuse for not taking the outburst seriously.[29]) She watched Michelle's relationships with her own mother and sister fall apart. The irony was staggering. They were two lesbian feminists who passionately believed in the importance of women living and working in harmony, but neither could have a valuable exchange with her mother or sister.

Adrienne struggled to get along with some of her lesbian friends, as well. During her first year in Montague, she got caught up in a mess involving a feminist journal called *Chrysalis*. She was close to the editors, Susan Rennie and Kirsten Grimstad, who had comforted her during the terrible time after she and Lilly ended their relationship. She had helped them brainstorm when they were planning *Chrysalis* and suggested they call it a magazine of women's culture so its contents could go beyond the arts. When Rennie and Grimstad moved to California, she donated three thousand dollars to help them launch the publication there.[30]

Starting with its inaugural issue in 1977, she had been a contributing editor, along with many others. Audre Lorde was poetry editor. Rich's essay "Disloyal to Civilization: Feminism, Racism, and Gynephobia" originally appeared in *Chrysalis;* this was the long essay about race relations that Lorde had sharply critiqued and Barbara Smith also helped her think through. Other leading feminists involved with the magazine included Mary Daly, Robin Morgan, Judy Chicago, and Marge Piercy.

Then plans were made for a special issue on women's poetry, and trouble ensued. In her examination of previous issues of the magazine, Lorde saw racism in the way Rennie and Grimstad printed poems by women of color, including a poem by June Jordan, a contributing editor, in the journal's pages. She expected them to handle things differently in the special issue.

Rich was slow to jump into this particular fray. Her politic approach aggravated Lorde, and when Lorde was upset, so was she. Eventually, Rich wrote a long letter to the editors, announcing her negative verdict. Rennie and Grimstad were shocked. They thought of her as a dear friend and ally. But Rich had had it with them and with *Chrysalis*.[31] Many years later, when they ran into her at a restaurant, she offered a perfunctory greeting. There was to be no forgiving, and no one had forgotten. Rennie and Grimstad felt the sting of the lost friendship all over again.[32]

Other friendships unraveled during Rich's time in Montague. For quite a while, she delighted in the company of Brady and McDaniel, the women behind the feminist press Spinsters Ink. A writer and physical therapist, Brady was awestruck when she heard Rich read from *Of Woman Born* in New York not long after its publication in 1976. After Brady and McDaniel, a literary scholar, became a couple, they began socializing with Adrienne and Michelle on a regular basis.

The two couples visited in Montague and at Brady and McDaniel's farmhouse in upstate New York. Drinking steadily, the four women talked late into the night. In Brady's recollection, Rich drank scotch before dinner and wine as the evening wore on. During her early visits to Montague, when it was finally time for bed, Brady lay awake listening to the bells ring on the hour and half hour at the Congregational church nearby. Tossing wakefully, she knew everyone in the house would have a hangover the next morning, but she expected Adrienne would pick up the thread of the previous night's discussion and continue it with dazzling new insights.[33]

The women's conversations ranged from high-minded debates about feminist politics to gossip about "the power women of the movement" who they thought had fallen short in one way or another. It seems Rich couldn't resist mocking and making fun of her famous peers, including Mary Daly, who Lorde had decided was the personification of white women's racism. "We'd reverse the motto—the personal is political—and study the inverse: 'the political is personal,' and wind up dissecting Mary's personal life insofar as we knew it," Brady recalled. "I didn't like setting my imagination to work on Mary's personal triumphs or failures, but neither did I want to check the hilarity of my mates as they made up scenarios and screeched with laughter."[34]

Because Brady suffered the lingering effects of a bad car accident, she and Adrienne commiserated on the subject of chronic pain. She advised Adrienne on proper care of her aching joints. At one point, Adrienne suggested they write a book together about arthritis and pain management: She would give her personal account and Brady would provide the medical perspective. Brady did not take her up on the intriguing proposal. Rich told Brady she didn't want to be defined by her disability, but she was beginning to mention her pain in her poems. It was part of who she was and how she experienced the world; to leave it out no longer made sense to her.

The two women also discussed the bafflement they felt when lesbians promoted sadomasochistic sex as a way to act out their fantasies—a hot topic in those years. They couldn't understand why anyone would court pain. And in their observation, women who professed to enjoy violent sex had no empathy for those who were in pain all the time. "Women like us were derided for having 'vanilla sex' with some contempt," Brady observed, "and we took personal offense at that, feeling our pain was being discounted, made into a form of stimulation, rather than the constant drain it was."[35]

Later on, after she had knee replacement surgery, Rich stayed for a week at Brady and McDaniel's home. They cooked and cared for her, and Brady spent hours each day helping her with physical therapy. Rich's correspondence reveals how grateful she was to them, especially Brady.[36]

The close friendship began to fray when McDaniel decided to quit drinking. After Adrienne and Michelle found out about this development, Michelle called and asked McDaniel to serve as her sponsor and help her get sober, too. But in Brady's recollection, it was too early in McDaniel's recovery for her to assist anyone else struggling with the addiction. Later, Brady also gave up drinking. When she told Adrienne she took comfort in the simplistic slogans she heard at support meetings, Adrienne's face reflected her disdain; she couldn't stand what she took to be the self-absorption and solipsism of New Age philosophies.

"I know she was trying to listen," Brady noted, "but her eyes glazed over and gazed away from mine. She seemed to be sitting on her hands to avoid making judgments, but I felt a wall of ice go up between us."[37]

Perhaps there was more to her response than a scornful reaction to sayings like "One day at a time." Brady wondered whether Rich felt threatened by her decision (and McDaniel's) to stop drinking, since alcohol had been integral to their shared social life. She also wondered whether her crumbling relationship with McDaniel posed a threat to Rich's hope of a lifetime with Cliff. Both Brady and McDaniel had indulged in affairs and would soon part ways.

Brady was on to something. When Rich learned that her friend Susan Wood-Thompson (now Susan Robinson), a scholar and writer who contributed work to *Sinister Wisdom,* and her partner, Betty Bird, had parted ways, she drove to McDaniel and Brady's home in a panic. Word got back to Wood-Thompson that Rich said she was afraid that if a partnership as seemingly solid as Wood-Thompson's with Bird could end, no lesbian relationship was safe.[38]

Whatever the primary cause of her fear or mistrust, Rich dropped Brady and McDaniel after they split up. In response to a letter from Brady in search of closure to their friendship, Rich responded with a one-two punch of nostalgic longing for their old days of camaraderie and a harsh critique of a short story Brady had published. Rich thought Brady's portrayal of a relationship ending had hewed too close to real life and didn't rise to the level of art. Brady was hurt by her words and shot back an angry reply that ended things once and for all.[39]

Friends in her inner circle, such as the biographer Blanche Wiesen Cook, saw a pattern in Rich's behavior.[40] She was willing to give her time, thought, and money—to say nothing of the glorious heft of her name—to her friends' various causes. She was exceptionally generous in that way. But when someone angered or disappointed her or just wore her out, she cut ties, often with little warning. It was not always obvious to those she spurned that she often did so as a matter of self-protection.

She was aware a great many women looked to her for guidance, courage, and tangible support, including book blurbs and letters of recommendation, which required a heavy investment of her time. It was the rare literary friend who hadn't benefited in some important way from her largesse. But she was neither a saint nor a superwoman, and she wouldn't pretend otherwise. She had to bow out every once in a while. She wrote to Tillie Olsen that there were times when she felt overwhelmed with everything she had taken on. As someone who could command the public's attention, she took her responsibility very seriously, but the stress was wearing her out.[41] This was a hint that she, too, suffered greatly when her friendships went awry.

That was certainly the case whenever she and Lorde were on the outs. Rich would do virtually anything for Lorde, as the *Chrysalis* episode illustrates, but a collaborative writing project that involved Rich interviewing her was almost more than their friendship could bear. Commissioned by the poet Marilyn Hacker for a book called *Woman Poet: The East*, the interview at Rich's home in Montague gave Lorde the floor, but Rich came up with the questions and was heavily involved in the editing process. Their correspondence indicates Lorde pushed back mightily during the time they were communicating about the written version of the interview.

Somehow, the two women came to a meeting of the minds. Part of the interview appeared in the book Hacker edited. A fuller version was published in *Signs* in 1981 and reprinted three years later in Lorde's *Sister Outsider: Essays and Speeches*. The longer version begins with Rich asking Lorde to talk about her childhood and her development as a poet. Lorde does most of the talking. But in the second half, the interview turns into an intensely personal conversation, a hashing out of differences. Important as it was to them, this exchange also modeled the way two lesbian feminists, one black and one white, could communicate with as much candor as they could muster.

At one point in the interview, Lorde announced she had "a lot of pieces of conversations" in her head with Rich, which she then wrote in her journal and viewed as occurring "in a space of Black woman/white woman where it's beyond Adrienne and Audre." Those mental conversations grew out of the "different pitfalls," as Lorde put it, the two of them encountered in actual life:

AUDRE: I've never forgotten the impatience in your voice that time on the telephone, when you said, "It's not enough to say to me that you intuit it." Do you remember? I will never forget that. Even at the same time that I understood what you meant, I felt a total wipeout of my modus, my way of perceiving and formulating.

ADRIENNE: Yes, but it's not a wipeout of your modus. Because I don't think my modus [is] unintuitive, right? And one of the crosses I've borne all my life is being told that I'm rational, logical, cool—I am not cool, and I'm not rational and logical in that icy sense. But there's a way in which, trying to translate from your experience to mine, I do need to hear chapter and verse from time to time. I'm afraid of it all slipping away into: "Ah, yes, I understand you." You remember, that telephone conversation was in connection with the essay I was writing on feminism and racism.[*] I was trying to say to you, don't let's let this evolve into "You don't understand me" or "I can't understand you" or "Yes, of course we understand each other because we love each other." That's bullshit. So if I ask for documentation, it's because I take seriously the spaces between us that difference has created, that racism has created. There are times when I simply cannot assume that I know what you know, unless you show me what you mean.[42]

For anyone who might never have encountered it in so raw a form, this was honest dialogue, and it wasn't easy or reassuring to read. The exchange showed how much Lorde and Rich thought about every single conversation they had, every piece of information transmitted back and forth. Viewing their friendship as a template for interracial dialogue raised the stakes for them considerably, something the interview cast in bold relief.

In talking about misfires and miscues, Rich revealed a few very interesting things about herself. She said she'd been told all her life she was "rational, logical, cool." As an emotionally volatile child, she was hardly a candidate for those labels at 14 Edgevale Road. Perhaps there had been a hint of that assessment in Auden's introduction to *A Change of World* and in early reviews of her poetry, but in more recent years she had been widely praised for her courage and passion. Most likely, she was thinking of her adversaries within and outside the movement who knew she could be judgmental and cool, even cold, at times—

---

[*] "Disloyal to Civilization: Feminism, Racism, and Gynephobia," collected in *On Lies, Secrets, and Silence.*

and people did talk. In any case, the accuracy of the description came through as she confessed that she often resisted Lorde's perceptions:

> They can be very painful to me. Perceptions about what goes on between us, what goes on between Black and white people, what goes on between Black and white women. So, it's not that I can just accept your perceptions unblinkingly. Some of them are very hard for me. But I don't want to deny them. I know I can't afford to. I may have to take a long hard look and say, "Is this something I can use? What do I do with this?"[43]

For Rich, everything was always material for her education and, by extension, her writing. Although she was sincere in trying to get past her admitted racism and other long-internalized biases, there remained something stubbornly colonialist about her. Just as she had decades ago when reading James Baldwin with more skepticism than she would want to admit these days,[*] she looked at her brilliant black lesbian friend Audre Lorde as source material, someone whose ideas and insights she might cherry-pick for her own use. For make no mistake: Writing is a blood sport, and if Rich got hold of a powerful idea she could use, she would pause to give credit and then run with it and make it her own.

The poet and scholar Elana Dykewomon, who became editor of *Sinister Wisdom* a few years after Rich and Cliff gave it up, said of Rich, "She was in a very uncomfortable position as an antihierarchal person placed in a very hierarchal position because of her talent."[44] But sometimes people felt uncomfortable around her because a very hierarchal person lurked just behind her antihierarchal mask and could peek out at any moment. Put another way, she was one part Frederick Douglass and two parts William Lloyd Garrison. Speaking out for equal rights didn't mean she wanted to cede her power and authority, even to someone she loved and respected as much as Audre Lorde.

---

[*] In a June 17, 1968, letter to Hayden Carruth, Rich wrote dismissively of Baldwin. She said she had not reread his early essays or his first novel, *Go Tell It on the Mountain* (1953), which she had found instructive five years earlier, and did not like his recent fiction. She later came around to being a strong proponent of Baldwin's writing.

Yet given the opportunity to take the stage on her own, no one could tell the truth about power more selflessly or eloquently than she could. When she read in Coolidge Auditorium at the Library of Congress in April 1981, the crowd was so large that some people had to sit in a separate room and watch the event on a monitor. In her introductory remarks, the Library of Congress's poetry consultant, Maxine Kumin, said, "We could have filled a football stadium with people who sought tickets to this event."

In the recording of her performance, Rich sounds delighted. There were few things she loved more than the chance to share her vision with a large, receptive audience. Except for the time spent in solitude writing at her desk, this was when she was doing what she knew she was put on Earth to do. She declared, "I write as a woman, as a lesbian, and as a feminist. I make no claim to be universal, neuter, or androgynous"—a remark that drew appreciative laughter.

As she worked her way toward "Power," the first poem she would read that evening, she spoke with passion of the large body of literature, including magazines and documentary histories, growing out of and invigorating the women's movement: "Probably never has a political movement gestated so vital a literature, and it is still growing. It is this literature, both the old, which has been and is being re-found, and the new, by women fifteen and twenty years younger than me, and also the new by women fifteen and twenty years older than me, which fires my blood and urges me on, gives me what I need to do my work—challenge, goad, inspiration."

She described the mingled triumph and bitterness of coming out on the other side of a patriarchal, racist education that devalued women and people of color at every turn: "In the process of unlearning the lies, breaking the silences, unlocking the taboos, I had finally and miraculously a political movement of women as my true university."

With that extraordinary statement ringing in the air, she acknowledged the role of Kumin in bringing her to speak at the Library of Congress along with "hundreds of women whose work, thinking, activism, imagination, militancy have taught me courage and spurred me to risk." This was the generosity on which Rich staked her reputation as a leader; she knew it would be unfair to the others working for the cause if she soaked up all the attention by herself. "I wanted to say all this because the impulse toward tokenizing, toward selecting some one of us, or a couple of us, to make visible is profound in patriarchy. And because the white fathers have always consolidated their power by allowing a few token women visibility."[45] Then she read "Power," the poem that in its closing lines seemed to point a finger right at her:

She died    a famous woman    denying
her wounds
denying
her wounds    came    from the same source as her power[46]

This poem, this occasion, was Rich in all her complicated glory. She spoke openly about the harm tokenism does to women, both those invited inside the male circles of power and the countless others excluded. But she loved her power. It was the reward she had lived for as a young child sitting at her desk writing a long play called "Suicide." If she could survive her childhood and devote every waking minute to making herself a writer worthy of renown, she would not have lived in vain. Standing before the crowd in her nation's capital, she figuratively extended her hands to the masses while rising above them at the same time. She knew her power came from the same source as her wounds. That was different from what the poem said, and it was that knowledge that pushed her ever onward. She would selectively expose her wounds and vulnerabilities as a means of consolidating her own power as a writer and leader. Picking her way through the minefields of her past and present life, she continuously asked herself, *What do I do with this? Is this something I can use?*

# CHAPTER 20

# ANGER AND TENDERNESS

*1981–1984*

In the fall of 1981, Rich published *A Wild Patience Has Taken Me This Far.* Her previous collection, *The Dream of a Common Language,* marked the transition from Lilly to Michelle. This new book was written with Michelle in her life from first page to last. For a poet who found so much to say about her complicated marriage to a man who committed suicide and her brief, tumultuous affair with Engler, the assumed permanence and relative stability of her relationship with Michelle presented a literary problem. She paid tribute to Cliff in "The Spirit of Place," as she had in "Transcendental Etude" at the end of *The Dream of a Common Language,* and she would continue to publish occasional love poems for her and meditations, sometimes enclosed within sequence poems, about their life together. But she had to be careful not to go too far. Michelle had her own stories to tell and was known for being a very private person. Bits of her life story come out in her own books and in a handful of interviews, but she was not a public figure the way Adrienne was, nor did she want to be. No doubt Rich took this into consideration as she wrote. She looked elsewhere for poetic material and found it in her vexed relationships with other people, some alive but no longer in her life and others who were deceased ancestors or historical figures. It does not seem too great a leap to say some of these poems were subtle, associative commentaries on the complexity of her relationship with Michelle, the person with whom she most wanted to connect.

As the poems "For Memory" and "Rift" reveal, Rich continued to do battle in her head with individuals with whom she was no longer on speaking terms. In "For Memory," she holds out hope for reconciliation with an unidentified but evidently very angry person, who could be her sister or a former lover or an amalgamation of the two: "I can't know what you know / unless you tell me / there are gashes in our understandings / of this world."[1] In "Rift," she sounds less hopeful: "When language fails us, when we fail each other / there is no exorcism. The hurt continues."[2]

These poems are the pained, at times beautiful by-product of her difficulty in maintaining the nurturing bonds that meant the world to her. Rich could not summon the words to fix all her broken relationships, but she had the language for poems describing the deprivation. Likewise, in "Mother-in-Law" and "Grandmothers," the communication is on the page, with herself and her readers, rather than with family members she did not particularly like. The same is true of "Heroines," addressed to white female abolitionists of the nineteenth century whose "partial vision" she could neither commend nor entirely discount.[3] In the late 1960s and into the 1970s, Rich had written with searing honesty about the problems of trying to talk to men. In *A Wild Patience,* she tacitly acknowledged the equally hard task of talking to women.

During the months leading up to her new book's publication in October 1981, she kept up her usual steady pace of traveling to college campuses to read and discuss her work. Her readings at Memphis State University (now the University of Memphis) and Delta State College (now Delta State University) were especially important to her, because she wanted to go into the Deep South and explore Mississippi, where her maternal ancestors were from. Her host at Delta State was a young English professor, Terry Everett, who loved her poetry and included Rich on the syllabus for his world literature class. In the weeks that preceded her visit, the class pored over her poems, and other students and faculty also prepared for a much-anticipated event.

On a bitterly cold February day in 1981, Everett met Rich in Memphis and drove her to Cleveland, Mississippi. Still weighing the possibilities that lesbian separatism offered her and other radical feminists, she nevertheless took an immediate liking to her friendly and accommodating host, who had agreed to take her sightseeing. When she discovered they could take a different route back to Memphis that evening, her response showed how excited she was about the trip and how comfortable she was with Everett. As he wrote in a magazine article about her visit, "She said that she was a person who liked to have it both ways when possible and asked if we could not come back the other way."[4]

Her energy and enthusiasm belied the disability that she could never escape. Before her afternoon reading, a Delta State student overheard her in the women's restroom exclaiming in pain, presumably due to her arthritis. When she appeared onstage, another student, Leigh Allen, was struck by her diminutive size and aged appearance. When Rich's cane fell to the floor, Allen remembered, the poet said sardonically that "it didn't want to be with her and she didn't want to be with it, either."[5]

A recording of her reading shows Rich dressed in a purple turtleneck sweater and dark pants, her hair cut short and her eyes bright. She does not appear to be in discomfort. Her distinctive voice sounds a little more southern than usual, perhaps in unconscious accord with her audience.

By way of introduction, she discussed her desire to "reclaim" her southern heritage, "which is, in fact, four grandparents, all of whom were Southerners, two parents who were Southerners, and a whole background, a whole mythology, some of which I tried to shrug off or lay aside as I was growing up and escaped into the world of New England, a world which had stood for me and stood often in the legendary mythology of having some innate moral superiority"—a superiority she no longer believed in.

With these opening remarks, she let it be known she had not come to condescend or valorize. Among the poems she read were "Hunger," "To a Woman Dead in Her Forties," and "Power," all from The Dream of a Common Language, and "Grandmothers," from A Wild Patience Has Taken Me This Far. After the reading, she took questions from the audience. A man's truculent inquiry explained why there were times she wanted to address only women. He asked whether the revolutionary empowerment of women she advocated could be accomplished "without physical violence." Modeling the "wild patience" she knew she needed on occasions like this, she refused to let him get away with implying that women, not men, were the real threat to peace and order:

Physical violence is going on right now. An inordinate amount of physical violence is going on right now. And I always feel astonished, really, at questions like that, because they suggest that we're living in a pacific world, in a pacific society. This is a totally violent society, and I'm speaking both locally about America, U.S., and I'm talking about our global society. And [that] there is global violence against women every day is a banal fact of life. There is imperialist violence. There is economic violence; there is medical violence against all kinds of people. I feel as if a response to that might be, what can be done about the violence through which we are now living?

And I think your question probably comes from some fear that there is suddenly going to be amazon brigades marching with castration tools or something like that. I think if we really seriously think about what has been going on, what has been perpetrated in a society ruled by men and mostly by white men, that this looks absurd. It just feels to me like a fantasy projection. And I really think it has to be examined as such.

We're living amid violence. Women are just beginning to feel that we have the right to resist. We are even just beginning to name the violence that's being done to us, in terms of things like rape, woman-beating, incest, child abuse, the seizure of our uteruses. I mean, that's the only answer I can give you. I'm forced to concentrate on the violence that already is. I wish I weren't. I would very much prefer to be in the situation where I could draw breath and contemplate some other blueprint.[6]

She was able to compartmentalize her anger, which did not affect the rest of a successful and memorable event. Allen, for one, came away filled with awe. Too shy to ask Rich to sign a book on that occasion, she spent the coming years following Rich's career and studying subjects discussed in her poems and essays. At a much later reading, she worked up the courage to request an autograph. She asked whether Rich remembered Terry Everett—and Rich did. But it was that first reading that made an indelible impression. Like many others hearing Rich for the first time, Allen recalled the experience as transformative.[7]

Everett and a colleague drove Adrienne back to Memphis in a borrowed car. She happily joined in as they traded quotations back and forth from the poetry of William Carlos Williams. At her request, they stopped in Ruleville so she could see the hometown of the civil rights activist Fannie Lou Hamer. She bought a pick—a comb—as a memento to give June Jordan, whose poem about Hamer she admired.[8]

Everett's adrenaline was flagging as the much-anticipated day wound down, but his prized guest was still in high spirits. She seemed unfazed when they made a wrong turn and then Everett's colleague mistakenly turned on the air conditioner instead of the defroster and caused their obstructed view to disappear altogether.

She had told Everett about "the most frightening incident in her life," when "two would-be rapists" pursued her and Michelle on a back road in Massachusetts.* With that story in mind, a tense Everett was afraid something bad would happen on the drive back to Memphis. The whole experience became strangely dreamlike as Rich remained unperturbed: "The poet's arthritic body melted into the darkness, and the soft round face seemed to grow younger, glowing with energy, illuminating the darkness. The bright mind ran on."[9]

Rich found her brief time in the Deep South immensely interesting and relevant to her further reflections on her southern ancestors. She later told her friend Mab Segrest, a lesbian writer in North Carolina and editor of *Feminary,* a southern feminist journal Rich admired, that she was trying to make sense of the ambivalence toward the South her father had instilled in her. "I was brought up to believe that the Confederacy was noble and elegant, but also with Southern self-hatred. I had to go to Radcliffe, but my father talked mockingly of 'that cow-college in New England.' (Jewish pride and self-hatred compiled with Southern pride & self-hatred is quite a mix.)"[10]

Over a period of three decades, she had evolved from a formalist poet attempting to see the world through a man's eyes to a self-consciously female poet seeing with a woman's eyes to a subversive token weighing the viability of androgyny. From there, she emerged as a lesbian and then declared herself a white lesbian of privilege trying to

---

* She documents this encounter in "The Spirit of Place," *CP,* 554.

understand women whose race, ethnicity, and social class did not match her own. By the early 1980s, she was deep into an exploration of her identity as the descendant of southerners, both Protestant and Jewish.

Of the two sides, her Jewish ancestry caught and held her imagination. Her relationship with her deceased father had actually taken a turn for the better. Maureen Brady recalled Adrienne's attitude toward the once-despised Arnold Rich as "fairly adoring" at the time.[11] Dead for more than a decade, he was easier to deal with than her living relatives.

Her living relatives, of course, included her three sons. Rich's correspondence makes it clear how much she loved them. They were in frequent contact with her, and she was delighted they were emotionally close to one another. But in an interview with a Canadian feminist publication called *Broadside,* she described them with unnerving objectivity. She said they were now "full grown, adult, white males whom I am very fond of and like very, very much; about whose feminism or pro-feminism I would not swear an oath on any account."

David, Pablo, and Jacob Conrad could not help that they were white men, but their mother nevertheless wanted them to recognize their advantages in life: "They are, I think, fundamentally decent people but have yet to understand, if they ever do, what their gender and skin color does for them. I don't think they can realize the doors that are open, the assumptions that are made, the privilege that goes with that."[12] Her sons had to be held just as accountable as everyone else; she insisted on it. Perhaps it was only fair, but such remarks made her sound cold.

Cold or not, Rich spoke her whole truth. She was not going to "tell it slant," as Emily Dickinson advised;[13] that was not her way. During her tour of England, she told *The Observer,* "It would interest me if I saw men, as groups or individuals, really being able to take the risks that women are taking, have taken, not just on our own behalf but on behalf of every movement against oppression, through all history. Men can be pro-feminist—usually they're involved with women who are strong feminists and, in order to have such relationships, they have to radicalize their politics. I'm perfectly willing to grant exceptions, but I don't think that's the point."[14]

Her searing directness sometimes alienated her audiences. During a lecture at North Texas State University, she told a group of students, male and female, they lived in a "woman-hating culture" and that popular media debased women. Most of the men reportedly left before she finished.[15] They weren't interested in what a furious lesbian feminist poet from New England had to say, and she wasn't interested in figuring out how to gain and hold the attention of students whose life experience was vastly different from her own.

During the Reagan era, hosting Rich on campus had the look of a bold stroke, and some schools courted her precisely because of her lesbian feminist politics. That seems to have been the case when Cornell University chose her as an Andrew D. White Professor-at-Large for a six-year term. There were faculty members who recognized the vital contribution she could make to campus conversations. One person involved in her selection indicated Rich's status as an out lesbian had worked in her favor.[16] Given that the job offered her a great deal of flexibility in the timing and brief length of her campus visits, Rich was happy to accept the prestigious appointment.[*]

In the spring of 1982, she titled her Cornell workshop "What Do We Mean When We Say We?" She allowed one man, a professor of African-American history, to be in an otherwise all-female class. Her description for the course read, in part: "Discussion on Difference in the Women's Movement. False Universals. Identity politics: grounding ourselves in recognition and understanding of our particular cultures and backgrounds, how assimilation affects perspective. How did we learn fear of difference and from whom?"[17]

The question was a profound one that reverberated in her life. Around the same time she was teaching her class at Cornell, Stanford's Center for Research on Women sponsored a conference titled "Women Writing Poetry in America." Among the speakers were Audre Lorde, Alicia Ostriker, Kathleen Fraser, Judy Grahn, Carolyn Kizer, and Denise Levertov, who taught at Stanford. A panel on "The Lesbian Writer" sparked some controversy. According to Levertov's biographer Donna Krolik Hollenberg, "The discussion heated up when, in response to the claim that heterosexual sex is 'oppressive,' an idea then current in some lesbian feminist circles, Denise objected from the audience: 'There are many women who love having sex with men, who think this is natural. The [lesbians] are angry at being told that their predilections are not

---

[*] Citing health problems, she resigned from her position at Cornell, which had begun in July 1981, before her six-year term ended.

natural. So okay. Why should they oppress other women by taking that attitude toward *them?*'"[18]

Whether it was lesbians debating sadomasochistic sex or straight women arguing with lesbians who had little use for heterosexual feminists, sex was getting in the way of the women's movement. Levertov was not the first to wonder why some lesbian feminists were hostile toward heterosexual feminists. But straight women did not have to endure the extra layer of misogynistic scrutiny applied to lesbians, and lesbians could tell when heterosexual women were uncomfortable around them, even if they didn't openly condemn lesbians as the "lavender menace," as Betty Friedan famously had. Further, radical lesbian feminists had a woman-centered vision of the future, and some did not believe straight women capable of joining them in making such a vision a reality. Maybe their skepticism was justified, but the reverse discrimination within the movement was as divisive in its own way as Friedan's homophobia.

As infighting signaled grave trouble within the mainstream women's movement, Rich began to look for other sources of political fulfillment. In that spirit, also in 1982, she wrote what was to be one of her most personal and frequently quoted essays, "Split at the Root: An Essay on Jewish Identity," for a collection of prose and poetry called *Nice Jewish Girls: A Lesbian Anthology,* edited by Evelyn Torton Beck, a women's studies scholar and Holocaust survivor. Other contributors included Irena Klepfisz, Elana Dykewomon, and Melanie Kaye/Kantrowitz, all of whom Rich published in *Sinister Wisdom.* Rich participated in public readings promoting *Nice Jewish Girls* and made it obvious to Beck she was deeply invested in the book.[19]

In her essay, unusual for her in that it is wholly autobiographical, she wrote about the difficulties of reckoning with her Jewish identity as the daughter of an assimilated Jewish man and Gentile mother. To write the essay, she declared, she would "have to claim my father, for I have my Jewishness from him and not from my gentile mother, and I have to break his silence, his taboos, in order to claim him. I have in a sense to expose him." She also would "have to face the sources and the flickering presence of my own ambivalence as a Jew; the daily, mundane anti-Semitisms of my entire life."[20]

She was doing exactly what Cliff had done in *Claiming an Identity*

*They Taught Me to Despise.* Cliff was the woman of color whose parents expected her to pass as white; Rich was the self-described *"Mischling, first-degree,"* now stepping forward as a Jew,[21] whose parents had schooled her in virtually everything except faith in general and Judaism in particular. Although she professed bafflement as to why the "question of Jewish identity" had begun to consume her the previous year, in 1981, it's hard to imagine Cliff's explorations (published in 1980) weren't influencing her own. In any event, Rich didn't point her readers in that direction. Instead, she cited "Readings of History," a 1960 poem in *Snapshots of a Daughter-in-Law,* in which she had written of herself: "Split at the root, neither Gentile nor Jew, / Yankee nor Rebel."[22] She said her questions about her Jewish identity had begun in the early 1960s.[23]

In the 1980s, a decade when Jewish feminists were organizing on their own and through local chapters of a national group called New Jewish Agenda, Rich was part of a groundswell of activism, just as she was when she announced herself as a feminist and later as a lesbian. She portrayed herself as an assimilated Jew who knew practically nothing about Judaism as a child, was shocked by the Holocaust and the realization as a teenager that she was no different from the Jews who were gassed to death, learned about the culture and traditions from Jewish friends in college, and then married an assimilated Jewish man. As she did when discussing racism, she candidly admitted old prejudices were part of who she was or at least who she used to be and revealed that while she and her husband had shared some of the traditions of Judaism with their sons, she had not discussed the Holocaust with them. She ended the essay by saying it represented beginnings for her rather than any definitive conclusion.

*Nice Jewish Girls* found a receptive audience and sold more than ten thousand copies its first year in print.[24] Its readership went beyond Jews and gay and lesbian readers. According to Beck, "In those years, the juxtaposition of 'Nice Jewish Girls' with 'lesbian' was such a shock and an anomaly that it held its own interest (and perhaps curiosity) to many. People used to ask, 'There are many?'" In an intriguing development across religious faiths, Beck learned that *Nice Jewish Girls* inspired the 1985 anthology *Lesbian Nuns: Breaking Silence.*[25]

The popularity of *Nice Jewish Girls* led to the formation of Jewish lesbian activist groups, including one called Di Vilde Chayes (Yiddish for "the wild beasts"), made up mostly of contributors to the anthology. Rich was one of seven members of Di Vilde Chayes spread out over a wide area who met periodically for a couple of years to discuss anti-Semitism within the women's movement and provide support for one another.[26] Di Vilde Chayes met at least once at Rich and Cliff's home in Montague. During the day, they discussed business matters; in the evenings, they relaxed by playing music and dancing. Adrienne's arthritis prevented her from dancing, but Beck recalled that "she loved watching and seemed to become part of our dancing as she swayed to the music."[27]

Di Vilde Chayes offered just the sort of brainy, contentious stew of politics, sexuality, and social justice issues that Rich loved, and it primed her to become further involved in Jewish feminism. Yet Beck sensed some trepidation. "When we were first embarking on Di Vilde Chayes and explorations of Jewish identity, and I said that I was scared of where it might take us," Beck recalled, "she said something to the effect that of course any such major shift in one's work had to be frightening. I think she herself was probably wondering how coming out as a Jew might affect her, where it might take her, but she never said this specifically." It was evident to Beck, however, that Di Vilde Chayes was very important to Rich.[28]

Rich went to Portland to read her poetry at Reed College early in 1982. Judith Barrington, a young poet she had met at a women's studies conference and with whom she corresponded, had offered to host her because she knew Adrienne needed quiet and privacy away from campus. When Barrington picked her up at the airport, she was shocked to see the poet making her way from the plane to the terminal in a wheelchair.

Barrington's partner, Ruth Gundle, recalled, "We were not teetotalers, but it did surprise us how much Adrienne drank. She carried a little flask with her." Before her campus reading, she invited Gundle and Barrington to share a drink with her in a coatroom. Adrienne drank rye whiskey from her flask, but in Gundle's recollection she did not appear intoxicated when she was onstage.[29]

At Barrington and Gundle's urging, Adrienne went to see a chiropractor friend of theirs during her visit. The chiropractor told her she should move to a warmer climate to preserve her health.[30] The value of cutting back on red meat and alcohol also came up in their conversations, and Adrienne took the advice to heart. An inveterate reader of cookbooks, known among friends for her appreciation of good food, she began experimenting with a healthier diet and massage therapy, both of which helped her feel better.[31] Rich's correspondence indicates she spent time in San Francisco during March 1982 and found a massage therapist who helped her tremendously. While on the West Coast, she also experimented with a raw foods diet and swam in a heated pool.[32] She was trying to take better care of herself. As she anticipated her second knee surgery in two years—a replacement of the 1966 prosthesis in her right knee—she continued getting massages once she returned home. She had begun to see there were things she could do to ease her pain that didn't involve medication.

That summer, she began telling friends, including Audre Lorde and Tillie Olsen, that she and Michelle missed being close to a city. Later, she went so far as to admit to Olsen that she loved New York "as much as ever" but couldn't handle living there.[33] California beckoned, and Rich and Cliff had Oakland in mind, probably due to its ethnic and racial diversity. A great deal was up in the air, including Michelle's West Coast job prospects, but when Scripps College offered Adrienne a monthlong teaching position, she welcomed the income and the chance to be in California; she added a speaking engagement at the University of California in Santa Cruz. She wrote Tillie Olsen that spending February 1983 at the women's college in Claremont would be "dull, probably, but good for my health."[34]

Her time in Claremont was not dull. She gave a brilliant lecture titled "Resisting Amnesia: History and Personal Life," which she would include in Blood, Bread, and Poetry. In the lengthy speech, she insisted on the vital importance of studying the past and making sure future generations had access to a history of women's lives and experiences that went beyond the mere recording of facts. "I would suggest that feminist history is history charged with meaning," she wrote. She exhorted women "to know the past in order to consider what we want to conserve and what we want not to repeat or continue."[35] And further, "This is one of the eroding effects of amnesia: we cannot build on what has been done before because we do not even know it is there to build on."[36]

As February drew to a close, she wrote Audre Lorde that she wanted to wrap up her class so her students would have plenty to think about. Certainly that was the case for anyone who had attended her lecture. She had not only met women who stimulated her thinking but also "touched on so many female worlds here (meaning California, not just Claremont)—so many forms of growth & stagnation." Intrigued, stimulated, in a climate that eased her arthritic pain, she felt much better than she had in Montague. "The SUN is HOT AND BURNING!" she announced happily to Lorde. "Spring is here—all the blossoms—I am sitting on the patio glider drinking it into my soon-to-be-shipped-back-to-New England bones."[37]

In July 1983, Rich was among two hundred intellectuals, half of whom were American, who gathered in Nicaragua for a cultural conference put together by a group of Sandinista rebels. Susan Sherman, a poet and founder of *IKON* magazine, had also been invited. She escorted Rich, who needed a traveling companion due to the hardship of her arthritis. The two poet-activists had known each other for a number of years through the women's movement. In Sherman's view, the trip to Nicaragua had a profound influence on Rich's worldview and subsequent writing. That observation is borne out in the essays "North American Tunnel Vision," "Blood, Bread, and Poetry: The Location of the Poet," and "Notes Toward a Politics of Location," all included in *Blood, Bread, and Poetry*—and all pointing to Nicaragua as an important touchstone in her evolving sense of herself as a North American poet with a global political sensibility.

While traveling around the country for a week, however, Rich had to concentrate on the immediate matters of safety and even survival. Much of her time during the day was spent in edifying meetings with Sandinista government leaders. But her off-hours proved hazardous. Sherman recalled that one night during their stay in the suburbs outside Managua, an earthquake struck. She hurriedly woke Rich and told her, "We've got to get outside." Although they were not harmed and the earthquake wasn't as bad as Sherman had feared, it was a traumatic night.[38]

On another occasion, Rich, Sherman, and Margaret Randall—a fellow activist and writer whose anthology of Cuban woman poets Rich greatly admired—traveled north on a side trip to the border with Honduras. Randall had organized the perilous excursion. In Randall's recollection, "The Contra war was in full swing, and the trip was not an easy one. Our small minivan or bus had a military escort, and I remember it was slow going, especially as we moved farther north and were more in danger of a possible ambush. Several of those who had signed up for that trip became quite fearful, perhaps wishing they had stayed in Managua. Adrienne provided a voice of commitment and sanity. She kept others calm. The experience couldn't have been easy for her, in light of the heat and danger and particularly because of her own disability, but her example went a long way toward keeping everyone in good spirits."[39]

Rich returned to Scripps College for another residency early in 1984. When she got home to Montague, she was met with a blizzard and word that a dear neighbor friend had died. She and Michelle decided to move to California, and on April 3, 1984, she wrote Tillie Olsen that there was a FOR SALE sign in their front yard.[40]

Their lovely, drafty old house had served its purpose as a place where she could work, but to further subject herself to winter in New England would be a violation of her body and soul. Moving away felt like a matter of survival. Twinklings of possibility made her feelings of resignation easier to bear. She would leave the little town, as she had left Manhattan, with more hope than regret. She would begin again in California, a place that had intrigued her for decades but had never felt, until now, like a place she might call home. Fueled by what she considered her defining traits of anger and tenderness, she would continue venturing out into the world even though the inner journey was the one she lived for. As she wrote in "Integrity,"

> but really I have nothing but myself
> to go by; nothing

stands in the realm of pure necessity
except what my hands can hold.

*Nothing but myself? . . . My selves.*
After so long, this answer.
As if I had always known
I steer the boat in, simply.
The motor dying on the pebbles
cicadas taking up the hum
dropped in the silence.

Anger and tenderness: my selves.
And now I can believe they breathe in me
as angels, not polarities.
Anger and tenderness: the spider's genius
to spin and weave in the same action
from her own body, anywhere—
even from a broken web.[41]

# CHAPTER 21

# WORDS THAT BLEW
# OUR LIVES APART

*1984–1990*

Moving to California was not a miracle cure, but it definitely improved the quality of Adrienne Rich's life. Gone were the long cold winters that plagued her body and soul; in came the Pacific warmth that eased her suffering and improved her mood. She and Cliff moved to 418 Frederick Street in Santa Cruz in time for the new academic year in 1984. Rich had been appointed Distinguished Visiting Professor at San Jose State University, and Cliff was working on a novel and piecing together teaching assignments at several different places. They chose Santa Cruz because Rich had enjoyed staying there during one of her extended visits to California, but they still planned to settle in Oakland.

Adrienne was fifty-five years old. She had endured physical pain for so long that any lessening of her arthritic symptoms felt like a new lease on life. With the help of health-care practitioners on both coasts, she had begun taking better care of herself. Basic things like massage therapy, a healthy diet, and exercise were making a real difference. These improvements, combined with a mild, sunny climate, were life-altering. She wrote to Audre Lorde that she was constantly struggling not to overdo it, now that she felt healthier and more energetic. In the company of younger, more physically vital friends, she had to pace herself and save her strength for writing.[1]

She was in the habit of retreating to Vermont when she needed long blocks of time to renew her strength. Now, though, she guarded her stamina every single day. To protect her writing time, she continued shedding people and projects that no longer engaged her. One of those projects was the fight against pornography. Before stepping away, she changed allegiances and stunned women who had counted on her for her support. Despite the astonishment and dismay of feminists whose prominence equaled hers, Adrienne held firm. It was not that she was suddenly "for" pornography. Rather, she had come to believe the attempts to quash it might imperil free expression by women, lesbians in particular. And in the context of her evolving thought at this time, it seems she had begun to feel, whether rightly or wrongly, that the anti-pornography movement was passé.

In 1985, the so-called "sex wars" heated up considerably when two of her friends, attorney Catharine MacKinnon, the driving force behind sexual harassment law, and Andrea Dworkin, the activist and author of *Pornography: Men Possessing Women*, began making inroads against pornography at the municipal level. According to the model ordinance MacKinnon and Dworkin drafted, pornography could be the basis for a civil suit alleging sex discrimination. Women harmed by a specific work could sue its producers and distributors in civil court. Minneapolis's city council passed the law, only to see it vetoed by the mayor. A similar law, also crafted by MacKinnon and Dworkin, passed in Indianapolis but was challenged by the American Booksellers Association, among other groups. A district court judge struck down the law as unconstitutional, but the city of Indianapolis appealed the decision to the Court of Appeals for the Seventh Circuit.

A group called the Feminist Anti-Censorship Taskforce (FACT), consisting mostly of women—many in academia, many of them lesbians—objected to the law in a "friend of the court" brief sent to the circuit court based in Chicago. The document warned against state control of pornography and the presumed censorship of material important to women. Survivors of sexual violence in which pornography played a significant role also submitted a "friend of the court" brief—in support of the ordinance.[2] In the end, to the satisfaction of those supporting the lengthy and opaquely worded FACT brief, the circuit court did not reverse the lower court's decision.

Rich and Cliff were among the prominent women who signed the

FACT brief.* Rich's name stood out from dozens of others because she had made a dramatic leap from one side of the debate to the other. Among the women shocked by her signature was Dorchen Leidholdt, a founding member of Women Against Pornography, who had read and loved Rich's books for years. Looking back, after nearly three decades as a feminist attorney, now running the largest legal services program in the country for survivors of gender-based violence, Leidholdt said that in signing the FACT brief, Rich had set back the entire women's movement, not just the antipornography coalition within it.[3] The gravity of that claim says a lot about the power and influence Rich wielded at that time. As for the members of FACT, who had sought her out, they were grateful for her support.[4]

When the radical feminist publication *off our backs* asked Rich to explain why she signed, she responded with an essay in which she said her "decision to sign was not a simple or hasty one."[5] She wasn't entirely sold on the FACT brief, which she felt put too much faith in the power of the First Amendment to protect women's freedom of expression, but she found the document otherwise persuasive. Some of her comments hewed closely to the brief itself; they showed how far she had come in accepting the adamantly held views of her sex-positive lesbian friends—what Leidholdt retrospectively deemed "group think."[6] For example, Rich favorably mentioned Joan Nestle's essay "My Mother Liked to Fuck" in her defense of signing the brief,[7] an indication Nestle was a key figure in bringing her to the other side of the debate. Rich had decided that laws intended to punish pornographers would harm women whose sexual desires fell outside the perceived norm. She believed such laws "would be used—with the same brazen complacency that allows an anti-abortion movement to name itself 'pro-life,' the same indecency that allows Reagan, on the day he visits the SS graves, to say 'I am a Jew'—by the most reactionary forces in the country."[8]

At the time, pornography already had begun its migration out of

---

* The women who signed the FACT brief included Rita Mae Brown, Cheryl L. Clarke, Jewelle Gomez, Judith McDaniel, Kate Millett, Joan Nestle, Minnie Bruce Pratt, Susan Sherman, and Barbara Smith. Among the notable feminists who did *not* sign: Susan Brownmiller, Mary Daly, Audre Lorde, Robin Morgan, Janice Raymond, and Gloria Steinem.

theaters and bookstores and into people's homes via videocassette. Anyone with a TV monitor and VCR could watch pornographic videos at home. In the not-too-distant future, the Internet would increase access to pornography beyond most people's wildest imaginings; children would be among the countless numbers viewing violent pornographic acts on personal computer screens. Even though she didn't know what the future held, Rich had come to believe pornography could not be stamped out. In a repressive political climate, furthermore, she feared the law MacKinnon and Dworkin were promoting would backfire. She surely had *Sinister Wisdom* and other lesbian-themed journals in mind when she wrote, "It would mean the loss of images, words, and information empowering to women, the loss of our counter-statements, the burial of the very dialogues we need to be having among our communities, in order to organize and act instead of collapsing in fragments."[9]*

According to Leidholdt, looking back many years later, Rich's concern "was groundless, since the ordinance was not a criminal statute that could be misused by the state but a civil rights law that opened the doors of the courts to harmed women in pursuit of justice."[10] The debate among feminists over pornography in general and the MacKinnon-Dworkin ordinance in particular succeeded in turning women against one another. In a letter published in the August–September 1985 issue of *off our backs*, Leidholdt, Mary Daly, Robin Morgan, and many other feminists vehemently objected to the FACT brief. The group wrote that FACT's authors and signatories had acted irresponsibly. Rich came in for special criticism: "Picture the next issue of *Playboy* with the headline 'Lesbian feminist poet Adrienne Rich defends women's access to pornography.'"[11]

The unfriendly spotlight would linger a while longer. In the October issue of *off our backs*, MacKinnon published an open letter to Rich. Like others whom Rich had spurned, MacKinnon was astonished to discover she had been cut off. "I wish you had responded to the letter Andrea [Dworkin] wrote you, or called me back like you said you would, after you signed the FACT brief," MacKinnon wrote. "I do not comprehend why you did not discuss your issues about our work against pornogra-

---

* By the early 1990s, Rich had joined an organization called Feminists for Free Expression as further proof of where her allegiances lay.

phy with Andrea or me, or seek out information like the Minneapolis transcripts, before you took a public position on something of such consequence."[12]

MacKinnon went on to challenge Rich's justifications for signing the brief. She pointed out the ordinance was a civil law, not a criminal one; it did not ban pornography but instead "defines a harm, like segregation in schools, and permits citizens to act against it."[13] Near the end of her letter, she wrote: "You say you know what subordination means, unlike the brief you signed. Unlike the brief you signed, you say the harm of pornography is real to you. Yet you still side with the status quo, with letting it go on, with doing nothing."[14]

Rich didn't answer MacKinnon's public rebuke, and the two internationally renowned feminists had no contact ever again. Looking back on her former ally's decision to sign the FACT brief, MacKinnon described it as "sickening" and "unthinkable." She acknowledged that Rich made "monumental" contributions to women in the years before she signed the FACT brief but said she could not stomach reading any of the books Rich published in subsequent years.[15]

Perhaps Rich had the dispute over pornography in mind when she wrote "For an Album," a poem published in *Time's Power: Poems 1985–1988*, her next volume of verse. It aptly conveys the drama and emotion that played out again and again in the women's movement:

Our story isn't a file of photographs
faces laughing under green leaves
or snowlit doorways, on the verge of driving
away, our story is not about women
victoriously perched on the one
sunny day of the conference,
nor lovers displaying love:

Our story is of moments
when even slow motion moved too fast
for the shutter of the camera:
words that blew our lives apart, like so,
eyes that cut and caught each other,
mime of the operating room
where gas and knives quote each other

moments before the telephone
starts ringing: our story is
how still we stood,
how fast.[16]

A glance, a signature, a phone call or an unreturned call—Rich knew this was the stuff of the movement as much as any image of solidarity. The "words that blew our lives apart" could foretell revelation or revolution—or both. With profound change comes upheaval, no matter whether that change is for good or ill. In the closing lines, standing fast can symbolize both immovable resolve and the swiftness of change. She had lived it: She knew.

⁂

By now, Rich was deeply alarmed by the direction in which the country was going under Ronald Reagan. She read with grave interest of right-wing groups in California and reassessed her responsibilities to the world and to herself. Corporate interests were gaining ground, while the social progress of the 1970s was imperiled. Recognizing this and pained by it, Rich craved new stimulation that would expand her sense of who she was and what she was meant to do with the rest of her life.

For fifteen years, that stimulation had come from the women's movement. But now, as second-wave feminism collapsed on itself, she looked outward and inward and realized the old synergy was no longer there. As a poet, she was in the business of creating personas and portraying her multiple "selves" in ways that were no less true for their changing nature. And so it was that she took off the mask of radical feminist that she had worn long and well and liberated herself from the women's liberation movement.

She did so because she had begun to question the basis for oppression. As she wrote to Mab Segrest, she no longer felt compelled to put her opposition to the oppression of women at the center of her ideology, though she knew that doing so had been essential to her and other feminists early in the women's movement.[17] She had not given up on feminism, but she could no longer countenance being identified primarily as a feminist. From now on, feminism would be a given in her life and her politics rather than her defining message.

She had made that clear in a lecture she gave at a feminist theory conference in Utrecht, Holland, in June 1984 and now strategically positioned as the final essay in *Blood, Bread, and Poetry: Selected Prose, 1979–1985*. In "Notes Toward a Politics of Location," she wanted it known that her politics were a work in progress, as was she. Addressing her European audience at the outset of the essay, she said that just a few years earlier, she would have spoken as a white American feminist "self-separated" from a violent, arrogant U.S. government and "quoting without second thought Virginia Woolf's statement in *Three Guineas* that 'as a woman I have no country. As a woman I want no country. As a woman my country is the whole world.'" But that was no longer accurate: "I come here with notes but without absolute conclusions. This is not a sign of loss of faith or hope. These notes are the marks of a struggle to keep moving, a struggle for accountability."[18]

Rich wrote that she was finding her way toward a new politics through a broader understanding of Marxism. Until recently, it had felt to her like a dead end for women because she considered the philosophy popularized by the New Left as narrow, overly certain, and resistant to reevaluation. But as she came to realize she, too, had been party to narrowness of thought and self-certitude, she could see what was right about the women's movement of the 1970s and what was terribly wrong with it: "[E]ven as we shrugged away Marx along with the academic Marxists and the sectarian Left, some of us, calling ourselves radical feminists, never meant anything less by women's liberation than the creation of a society without domination; we never meant less than the making of all relationships. The problem was that we did not know whom we meant when we said 'we.'"[19]

That was the crux of the matter for Rich. She wrote that the powerful books, speeches, and lectures by people of color, the poems of contemporary Cuban women, and her travels in Nicaragua had forced her to confront the self-presumed importance of her political identity as a middle-class white American. In Nicaragua, "a tiny impoverished country, in a four-year-old society dedicated to erasing poverty, under the hills of the Nicaragua-Honduras border," she had begun to realize she had to take responsibility for being part of the problem: "I could physically feel the weight of the United States of North America, its military forces, its vast appropriations of money, its mass media, at my back;

I could feel what it means, dissident or not, to be part of that raised boot of power, the cold shadow we cast everywhere to the south."[20] Equally burdened and empowered by this new, visceral understanding of herself and the country she and her fellow citizens had been taught since childhood was the greatest, most honorable place on Earth, she stepped into a new phase of her life as a responsible, responsive member of many concentric societies, no one more important than the next, all surrounding her breathing, pulsing human body. She was intent on knowing her place, so to speak, in ways that would forever alter the sense of entitlement that had enabled her to speak with extraordinary conviction throughout her most influential years as a radical feminist leader. In the name of a "society without domination," she was willing to give up power for the greater good.

From the standpoint of her career, it was very possibly a tactical error. She had opened so many minds and positively changed so many lives as a high-flying eagle of white American feminism. For countless readers, her woman-centered poems in *Diving into the Wreck* and *The Dream of a Common Language* inspired nothing short of awe. Along with her poetry, *Of Woman Born* and essays such as "Compulsory Heterosexuality and Lesbian Existence" had added range and considerable depth to the interdisciplinary field of women's studies and given scholars of lesbian identity and lesbian politics substantive arguments to build on or refute, as they pleased.[21] Rich, then, was a feminist heroine and lesbian icon. For many, that's who she always would be—and that was a lot.

But that was no longer who she wished or intended to be. Citing the contributions of black feminists "Gloria I. Joseph, Audre Lorde, Bernice Reagon, Michele Russell, Barbara Smith, June Jordan, to name a few of the most obvious," she argued in "Notes Toward a Politics of Location" that white feminists baffled or offended by black women's political writings made it obvious their "white feelings remain at the center." She would no longer allow that to be true of her: "Yes, I need to move outward from the base and center of my feelings, but with a corrective sense that my feelings are not *the* center of feminism."[22] Though she wasn't forsaking feminism, the morass of abstractions that the term embodied no longer served her vision of equality and inclusion the way it once had, if it ever had.

She understood what Ronald Reagan was doing and saw in a flash of self-abnegating genius a parallel in her recent past. She expressed it as a question she had evidently already answered: "Is there a connection between this state of mind—the Cold War mentality, the attribution of all our problems to an external enemy—and a form of feminism so focused on male evil and female victimization that it, too, allows for no differences among women, men, places, times, cultures, conditions, classes, movements? Living in the climate of an enormous either/or, we absorb some of it unless we actively take heed."[23]

Who would Adrienne Rich become now? Which one of the many selves she alluded to in "Integrity" would step to the fore? The answer had been in the works for a while, ever since she wrote "Split at the Root" for *Nice Jewish Girls* and began thinking of herself as a Jewish lesbian feminist. After decades of contemplating her Jewish ancestry and trying to make sense of the choices her tormented Jewish father and husband had made, she was ready to put this part of her identity front and center. Just as she had come out as a woman no longer hiding behind a male viewpoint in her poems and then as a lesbian unwilling to camouflage herself behind her married, heterosexual past, now she placed her surname, Rich, in the historical and cultural context it had telegraphed all along. This was how she was actively taking heed and embracing "both/and" rather than "either/or." In Hitler's formulation, her status as a *mischling*, a child of mixed Jewish and Gentile ancestry, didn't exclude her from persecution. Being both therefore meant being a Jew, even if Jewish law decreed that Jewishness was determined by the maternal line. Identifying publicly as a Jew was a way of putting herself in the line of fire yet again, but it also was a way of divesting herself of some, if not all, of the white privilege she chafed against. Her Jewish identity was "the thing itself and not the myth,"[24] and she would make sure people knew.

For it was always the Jew in her, even more than the woman, the lesbian, the radicalized mother, who yearned and needed to be heard and seen, no matter the consequences. The Jew in her was the child of Arnold Rich, from whom she had inherited an extraordinary intellectual capacity and practically superhuman energy that won out time and again over the formidable opponent of her physical pain. Being a Jew opened a new path of communication with her long-dead father. In a prose section of "Sources," soon to appear in *Your Native Land, Your Life: Poems* (1986), she addressed Arnold Rich directly and found a way to view him, at last, with compassion. She realized she had seen only the "power and arrogance of the male" in him and had overlooked "the suffering of the Jew" because he had hidden that from her: "It is only now, under a powerful, womanly lens, that I can decipher your suffering and deny no part of my own."[25]

She had made a Talmud out of her life, the multiple meanings of which demanded endless study, debate, and interpretation. When a biographer friend described her struggle to convey the life of her subject, Rich told her she might not be able to get the story exactly right, but she could get it "righter."[26] That was what Rich herself was doing as she came out again and again, endlessly writing and rewriting, righting and re-righting the truths of her own story, her life.

By 1985, she was a prominent member of New Jewish Agenda. Founded in 1980, it placed a strong emphasis on gay and lesbian rights, as evidenced by the selection of Rich's friend Irena Klepfisz, a lesbian poet-scholar, as its executive director. The elements of inclusion and collective action were central to its platform and no doubt inspired Rich to join. In her keynote speech at NJA's national convention in the summer of 1985, she traced the path that had led her home to her Jewish self:

> It is feminist politics—the efforts of women trying to work together as women across sexual, class, racial, ethnic, and other lines—that have pushed me to look at the starved Jew in myself; finally, to seek a path to that Jewishness still unsatisfied, still trying to define its true homeland, still untamed and unsuburbanized, still wandering in the wilderness.[27]

That starved Jew was a stark manifestation, as evocative as a Käthe Kollwitz etching, of what had been withheld from her in childhood. She had once written with heartbreaking bitterness that her parents never gave her the choice to be a Jew. But now she saw being a Jew not as a choice but as a wondrous, nonnegotiable truth that expanded her sense of shared purpose in preserving and fighting for all that was good in humanity. In her speech, she declared:

> We are women and men, *Mischlings* (of mixed parentage) and the sons and daughters of rabbis, Holocaust survivors, freedom fighters, teachers, middle- and working-class Jews. We are gay and straight and bisexual, older and younger, differently able and temporarily able-bodied; and we share an unquenched hope for the survival and sanity of the human community. Believing that no single people can survive being only for itself, we want a base from which to act on our hope.[28]

Rich was well received by progressive Jewish audiences. After she spoke at the University of California at Santa Barbara, the rabbi for the campus Hillel Foundation felt moved to write an essay for the student newspaper. "She spoke of the Holocaust, and of the fierce Zionist pioneer women, and of Yerushalayim . . . our name for Jerusalem," wrote Rabbi Steve Cohen, who knew and admired Rich's poetry. "My heart was bursting, to hear her speak so movingly of what is most important to me; but even more, out of the joy of watching a Jewish mother/sister stand up and powerfully bear witness to being Jewish."[29] Once again, Adrienne Rich was as an emblem of possibility.*

The year 1986 was a notable one for her. She published *Your Native Land, Your Life: Poems,* and her third book of prose, *Blood, Bread, and Poetry.* Norton issued a tenth-anniversary edition of *Of Woman Born.* And, after teaching for two years at San Jose State, she accepted a position at Stanford University. Her seven years as professor of English and feminist studies at Stanford gave her the financial security and health-insurance benefits she needed, along with the academic standing appropriate for someone of her renown.

---

* In 1988, Rich and Ruth Atkin launched *Gesher* (Hebrew for "bridge"), a Jewish feminist newsletter, and in 1990, Rich was one of seven women who founded *Bridges: A Journal for Jewish Feminists and Our Friends.*

In addition to "Sources," the long autobiographical poem drawing on Rich's historical and familial past, *Your Native Land, Your Life* included other poems, such as "North American Time," "Virginia 1906," "Upcountry," "Baltimore: A fragment from the Thirties," and "New York," that reveal a consuming preoccupation with place in relation to identity. In her jacket copy for the book, Rich wrote, "In these poems I have been trying to speak from, and of, and to, my country. To speak a different claim from those staked by the patriots of the world; to speak of the land itself, the cities, and of the imaginations that have dwelt here, at risk, unfree, assaulted, erased."

Also in 1986, she received the inaugural Ruth Lilly Poetry Prize of $25,000 for lifetime achievement. The prize was the largest cash award she had received, up to that point, for her writing.[30] The windfall was well timed, since it enabled her and Michelle to buy a home in Santa Cruz. They had to drive an hour and a half to get to the Bay Area, but Adrienne had decided she preferred the relaxed atmosphere of Santa Cruz to urban life in Oakland or San Francisco. It was easy to get around in Santa Cruz, a small city with a population under fifty thousand in her early years there. Located on Monterey Bay, it gave her whole new vistas to contemplate and write about, and it was very much a poetry town. For her first several years there, Lucille Clifton taught at the University of California, Santa Cruz, and became one of her good friends. William Everson also lived in Santa Cruz. Other notable local poets included Ellen Bass, Stephen Kessler, Gary Young, and Joseph Stroud. A couple of independent bookstores frequently hosted poetry readings, and Rich was likely to run into fellow poets and other writers during her regular visits. When she wanted to be around other poets, they were easy to find.

The house where she and Michelle would live the rest of their days was located at 2420 Paul Minnie Avenue. The unusual street name attracted inquiries from friends, including Donald Hall, who wanted to know who Paul Minnie was. In response, Adrienne explained that a pair of long-ago homesteaders, Paul and Minnie, had built a chicken ranch on the street—hence the name. Her own home was once a chicken ranch, before the property was subdivided and the house updated.[31]

Built in 1909, it is eighteen hundred square feet with a wraparound back deck. While Adrienne and Michelle lived there, it was painted green, with yellow trim. As in Montague, each of them had a study.

Michelle's opened onto the deck and had a skylight; Adrienne's was off the living room. Their bedroom was sparsely furnished, with a large bed, a dresser, and, for a while, a woodstove in the corner. At some point, they added a furnace, positioned awkwardly in a closetlike structure in the living room, and had the woodstove removed. They did little remodeling beyond the addition of kitchen counters topped with tile and, in the living room, an enormous wooden display case for books and art objects. Opposite the sitting area, they had another massive bookcase filled with books. The artwork on the walls included cover designs for their books, some that made it into print and some that did not. Michelle kept a vegetable garden in the backyard, and they gradually amassed a collection of succulents they kept in pots on the deck. The path leading around the house to the backyard was filled with cacti, which caught on people's clothes and scratched their legs. In the backyard, a plum tree flowered and bore fruit, and a tall hedge of bottle-brush shrubs screened most of the house from Paul Minnie Avenue.[32] It was an unassuming, modest residence for someone of Rich's stature, but she and Michelle were comfortable there, and its value rose with the stock market.

They liked the unpretentious neighborhood and got along well with their neighbors, who found them approachable and friendly. Robin Riviello and her family lived in the house behind theirs and shared a driveway with them; they had moved in around the same time as Rich and Cliff. Through mutual acquaintances, Riviello heard the writers weren't happy about living in close proximity to young children, but the two households soon developed a warm relationship.

Michelle especially made a point of getting to know Riviello's children and playing with them. A couple of times, she buried coins in the family's yard and presented the children with a handmade treasure hunt map burned at the edges to give it an aged, authentic look. The children became so fond of Michelle, they would call out to her to come over when they saw her in the driveway. On Halloween, Michelle greeted trick-or-treaters while wearing a hat that made it appear an arrow was sticking through her head.

Still, there were boundaries. The literary couple let their neighbors know they wrote every day from 9:00 a.m. to 3:00 p.m. and wanted to be left alone during that time, if at all possible. On one occasion, when Riviello had to rush a child to the doctor, Adrienne and Michelle agreed to tend to the other three Riviello children, all very young. In Riviello's recollection, the babysitting required about an hour of the couple's time. When she got back, Adrienne and Michelle said they couldn't help out like that again—it was more than they could take on.[33]

While Rich was teaching at San Jose State, a Stanford student named Sue Reinhold helped jump-start the effort to bring her to Palo Alto. One of a handful of feminist studies majors and a prominent student leader, she was introduced to Rich's writing by Diane Wood Middlebrook, a powerhouse English professor who would later publish her biography of Anne Sexton to great acclaim and controversy. Middlebrook's lecture on Rich and Virginia Woolf during Reinhold's freshman year had greatly impressed her. When she found out Rich was teaching not far away, she began talking with Middlebrook and others in the English department about bringing her to Stanford. Soon, the department invited Rich to campus and "really courted her," in Reinhold's recollection. When the star student had the opportunity to meet the famous poet, she was "quaking in my boots, meeting this legend." Yet inspiration struck: She brought up Muriel Rukeyser's poetry, and Rich was delighted to talk to her about the elder poet, whom Rich was intent on bringing back into the public eye.[34]

Rich was appointed professor of English and feminist studies at Stanford in 1986. But before she received the official offer, her old friend Albert Gelpi, chair of the English department, asked Denise Levertov how she would feel about having Adrienne as a colleague. Levertov was distinctly unenthusiastic. She didn't want to teach during the quarters when Rich was on campus and suggested Rich's public advocacy for lesbianism was "potentially not a good influence for young women eager to be good feminists." If college-age women were in thrall to Rich, they might "make sexual decisions for ideological reasons" and find themselves trapped in sexual identities that would be hard to escape. However, she knew Al and Barbara Gelpi were Catholics who fully accepted Rich and her views. She would neither condone nor stand in the way of Rich's appointment.[35]

Rich probably never knew Levertov had such strong reservations about her, nor did she know the politically conservative poet Dana

Gioia lobbied on her behalf for a major honor. In June 1987, she flew to the East Coast to accept the Brandeis Medal for the Creative Arts. The judges on the selection committee included Gioia, a New Formalist poet and corporate businessman, and Howard Moss, *The New Yorker*'s poetry editor, whom Rich didn't like.

Known for his lyric poems adhering to a rhyming, metrical style Rich had given up long ago, Gioia lobbied hard for her: "We were looking at lifetime achievement, and it just struck me that Rich was the most overwhelmingly deserving of it." Other judges, including Moss, weren't so sure, but Gioia prevailed and wrote the award citation. At the ceremony, Rich was "quite cordial to me," he recalled, though he assumed (correctly) that she didn't see him as an ally.[36]

Back at Stanford, Rich and Levertov were moving toward a détente. The campus connection and their mutual friendship with the Gelpis provided an opening. When *Your Native Land, Your Life* came out, a peacemaking Levertov made sure to express her admiration. She told Al Gelpi she saw a similarity between Rich's embrace of Judaism and her own belated acceptance of Christianity, the faith of her parents.[37]

Things were looking up in this long-idle friendship that meant a great deal to Rich, but she showed her own signs of hesitation and rivalry. In the poetry and poetics course she taught in the fall of 1987, she compiled a booklet of poems that students were required to purchase at a copy shop. The collection contained a marvelous array of mostly modern and contemporary poets but no Levertov.[38] In 1988, however, they traded confidences about family illness. Rich's eldest son, David, was ill, and Levertov's son, Nick, also had been seriously ill. After that, there was a warming trend. The two women got together on occasion and exchanged some friendly notes and letters.[39]

By the summer of 1988, David was recovering. Adrienne made plans to meet her sons in Vermont for Labor Day weekend and then go to Cambridge to celebrate her mother's ninetieth birthday. In the fall, she and Michelle co-taught a class at Stanford on women artists, including Virginia Woolf, Lillian Smith, Helen Keller, Frida Kahlo, and Billie Holiday. Rich very likely requested the co-teaching arrangement. Michelle had taught briefly at the University of California at Santa Cruz but was turned down for a tenure-track appointment. The rejection had embittered her.[40] With both of them at Stanford, they could share the commute, and Michelle could position herself for a permanent job at Stanford or somewhere else.

Like many prominent artists and scholars allowed to make their own schedules in exchange for the luster they brought to a college campus, Rich didn't teach every quarter, nor did she go out of her way to make herself available to students. In class, she was a focused, serious presence; her occasional acerbic zinger didn't necessarily register on everyone in the room. She wasn't looking to get to know her students the way she had early in her career when she taught in the MFA program at Columbia, but her thoughtful, if brief, comments on their papers showed she saw them as individuals.

Given the opportunity to teach feminism, she threw herself into the task and made sure her students read the small-press publications central to the movement in the 1960s and 1970s. She was determined to teach them important recent history they otherwise might never have known about. She also required them to reflect deeply on the prejudices that informed their judgments. For the children of affluent families, this was often the first time they had questioned their social advantages and privileges. In the class Reinhold took with Rich, about half of the fifteen or so students were lesbians. To her, it seemed Rich was putting everyone through "a good old-fashioned feminist consciousness raising." Her approach made for some difficult days. "A lot of people ended up crying in the class. We were doing very personal work. She was asking us to do some tough stuff—look at privilege, family origins, points of pain, points of vulnerability," Reinhold said.

The eminent professor, leaning on her cane as she arrived for class, remained a remote figure. Students who took her courses in hopes of getting to know her were disappointed. Instead, she insisted they get to know themselves. Reinhold wrote her final paper on "what I'm going to do, the tussle I was in, reaching for hyper-elite status." She saved the paper and drew strength from Rich's brief comment on it: "I believe you will invent the methods you need."[41]

The job at Stanford meant Rich had a commute of an hour each way on her teaching days. During the winter, sometimes it took longer when she got caught in heavy rain on Route 17. The sight of wrecked cars littering the highway unnerved her. To calm herself, she recited Yeats's "An Irish Airman Foresees His Death"—not because she thought she was going to die but "because the measure of the poem kept my hands on the wheel and kept me focused."[42]

Hard rain wasn't the only hazard of the drive. On October 17, 1989, she was among many thousands of people who experienced the Loma Prieta earthquake, which registered a magnitude of 6.9 on the Richter scale. When it rocked California a few minutes after 5:00 p.m., Rich was on the highway between Palo Alto and Santa Cruz. That put her perilously close to the epicenter, which was near Loma Prieta, the highest peak in the Santa Cruz Mountains, and about ten miles northeast of Santa Cruz. Her car slid, but she came through unscathed. In the aftermath, she had to take a different, longer route to Stanford. The change in circumstances meant she had little time for anything besides preparing for her classes,[43] but in the meantime, the disaster helped her realize how invested she was in the community and state she'd called home for five years.

The earthquake killed sixty-three people, injured thousands, and interrupted the World Series between the San Francisco Giants and the Oakland A's.[44] It wrecked Santa Cruz's downtown shopping area and killed three people at a coffee roaster next door to Bookshop Santa Cruz. In the lengthy period before the downtown was rebuilt, the bookstore and other businesses operated out of large tents. Rich made a point of patronizing "Book Tent Santa Cruz," as the store's jauntily altered sign read. She lined up to buy books along with her Santa Cruz friends and neighbors and later participated in readings in solidarity with the community.

While waiting in line at the book tent one day, she met Gary Young, Santa Cruz's first poet laureate. Someone nearby asked Young if he knew Rich, and when he said no, he learned she was standing right behind him. He introduced himself and asked if she would sign the book of hers that he was about to buy. After that, they became friends and sometimes read at the same events, including readings intended to unify the community after the earthquake.

Young remembered Rich as "really delightful, very quiet but very intense." Although she was capable of small talk, she avoided it whenever possible: "She was always ready to talk about deep issues and bigger pictures." Since he, too, suffered from rheumatoid arthritis, they often discussed new treatments becoming available and commiserated over the hardships of the affliction. There were times when he saw her at readings and she confided she was having a bad day. Although he didn't think of her as reclusive, he recognized it sometimes took enormous effort for her to be out in public. Her efforts to restore her health could not stave off bad flares of pain. It seemed to Young that many people in the community didn't realize how much physical suffering she endured.[45]

In 1989, Rich published *Time's Power: Poems 1985–1988*. It was her twelfth full-length volume of verse and, including her works of prose and chapbooks, her seventeenth book in thirty-eight years. She told Levertov that writing poems kept getting harder.[46] Nevertheless, she was averaging a new poetry collection every several years. The new book was dedicated to Michelle, whose presence in Adrienne's life was a continuing source of wonder and consternation. In "Love Poem," she describes her lover's green eyes, "fierce curls," and the "delicate / coffee-bushes" of her nude body. The poem, dated 1986, acknowledges her continuing sexual attraction mingled with an awareness of the differences in origin and perception—"dark blood under gold skin"— informing Michelle's restless vision of the world they shared. After a decade together, a new topic has infiltrated their conversations: "we're serious now / about death we talk to her / daily, as to a neighbor." Given that Adrienne was nearly twenty years older and her health was far from robust, they needed to talk about what would happen if she died and left Michelle a young widow. But the poem is not exactly about that. Instead, it implies they were beginning to accept the fact that both of them would die someday: death "has the keys / to this house if she must // she can sleep over."[47]

Michelle's other appearances in the volume reveal Adrienne's anxiety about their relationship. She was trying to find the poetry within their struggles, battles, and differences, just as she had during her marriage to Alf and later in her love affair with Lilly Engler. "I will not be the dreamer for whom / you are the only dream / I will not be your channel / I will wrestle you to the end / for our difference (as you have wrestled me)," she wrote in the fifth section of "Sleepwalking Next to Death," dated 1987. In the seventh section, the burden of living with another writer comes into full view: "Calmly you look over my shoulder at this page and say / *It's all about you None of this / tells my story.*" The lines expose the tensions in their household.

Adrienne had once described herself as a sleepwalker mindlessly fulfilling societal expectations in the early years of her marriage, and now, using the same metaphor, she feared she was overlooking something important in her life with Michelle. In the tenth section of "Sleepwalking," she writes with apprehension of the border patrol, which she would have encountered as a California resident traveling south to Mexico. It is not the actual guards she fears but, rather, "the sleepwalker in me" and "the loner in you."[48] Perhaps she worried this relationship was doomed, just like her marriage to Alf and her love affair with Lilly: She would miss some crucial piece of information, and the distance between her and her partner would become insurmountable. If the poems that Michelle inspired never achieved quite the same grandeur as "Twenty-One Love Poems," the sequence based on Rich's relationship with Engler, it was perhaps because the material for grandeur simply wasn't there. But this was the romance in her life that lasted. Her life with Michelle didn't dominate her poems, but when it surfaced, it reminded readers she was in an enduring lesbian relationship that shaped who she was and how she saw the world.

Rich became friends with some of her lesbian colleagues at Stanford, and these women saw trouble flaring at 2420 Paul Minnie Avenue, just as other friends had seen unrest in Montague. Interspersed among relaxed and happy gatherings were times when a hard-drinking Michelle picked fights with guests sharing a meal with her and Adrienne. Those women and their partners were not invited back. There were rumors that both Michelle and Adrienne had flirtations and affairs. On one occasion, Michelle confided to a Stanford colleague that she and Adrienne had an open relationship, the implication being that she was available if the woman wanted to pursue an affair.[49] Open or not, the relationship endured. If there was friction between them, if one or both of them drank too much, if there were romances on the side—none of it was a deal breaker.

In 1990, Michelle found an academic home on the other side of the country, at Trinity College in Hartford, Connecticut. She started out as a visiting lecturer and came back in 1992 and 1993 in that same capacity. Then, beginning in 1993–1994, she held an endowed position that required her to teach one semester every year. Her course offerings included creative writing seminars and classes on Virginia Woolf, historical fiction, and Caribbean literature.

She was well received at Trinity, a private liberal arts college a couple of hours north of New York City. Her department chair, Ron Thomas (who later became president of the University of Puget Sound), remembered her fondly. He was impressed by her output, including scholarly articles in addition to her novels and short stories, and considered her an excellent teacher. Of the colleague he came to know as a dear friend, Thomas said, "Michelle demonstrated a remarkable ability to bring to bear in the classroom her practice as a novelist and poet. She was able to attract young writers as a trusted and respected mentor and confidante, and invariably displayed a sharp wit and deep intelligence in her courses." According to Thomas, student evaluations indicated "Michelle never shrank from expressing strong convictions about social justice or asking for (and getting) a high level of performance" from them.[50]

Cliff's literary reputation was growing. In 1982, Norton had published the volume by the southern writer Lillian Smith that she edited, *The Winner Names the Age: A Collection of Writings.* She had published two books with small feminist presses and then risen in stature with *Abeng* (1985), *No Telephone to Heaven* (1987), and *Free Enterprise* (1993), novels issued by trade publishers. She gave guest readings and heard from scholars writing about her work. Although she was not destined to achieve her partner's level of fame, at least not in her lifetime, she had achieved noteworthy success as a writer and professor.

Thomas's impression was that Cliff deeply missed Rich when they were apart.[51] The couple got together in New York or Vermont when Rich's travels brought her East. When Cliff returned home to Santa Cruz, Rich wrote to Donald Hall that they resumed their shared life with ease.[52]

Rich met Frances Goldin, her future literary agent, at a dinner the night before a book awards ceremony in New York in the late 1980s. In Goldin's recollection, "We bonded, because we had similar politics, and we had wanted to meet each other for some time. And when the meeting was over, I said to her, 'Can I hug you?' And she said, 'It would be a pleasure.' And we hugged. And then I said, 'Well, if we can hug, can I kiss you? And she said, 'I would love to.' And we left, and that happened."

The hug and the kiss didn't quite seal the deal. Goldin said she pursued Rich for a couple of years in hopes of acquiring her as a client. When a poster of Rich appeared inside New York City buses as part of a promotion recognizing poets, Goldin sent her a photograph of the poster with a note saying, "Millions of people in New York know about you because you were on the bus this morning." Then a time came when Rich needed help deciding which of two British publishers she should choose for a book Norton had issued in the United States. She consulted with Goldin by phone, and after a successful resolution of the matter, Rich asked if Goldin would represent her next book. "And I said, 'Does night follow day?' "[53] She served as Rich's agent from then on.

Because they lived on opposite coasts and Rich liked to have everything in writing, most of their contact was by letter or email. Goldin liked her new client's poetry, which she considered accessible and politically relevant. The mother of two lesbian daughters, Goldin marched every year in New York City's Pride March in their honor. When she visited Adrienne and Michelle in Santa Cruz, the only time she saw them at their home, she thought they were a good couple. As Rich removed a casserole from the oven, Goldin was moved by the sight of her friend and client's gnarled hands. That was the image that kept coming to mind years later when she reminisced about the woman whom she represented for more than two decades.[54]

By now, major honors were coming Rich's way thick and fast. In 1989, she received the National Poetry Association's Award for Distinguished Service to the Art of Poetry as well as New York University's Elmer Holmes Bobst Award in Arts and Letters. From the late 1980s through the early 1990s, she received honorary doctorates from Brandeis, City College of New York, and Swarthmore—all schools where she had taught. Although she claimed the honorary degree from CCNY meant more to her than any other such honor, the one from Harvard University in 1990 was certainly significant. This, after all, was the school that had indelibly shaped her thinking and writing as an undergraduate and then caused her no end of irritation when she was a faculty wife expected to support her husband's career above all else. Rich had stayed in regular contact with people at Harvard throughout her career. She was a blunt critic at times, but the bridge of her relationship with her alma mater was one she took care not to burn. As much as she railed against the university practices and policies she found objectionable, Harvard was impossibly dear to her; it always would be part of who she was. By donating her papers to Harvard's Arthur and Elizabeth Schlesinger Library on the History of Women in America, she ensured, in effect, that she would always be in residence there.

Adrienne pushed on. The magnetic pull of each day drew her into the world. Work was everything. The requests for her assistance—from writers, editors, and activists—kept coming. Even if she no longer had the power she wielded when she was at the center of the women's rights movement from the early 1970s through the mid-1980s, her name still had enormous cachet. In the dusk of late middle age, she didn't write to win honors or awards; she did so because she still found truth in poetry. At a time when she viewed national politics as completely craven, she needed that truth more than ever. Questioning, seeking, clawing at the mysteries inside and all around her, she looked to the ocean, the sky, and the earth and then turned back to her desk. She was no sleepwalker. Woman, lesbian, Jew, poet, cripple—she conserved her strength, made time, and wrote.

CHAPTER 22

# CITIZEN POET

## *1991–1998*

In the May 1991 issue of *The Atlantic*, Dana Gioia published a widely read and controversial essay titled "Can Poetry Matter?" He indicted academia for creating a self-rewarding subculture of mediocre poets scrambling for tenure-track jobs. Although Gioia sympathized with anyone who wanted to live a middle-class life rather than suffer in near poverty while writing poems, he argued that English departments had bred countless so-so poets whose fame was limited to MFA classrooms and the college poetry-reading circuit. In his view, the funding agencies that subsidized poets added to a culture of entitlement. He pointed out that most general-interest publications had stopped publishing poems, and he felt the little magazines dedicated to poetry would be more interesting if they contained a miscellany of verse, fiction, and stringently honest book reviews. Further, he suggested that anthology editors were publishing teacher-poets of questionable talent in hopes those teachers would require students to buy the books. Still, he wrote, there were truly notable voices out there: "Adrienne Rich, for example, despite her often overbearing polemics, is a major poet by any standard."[1]

"Can poetry matter?" was not the sort of question Rich would ask, since nothing mattered to her more than poetry. But an existential question lurked just below the surface of Gioia's crisp prose: How long could Rich matter if her politics were woefully out of tune in a conservative age?

Rich disliked the New Formalist use of strict meter and rhyme, techniques she had discarded decades ago.* To her, it was old news, very much in keeping with what she considered the regressive politics and policies of the new decade under way.[2] As for Gioia's charge that she was a polemicist, it was not without truth. But subtlety wasn't her style when it came to exposing corporate and military power grabs and their deadening impact on the human spirit. American politics of the early 1990s left her disgusted and barely able to maintain her bedrock optimism, and she saw no reason to keep her opinions to herself.

She declared the Gulf War that George H. W. Bush launched in 1990 "an absolute failure of imagination, scientific and political,"[3] and pointed out that the booming economy only widened the gap between the rich and poor. At a time when the Internet was just heaving into view, she recognized that popular media could have a soul-deadening effect. In the mirrors the media held up to the country, she wrote in *What Is Found There* (1993), "[O]ur lives are reflected back to us as terrible and little lives. We see daily that our lives are terrible and little, without continuity, buyable and salable at any moment, mere blips on a screen, that this is the way we live now. Memory marketed as nostalgia; terror reduced to mere suspense, to melodrama."[4] It was hard for any one citizen to say or do anything truly meaningful under such cynical conditions, and things would only get worse in the age of social media.

Racism, sexism, and homophobia—they were everywhere, and Rich felt compelled to admit to her readers, "You are tired of these lists; I am too."[5] An interviewer asked whether she ever wanted to opt out of politics altogether. In reply, she said, "I'm not tired of the issues; I'm tired of the lists—the litany. We're forced to keep naming these abstractions, but the realities behind them are not abstract. The writer's job is to keep the concreteness behind the abstractions visible and alive. How can I be tired of the issues? The issues are our lives."[6]

She could not single-handedly wipe out racism or stanch the blood flowing from one violent crime after another, but she could rededicate herself to the art of political poetry. In her early sixties, she intended to name the disquieting truths that had made her country what it was and helped make her who she was. In some respects, this was business as usual for her, but a new era required new vigilance and new questions.

---

* There are rare exceptions, such as the rhyming "Rhyme" in *Telephone Ringing in the Labyrinth: Poems 2004–2006.*

With Muriel Rukeyser and Whitman among her models, she began asserting her identity as an American in ways she hadn't done before: "I've been coming out as a poet, a poet who is a citizen, a citizen who is a poet. How do those two identities come together in a country with the particular traditions and attitudes regarding poetry that ours has?"[7]

That was the question animating *An Atlas of the Difficult World: Poems 1988–1991*. In this poetry collection, dedicated to the memory of John Benedict, her longtime poetry editor, whom she had relied on and loved, Rich explained, "I was trying to talk about the location, the privileges, the complexity of loving my country and hating the ways our national interest is being defined for us."[8] In sprawling, long-lined poems of multiple sections, she eulogized women and men whose suffering personified a nation in crisis. Whitman was everywhere in the volume, especially in the lengthy title poem. In its eleventh section, as she addresses the question of "what it means to love my country," she contemplates the physical world, the cities, and the purported values of a nation before considering herself and other citizens:

> Minerals, traces, rumors I am made from, morsel, minuscule
> fibre, one woman
> like and unlike so many, fooled as to her destiny, the scope of
> her task?
> One citizen like and unlike so many, touched and untouched in
> passing
> —each of us now a driven grain, a nucleus, a city in crisis
> some busy constructing enclosures, bunkers, to escape the
> common fate
> some trying to revive dead statues to lead us, breathing their
> breath against marble lips
> some who try to teach the moment, some who preach the
> moment
> some who aggrandize, some who diminish themselves in the face
> of half-grasped events
> —power and powerlessness run amuck, a tape reeling backward
> in jeering, screeching syllables—
> some for whom war is new, others for whom it merely continues
> the old paroxysms of time

some marching for peace who for twenty years did not march for
         justice
some for whom peace is a white man's word and a white man's
         privilege
some who have learned to handle and contemplate the shapes of
         powerlessness and power[9]

She pointed a finger at her enemies, real and imagined, when she described herself as made of "rumors." Easily hurt, she raged against anyone who took exception to her views, and she assumed, correctly, that
people talked about her behind her back. One wonders what she meant
when she described herself as "fooled as to her destiny, the scope of her
task." Perhaps she saw her destiny as greater than ever before and her
task much larger. But the ambiguous phrasing leaves open the possibility that a disillusioned Rich felt the scope of her influence was smaller
than she had once believed.

*Atlas* was a deserving finalist for the National Book Award, but it had
detractors who wanted her to write other poems in other ways. To the
critic writing for the *Harvard Review,* her new poems felt "willed and
programmatic" and not as good as those in *Time's Power,* where Rich
spoke as "a woman rather than a dogma, a person rather than agenda."[10]
Further objections came from her old nemesis Helen Vendler. Critic
and poet were capable of a civil exchange on the rare occasions when
they met. They acknowledged a shared love of Wallace Stevens, but
beyond that, they were in very different camps. Like Gioia, Vendler
thought Rich had become doctrinaire.

The charge would have carried more weight if Rich had *only* been
doctrinaire. But her Whitmanian rants, with a soupçon of Ginsberg,
were but one of countless experiments she made in style and subject
matter. There was no such thing as an "Adrienne Rich poem," because
she was always trying out new personas and themes and drawing on a
myriad of sources. She knew as well as anyone else that *An Atlas of the
Difficult World* was a very different book from *Time's Power;* she wanted
it that way. What sounded doctrinaire in *Atlas* was also doctrinal—
essential, that is, to Rich's evolving ethos as expressed in verse, her
own *Leaves of Grass.*

Vendler didn't buy it. In *An Atlas of the Difficult World,* she saw not a citizen poet but a heavy-handed moralist and social reformer who, not so secretly, felt sorry for herself. She was unimpressed by Rich's sympathy for marginalized individuals and groups and thought the poet invoked these figures as a means of "pitying herself (indirectly) in others." For Vendler, identity politics stifled art. Nothing would have pleased her more than if Rich had written a poem empathizing with a straight white man or a wealthy Christian: Why couldn't Rich see beyond the historic categories of oppression and write about good and evil at war in an individual human psyche? Barring that, she wanted "the real and complex Rich" to go ahead and talk about herself rather than pushing her feelings off on "her allegorical surrogate victims."[11]

Rich's old friend Philip Levine took a very different view of her new book. When he was named the winner of the National Book Award for *What Work Is,* Levine "approached the podium in obvious disbelief" and said he'd expected Rich to win. He continued to praise her at a press conference, saying he'd given Rich's new book "to a young friend of his, a poet, who was dying, and was pleased that the last book his friend read was Ms. Rich's study of life and death," according to *The New York Times.*[12] Perhaps in the back of his mind, Levine was recalling his role in the 1974 edition of the NBA, when Rich and Ginsberg were cowinners in the Poetry category, apparently due to Levine's advocacy for Ginsberg. In any case, he was on Rich's team now.

The two had been out of contact during the years when she cut off many of her male friends, but she had written him a warm letter in 1990 after he praised her in *The Kenyon Review.*[13] On November 27, 1991, a week after the ceremony, she sent him a postcard expressing her appreciation for the "extraordinary generosity" of his comments, which she considered unprecedented at such occasions. She felt his spontaneous remarks, "in these mean-spirited times," reflected well on the art form and the community of poets that meant so much to both of them.[14]

Rich was still in touch with other old friends, notably Hayden Carruth. By now, he and Rose Marie had been divorced for a long time. Hayden's infidelities and general unreliableness had caused her to leave him and begin a new life on her own, as a high school German teacher. Hayden eventually married Joe-Anne McLaughlin, a poet whom he had known as a friend and correspondent for many years. McLaughlin had attended a reading Rich gave in the mid-1970s at Stockton University, when she was an undergraduate there. She came away greatly impressed. Years later, Rich's faith in Carruth made a difference to McLaughlin as she decided whether to make a life with him.

McLaughlin had corresponded with Carruth for nearly a decade when he called her from the hospital after a failed suicide attempt: "He said I needed to come to Syracuse and save him." She made the trip, married him a year later, and found he was in much better spirits for the first year or two after he'd nearly killed himself than she'd ever seen him. She took no credit for the transformation and instead believed it was a "physiological" change brought on by the failed suicide.

Hayden continued to publish books of poetry, but his eccentricities and social anxiety made his public readings and related appearances problematic. Making things worse, he was drinking again, something he had avoided for many years. When his publisher, Copper Canyon, sent him on a tour in 1992 in support of his new collected volume of short poems, he traveled to California and gave a reading at Stanford that Rich attended and had very likely arranged. At a dinner afterward, he decided it would be fun to go outside and break glassware taken from the restaurant. McLaughlin left because she had no desire to join in.

Rich later hosted the couple at her home for lunch; Cliff was not there. During the visit, Hayden drove around Santa Cruz with Rich and McLaughlin as his passengers. The drive did not go well. In McLaughlin's recollection, "Hayden was driving aggressively. Adrienne screamed at him and told him to stop. I jumped about three feet in the air. She was really, really furious. It was a memorable moment for me. I think it impressed Hayden. I had not seen her out-of-control angry before." Despite that low point, Adrienne did everything she could to ensure that Hayden and Joe-Anne had a good time in California. She paid for them to travel to San Francisco by limousine and had rented a place for them to stay at Big Sur. In the end, although they made it to San Francisco, Hayden was beginning to get sick from pneumonia. He and Joe-Anne weren't able to go to Big Sur.[15]

Adrienne's relationship with Michelle was now in its second decade. Michelle had found a niche audience for her novels about Jamaican life, but she was not as famous or anywhere near as big a draw on the lecture circuit as Adrienne was. When Adrienne was invited to teach in a weeklong women's writing workshop in the summer of 1992, she declined and proffered Michelle instead. Neither Adrienne nor the workshop leaders could foresee the disaster that would unfold.

The organizers of "Flight of the Mind" on the McKenzie River in Oregon were Ruth Gundle and Judith Barrington. The couple had hosted Rich on her visit to Portland in the early 1980s and introduced her to the chiropractor who recommended she leave New England to protect her health. They liked and greatly admired Adrienne and were happy to offer Michelle a job teaching during one of their summer workshops, intended to be safe zones where women could write in a beautiful setting and get constructive criticism from accomplished authors.

Michelle's alcoholism was an open secret, especially in lesbian literary circles, but Gundle and Barrington hadn't gotten the word. They didn't vet her, since she was Adrienne's partner—that was sufficient recommendation. But from the start, Michelle seemed bent on contributing to the "mean-spirited times" Adrienne had lamented in her note to Levine. When Michelle didn't show up one morning as expected, Barrington set out to check on her.

In Gundle's recollection, "Judith went to Michelle's cabin on three consecutive mornings, and each time Michelle was drinking from a different bottle of booze." Thus fortified, she taught her workshop. "To say that she was drunk during the class hardly says it. She was plastered. We could hardly believe it—first that she was drinking so much, but also that she was starting in the morning. She must have had a very high tolerance, as she never appeared drunk."[16]

The women of color eager to study with a Jamaican-born author were surprised to discover, first of all, that Michelle could pass for white and, second, that she could be abrasive and insensitive. The codirectors learned that one woman had written about sexual abuse in response to an assignment Michelle had given in class. When the woman's turn came to read her draft aloud, an impatient Michelle cut her off: "'I'm so sick of hearing about that. Next!'" Complicating matters and raising uncomfortable questions about Cliff's views on race, she lavished attention on a white woman enrolled in her class, although Gundle and Barrington had told teachers not to play favorites or work with students outside workshop hours.

About half of Cliff's students felt so disparaged that they left her class. Barrington taught them in a separate group, and they were offered the chance to return the following summer at no cost. Barrington and Gundle tried to contain Michelle so she wouldn't ruin the workshop for all eighty or so participants, but they could not stop her from making fun of prominent black writers—including Alice Walker, whose novel *The Color Purple* she derided as "Colored People"—during a meal Michelle attended along with women of color enrolled in the workshop. Her aura of disdainful superiority was the opposite of what Gundle and Barrington wanted in their instructors. In the evening, back in their own quarters, the couple wept in frustration.

After the workshop ended and Cliff went home, Gundle and Barrington received an angry letter from her accusing them of things that had no basis in reality. They heard not a word from Rich, who stood in solidarity with her partner and stopped sending them the friendly notes and complimentary tickets to her readings they had grown accustomed to. Wounded and disappointed, the two women continued to follow Rich's career and read her books. Years would pass before circumstances would require Adrienne to reciprocate their continuing goodwill toward her (if not toward Michelle).* For the time being, both couples retreated to their corners.

Also that summer, Rich and Levertov were in communication about an essay by Levertov called "Biography and the Poet." In response to the draft Levertov had sent her, Rich wrote a three-and-a-half-page, single-spaced letter covering many topics related to poetry, just as they had in the old days. Like Levertov, Rich was inclined to think biographies of poets were fraught with peril. She wrote that she didn't like their Stanford colleague Diane Wood Middlebrook's recent biography of Anne Sexton.

Although she didn't say so in her letter to Levertov, Middlebrook's use of recordings that Sexton's psychiatrist had made during his meetings with Sexton must have concerned her. Rich had a long history of therapy, including her time as the patient of Lilly Engler. "Twenty-One Love Poems" alludes to tape recordings, and if indeed the lovers had

* On that later occasion, in 2006, Barrington introduced Rich at a reading she gave in Portland. Face to face with Barrington and Gundle at a dinner accompanying the event, Rich was nonplussed, but she eventually warmed up and engaged them in friendly conversation. Ruth Gundle, email message to author, May 18, 2017.

made recordings of their therapeutic sessions, Engler still may have had them. If Middlebrook had gained access to Sexton's confidential records, who was to say Rich's own would be off-limits? In her letter to Levertov, Rich also had choice words of criticism for *Poets in Their Youth,* by Eileen Simpson, John Berryman's wife. She felt Simpson had strayed too far from the poems and indulged in gossip.[17] Levertov's proscriptive essay and Rich's own fears about what could go wrong in a biography evidently weighed on her mind. Ever since her girlhood, she had craved a place in posterity, but she wrestled with the idea of someone else shaping the narrative of her life.

On November 17, 1992, Rich was presented with the Lenore Marshall Poetry Prize at the National Arts Club in New York. Sponsored by *The Nation,* the prize came with ten thousand dollars. She had long been fond of *The Nation,* where she had begun publishing her poems in the 1960s, around the time she spurned *The New Yorker.*

On the same day, Audre Lorde died of liver cancer at age fifty-eight in Saint Croix, where she was living with Gloria Joseph. In her final years, Lorde had ended her relationship with Frances Clayton, her longtime partner, and chosen to be with Joseph, a Caribbean-born black woman, with whom she felt a strong kinship.

Her passing brought to an end one of the most significant relationships of Rich's life. Adrienne had loved her passionately, even though she didn't reciprocate Audre's sexual desire. Each was an indispensable friend to the other. In "Hunger," a poem from the mid-1970s dedicated to Lorde, Rich wrote, "Until we find each other, we are alone."[18] The continuing process of finding each other—achieving that elusive mutuality they both craved—had meant the world to both of them. Separately, they were riveting exemplars of courage, frailty, bluster, and brilliance. Together, they belonged in a Wagnerian opera, one's aria barely ending before the other's began.

In the early years of their friendship, Rich had been the more lauded and famous of the two, and there were occasions when her greater renown irritated Lorde. But in time, Lorde caught up and achieved international stature. She read and lectured in Europe, Australia, and New Zealand, as well as in the United States, and developed an extremely loyal following. She held a distinguished professorship at her under-graduate alma mater, Hunter College, which further recognized her with the establishment of the Audre Lorde Women's Poetry Center. She had her own power, distinct from Rich's, and both of them knew it.

After Audre's death, Adrienne grieved privately. She edited her friend's posthumous collection of poems, titled *The Marvelous Arith-metics of Distance,* and frequently quoted her in interviews and essays. Lorde's reputation would grow in the coming years. Rich did her part to keep her beloved friend's memory alive.

Near the end of 1992, Adrienne had spinal surgery on her neck. After the operation, she was temporarily outfitted with a halo brace, which kept her spine properly aligned and prevented her from turning her head. A metal band encircled the crown of her head and was secured by screws drilled into her skull; long metal pins connected the halo to a vest she wore. After the surgery, Michelle went to Trinity College in January for her annual semester of teaching, and Adrienne asked several friends to stay with her on a rotating basis.

For decades, countless women had relied on her for recommenda-tion letters, blurbs for their books, moral support, and generous checks helping them accomplish their goals. She rarely asked for anything in return, but now she needed help. In a letter to Elly Bulkin, Irena Klep-fisz, and Minnie Bruce Pratt, she focused on her concrete needs rather than her vulnerability: "Twice a day the pins holding the 'halo' to my head need to be sterilized with peroxide / saline solution and Betadine. I can't see or reach them but can give instructions."

Of course she would give instructions. Even in a severely compro-mised state, she remained as in control as circumstances allowed. She told her friends she would require help loading and unloading the dryer, but she could handle the washing machine on her own. With an actual halo screwed into her head, Adrienne Rich was martyr and boss: "I can do cleaning except for floors (vacuuming and mopping) and areas too high or low for me to reach."[19] She needed love and moral support in her partner's absence, but what she asked for was maid service.

During her recuperation, her friend Bettina Aptheker, a feminist scholar and author who taught at UC Santa Cruz, paid her a visit. When

Rich answered the door, Aptheker was stunned by the sight of her wearing the halo brace: "We both stood there and then she started to laugh. She said to me, 'Oh, it's nothing. The forehead is the thickest part of the brain.'" Aptheker learned that Rich wasn't allowed to take off the brace even while sleeping.[20]

Once she had gotten past the early stages of recuperation, Rich made a trip to New York. Although it strains credulity to think her doctors cleared her for cross-country travel, she wanted to go. She visited with Robin Morgan, who was worried and embarrassed for her as people on the street stared at the small woman wearing what appeared to be a medieval torture device on her head.[21]

By summer, she had recovered and felt much stronger, though arthritic pain remained a constant in her life. *What Is Found There* was due out in the fall, and she had a wildly busy book tour ahead of her. For the time being, she worked on new poems, read, and tended her collection of cacti and other succulents. Adding to the pleasures of a relaxed summer were her long conversations with Michelle, home from Connecticut and anticipating publication of her new book, *Free Enterprise: A Novel of Mary Ellen Pleasant*. Adrienne treasured their quiet time together and loved having Michelle once again by her side.

Yet both of them dreaded the formulaic marketing process that would accompany publication of their books. The question, Rich wrote, was "how to resist [the hype] yet go forth into the world with one's love-child." She was well aware that publishers had to make a profit, but as an artist she had always seen herself as the driving force that set the wheels of a publication into motion. She had never gushed with gratitude to her editors and publishers, because she believed they were the ones who should be grateful to her. Now she saw how the corporatization of the industry had made profit the be-all and end-all of an author's value to her publisher. She had warm friendships with editorial and production staff members at Norton and made a point of visiting with them on her trips back to New York, but the trends in the overall industry incensed her, and as she prepared to travel the country promoting her new book of essays, she couldn't escape the feeling she was complicit in those trends. She believed art was "a kind of last frontier of resistance in this country" against dehumanizing corporate greed,[22] but she was aware her power had diminished and she was a very small cog in the vast system she loathed. She and Cliff talked about such things at length; their angry frustration united them even as it muddied the beauty of their days.

Nevertheless, Rich found things to enjoy during her book tour, which took her to Baltimore. It had been fifteen years since she had been back in the city of her birth. As usual, she used her travels as a way to think about history and her place in it, and interviews as an opportunity to reach people who might not have thought about the issues that consumed her. "This visit has really started me focusing on growing up in Baltimore," she told a reporter for *The Baltimore Sun*. Gliding past the complexities of life at 14 Edgevale Road, she praised her childhood while allowing that there were gaps in her early education. In retrospect, she realized that "of the eight to ten people who were part of my regular high school group, three of us were gay." She also touched on racism and class divisions in her recollections of Baltimore, but another topic she brought up surprised and charmed her interviewer. "Who sells the best crab cakes in the city now?" asked Rich.[23] She couldn't live by poetry and politics alone.

As she had since early in her career, Rich treated conversations with reporters the same way she did correspondence with her poet friends: as a means of working out ideas she might develop in more detail elsewhere. In a lengthy interview with *The Progressive*, in January 1994, the conversation inevitably circled around to feminism. Rich announced she was dispensing with "feminism" and going back to "women's liberation." Pressed to explain, she said, "Women's liberation is a very beautiful phrase; feminism sounds a little purse-mouthed. It's also become sort of meaningless. If we use the phrase women's liberation, the question immediately arises, 'Liberation from what? Liberation for what?' Liberation is a very serious word, as far as I'm concerned."

In the *Progressive* interview, she recalled reading an article in *Harper's* around 1970 declaring the death of the movement just as she saw it flowering all over the country. Despite repeated claims of a collapse, she believed resurgent efforts to empower women were "unquenchable and unkillable," and aided by global communications. For anyone who still didn't get why she put social justice front and center, she explained it succinctly in the interview: "I really believe that justice and creativity have something intrinsically in common. The effort to make justice and the creative impulse are deeply aligned, and when you feel the necessity of a creative life, of coming to use your own creativity, I think you also become aware of what's lacking, that not everyone has this potentiality available to them, that it is being withheld from so many."[24] She would return to this idea a few years later, when she had the whole nation's attention.

In June 1994, Rich received word she had won a MacArthur Fellowship, informally known as a "genius grant," for her writing. The amount of the no-strings-attached awards ranged that year from $235,000 to $375,000, paid over five years. During the thirteen years the program had existed up to that point, she was among forty-seven poets honored. Of those poets, only seven were women, all of whom were white. Out of her fellowship class of twenty, she was the only poet and one of seven women. For anyone paying attention, it was obvious that what Rich had been saying for decades was still true: The odds of winning an award for creative or intellectual achievement—for anything, really, other than a beauty pageant—were stacked against women, especially women of color.

But change was afoot. Nine of the recipients in her fellowship year were minorities, including dancer and choreographer Bill T. Jones, jazz composer and musician Ornette Coleman, and Janine Pease, former president of Little Big Horn College in Crow Agency, Montana. Also of note, the MacArthur Foundation director was Catharine R. Stimpson, a lesbian literary scholar with whom Rich was acquainted. Stimpson was steering the fellowship program toward a broader representation of creative genius. In any case, Rich was happy to accept the award. She had never been wealthy, and while the MacArthur would not change that, it certainly helped.

Rich and Cliff's neighbor who lived in the house behind theirs, Robin Riviello, continued to see them regularly. She observed that the couple kept their living room dimly lit, the blinds closed to the sun. Books were everywhere, in large bookcases in the living room and in their separate studies. Getting to the driveway from the back door involved a short flight of steps, which Rich found increasingly hard to navigate. She and Cliff had a lift installed, and Rich used it first with her walker and later a wheelchair.[25] It had a serious purpose, but the couple allowed the neighbor children to play on it.

Rich and Cliff were warmhearted neighbors. When Riviello was going through a divorce, both women offered their encouragement and emotional support, and when Riviello was devastated by the death of her father, Rich told her with great kindness, "I wish I could cry with you." Riviello recalled the empathy of that long-ago remark with tears in her eyes. Cliff in particular listened and counseled Riviello when her children were older and going through hard times. In Riviello's recollection, Cliff "was moody, but she had a really good, generous heart. And then she had her own problems at times, like everybody does. But we had a lot of good years together as neighbors."[26]

Thom and Nancy Kerr, who lived next door, also enjoyed a friendly relationship with Rich and Cliff and were in frequent contact with them. When Thom Kerr began writing short stories, both women took an interest and recommended authors for him to read. They were accessible enough that Nancy Kerr felt comfortable knocking on their door if she was short on an ingredient she needed for a recipe, and Rich and Cliff did the same. Raising the stakes on one memorable occasion, Rich called to say she'd been stung on the forehead by a bee. Nancy Kerr told her to come over so Kerr could slice the stinger off without allowing it to release any toxins. The two couples often chatted about local goings-on and traded tales about a neighbor none of them liked. Nancy Kerr recalled with laughter that Rich and Cliff told her they'd had a cat that "came with the house" when they bought it and the cat would wander off, only to return home without fail when the two women turned on the TV to watch *The Golden Girls*.

When the Kerrs' daughter became pregnant while she was single, there was no hint of disapproval from Rich and Cliff. Cliff and Nancy Kerr met up by the mailboxes one day, and Cliff asked for an update. When Kerr said she was "a proud grandmother," Cliff responded with a grin and a pronouncement—"I'm going shopping!"—before immediately heading out to buy a gift for the new mother and her baby.

In the evenings, the Kerrs often heard the two women chatting and laughing together on their deck. Every once in a while, they overheard Adrienne chiding her partner: "Oh, *Michelle!*" For a long time, Cliff and Rich hosted a monthly Sunday luncheon, with Cliff preparing the refreshments. Guests would circulate in and around the house, and the Kerrs would glimpse the activity between the trees and shrubs separating the two yards.[27]

TV journalist Bill Moyers announced plans for a PBS eight-part series on contemporary poets that would draw its subjects from the popular Geraldine R. Dodge Poetry Festival in Morristown, New Jersey, and air in 1995. Rich was a natural for both the festival and the series, and she was selected to appear in an installment with the Puerto Rican–born Victor Hernández and the African-American poet Michael S. Harper. Despite her deep skepticism of mainstream media, the series presented her with an opportunity to reach an audience of millions. She agreed to be interviewed at the Dodge festival in the fall of 1994.

During her televised conversation with Moyers on the program *The Language of Life,* Rich offered a view completely antithetical to Dana Gioia's. When Moyers asked her why poetry "has such a hard time getting a hearing in this culture," she said, "I have been seeing and noting a tremendous renaissance of poetry in the United States, over the past ten, twenty years. Watered and nourished by the voices of many groups which had been silenced before that. Watered and nourished by the voices of women, by the voices of people of color, by the voices of gay men and lesbians, by the voices of working class white Americans, and there is the seething, burgeoning, poetry out there, but it's many poetries." It was a deft parry. In other interviews, she talked bluntly about the poor quality of so much of the poetry she read. In that respect, she and Gioia were of like minds. But on this occasion, she was resolutely upbeat about poetry; she would not be put on the defensive about the art form that had defined her life.

She made sure Moyers knew she was not grateful for the opportunity to appear on TV. Just as she had asserted her equal standing in her earliest dealings with prominent magazine editors, now she wanted the avuncular Moyers to acknowledge the corporate motive behind *The Language of Life,* and behind virtually everything else on TV, including public television. She spoke bitterly about a commercial she had seen advertising a book called *Die Rich: How to Avoid Estate Taxes.* It was not just the cynical, soulless nature of the book that sickened her but also the medium that brought word of the book to her. Given the stranglehold that "corporate capitalism" had on TV programming and the "contempt for humanity" embodied in its base messages, she wondered how a show about poetry could remain unscathed.

The journalist in Moyers saw an opportunity. He asked her, "What does poetry have to say to just that?" Rich's spontaneous reply crackled with logic and wisdom that muted the tinny noise of TV pitchmen and poetasters alike: "Well, I believe that poetry that is poetry, is asking us to consider the quality of life. And it is reflecting on what makes it possible for us to continue as human. Under the barrage of brute violence, numbing indifference, trivialization, shallowness, that we endure."[28] This was her answer—this was *the* answer—to the valid but insidious question, "Can poetry matter?"

In 1995 and 1996, Rich made news on several different fronts. Given her productivity and stature, two of the news items were routine. In 1995, she published *Dark Fields of the Republic: Poems 1991–1995,* and in 1996, she received the Tanning Prize, a staggeringly generous award of $100,000 for "excellence in poetry" from the Academy of American Poets. The publication of a new book was business as usual for her, and the prize was further evidence that she was the go-to choice for committees looking to honor a living poet. The most prestigious honors— the Nobel, the Pulitzer, a National Book Award she didn't have to share with another poet—continued to elude her, but it seemed that sooner or later virtually every other prize would come her way.

The vision behind *Dark Fields of the Republic* is bleak, with a few saving shafts of light. The title comes from a passage in Fitzgerald's *The Great Gatsby.* Describing his doomed title character, Fitzgerald writes that Jay Gatsby didn't know his dream "was already behind him, somewhere back in that vast obscurity beyond the city, where the dark fields of the republic rolled on under the night."[29] In poem after poem, Rich explores the perils of what felt to her like a very ominous era. "In Those Years" imagines a time in the future when people will look back on the early 1990s and realize they had ignored "the great dark birds of history" tearing "along the shore, through the rags of fog / where we stood, saying *I*."[30] In "Deportations," she describes people being removed from their homes and jobs, along with children snatched from schoolyards: "There are far more of the takers-away than the taken / at this point anyway." Then in a "dream-cut," she imagines a group of faceless men who "have come for us, two of us and four of them." She expects any attempt to engage them in meaningful conversation, "as if trying to appeal to a common bond," will be useless and too late: "as if I were practicing for something / yet to come."[31]

"Calle Visión" is one of several long sequence poems in *Dark Fields*. In her published notes elucidating the poem, she explains that the title refers to "the name of a road in the southwestern United States—literally, 'Vision Street.'"[32] She writes from the perspective of someone in terrible pain trapped in a terrible dreamscape. It is part hell and part hospital planted in the desert. Amid a rush of apocalyptic images ("dead birds coming at you along the line" and "fire in the chicken factory fire / in the carpal tunnel     leaping the frying vats"), she pauses to note a time when "once we were dissimilar / yet unseparate     that's beauty     that's what you catch // in the newborn's midnight gaze / the fog that melts the falling stars."[33] In a world where beauty itself appears to be the lost dream, Rich refuses to give up or give in. Near the end of the poem, she writes:

> This place is alive with the dead and with the living
> I have never been alone here
>
> I wear my triple eye as I walk along the road
> past, present, future all are at my side
>
> Storm-beaten, tough-winged passenger
> there is nothing I have buried that can die[34]

In a hard, upsetting poem, these lines stand out. Rich endured chronic physical pain that seemed to sharpen her awareness of the pain and suffering in the world. For her, pain was twinned with vitality. Just as her body refused to stop hurting, so she refused to stop seeing, knowing, and recording the suffering she saw. In "Calle Visión," she takes her place in posterity, long before her death, in a long line of artist-witnesses. She glories in the continuum of time stretching endlessly behind and ahead of her. She, too, will die, but in her fluid conception of time, she's not exactly going away.

The publication of the 1996 edition of the anthology *The Best American Poetry*, which Rich edited, tipped off a rip-roaring controversy about the nature of poetry, just the sort of debate she loved. David Lehman, the series editor, had approached her about editing the new entry in the series. Once she was certain he would give her complete freedom in her selections, she read through scores of journals from the previous year in search of the "best" poems. It went without saying that she would choose poems by women, racial and ethnic minorities, and gay men and lesbians. She also selected poems by prisoners and teenagers. The firestorm of criticism following the book's publication might have led one to believe Rich had set out to erase everyone else, but that was not the case.

Men and women are equally represented in the collection. The book's white poets include Stanley Kunitz (her Columbia colleague, whom she had never liked), James Merrill, Reynolds Price, Diane Wakoski, Margaret Atwood, and her old friends W. S. Merwin and Jean Valentine. English professors who had published at least one book of poems are well represented. The anthology is not unbalanced; it is balanced in a way that many readers of poetry at the time were not used to seeing.

Her old nemesis John Simon found the book largely devoid of art. In a lengthy review in *The New Criterion*, he took the essence of a line from John Ciardi about a camera "only" photographing the photographer and observed that "an anthology photographs the anthologist." (The review, by extension, was a self-portrait of him.) In his view, *The Best American Poetry: 1996* was a self-portrait of Rich, whose politics he didn't share and whose choice of poems he mostly despised. Though there were a few poems he liked, he came away feeling the anthology reflected the sorry state of poetry. "Have all, or almost all, poems been written? Are there only epigones left, now and then finding a grain left unpicked? Is most of what we can get in 1996 and hereafter either reheated leftovers or wanderings far afield from real poetry? I do not know the answers. But I worry."[35]

Harold Bloom, a Yale English professor whose thoroughly engaging *Anxiety of Influence* and grand mal bloviation brought him fame beginning in the 1970s, also weighed in on Rich's selections. In a fit of jowly pique, Bloom declined to include a single poem from her anthology in his own entry in Lehman's series, *The Best of the Best American Poetry: 1988–1997*. As Sandra M. Gilbert observed in a review of several anthologies, Bloom "refuses to identify Rich as the editor of the offending collection, as if even to say her name would be to besmirch the purity of one who boasts of being 'a lifelong aesthete at the age of sixty-seven.' Or perhaps, more accurately, as if to say 'Adrienne Rich'— the name, after all, of a poet of his generation whose art and thought have clearly made her one of his own 'strong equals'—would be to concede the power as well as the existence of an enemy he longs to annihilate."[36]

Gilbert was not entirely in Rich's camp. She suggested Rich had gone too far in her introduction by claiming that racism prevailed at every turn: "I can't help wondering, for instance, if such recipients of high literary honors as—just to mention a few—Maya Angelou, Rita Dove, Yusef Komunyakaa, Derek Walcott, and Toni Morrison would appreciate Rich's silent dismissal of their achievements, even in several cases her withholding of their names ('Need I add that when in 1992 an African-American woman delivered her verse at a presidential inauguration, and another African-American woman was named Poet Laureate of the United States, these events did not vitiate the racist policies of the state')."[37]

Gilbert had a point. No one could reasonably expect Angelou's reading at Bill Clinton's first inauguration or Dove's appointment as poet laureate to put the kibosh on racist policies in place for decades and dismantle racism that had existed for centuries. But Dove and Angelou deserved the honors they had received. To imply they were mere tokens was to overlook the impact they had on people moved and thrilled by their official recognition. Dove, Angelou, and many other writers of color were being taught, furthermore, in classrooms across the country, and the public was buying and reading their books—and many people would buy and read the anthology Rich had edited. There had been progress, even if it wasn't as dramatic or unqualified as what Rich wanted.

For every Harold Bloom or John Simon trying mightily to knock her down a peg, and for every Sandra Gilbert who offered her a genuinely thoughtful assessment, Rich had numerous, largely uncritical admirers. As the AIDS crisis wore on, gay men were increasingly among her fans. Most of them would not have known about her harsh words from earlier decades, when she condemned rough gay male sex as an expression of patriarchal violence. Instead, they knew her as their advocate and a compassionate friend to AIDS victims, as evidenced by her poem in *Time's Power,* "In Memoriam: D.K.," memorializing her old friend David Kalstone, the Rutgers professor and scholar of her poetry who had died of AIDS. In March of 1996, the Gay Men's Chorus of Los Angeles commissioned and performed *Mornings Innocent,* a song cycle for male chorus, oboe, cello, harp, and piano, with words by Rich, among other poets, and music by Thomas Pasatieri. Although Rich didn't attend the concert, she received a warm letter from the artistic director, Jon Bailey, saying the chorus planned to record the piece for an album titled *Songs of Love.*[38]

While Adrienne continued to suffer from rheumatoid arthritis and dealt with various other ailments, her mother enjoyed remarkably good health. Now in her nineties, Helen Rich had remained in Cambridge even though both her daughters had moved away a long time ago. Independent, friendly with her neighbors, and close to her granddaughter, Valerie Glauber (Cynthia Rich's daughter), she was a prodigious walker and lifelong student who took advantage of community course offerings in Cambridge. She studied Italian, among other subjects, and earned high praise from her professors. Adrienne visited her mother when her reading tours took her back east, but they were not on good terms.

Thinking back on her childhood and reading about the various forms emotional abuse of children could take, Adrienne viewed her mother through a lens of anger and hurt. It was her mother, after all, who had locked her in the closet when she was a misbehaving little girl (at Arnold Rich's bidding). For all the time Adrienne had put into thinking and writing about the hardships of motherhood, she couldn't forgive Helen for her flaws and shortcomings. In a letter to Audre Lorde mentioning "[t]his stuff with my mother," she wrote, "Some of the writing I've read on child abuse has helped me think about what is not active abuse but passivity and indifference, which takes a long time to name and discern. Hard when others don't see her that way, but as a triumphant independent old lady."[39]

Adrienne was still in touch with Alf's parents and his brother, Morris, more than twenty-five years after Alf's suicide, and she got along better with them than she did with her mother or Cynthia, from whom she remained estranged. Her long-ago visits to the Cohen household in Brooklyn had immersed her in Jewish culture. The bountiful family meals her mother-in-law prepared and her in-laws' observance of Jewish holy days were instructive, as was their acceptance of Alf, who had changed his surname and undergone cosmetic surgery so he would look less Jewish. Alf had rejected their religious faith, but they had not rejected him. Nor had they rejected Rich, whose life had changed so dramatically after their son's death.

Emanuel Cohen died at age one hundred in April 1996, and his wife, Anna, was ninety-seven when she died in late December of the same year. Each had lived the extremely long life that Alf had once predicted for himself, based on family history. After her mother-in-law's death, Adrienne felt an era had ended for her and her sons. To her old friend Helen Margolis Smelser Daube, she wrote that she had gone to Brooklyn to stay with her middle son, Pablo, and his wife, Diana, after Anna died. By the time she got to her in-laws' apartment on Plaza Street, the mirrors had already been covered, in keeping with Jewish tradition. Pablo and her eldest son, David (who also lived in Brooklyn), were organizing food for a meal after the burial service in Queens, and her youngest, Jacob, flew in from California. Adrienne accepted Morris's invitation to speak at the funeral. As it turned out, she was the only speaker other than the rabbi.

In her remarks, she had recalled the hardships her mother-in-law had endured, including repeated bouts of clinical depression and electroshock therapy, but she also talked about Anna's "great capacity for pleasure, for gaiety, a kind of flirtatiousness which shows in certain photographs, fastidiousness and love of pretty things, appreciation of life. How at the end of her life she loved to be touched, and would sit holding someone's hand and saying over and over, 'I love you.' "[40]

Her eulogy showed how well Adrienne had known Anna and how closely she had observed her. Though she had not always viewed her mother-in-law charitably, as her aggrieved 1980 poem "Mother-in-Law" reveals, Anna's passing was a solemn family milestone. Without a loving connection to her mother or her sister, and with Michelle estranged from her family, Adrienne took solace in the closeness she and her sons felt to the Cohens.

Rich was again in the news in July 1997, and this time the controversy went beyond the world of English departments and partisan bickering over anthology selections. When she received a phone call from the National Endowment for the Arts informing her that she was among twelve recipients of the National Medal of Arts, Rich seized the opportunity to reject the prize. With the high-minded opprobrium that made her adversaries groan, she fired off a letter to Jane Alexander, head of the NEA at the time, and shared it with the press. In the letter, copied to Bill Clinton, she said she had immediately turned down the award because "I could not accept such an award from President Clinton or this White House because the very meaning of art, as I understand it, is incompatible with the cynical politics of this administration."

She reminded Alexander of her history as a political poet and asserted her continuing faith in the power of art to effect social change. From that vantage point, she refused to overlook "the increasingly brutal impact of racial and economic injustice in our country." In the most frequently quoted lines from her brief letter, she declared, "There is no simple formula for the relationship of art to justice. But I do know that art—in my own case the art of poetry—means nothing if it simply decorates the dinner table of power which holds it hostage."

She was aware of Alexander's "serious and disheartening struggle" to convince Republican leaders not to eliminate the NEA altogether, but her awareness was the extent of her sympathy. She loathed the Clinton administration, which she viewed as complicit in policies of economic disparity: "My concern for my country is inextricable from my concerns as an artist. I could not participate in a ritual which would feel so hypocritical to me."[41]

This was vintage Rich, showing her mettle as she turned down the medal. She was not the first to reject this particular honor and the accompanying invitation to dinner at the White House; in 1989, Leonard Bernstein had said no to President George H. W. Bush. But her statement was so severe, so principled, that it became the rejection letter read 'round the world. In this defining moment in her long war against the many-headed serpent of the patriarchy, Rich showed there were other kinds of power besides that which the American government wielded. She let it be known that poetry, real poetry, was not an adornment, and as a real poet, she would not stay quiet in exchange for a bauble and a fancy meal. For anyone wondering: Yes, damn it, poetry mattered.

In late 1997, she learned of the death of Denise Levertov. Their friendship had once been enormously important to both of them, but after they quarreled in the mid-1960s, things were never the same, though both made an effort to be cordial during their overlapping years at Stanford. Rich's side of the correspondence shows how much she wanted Levertov to be part of her life. Levertov was spontaneous and epiphanic, a born wanderer and mystic; whereas Rich was the poet-scholar, her study lamp always turned on. She settled in one place and lived there as long as she could stand it. In place of Levertov's religiosity, she had her Jewish father's faith in the holiness of the natural world, yet in belatedly claiming her ancestral Judaism, Rich had joined Levertov in making a familial religious heritage part of her story. They were both political poets; both had difficult marriages to anguished Harvard graduates who lacked their wives' drive and genius. They could have learned much more from each other had they stayed close, mutually supportive friends.

In "Negotiations," Rich may be writing about her longing to reunite with Levertov, though the poem could be about many of her writer friends with whom she was no longer in regular contact. In the last two stanzas, she writes:

Someday if there's a someday we will
bring food, you'll say I can't eat what you've brought
I'll say Have some in the name of our
trying to be friends, you'll say What about you?
We'll taste strange meat and we'll admit
we've tasted stranger

Someday if someday ever comes we'll go
back and reread those poems and manifestos
that so enraged us in each other's hand
I'll say, But damn, you wrote it so I
couldn't write it off    You'll say
I read you always, even when I hated you[42]

Rich's willingness to review *The Letters of Robert Duncan and Denise Levertov* was an act of posthumous loyalty. She knew Levertov's friendship with Duncan had ended painfully. After his death in 1988, she had written Denise a letter of nuanced condolence. Now, in the pages of the *Los Angeles Times Book Review,* she contemplated this complicated friendship from a literary remove. It was an interesting experiment, since their correspondence approximated what she and Levertov also had— and also lost. She wrote, "These were two people of strong opinions on more than poetry. A close, mutually confirming artistic relationship may be like a marriage: until a crisis, underlying tectonic shifts don't get talked out. In our plot-driven world we may assume that the crisis is the 'real' story." Rather than dwell on the crisis, Rich said she was more interested in how the two poets tried "to work out, with and against each other, the values and processes of their art. Up to the eventual rift, there was passionate trust in their dialogue, and they bequeathed much to the future, saving almost all of each other's letters."[43]

She could have written the same of herself and Levertov. They, too, had worked things out, with and against each other. Rather than the mutually devastating rift, Rich would concentrate on the passionate trust they had shared for a long, meaningful time.

# CHAPTER 23

# I AM MY ART

## *1999–2012*

Between 1999 and 2010, the year she turned eighty-one, Adrienne Rich's productivity was remarkable. Drawing on a wellspring of creative energy phenomenal for someone crippled and in pain, she published four volumes of new poetry, a compilation covering a half century of her verse, and three collections of essays.[*] She was averaging a new book practically every year, while still traveling widely to give readings and talks. Concentrating on her work may have been a way to block out the physical suffering she endured,[1] but it probably never occurred to her to stop. To keep writing and publishing was to keep being Adrienne Rich.

As the new decade and new century approached, Rich and Cliff recalibrated their lives. Cliff resigned from her endowed professorship at Trinity College in 1999, the year she turned fifty-three. From now on, they would be together year-round. Rich had banked several lucrative prizes, and she had income from her many books, a number of which

---

[*] During this period, Rich published *Midnight Salvage: Poems 1995–1998; Fox: Poems 1998–2000; The School Among the Ruins: Poems 2000–2004; Telephone Ringing in the Labyrinth: Poems 2004–2006; The Fact of a Doorframe: Poems Selected and New, 1950–2001; Arts of the Possible: Essays and Conversations* (2001); *What Is Found There: Notebooks on Poetry and Politics* (2003, an expanded edition of the 1993 edition); and *A Human Eye: Essays on Art and Society, 1997–2009.*

had been translated into foreign languages. She was eligible for Medicare, so her concern about health insurance was presumably over. The two women didn't comingle all their funds, as evidenced when Adrienne told a friend she'd given Michelle money so she could get her car repaired.[2] But at this point, they could get by without either one holding a salaried teaching position.*

Adrienne's continuing devotion to Michelle came through in book dedications and poems. In her seventy-second year, she dedicated her poetry collection *Fox*, *"For Michelle, again, after twenty-five years."* A few years later, she portrayed a balanced, companionable, and still sexual relationship in a poem called "Memorize This": "One oils the hinges one edges the knives / One loses an earring the other finds it / One says I'd rather make love / Than go to the Greek festival / The other, I agree."[3] For readers such as Helen Vendler who wanted wrenching, personal truths from Rich, there was "Bract," a poem about Michelle, a temperamental woman whose furies sometimes complemented and sometimes collided with Adrienne's own:

> Stories of three islands
> you've told me, over years
> over meals, after quarrels,
> light changing the spectrum of your hair
> your green eyes, lying on our backs
> naked or clothed, driving
> through wind, eighteen-wheeler trucks
> of produce crates ahead and behind
> you saying, I couldn't live long
> far from the ocean
>
> Spring of new and continuing
> war, harpsichord crashing
> under Verlet's fingers

---

* The story about the car repairs notwithstanding, Cliff was not without her own resources. She had income from her book publications, and neighbors in Santa Cruz said she was generous in her gifts.

I tell you I could not live long
far from your anger
lunar reefed and tidal
bloodred bract from spiked stem
tossing on the ocean[4]


Like Yeats beholding Maude Gonne, Adrienne found much to love in Michelle's anger. For her, it was noble. Not everyone thought so. But Adrienne herself was famous for the passionate anger behind her dissection of the forces of oppression and corruption. Among her friends, Adrienne was known for her humor and frequent laughter. She was gentle and even-tempered until something raised her ire—and then there was trouble. She could be judgmental, and she could lash out. Well into her later years, she continued to drop friends who displeased her or took up too much of her time.

In her lover, Adrienne saw something of herself and something quite different. Michelle's diasporic vision complemented her own. Like Adrienne, Michelle was on a painful quest to understand who she was in an unloving world that had made her uncomfortable in her own skin. The humor that friends always described as wicked and biting made Adrienne laugh loudly and long. Michelle had a way of cutting through the smog of outrage and self-righteousness that sometimes enveloped both of them.

To all appearances, Adrienne and Michelle had a good life together, but Adrienne remained vigilant in her awareness of their different backgrounds—hers as a privileged, highly successful white woman, Michelle's as a light-skinned Jamaican-American, also privileged in many ways, who could never shake the self-loathing that came with her childhood indoctrination into racism and homophobia. In a 2001 interview, Rich said, "I think it's very dangerous for two people in love not to think about the ways that their relationship is culturally biased." She thought each person needed to be aware of the "cultural framework" shaping his or her expectations and feelings, no matter what that person's background was. "To be conscious of that is work. It takes work, particularly when you're in love."[5] She was right, but her remarks were a poignant sign she would never ease up on herself. Ever since her father had instilled it in her as a young child, she had believed hard work was the solution to virtually every problem. Perhaps it was.

In her later volumes, she continued to rage, elucidate, and float fragments of her life in the larger currents of history. There would be no taming, no holding back. She wasn't done, not yet. She continued to write long sequence poems that followed intricate, winding paths of thought. The title sequence in *Midnight Salvage* (1999) is characteristic of this mode in that it moves back and forth between private, at times impenetrable reveries and moments of ineluctable clarity. In the sixth and most compelling of its eight sections, Rich writes of "the old craftsman" killed in the road near a junkyard called Midnight Salvage. "The young driver" was unfamiliar with the road's sharp curves and the local residents' habit of sometimes walking right in it: "such skills he did not have being in life unpracticed." There is a hint of drollery in her inverted phrase, as if Rich knows she has the materials for a rustic ballad. But this is a road she knows well, and the poem suddenly veers away from a sad moment in local history and into deeply personal terrain:

> but I have driven that road in madness and driving rain
> thirty years in love and pleasure and grief-blind
> on ice I have driven it and in the vague haze of summer
> between clumps of daisies and sting of fresh cowflop odors
> lucky I am I hit nobody old or young
> killed nobody left no trace
> practiced in life as I am[6]

Rich had traveled the road to West Barnet with her husband by her side from 1966 to 1970. She had spent the last three decades making the trip without him, and his lingering absence was the great sorrow behind every tree and cloud.[*] Still, Rich loved her home there and the road leading to it. She had written thousands of pages in that house; the slant of sun through the windows, the beat of rain on the roof had infused every syllable. Though she still felt the need to declare she had

---

[*] Also in *Midnight Salvage*, "Shattered Head" leaves no doubt that Rich remained transfixed by Alfred's death.

"killed nobody"—a superfluous confession unless she still felt some cul-
pability in Conrad's death—it was a true statement. Was it also true she
had "left no trace"? Maybe. Her presence on the road to West Barnet
was no more or less real than anyone else's. But what that road meant
to her forever unwound in her poems and prose, the long ribbon of her
memory. Though no one could see a trace of her on the road, the road
had imprinted itself on her life and legacy.

Although she had claimed her Jewish ancestry, no formal religion,
Jewish or otherwise, had ever claimed her. That is not to say she lived
and wrote in a narrowly secular realm—far from it. The glimmerings
of spirituality in her later poems offer crucial insights into her understanding of the world beyond the planet she walked on. A poem in *Fox*,
for instance, describes an outing she took with Jacob and his family to a
tourist site called the Mystery Spot, which bills itself as "a gravitational
anomaly located in the redwoods outside of Santa Cruz."[7] "Waiting
for You at the Mystery Spot" is unusual for Rich in that it mentions her
family members by name and positions her as a grandmother.

While she is waiting out the pilgrimage that her family makes to
a high peak, she glimpses something of a real mystery as she watches
"the miraculous migration" of sunlight filtering between the leaves of
redwood trees above her, "the great spears folding up / into letters from
the sun deposited through dark green slots / each one saying / *I love you
but / I must draw away    Believe, I will return.*"[8] It was in strange, beautiful images like these that Rich reached as far as she could into worlds
beyond her mortal grasp. For someone for whom correspondence had
been a lifelong occupation and a lifeline, it was no accident she imagined letters being written and delivered in the liminal space between the
known world of the mind and body and the occluded one of the spirit.
That was the sign of the sacred.

There is something Christ-like in the message she imagined coming
not from the Son of God and Man, but the sun. And since Rich was sitting apart, unable to make the hike up the hill, there is something of her
in the message, too. She couldn't stay on Earth with her family forever.
Although she had twelve more years to live when she wrote the poem,
she knew the time would come when she would "draw away." More
than a decade earlier, she had addressed "the place beyond all places, / /
beyond boundaries . . . the place beyond documents," and questioned

her fruitless efforts to read the name of an unnameable "you."[9] But as much as she wanted to, as much as she might try, she couldn't know the unknowable.

She believed not in God but in History, the continuation of the living story. History was what had happened a thousand years ago; it was what had happened in the past few seconds, her own inhalations and exhalations, the slight turning of the breeze and the light. And History kept coming back, in messages from the sun and the words of women and men long known and others recently uncovered or rediscovered. In all of that, she believed. And in believing, she felt she, too, would return, in her poems and other writings and perhaps in some other form as well, in messages to her descendants and others who caught the edge of her words in their thoughts and dreams.

For most of her adult life, Adrienne had needed more medical attention than her mother did. If the poet had died in her sixties, the audiences that had seen her crippled frame braced behind a lectern would not have been shocked. As she entered her seventies, she met her mother, now blind, in old age. Both of them were struggling.

Adrienne and Cynthia visited Helen separately on a couple of occasions before she died. The estranged sisters had a few phone conversations, in Cynthia's recollection, as they discussed their mother's care and began planning for a memorial service. Helen Jones Rich's generally good health had lasted until just a few months before her death at 102 on October 24, 2000.[10] Rich was seventy-one. When the time came for the memorial service, she and her sons attended, along with Cynthia's daughter and son, Helen's longtime caregiver, and a couple of Helen's neighbors with whom she was good friends. Michelle did not attend, nor did Cynthia, who was living in San Diego and had visited Helen shortly before her death. Several months earlier, Cynthia had lost her partner, Barbara Macdonald, who suffered from Alzheimer's disease for many years. Adrienne had marked the loss with a letter of sympathy that Cynthia had read as cold and perfunctory. The sisters remained at odds, even in the most profound times of need and loss.

᠅

Rich's mind continued to sprint; her insights glittered with pre-science. That was evident in March 2001, when she published an essay titled "Credo of a Passionate Skeptic" in the *Los Angeles Times* in advance of the publication of *Arts of the Possible*. Citing Marx, a major influence on her critical thinking for two decades, she contemplated the women's movement of the 1970s. She observed that "one period's necessary strategies can mutate into the monsters of a later time," and she took responsibility for her indirect role in calling monsters forth:

> Feminism has depended heavily on the concrete testimony of individual women, a testimony that was meant to accumulate toward collective understanding and practice. In "When We Dead Awaken," I borrowed my title from Ibsen's last play, written in 1900. Certainly the issues Ibsen had dramatized were very much alive. I "used myself" to illustrate a woman writer's journey, rather tentatively. In 1971 this still seemed a questionable, even illegitimate, approach, especially in a paper to be given at an academic convention.
>
> Soon thereafter, personal narrative was becoming valued as the true coin of feminist expression. At the same time, in every zone of public life, personal and private solutions were being marketed by a profit-driven corporate system, while collective action and even collective realities were mocked at best and at worst rendered historically sterile.
>
> By the late 1990s, in mainstream American public discourse, personal anecdote was replacing critical argument, true confessions were foregrounding the discussion of ideas. A feminism that sought to engage race and colonialism, the global mono-culture of United States corporate and military interests, the specific locations and agencies of women within all this was being countered by the marketing of a United States model of female—or feminine—self-involvement and self-improvement, devoid of political context or content.[11]

Rich was making this case before social media irreparably changed public discourse. She saw what was happening and sensed worse things to come. She acknowledged her role in contributing to the mode of self-revelation that a shape-shifting patriarchy had manipulated for its own ends. No matter its pretensions or evasions, that patriarchy would never have women's interests at heart. Its minions, including women starved for a smidgen of power, would seize any opportunity to debase and control, to distort and undercut. Rich saw all of that very clearly. It angered her that so few others bothered to look, let alone see.

In April 2001, Adrienne went to Santiago, Chile, to participate in an international poetry festival called "ChilePoesía." During an interview conducted by fax before she arrived for the conference, she responded to questions from Magdalena Edwards, a young Chilean-born Harvard graduate. Rich spoke about distortions of language and the motives behind them: "One of the insidious rhetorical devices of the U.S. Right has been to claim (for example) that empathy with others is merely 'liberal guilt' or 'political correctness,' that compassion is merely sentimental or even hypocritical. I see it as an entirely cynical view that underscores the profit motive as the only real basis for human relationships."[12] She was exposing a problem that would grow exponentially worse in the coming decades.

One of her readings in Santiago took place in an elegant building at the University of Chile overflowing with people seated in a theater and in the surrounding balconies. Wearing festive, dangly earrings, she sat at a desk onstage and put on large glasses before she began to read. She spoke somewhat haltingly in Spanish, in solidarity with her host country, before reading "Planetarium." Her warm smile and the pleasure in her voice reflected her joy in the occasion.[13]

Another festival reading featured all the participating poets and took place in the Moneda Palace in downtown Santiago. Recalling that occasion, Edwards said, "ChilePoesía's organizers sought to reclaim the space, to take it over with poetry, a gesture meant to highlight and reframe the historic bombing of the Palace on September 11, 1973, which ushered in the Pinochet regime. Their ambition was political and grandiose, but the execution was subtle and transformative. One by one, the poets took turns reciting their works from the building's balconied windows, and as one window went dark at the end of a final verse, another lit up. The crowd, young and old, stood below in silence. We were listening."[14]

When Rich returned home, she wanted to talk about Chile and the nation's love of poetry. In remarks at Stanford, she said, "Chile is now in the process of re-gathering its identity as a democracy after the horrible years under Pinochet. It's a process also of acknowledging and recognizing and discovering what was done in those years in very specific terms. So there is this painful recognition going on at the same time that there is a spirit of hope."

As a striving girl with a long life ahead of her, she had loved all that Harvard, and the surrounding neighborhood, offered her as a poet and intellectual. In the mid-1960s, she had exulted in the sophistication and teeming intelligence of Manhattan. Her home in West Barnet, Vermont, always fed her spirit. These were all places she needed. Now, to her amazement, she discovered she needed Chile. Its recent sordid history soaked the air, yet huge crowds came together in the name of the art Rich lived for.

Audiences at the festival's poetry readings ranged from a thousand people in smaller venues to fifty thousand in public plazas. In an era when cell phones were just beginning to be common, she looked on in approval as people paid rapt attention to the poets onstage and ignored their phones: "It was evident that these audiences had a sense of what poetry could mean to them or meant to them, and to me this was an almost overwhelming experience. It was something that I had known was possible, but I had never thought I would see it in my physical body—experience it in my life. To feel oneself part of a poetic and political tradition—part of something much greater than one's own individual career, one's individual poetry, one's individual time—is a very remarkable experience."[15]

She was describing a culminating moment in her lifetime. In Chile, she knew with every cell of her being that she was a mortal link in an immortal chain. Speaking before the masses, she was able to "see it in my physical body"—to enter the river, the flood tide, and feel large and small at the same time. It was always the poetry that kept her going, kept her alive; this was who and what she was.

Not six months later, after the terrorist attacks on September 11, 2001, she saw who and what her country was. This, too, was a culmination, though of a very different kind. The title poem in *The School*

*Among the Ruins: Poems 2000–2004,* written the summer before 9/11, anticipated the violence and its traumatic, endless aftermath. She later told a reporter she had spent that summer reading "accounts of 'civilian agonies' in Sarajevo, Baghdad, Bethlehem, Kabul—including Palestinian poet Mahmoud Darwish on the Beirut bombing of 1982."[16] She refused to put the United States before all other nations or to assume the horrors of current headlines were any worse than those of previous times or times yet to come. When the Twin Towers collapsed, she was as shocked as everyone else, but she had sensed impending danger. Immune as ever to unexamined patriotism (as seen in the post-9/11 proliferation of American flags), she refused to feel sorry for a country that had courted retribution for so long.

A section of *The School Among the Ruins* titled "USonian Journals 2000"[*] reflects her fury at a country whose self-absorption she found excruciating. Written almost entirely in prose and dated 2000–2002, the "Journals" consist of short passages in journal form. A section titled "Voices" portrays the erosion of conversation, the most basic unit of communication. Rich contrasts conversations in which people genuinely listen to one another or speak collaboratively with a "newer conversation" in which a rush of serial stupidities issues from a seemingly unshuttable mouth. She then quotes a man profanely bleating his personal problems over his cell phone in a "voice that penetrates kitchen-window glass" before moving on to another cell phone user, in a restaurant, shouting out his possibly shady business maneuvers, oblivious to the people around him. The section ends on a furious note of condemnation in which Rich surely hoped some of her readers would recognize themselves and change their ways:

> USonian speech. Men of the upwardly mobilizing class needing to sound boyish, an asset in all the newness of the new: upstart, startup, adventurist, pirate lad's nasal bravado in the male vocal cords. Voices of girls and women screeking to an excitable edge of brightness. In an excessively powerful country, grown women sound like girls without authority or experience. Male, female

---

[*] In a note below the section title she wrote that *Usonian* was Frank Lloyd Wright's term for "his prairie-inspired architecture." Her variation, "USonian," stood for "*of the United States of North America.*" *CP,* 911.

voices alike pitched fastforward commercial, one timbre, tempo, intonation.[17]

Some might say any given population's speech patterns, pitch, and cadences inevitably change over time and cannot or should not be judged or found wanting. But Rich, as always, was on to something. It wasn't just the content but the sound of so much American conversation that to her ear had grown annoying and bratty; each voice was heartbreakingly indistinct from the next, and there were too many voices slurring away into a cacophony of the forgettable and already forgotten. She'd heard enough to know the changes were real and pervasive. To her, they signaled both a wielding of power behind a vocal mask of cloying boyishness and a yielding of power implicit in the babyish "screeking" of women woefully unable or unwilling to grow up.

In 2002, Rich's long, complicated friendship with Hayden Carruth ended, and it was Carruth's fault. In the years preceding the appalling denouement, she had corresponded with him and gone out of her way to be kind to his family. She wrote a blurb for McLaughlin's first book of poetry and, in 2000, sent her a check for five thousand dollars so McLaughlin could visit her baby grandson. For McLaughlin, this was material evidence of Rich's generosity in all things. Going further in the same vein, Rich organized and participated in a panel of readings and discussion in New York in honor of Hayden's eightieth birthday in 2001. It seemed her kindness to him and his family knew no bounds.

In 2002, in a cruel turnabout, Hayden talked unrestrainedly to a reporter writing a long profile of Rich. McLaughlin was in the room for part of the time he was on the phone with the *Guardian* reporter calling from London. From Carruth's side of the conversation, including his tone of voice and "conspiratorial laughter," she could tell the reporter had jollied him into discussing private details about Rich's marriage and its aftermath. When the lengthy article appeared in the June 14, 2002, issue of *The Guardian*, Rich was enraged. One of the few people in whom she had confided in the days right before and after her husband's suicide, Carruth told the reporter, a stranger to him, that Conrad had thought Rich was going mad. In the wake of his own suicide attempt,

Carruth made Rich sound like a harridan whose feminist rantings were too much for any man to bear. McLaughlin believed that out of her husband's desire to be a member of the "boys' club," born of a lifetime of feeling like he didn't fit in, he had betrayed a friend he professed to love and care about. She took Rich's side in the matter,[18] but there was no way to undo what Carruth had said.

On the same day the *Guardian* profile appeared, June Jordan died. The sixty-five-year-old Jordan had been one of Rich's closest friends and had been her lover for a brief time. In a characteristic act of loyalty, Rich wrote the foreword to the posthumously published *Directed by Desire: The Collected Poems of June Jordan.* She recognized the seriousness of purpose that accompanied Jordan's effervescent wit. Her description of Jordan revealed their kinship as political poets and hinted at how much she had learned from Jordan during a friendship spanning nearly three decades: "She wanted her readers, listeners, students to feel their own latent power—of the word, the deed, of their own beauty and intrinsic value; she wanted each of us to understand how isolation can leave us defenseless and paralyzed," Rich wrote. "She knew, and wrote about, the power of violence, of hate, but her real theme, which infused her style, was the need, the impulse, for relation."[19] The recognition of power in all its dimensions, twinned with the pursuit of meaningful relationships, was inherent in Rich's own thought.

The honors continued to roll in. The 2003 Bollingen Prize for Poetry earned her fifty thousand dollars. Yale University's Beinecke Rare Book and Manuscript Library awarded the prize biennially to an American poet for either an exceptional book published in the past two years or lifetime achievement in poetry. The press release indicated Rich had won for both. The three judges that year were the poet John Hollander; Willard Spiegelman, a professor of English at Southern Methodist University; and Louise Glück, who had unhappily audited Rich's poetry writing class in Columbia's MFA program decades earlier. In the years since, Glück had enjoyed a highly decorated career of her own: she won the Pulitzer Prize for Poetry in 1993 and the Bollingen in 2001; she was named U.S. poet laureate in 2003.

When Glück and the other judges met to compare notes, Rich was discussed as a possible winner. She was not Glück's first choice, but she was the "obvious person on whom we all agreed." Then, Hollander had a change of heart. In Glück's telling, he was convinced Rich would "refuse the award and humiliate us all," in keeping with her history of turning down awards and rebuking the organizations that wanted to honor her.

Glück disagreed with her fellow judge's premise. In a situation similar to Dana Gioia's, when he advocated for Rich as the deserving winner of the Brandeis medal, she fought for Rich as a candidate deserving the honor, no matter how Rich might respond to it. In her recollection, Spiegelman watched in dismay as his fellow judges dug in. Glück eventually prevailed and the prize went to Rich, who accepted it with no caveats or complaints. Glück recognized her elder's valuable contributions to the art form they both lived for: "I saluted a companion in the journey." After the honor was announced, she and Rich talked by phone. "She seemed moved that I had been on that committee," Glück recalled. "I was moved that she was moved."[20]

Still, Adrienne wrote poems and essays; still, she traveled to faraway places to give lectures. At a conference in Scotland in 2006, she outdid herself with a lecture of extraordinary breadth and foresight. In "Poetry and the Forgotten Future," she began by reading from "The Kind of Poetry I Want," by Hugh MacDiarmid, whom she identified as the "great Scottish Marxist bard." Anyone who knew her could understand why she admired this poem. She, too, wanted "words coming from a mind / Which has experienced the sifted layers on layers / Of human lives—aware of the innumerable dead / And the innumerable to-be-born."

In the course of her lengthy speech, she laid out the global poetics she had been developing over the past twenty years. She reminded her audience that Shelley's famous line about poets being "the unacknowledged legislators of the world" meant little without its framing ideology: "For him there was no contradiction among poetry, political philosophy, and active confrontation with illegitimate authority. [. . .] Shelley, in fact, saw powerful institutions, not original sin or 'human nature,' as the source of human misery. For him, art bore an integral relationship to the 'struggle between Revolution and Oppression.' His West Wind was the 'trumpet of a prophecy,' driving 'dead thoughts . . . like withered leaves, to quicken a new birth.' He did *not* say, 'Poets are the unacknowledged interior decorators of the world.'"

Likewise for Rich, poetry was an instrument of prophecy, inseparable from politics. She had long known it; in Chile, she had seen it. For her, the future would always be the playing field of the poet's imagination. She entreated her audience in Scotland to remember the possibilities the future held:

> For now, poetry has the capacity—in its own ways and by its own means—to remind us of something we are forbidden to see. A forgotten future: a still-uncreated site whose moral architecture is founded not on ownership and dispossession, the subjection of women, torture and bribes, outcast and tribe, but on the continuous redefining of freedom—the word now held under house arrest by the rhetoric of the "free" market. This ongoing future, written off over and over, is still within view. All over the world its paths are being rediscovered and reinvented: through collective action, through many kinds of art. Its elementary condition is the recovery and redistribution of the world's resources that have been extracted from the many by the few.[21]

Rich was seventy-seven years old when she delivered this speech. She was eighty when the essay appeared in *A Human Eye: Essays on Art and Society, 1997–2008.* She was not one for conventional nostalgia; it was the future that entranced her.

With the future in mind, she sought out gifted younger poets and became close to those able to overcome their awe of her. She advised them, listened to them, and made sure they knew she took them and their work seriously. Among those she befriended was Marilyn Chin. After she attended a poetry reading Chin gave in Santa Cruz in 1987, early in Chin's career, the two became friends and met for dinner on several occasions in southern California. In Chin's recollection, "She mentored me and also admonished me." Although Rich also cultivated the friendship of the poet Ed Pavlić, Chin sensed she had a special interest in nurturing the careers of young women poets.

In all of her friendships with younger poets, both male and female,

Rich was cementing the lineage from one generation to the next. She wanted to know them; she also wanted them to build on the legacy she was imparting to them. As Chin surmised, "People don't understand how revolutionary her poetry is. Maybe that's why she was seeking me out for those one-on-one sessions—because I know; I carry the code with me. She wanted to have a new progeny of women poets to carry the work of poetry."[22]

Her own work continued in *Tonight No Poetry Will Serve: Poems 2007–2010.*[*] As she looked back at the astonishing arc of her life, the old currents of desire surged anew. In "Ever, Again," a poem from 2006, she yearns to go back to her quiet summers in West Barnet with her sons after Alf had died. In those seasons of private tumult, the everyday routines of rural life had provided ballast. She imagines driving up the long driveway, running water from the kitchen sink, inhaling the aroma of freshly mowed grass, and unpacking groceries, the local newspaper, and a flask of Portuguese rosé. She would set up her Olivetti typewriter next to "the stack // of rough yellow typing paper" before yielding to "voices of boys outside / proclaiming twilight and hunger."[23] As the poem closes, Rich's life at the time unfolds with quiet splendor. Hard as it was, she would live it again, if only she could:

> Pour iced vodka into a shotglass
> get food on the table
>
> sitting with those wild heads
> over hamburgers, fireflies, music
>
> staying up late with the typewriter
> falling asleep with the dead[24]

She had lived through that time; it had lived through her. The sons who stole her away from her writing in their toddlerhood had kept her alive to the present in their teen years. The boys, too, fell asleep with

---

[*] The book's ambiguous title suggests that in the worst of times, it may seem as if poetry doesn't offer the solace or spur to action one might crave from it. But then again, perhaps great poetry refuses to serve the interests of a violent world and thus embodies ennobling courage and resistance.

the dead, in the house their father had loved, near the meadow where he had ended his life.

In her final years, Adrienne continued to mourn that defining loss. Her last poems were private and mysterious, as she traveled alone down a darkening road toward death. Always, Alfred Conrad was ahead of her, the mysteries of his foreshortened life pulling her toward him and then pushing her away. In "Winterface," dated 2009, a letter inquiring about Alfred's theories on the economics of slavery prompts a fragment of elegy:

You left your stricken briefcase here
no annotations

phantom frequencies stammer
trying to fathom

how it was inside alone where you were dying[25]

Now, Adrienne knew her own life would be ending soon. In one of her last trips, she and Michelle went to Toronto in June 2010 so Adrienne could receive a lifetime achievement award from the Griffin Trust, a major benefactor of poetry. Rich's hair was tinted reddish brown and her voice was as strong as ever. She read briefly and expressed gratitude to her hosts.

She gave poetry readings as long as she could. The Kerrs, her next-door neighbors, attended one with their young grandson. As they walked around the bookstore before the event began, they came upon Rich sitting in a secluded corner, going over her notes. Nancy Kerr was quick to tell her grandson they needed to leave her alone so she could prepare, but Rich didn't mind the intrusion and wanted to chat with the boy.[26]

By the time she had turned eighty, her eyesight was failing. To read and write on the computer, she needed to have the text greatly enlarged. That was an easy solution. Still, she felt the visual world slipping away. While visiting the poet Doren Robbins and his wife, the writer and artist Linda Janakos, at their home in Santa Cruz, the conversation took an unusually solemn turn. "She said the hardest thing about growing old was the dimming of the light," Janakos recalled. She meant it literally,

Janakos said, though Robbins suggested there also was a metaphorical layer to Rich's admission.[27]

There began to be times when her mental acuity appeared to be slipping. Her longtime copy editor at Norton, Carol Flechner, remembered one such occasion at a reading Adrienne gave in New York. She felt Adrienne was "out of it" as she read. Afterward, when Flechner spoke to her, Adrienne didn't seem to recognize her.[28] Old friends who hadn't seen her for a long time got the same impression during chance meetings. Possibly, she couldn't see them well enough to recognize them, and there may have been times she was on pain medication that dulled her sensibilities—or in too much pain to respond.

To get around, she relied on a walker, a wheelchair, and Michelle. Elana Dykewomon recalled seeing the couple at a public event and noticing that Michelle's expression betrayed her exhaustion.[29] In her sixties and struggling with alcoholism, she was determined to shepherd her frail partner through the crowd. She had become Adrienne's round-the-clock caregiver. Watching helplessly as her partner lost the vitality that had enabled her to survive crippling arthritis for sixty years, Michelle had "some rough, lonely days," their neighbor Robin Riviello observed. It was only at the very end that hospice came to 2420 Paul Minnie Avenue to assist.[30]

Rich's friend and former student Jack Litewka and his wife visited Adrienne a couple of months before she died. In his recollection, "It was clear to me that she was very frail, and that this was probably the last time that we would see her because she made it clear that it was time for her to hunker down with Michelle and her three sons who visited from New York and Los Angeles almost on a weekly basis to make some decisions so that others would not be left with a mess to clean up." They talked briefly about her physical condition but then moved on to literature, politics, and other topics, as if it were an ordinary visit.[31]

On March 27, 2012, at 5:30 in the afternoon, Adrienne Cecile Rich died at home at the age of eighty-two.[*] David Conrad walked over to Riviello's house to tell her Adrienne was gone. Michelle later told

---

[*] Her family announced the cause of death as complications from rheumatoid arthritis. Her death certificate specifies several afflictions, including erosive rheumatoid arthritis, osteoporosis, and lumbar spinal stenosis, which causes compres-

friends that Adrienne had died in her arms. In the coming days, word of Rich's passing traveled around the world. Her death was announced on news programs and in newspapers far and wide. Numerous tributes appeared on social media.

Cynthia Rich, at home in San Diego, learned of her sister's death from a radio broadcast.[32]

A poetry reading in Rich's memory was held at Santa Cruz's public high school. A crowd of her local friends, including her neighbors and a number of poets, turned out, along with many people who wanted to honor the city's most famous resident. Bettina Aptheker expressed her condolences to Cliff, whose face was "gray with grief."[33] She was lost without her partner of thirty-six years. She later told Linda Janakos she felt the ghostly pressure of Adrienne's feet pressed against hers in bed every night.[34]

Rich had completed a final book in her last months, *Later Poems: Selected and New, 1971–2012*, which came out the year of her death. In 2016, her *Collected Poems: 1950–2012* was published. Edited by Pablo Conrad, the volume includes an introduction by Claudia Rankine and thus marks the first volume of her poetry since *A Change of World* where another poet's words frame Rich's own.

Michelle Cliff died on June 12, 2016, at age sixty-nine. The immediate cause of death listed on her death certificate was liver failure; alcoholic hepatitis and chronic alcohol abuse were identified as conditions leading to the cause of her death.

*Who was she? Who was she really?* Some fourteen years before her death, Adrienne Rich appeared to be closing in on an answer in "A Long Conversation," a sequence poem dated 1997–98. The relevant passage appears in a section titled "Brecht Becomes German Icon Anew Forgiven Marxist Ideas." As is often the case, Rich speaks her personal truth through the guise of a persona: "I am my art: I make it from my body and the bodies that produced mine. I am still trying to find the

---

sion of nerves in the lower back. The certificate also notes that Rich was to be cremated and her ashes taken to the family home in West Barnet.

pictorial language for this anger and fear rotating on an axle of love."[35] She had spent her life searching for a viable identity and never found one that fully fit. Even the notion of having multiple selves was not quite what she was after.

What she ultimately came to realize was that the answer to her all-consuming question had been right before her eyes all along. Her strengths and her wounds were all there on the page: *I am my art.* That is the power of Adrienne Rich, her triumph. Freed from earthly suffering, perhaps sending letters of light through the redwoods of Santa Cruz, the touch of her fingers still imprinted on the doorknobs of an old house in Vermont, she is her art. That is who and what she is.

# ACKNOWLEDGMENTS

To everyone I interviewed for this biography, I offer my deep thanks. For their extensive commentary and the time they put into helping me, I owe special gratitude to Rose Marie Carruth, Helen Margolis Smelser Daube and her daughter, Tina Smelser, Susan Griffin, Donald Hall, Florence Howe, Catharine MacKinnon, Robin Morgan, Bettina Aptheker, and Cynthia Rich.

I also thank my sister Julia Holladay Mann, who has been enthusiastic and supportive from the very beginning of my research, and her husband, Fred; and my sister Cary Holladay, a superb listener and sounding board, and her husband, John Bensko. And I thank Kesia Carlson, a recent arrival on this particular odyssey, whose love has given my life new meaning and purpose.

Colleagues and friends also have been extremely helpful and encouraging. For reading chapters of the book and offering incisive suggestions, I thank Paul Mariani, Amanda Golden, Elizabeth Howard, and Roberta Culbertson. For graciously hosting me at various times while I was working on the book, I'm grateful to Ronna Johnson and Gerry Mabe of Watertown, Massachusetts; Laura and Randy Sellers of Chapel Hill, North Carolina; Cheryl Hollatz-Wisely and Kate Gray of Portland, Oregon; and Richard Pickering of Wellfleet, Massachusetts. For her expertise in tracking down elusive genealogical details, I salute genealogist Deb Stone of Portland, Oregon.

In gratitude for all the good conversations and wise counsel over many years, I thank my friends Keith Clark, Cheryl Hollatz-Wisely, Upāsikā tree turtle, and Toine Wyckoff. I also thank my local friends, Ashe and Tracy

Laughlin, Angus and Marjorie Macdonald, Suzanne Wilmoth, and Jeff Poole, for their kindness, good humor, and interest in my work on Adrienne Rich. In gratitude for her wisdom, breadth of knowledge, and generous heart, I have dedicated this book to my beloved friend, Roberta Culbertson.

Finally, to my agent, Janet Reid, for her unfailing ability to keep me focused; assistant editor Carolyn Williams, for her prompt and gracious answers to all my questions; and my editor, Nan Talese, who has just the right touch in all things: my sincere thanks and deep appreciation.

Special acknowledgment is made to the Adrienne Rich Literary Estate for permission to use previously unpublished writing by Adrienne Rich.

# NOTES

### ABBREVIATIONS

Adrienne Rich, AR; Cynthia Rich, CR; Helen Jones Rich, HJR; Donald Hall, DH; Denise Levertov, DL; Hayden Carruth, HC.

### BOOKS BY ADRIENNE RICH

AP—*Arts of the Possible*
BBP—*Blood, Bread, and Poetry*
CP—*Collected Poems: 1950–2012*
HE—*A Human Eye*
LSS—*On Lies, Secrets, and Silence*
OWB—*Of Woman Born*
WIFT—*What Is Found There*

### MANUSCRIPT COLLECTIONS

AL Papers—Audre Lorde Papers
AR Papers—Adrienne Rich Papers
BRC Papers—Bernard Roland Crick Papers
DL Papers—Denise Levertov Papers
HC Papers—Hayden Carruth Papers
HJR Papers—Helen Jones Rich Papers
MBP Papers—Minnie Bruce Pratt Papers
MS Papers—Mab Segrest Papers
TO Papers—Tillie Olsen Papers

## PREFACE

1 CR, email message to author, Apr. 23, 2014.

2 "Snapshots of a Daughter-in-Law," *CP*, 121.

3 "Planetarium," *CP*, 302.

4 Rich lived on Main Street in Montague, Massachusetts, when she wrote "Power." A fellow resident of Main Street, the poet and biographer Paul Mariani, writes that amber bottles had been found in the neighborhood: "Years ago, back in the 1970s, I remember a young man, a teenager, who had grown up here, digging in the grass and tree branch piles on the property behind my house, looking for tonic bottles, many of them a dark brown. These were bottles labeled as health tonics for women, but they were actually pint bottles of alcohol, which the ladies would discard in the old trash heaps to keep them hidden from prying eyes. There was a strong temperance movement here in town back in the early 1900s and the tonics were the women's way of getting around the social issues of the time. [. . .] If I knew about these bottles, my guess is so did Adrienne." Paul Mariani, email message to author, Nov. 23, 2019.

5 "Power," *CP*, 443.

6 "Sources," *CP*, 575.

## CHAPTER 1: Baby Genius

1 *Poems by Adrienne Cecile Rich* (bound typescript volume). No book publication date, but final poem dated "Baltimore October 14, 1935," folder 12v, AR Papers.

2 R. W. Emerson, "Letter to Walt Whitman," July 21, 1855, Walt Whitman Archive, whitmanarchive.org.

3 CR, email message to author, July 25, 2014. Unless otherwise cited, details in this chapter about the Rich family, including the inspiration for AR's first name, are drawn from the author's extensive email correspondence with CR, from April 2014 through the fall of 2019.

4 Arnold Rich to William Jones, May 20, 1929, file 5.14, HJR Papers.

5 AR's mother, quoted in "The distance between language and violence," *WIFT*, 184.

6 Stories written by Adrienne, 1933, folder 10v, AR Papers.

7 "The distance between language and violence," *WIFT*, 182.

8 Kiki Borchardt and Mary Munsil, "Scripps Q&A: Adrienne Rich" (n.d., but included with published interviews, 1980–1987), 8–9, folder 3, AR Papers.

9 Mary Gravely Jones to HJR, Sept. 17, 1935, file 1.6, HJR Papers.

10 Mary Gravely Jones to Hattie Rich, Sept. 17, 1935, file 8.7, HJR Papers.

11 AR, "The distance between language and violence," *WIFT*, 184.

12 Childhood writings, series 1, AR Papers. The young AR refers to typing at her desk.

13 "Solfeggietto," *CP*, 660–61.

14 Journal, June 1945, folder 33v, AR Papers.

15 "Split at the Root: An Essay on Jewish Identity," *BBP*, 113.

16 Journal, June 1945, folder 33v, AR Papers.

17 "Split at the Root," *BBP*, 113.

18 Gerald Spear, M.D., email message to author, Apr. 4, 2014.

19 Nan Robertson, "A Poet's Political and Literary Life," *New York Times*, June 10, 1987.

CHAPTER 2: The Patriarch and
the Woman in the Black Dress

1 Biographical material about Arnold Rich and his ancestry comes from email correspondence with CR; the author's genealogical research on the Rich family; and Ella H. Oppenheimer, *Arnold Rice Rich, 1893–1968* (Washington, D.C.: National Academy of Sciences, 1979), nasonline.org.

2 Biographical Files, Series R, Rich, Arnold R., file 1, General, Alan Mason Chesney Medical Archives, Johns Hopkins Medical Institutions.

3 CR, email message to author, July 15, 2014.

4 "Split at the Root: An Essay on Jewish Identity," *BBP*, 102.

5 CR, email message to author, July 15, 2014.

6 Oppenheimer, *Arnold Rice Rich*, 332.

7 Encyclopedia of Southern Jewish Communities—Charlottesville, Virginia, isjl.org.

8 "Split at the Root," *BBP*, 102.

9 Karl Shapiro, "University," Poetry Foundation, poetryfoundation.org. AR refers to this poem in "Split at the Root," *BBP*, 102.

10 Thomas Bourne Turner, M.D., *Part of Medicine, Part of Me: Musings of a Johns Hopkins Dean* (Baltimore: Johns Hopkins Medical School, 1981), 142.

11 Oppenheimer, *Arnold Rice Rich*, 333.

12 Ivan Bennett, M.D., "Arnold Rice Rich, 1893–1968," presented to Advisory Board, May 27, 1968, Alan Mason Chesney Medical Archives, Johns Hopkins Medical Institutions.

13 AR to Susan Griffin, June 26, 1975, Susan Griffin personal collection.

14 In "Sources," AR addresses her deceased father: "For years all arguments I carried on in my head were with you," *CP*, 576–77.

15 HJR, "Where Are the Great Women Composers?" typescript of essay published in *Maenad* 2.1–2 (1981), file 1.3, HJR Papers.

16 Arnold Rich to Helen Jones, Aug. 1917, file 3.1, HJR Papers.

17 CR, email message to author, July 22, 2017.

18 "Re-Forming the Crystal," *CP*, 415.

19 HJR, "Talk re: Arabs at Roland Park Country School," 1939, file 5.2, HJR Papers.

20 CR is the source for this anecdote about Helen Rich's meeting with a professional composer. CR, email message to author, July 20, 2014.

21 Files 1.1 and 1.2, HJR Papers. Samples of HJR's household expense records,

including lists of groceries purchased, are included in her papers, along with itemized lists of the family silver and other valuables. She wrote some of these in French.

22 "Split at the Root," *BBP,* 117.

## CHAPTER 3: Kingdom of the Mind

1 CR provided the detail about the condolence cards. CR, email message to author, Mar. 19, 2020.

2 CR, email message to author, Mar. 19, 2020.

3 "Tear Gas," *CP,* 294.

4 "Blood, Bread, and Poetry: The Location of the Poet," *BBP,* 170.

5 "The distance between language and violence," *WIFT,* 183.

6 AR acknowledges this feeling of abandonment in "The distance between language and violence," *WIFT,* 184.

7 CR, email message to author, Mar. 19, 2020.

8 Mary Gravely Jones to HJR, Sept. 19, 1935, file 1.6, HJR Papers.

9 Elizabeth Evitts Dickinson, "Roland Park: One of America's First Garden Suburbs, and Built for Whites Only," *Johns Hopkins Magazine* (Fall 2014), jhu .edu.

10 Deed and Agreement between the Roland Park Company and Edward H. Bouton, Containing Restrictions, Conditions, Charges, Etc. Relating to Guilford. July 1, 1913, guilfordassociation.org.

11 *The Baltimore Book,* quoted in Michael Olesker, "Synagogue Move Recalls a Sad Time of Restriction," *Baltimore Sun,* Aug. 3, 2000, baltimoresun.com.

12 "School Destroyed by 5-Alarm Fire in Roland Park," *Baltimore Sun,* June 5, 1947.

13 Peggy Webb Patterson, phone interview with author, May 1, 2016.

14 AR to family, May 29, 1950, folder 93, AR Papers.

15 This description is drawn from AR's childhood journals, CR's email correspondence with author, and Patterson phone interview.

16 Diary, July–Sept. 1944, folder 33v, AR Papers.

17 AR to Denise Levertov, July 7, 1992, DL Papers.

18 Journal, June 1945, folder 33v, AR Papers.

19 CR to AR, 1947, Cynthia Rich and Barbara Macdonald Papers.

20 Journal, July 10, 1950, file 40, AR Papers.

21 Terry Castle, phone interview with author, Aug. 14, 2014.

22 Tim Warren, "Rich, With Memories and a Passion for Poetry," *Baltimore Sun,* Oct. 16, 1993, baltimoresun.com.

23 HJR to Cecile Rich Weil, Feb. 7, 1978, file 2.5, HJR Papers.

24 AR to Susan Griffin, July 21, 1974, Susan Griffin personal collection.

25 AR to Susan Griffin, Mar. 22, 1980, Susan Griffin personal collection.

26 CR, email correspondence with author.

27 AR to Margareta Faissler, Jan. 9, 1964, folder 112, AR Papers.

28  AR to Margareta Faissler, Dec. 13, 1979, folder 112, AR Papers.

29  Diary, 1943–1944, folder 32v, AR Papers.

30  Peggy Webb Patterson, phone interview with author, May 1, 2016.

31  Journal, July–Sept. 1945, folder 33v, AR Papers.

32  Lou Pine, phone interview with author, May 29, 2016.

33  "Sonnet in Time of Battle," *The Red and White*, May 1945, Roland Park Country School Archives.

34  Unsigned [but probably by AR], "Backstage of 'Romeo and Juliet,'" *The Red and White*, Jan. 1945, Roland Park Country School Archives.

35  "Seventh Main," *Quid Nunc* (1946), 44, Roland Park Country School Archives.

36  Unsigned essay, *Quid Nunc* (1947), 39, Roland Park Country School Archives.

37  Typed sheet appended to back of journal entries for Mar. 30–Apr. 1, 1950, folder 40, AR Papers.

38  CR, email message to author, July 31, 2015.

39  "Adrienne Cecile Rich," *Quid Nunc* (1947), 28, Roland Park Country School Archives.

40  Journal, May 8, 1950, folder 40, AR Papers.

41  "Adrienne Cecile Rich," *Quid Nunc* (1947), Roland Park Country School Archives.

42  "Split at the Root: An Essay on Jewish Identity," *BBP*, 105.

43  Journal, Aug. 14, 1945, folder 33v, AR Papers.

44  "Split at the Root," *BBP*, 106.

45  "Split at the Root," *BBP*, 107.

46  CR, email message to author, July 15, 2014.

47  Journal, June 5, 1947, folder 33v, AR Papers.

## CHAPTER 4: The Girl Who Wrote Poems

1  AR to Arnold Rich, Feb. 2, 1952, folder 95, AR Papers.

2  AR mentioned her college writing routine in an early interview. "Poetess of 23 Finds Life a Study of Things, People—and Hard Work," *Baltimore Sun*, Sept. 17, 1952, folder 283, AR Papers.

3  AR to family, Oct. 23, 1947, folder 89, AR Papers.

4  AR to CR, Oct. 15, 1947, folder 89, AR Papers.

5  AR to Arnold Rich, Oct. 29, 1947, folder 89, AR Papers.

6  AR to Arnold Rich, Jan. 12, 1948, folder 90, AR Papers.

7  AR to her parents, Oct. 16, 1947, folder 89, AR Papers.

8  AR to Arnold Rich, May 20, 1950, folder 93, AR Papers.

9  AR to Arnold Rich, Hattie ("Anana") Rich, and CR, Oct. 26, 1947, folder 89, AR Papers.

10  AR to Arnold Rich, Oct. 29, 1947, folder 89, AR Papers.

11  Typescript of "To a Young Minstrel," Nov. 19, 1947, folder 54, AR Papers.

12  AR to parents, Apr. 27, 1948, folder 90, AR Papers.

13  Peggy Webb Patterson, phone interview with author, May 1, 2016.

14  AR to parents, Apr. 27, 1948, folder 90, AR Papers.

15  AR to parents, Apr. 27, 1948, folder 90, AR Papers.

16  "Amateur," 1948, Radcliffe papers, folder 55, AR Papers.

17  AR to parents, May 12, 1948, folder 90, AR Papers.

18  Jane Roland Martin, interview with author, Lexington, MA, May 18, 2016; Jane Williams, interview with author, Cambridgeport, MA, May 19, 2016.

19  AR to parents, Mar. 17, 1952, folder 95, AR Papers.

20  Jean Wilson, "Adrienne Rich: Journey Towards a Common Language," *Broadside* 2.9 (July 1981): 8.

21  "Stepping Backward," *CP*, 23–25.

22  Drew Gilpin Faust, "Mingling Promiscuously: A History of Women and Men at Harvard," in *Yards and Gates: Gender in Harvard and Radcliffe History*, ed. Laurel Ulrich (New York: Palgrave Macmillan, 2004), 454, 458, dash .harvard.edu.

23  Kiki Borschardt and Mary Munsil, "Scripps Q & A: Adrienne Rich" (n.d., but included in published interviews 1980–1987), folder 3, AR Papers.

24  AR to CR, Oct. 15, 1947, folder 89, AR Papers.

25  AR to Arnold Rich, Hattie Rich, and CR, Oct. 26, 1947, folder 89, AR Papers.

26  "Blood, Bread, and Poetry: The Location of the Poet," *BBP*, 172.

27  Theodore Morrison quoted in "On an Author," *New York Herald Tribune Book Review*, Mar. 1, 1953, folder 282, AR Papers.

28  Joyce Johnson, *Minor Characters* (New York: Washington Square Press, 1983), 84–85.

29  Jane Williams, email message to author, May 10, 2016.

30  Jane Roland Martin interview with author, May 18, 2016.

31  "The Yearbook Poll," *The Radcliffe Yearbook of 1951*, 109–17.

32  AR to parents, May 29, 1950, folder 93, AR Papers.

33  "When We Dead Awaken: Writing as Re-Vision," *AP*, 19.

34  Journal, Jan. 29, 1950, folder 40, AR Papers.

35  Sylvia Plath, *The Unabridged Journals of Sylvia Plath, 1950–1962*, ed. Karen V. Kukil (New York: Anchor, 2000), 201.

36  Journal, Jan. 24, 1950, folder 40, AR Papers.

37  Journal, May 8, 1950, folder 40, AR Papers.

38  Journal, Feb. 28, 1950, folder 40, AR Papers.

39  AR to parents, Jan. 24, 1950, folder 93, AR Papers.

40  AR to family, Nov. 10, 1950, folder 93, AR Papers.

CHAPTER 5: The Making of Adrienne Rich

1  Journal, Feb. 24, 1950, folder 40, AR Papers. Her journal from this period suggests Ted Morrison may have submitted poems to *The Virginia Quarterly Review* and other distinguished publications on her behalf. His written comment on one of her stories—"We'll try The New Yorker"—furthers that impression.

2  "When We Dead Awaken: Writing as Re-Vision," *LSS*, 40.

3 Journal, Feb. 28, 1950, folder 40, AR Papers.

4 Journal, Mar. 9, 1950, folder 40, AR Papers.

5 Journal, Mar. 23, 1950, folder 40, AR Papers.

6 Journal, Mar. 31, 1950, folder 40, AR Papers.

7 "F. O. Matthiessen Plunges to Death from Hotel Window," *Harvard Crimson*, Apr. 1, 1950, thecrimson.com.

8 Journal, Apr. 1, 1950, folder 40, AR Papers.

9 Letter to family, Oct. 28, 1950, folder 93, AR Papers.

10 Letter to family, [Mar.–Apr. 1950], folder 93, AR Papers.

11 Letter to family, Apr. 12, 1950, folder 93, AR Papers.

12 Letter to family, Apr. 12, 1950, folder 93, AR Papers.

13 Journal, May 15, 1950, folder 40, AR Papers.

14 Journal, May 17, 1950, folder 40, AR Papers.

15 Journal, May 19, 1950, folder 40, AR Papers.

16 Letter to Arnold Rich, May 20, 1950, folder 93, AR Papers.

17 Journal, May 19, 1950, folder 40, AR Papers.

18 Journal, July 6, 1950, folder 40, AR Papers.

19 Journal, July 31, 1950, folder 40, AR Papers.

20 W. H. Auden letters to AR, Aug. 1950, folder 136, AR Papers.

21 Journal, July 6, 1950, folder 40, AR Papers.

22 Journal, Aug. 30, 1950, folder 40, AR Papers.

23 Journal, Jan. 22, 1950, folder 40, AR Papers.

24 AR to family, Oct. 28, 1950, folder 93, AR Papers.

25 AR to family, Sept. 26, 1950, folder 93, AR Papers.

26 AR to family, Nov. 10, 1950, folder 93, AR Papers.

27 AR to family, Sept. 26, 1950, folder 93, AR Papers.

28 AR to family, Oct. 28, 1950, folder 93, AR Papers.

29 John Simon, "The Multicultural Muse," *The New Criterion* 15.1 (Sept. 1996), newcriterion.com.

30 John Simon, phone interview with author, Feb. 7, 2016.

31 AR to family, "Friday night" [1950], folder 93, AR Papers.

32 AR to family, Nov. 29, 1950, folder 93, AR Papers.

33 AR to family, Dec. 14, 1950, folder 93, AR Papers.

34 "Poems," *Radcliffe Quarterly* 35.1 (Jan. 1951): 22.

35 "The House at the Cascades" and "Prisoners," *Radcliffe Quarterly* 35.1 (Jan. 1951): 23.

36 AR published "The House at the Cascades" and "Prisoners" in her *Collected Early Poems* and *CP*.

37 Unsigned, "An Interview with Adrienne Rich," no author listed, *The Island* 3 (May 1966): 3, folder 190v, AR Papers.

38 "An Unsaid Word," *CP*, 20.

39 W. H. Auden, "Foreword to *A Change of World*," in *Reading Adrienne Rich: Reviews and Re-Visions, 1951–81*, ed. Jane Roberta Cooper (Ann Arbor: University of Michigan Press, 1984), 209–11.

40 AR to family, May 29, 1951, folder 94, AR Papers.

41 Alfred Kreymborg, "Voices That Speak in Verse," *The New York Times Book Review*, May 13, 1951, file 283, AR Papers.

42 Louise Bogan, "Verse," *The New Yorker*, Nov. 3, 1951.

43 CR, email message to author, May 1, 2016.

44 AR to Mab Segrest, Oct. 24, 1982, box 2, file 6, MS Papers.

45 CR to parents and Hattie Rich, June 1951, Cynthia Rich and Barbara Macdonald Papers.

46 AR to Arnold Rich, Feb. 2, 1952, folder 95, AR Papers.

47 Celia B. Betsky, "Adrienne Rich: Some Kind of Hetaira," *Harvard Crimson*, June 14, 1973.

48 "Foreword," *Collected Early Poems:1950–1970* (New York: Norton, 1993), xx.

## CHAPTER 6: *Toute la Gloire*

1 AR to father, May 3, 1951, folder 94, AR Papers.

2 Roberta Yerkes, associate editor, Yale University Press, to AR, July 24, 1951, folder 136, AR Papers.

3 T. S. Eliot to Chester Kerr, secretary of Yale University Press, Aug. 17, 1951, folder 136, AR Papers.

4 CR, email message to author, Dec. 17, 2016.

5 Peggy Webb Patterson, phone interview with author, Aug. 25, 2016.

6 AR to father, Nov. 5, 1951, folder 94, AR Papers.

7 "Alone," Oct. 22, 1947, folder 54, AR Papers.

8 AR to father, Nov. 5, 1951, folder 94, AR Papers.

9 AR to father, Nov. 5, 1951, folder 94, AR Papers.

10 Journal, Mar. 5, 1950, folder 40, AR Papers.

11 Bernard Crick to Francis Celoria, Nov. 7, 1952, BRC Papers.

12 Draft of Guggenheim application [1951 or 1952], folder 77, AR Papers.

13 W. M. Stucky, "Just a Few Lines On . . . A Young Poet Whose Effects Are Honest and Whose Perceptions Are Remarkable," *Lexington (KY) Herald-Leader*, May 6, 1951, folder 283, AR Papers.

14 Journal, Nov. 1, 1951, folder 41, AR Papers.

15 AR to father, Mar. 17, 1952, folder 95, AR Papers.

16 CR, email message to author, Mar. 19, 2020.

17 AR quoted in Maureen Brady, "Adrienne Rich: Friendship Doubles My Universe," *Sinister Wisdom* 95 (2015): 65.

18 CR, email message to author, July 15, 2014.

19 AR to father, Feb. 6, 1952, folder 95, AR Papers.

20 AR to father, Feb. 6, 1952, folder 95, AR Papers.

21 AR to father, Feb. 6, 1952, folder 95, AR Papers.

22 AR to father, Feb. 6, 1952, folder 95, AR Papers.

23 "Double Monologue," *CP*, 127.

24 "Rich, 'Cliffe Poetess, Will Read Work Today," *Harvard Crimson*, Feb. 14, 1952.

25  John Simon, "The Multicultural Muse," *The New Criterion* 15.1 (Sept. 1996), newcriterion.com.

26  CR recalled AR saying that she generally didn't like other women. CR, email message to author, Aug. 12, 2015.

27  Journal, Feb. 28, 1952, folder 95, AR Papers.

28  Journal, Feb. 28, 1952, folder 95, AR Papers.

29  Journal, Feb. 28, 1952, folder 95, AR Papers.

30  Journal, Feb. 28, 1952, folder 95, AR Papers.

31  I'm indebted to genealogist Deb Stone for locating biographical information on Emanuel Cohen's life and Alfred Conrad's tenure as a Harvard student. Details in this paragraph come from Harvard yearbooks and newspaper articles available on newspapers.com.

32  "Colleagues Mourn Schumpeter Loss, Join in Tributes," *Harvard Crimson*, Jan. 9, 1950.

33  "Sources," *CP*, 584.

34  The sources for the discussion of nose surgery are CR, email message to author, Dec. 17, 2016; Frances Strum Gilmore (Annette's youngest sister), phone interview with author, July 2, 2016; and Roland Vernei (Annette's son from her second marriage), phone interview with author, Nov. 5, 2019. Vernei said his mother had rhinoplasty "right at the end" of World War II, which would indicate that Conrad knew her both before and after she had the surgery done. I'm grateful to genealogist Deb Stone for identifying Annette Strum by name and helping me locate her surviving relatives.

35  Frances Strum Gilmore, phone interview with author, July 2, 2016.

36  The descriptions of Alfred Conrad, his family background, and Annette Strum are drawn from AR's journal, Feb. 27, 1952, folder 95, AR Papers; AR's later correspondence with friends; and the author's phone interviews with Strum's relatives.

37  Journal, Feb. 27, 1952, folder 95, AR Papers.

38  Journal, Feb. 28, 1952, folder 95, AR Papers.

39  Journal, Feb. 28, 1952, folder 95, AR Papers.

40  Journal, Mar. 6, 1952, folder 95, AR Papers.

41  Journal, Mar. 9, 1952, folder 95, AR Papers.

42  Journal, Feb. 28, 1952, folder 95, AR Papers.

43  Journal, Mar. 10, 1952, folder 95, AR Papers.

44  Journal, Mar. 11, 1952, folder 95, AR Papers.

45  AR to family, Mar. 11, 1952, folder 95, AR Papers.

46  AR to family, Mar. 11, 1952, folder 95, AR Papers.

47  AR to family, Apr. 10, 1952, folder 95, AR Papers.

48  AR to family, Apr. 10, 1952, folder 95, AR Papers.

49  Robert Solow, email message to author, Jan. 18, 2016, and phone interview with author, Jan. 17, 2016.

50  AR to family, May 2, 1952, folder 95, AR Papers.

51 Celia B. Betsky, "Adrienne Rich: Some Kind of Hetaira," *Harvard Crimson,* June 14, 1973.

52 Journal, June 21, 1952, folder 95, AR Papers.

53 Journal, July 6, 1952, folder 95, AR Papers.

54 Journal, July 6, 1952, folder 95, AR Papers.

55 Journal, July 13, 1952, folder 95, AR Papers.

56 J. Donald Adams, "Speaking of Books," *The New York Times Book Review,* Feb. 22, 1953.

57 Andy McCord, "Adrienne Rich: A Wild Patience at Delta State," *Delta Democrat-Times,* Feb. 21, 1982, folder 365, AR Papers.

## CHAPTER 7: Cleopatra of Oxford

1 AR to May Sarton, Feb. 15, 1953, May Sarton Papers.

2 Dana Greene, *Elizabeth Jennings: "The Inward War"* (Oxford: Oxford University Press, 2018), 37.

3 AR to DH, Feb. 16, 1953, and May 9, 1953, DH Papers.

4 "Day-Dreams and Fantasy," *The Times Literary Supplement,* Feb. 6, 1953.

5 Katharine S. White to AR, Nov. 19, 1952, folder 145, AR Papers.

6 These lapses are noted in Rich's correspondence with Katharine S. White and Howard Moss, folder 145, AR Papers.

7 Katharine S. White to AR, Feb. 19, 1953; AR to Katharine S. White, Mar. 7, 1953; Katharine S. White to AR, Mar. 24, 1953, folder 145, AR Papers.

8 Katharine S. White to AR, Feb. 19, 1953, folder 145, AR Papers.

9 AR to DH, May 9, 1953, DH Papers.

10 AR to DH, May 10, 1954, DH Papers.

11 Bernard Crick to Francis Celoria, Nov. 7, 1952, BRC Papers.

12 Bernard Crick to Francis Celoria, Nov. 7, 1952, BRC Papers.

13 Francis Celoria to Bernard Crick, "No. 2 letter, Monday, 9.30," BRC Papers.

14 Bernard Crick to Francis Celoria, Nov. 7, 1952, BRC Papers.

15 Francis Celoria to Bernard Crick ("& Sumner"), "Letter 3, Tuesday 13 (Morning)," BRC Papers.

16 Francis Celoria to Bernard Crick and Sumner Powell, "LETTER 5," Nov. 16, 1952, BRC Papers.

17 Sumner Chilton Powell to Bernard Crick, Nov. 30, 1952, BRC Papers.

18 Francis Celoria to Bernard Crick, "Monday 24" [Nov. 24, 1952], BRC Papers.

19 Francis Celoria to Bernard Crick, "Monday 24" [Nov. 24, 1952], BRC Papers.

20 Francis Celoria to Bernard Crick, "Monday 24" [Nov. 24, 1952], BRC Papers.

21 Sumner Chilton Powell to Bernard Crick, Jan. 11, 1953, BRC Papers.

22 CR, email message to author, Mar. 19, 2020.

23 "Sources," *CP,* 583.

24 Journal, May 1, 1953, folder 42v, AR Papers.

25 DH, email message to author, June 15, 2016.

26 "For Ethel Rosenberg," *CP,* 540.

27 AR to DH, May 9, 1953, DH Papers.

28 Journal, June 4, 1953, folder 42, AR Papers.

29 Journal, June 6, 1953, folder 42v, AR Papers.

30 "The Tourist and the Town," *CP*, 54.

31 "Notes," *Collected Early Poems: 1950–1970* (New York: Norton, 1993), 423.

32 "Blood, Bread, and Poetry: The Location of the Poet," *BBP*, 175.

33 CR, email messages to author, Aug. 6, 2014, and Feb. 28, 2017.

34 "For L.G.: Unseen for Twenty Years," *CP*, 421–24.

35 AR to DH, Feb. 15, 1968, DH Papers.

36 AR to Katharine S. White, Apr. 20, 1953, folder 145, AR Papers.

37 Arnold Rich kept copies of the vicious letters he sent to Adrienne after he learned of her engagement, but CR recalled destroying those copies in her parents' papers, because she thought the content was abhorrent. CR, email message to author, Mar. 19, 2020.

38 "Split at the Root: An Essay on Jewish Identity," *BBP*, 114.

39 Copy, Record of Marriages, Alfred Haskell Conrad and Adrienne Cecile Rich, City of Cambridge (MA), County of Middlesex, volume 35, folio 217.

## CHAPTER 8: The Unborn Self

1 AR to DH, Oct. 30, 1953, DH Papers.

2 Claudia Goldin, "Cliometrics and the Nobel," *Journal of Economic Perspectives* 9.2 (Spring 1995): 191. As Goldin notes, "cliometrics" pays tribute to Clio, the Greek muse of history.

3 "Econometrics," Investopedia, investopedia.com.

4 Robert Meyer, email message to author, Sept. 6, 2016.

5 AR to DH, Aug. 12, 1955, DH Papers.

6 Peggy Webb Patterson, phone interview with author, May 1, 2016.

7 Peter Davison, *The Fading Smile: Poets in Boston from Robert Lowell to Sylvia Plath* (New York: Norton, 1994), 193.

8 Kathleen Spivack, *With Robert Lowell and His Circle: Sylvia Plath, Anne Sexton, Elizabeth Bishop, Stanley Kunitz, and Others* (Boston: Northeastern University Press, 2012), 100.

9 CR, email message to author, Aug. 6, 2014.

10 DH, email message to author, June 15, 2016.

11 AR to DH, Nov. 6, 1953, DH Papers.

12 AR to DH, Oct. 30, 1953, DH Papers.

13 AR to DH, Jan. 7, 1954, DH Papers.

14 In later collected editions of her poetry, Rich shortened the title and referred to her second book simply as *The Diamond Cutters*.

15 Alfred Conrad to Elizabeth Lawrence, Apr. 1, 1955, folder 138, AR Papers.

16 "Anger and Tenderness," *OWB*, 26.

17 "Mother and Son, Woman and Man," *OWB*, 193.

18 "Anger and Tenderness," *OWB*, 25.

19 John Holmes, "Three Voices," *The New York Times Book Review*, Apr. 8, 1956.

20 Rich saved many of her reviews. A look at the early reviews reveals that critics writing for regional newspapers often saw the same strengths in *The Diamond Cutters* that her poet friends pointed out in their reviews for elite literary publications. However, these unknowns sometimes voiced objections her friends probably wouldn't have felt comfortable making. In doing so, they implicitly made a case for the value of choosing reviewers with no personal ties to their subjects. Folder 284, AR Papers.

21 Helen Vendler, "Ghostlier Demarcations, Keener Sounds," in *Adrienne Rich's Poetry*, ed. Barbara Charlesworth Gelpi and Albert Gelpi (New York: Norton, 1975), 164.

22 "The Middle-Aged," *CP*, 94–95.

23 "Living in Sin," *CP*, 71.

24 "The Diamond Cutters," *CP*, 104–105.

25 Note to "The Diamond Cutters," *Collected Early Poems: 1950–1970* (New York: Norton, 1993), 423.

26 "Foreword," *Collected Early Poems*, xix.

27 DH, "A Diet of Dissatisfaction," *Poetry* 87.5 (Feb. 1956): 301–302.

28 AR to DH, Feb. 29, 1956, DH Papers.

29 Randall Jarrell, *Poetry and the Age* (New York: Knopf, 1953), 165–66.

30 Randall Jarrell, "New Books in Review: Five Poets," *The Yale Review* 46.1 (Sept. 1956): 100–103.

31 Untitled tribute to Randall Jarrell, *Alumni News*, University of North Carolina at Greensboro (Spring 1966): 5.

32 AR to Jack Sweeney, Jan. 25, 1956, Papers of John L. (Jack) Sweeney and Máire MacNeill Sweeney.

33 AR to DH, Jan. 26, 1956, DH Papers.

34 Barbara Charlesworth Gelpi, "Introduction," "Reading at Stanford, 1973," audio recordings of Adrienne Rich, Penn Sound, Center for Programs in Contemporary Writing, writing.upenn.edu/pennsound.

35 Howard Moss to AR, Oct. 25, 1957, folder 145, AR Papers.

36 AR draft of letter to Howard Moss [1958], folder 145, AR Papers.

37 I'm indebted to CR for this insight. CR, email message to author, Apr. 23, 2017.

38 F. W. Dupee, "The Muse as House Guest," *Partisan Review* offprint (n.d.), 458, folder 145, AR Papers.

39 Sylvia Plath to Gordon Lameyer, quoted in Linda W. Wagner-Martin, *Sylvia Plath: A Biography* (New York: St. Martin's Press, 1987), 118. The original source is "Letters from Sylvia," an essay that Lameyer published in the *Smith Alumnae Quarterly* 16 (Feb. 1976): 3–10.

40 AR to DH, Feb. 29, 1956, DH Papers.

41 *Selected Poems* (London: Chatto & Windus, 1967) includes "Boundary" and "The Springboard" from *A Change of World*, and "Lucifer in the Train," "Concord River," and "The Middle-Aged" from *The Diamond Cutters*.

42 Davison, *The Fading Smile*, 194–95.

43  AR to DH, Aug. 23, 1955, DH Papers.

44  Robert Lowell, "Memories of West Street and Lepke," *Selected Poems*, rev. ed. (New York: Noonday, 1977), 91.

CHAPTER 9: Bursting with Benzedrine and Emancipation

1  Sylvia Plath, journal entry, Apr. 13, 1958, *The Unabridged Journals of Sylvia Plath, 1950–1962*, ed. Karen V. Kukil (New York: Anchor, 2000), 367.

2  Jean Valentine recounts the anecdote about Rich's use of the Poetry Room. Christina Davis, "Oral History Initiative: A Conversation with Jean Valentine," Mar. 12, 2017, woodberrypoetryroom.com.

3  Plath, journal entry, Apr. 13, 1958, *The Unabridged Journals*, 367–68.

4  Plath, journal entry, Apr. 13, 1958, *The Unabridged Journals*, 368.

5  Plath, journal entry, Apr. 13, 1958, *The Unabridged Journals*, 369. Conrad's frequent business trips to countries in South America and the Middle East may explain his suntan.

6  Plath, journal entry, Apr. 13, 1958, *The Unabridged Journals*, 369.

7  Sylvia Plath to Jack Sweeney, Apr. 27, 1958, Papers of John L. (Jack) Sweeney and Máire MacNeill Sweeney.

8  AR to Jack Sweeney, Feb. 20, 1959, Papers of John L. (Jack) Sweeney and Máire MacNeill Sweeney.

9  Sylvia Plath, journal entry, Apr. 17, 1958, *The Unabridged Journals*, 371.

10  AR to Diane Wood Middlebrook, Aug. 9, 1989, folder 6, AR Papers.

11  "Anger and Tenderness," *OWB*, 28–29.

12  "Anger and Tenderness," *OWB*, 27.

13  Guggenheim Foundation, 1951–1959, folder 77, AR Papers.

14  Jed Rasula, *The American Poetry Wax Museum: Reality Effects, 1940–1990* (Urbana, IL: National Council of Teachers of English, 1996), 60.

15  "An Interview with Adrienne Rich," no author listed, *The Island* 3 (May 1966), 3, folder 190v, AR Papers.

16  Robert Lowell to Elizabeth Bishop, Oct. 16, 1958, *The Letters of Robert Lowell*, ed. Saskia Hamilton (New York: Farrar, Straus and Giroux, 2005), 328.

17  AR to Jack Sweeney, Feb. 20, 1959, Papers of John L. (Jack) Sweeney and Máire MacNeill Sweeney.

18  "The Independent School for Girls in the Contemporary World: Its Singular Challenge" (booklet commemorating 50th anniversary of Roland Park Country School), Oct. 11, 1958, folder 352, AR Papers.

19  "The Independent School for Girls in the Contemporary World," folder 352, AR Papers.

20  "Anger and Tenderness," *OWB*, 29–30.

21  CR, email message to author, Apr. 23, 2017.

22  AR to Margareta Faissler, undated but annotated "[1959?]," folder 112, AR Papers.

23  AR to Margareta Faissler, Mar. 16, 1959, folder 112, AR Papers.

24  AR to DH, Feb. 15, 1968, DH Papers.

25 Guggenheim Foundation, 1951–1959, folder 77, AR Papers.

26 AR to Jack Sweeney, Apr. 17, 1959, Papers of John L. (Jack) Sweeney and Máire MacNeill Sweeney.

27 Diane Wood Middlebrook, *Anne Sexton: A Biography* (Boston: Houghton Mifflin, 1991).

28 AR quoted in Peter Davison, *The Fading Smile: Poets in Boston from Robert Lowell to Sylvia Plath* (New York: Norton, 1994), 203–204. The comment originally appeared in Middlebrook, *Anne Sexton.*

29 Elizabeth Bishop, quoted in Heather Treseler, "One Long Poem," *Boston Review,* Aug. 17, 2016, bostonreview.net.

30 Kathleen Spivack, *With Robert Lowell and His Circle,* 84–85.

31 AR to Denise Levertov, May 27, 1960, DL Papers.

32 Arnold Rich to AR [undated], enclosed with program for the National Academy of Arts and Letters and the National Institute of Arts and Letters Ceremonial, May 25, 1960, folder 78, AR Papers.

33 AR to Denise Levertov, Nov. 29, 1960, DL Papers.

34 "A Marriage in the 'Sixties," *CP,* 137–39.

35 AR to Denise Levertov, Mar. 17, 1961, DL Papers.

36 CR, email message to author, Apr. 22, 2017.

37 AR to Denise Levertov, Sept. 1, 1961, DL Papers.

38 AR to Denise Levertov, Sept. 1, 1961, DL Papers.

39 AR to Jack Sweeney, May 23, 1962, Papers of John L. (Jack) Sweeney and Máire MacNeill Sweeney.

40 Ted Hughes to AR [Mar. 1961], folder 127, AR Papers. Hughes wrote that Plath had gone to the hospital the previous day to have her appendix removed, and he was at home tending to their daughter. Plath's hospital stay was the catalyst for "Tulips," a meditation on oblivion and death that laid the poetic groundwork for many of her poems in *Ariel.*

41 Ted Hughes to AR, Sept. 9, 1962, folder 127, AR Papers.

42 Sylvia Plath, "Daddy," *Collected Poems* (New York: Harper & Row, 1981), 223.

43 Sylvia Plath, "Lady Lazarus," *Collected Poems,* 246.

44 AR, typed lecture titled "The Man of Noon: Masculine Figures in the Poetry of Women" 2: Sylvia Plath and Diane Wakoski, [undated, mid-1970s], folder 354, AR Papers.

45 AR published *A Wild Patience Has Taken Me This Far* in 1981.

46 Plath, "Lady Lazarus," *Collected Poems,* 244–47.

CHAPTER 10: Pessimistic Optimist

1 "Foreword," *Collected Early Poems: 1950–1970* (New York: Norton, 1993), xx–xxi.

2 AR quoted in David Kalstone, "Talking with Adrienne Rich," *Saturday Review* (Apr. 22, 1972), 57.

3 AR was not alone in dating her poems. Allen Ginsberg, for example, did

the same, and in his later collected editions, he provided explanatory notes, just as AR did in hers. Both poets were meticulous curators of their own work.

4  AR to Robert Lowell, May 30, 1962, Robert Lowell Papers.

5  Jacket copy, *Snapshots of a Daughter-in-Law* (New York: Harper & Row, 1 963).

6  AR, "Pages from a Memoir of the Forties," folder 26, AR Papers.

7  Rachel Blau DuPlessis, *Writing Beyond the Ending: Narrative Strategies of Twentieth-Century Women Writers* (Bloomington: Indiana University Press, 1985), 125.

8  DuPlessis, *Writing Beyond the Ending,* 126.

9  "Snapshots of a Daughter-in-Law," *CP,* 121.

10  "Adrienne Rich and Robin Morgan Talk About Poetry and Women's Culture," in *New Women's Survival Sourcebook,* ed. Kirsten Grimstad and Susan Rennie (New York: Knopf, 1975), 107.

11  Lucy Freeman, "Among the Recent Books: A Digest of Reviews," *New York Times,* Apr. 7, 1963.

12  R. W. Flint, *The New York Review of Books,* Feb. 1, 1963, www.nybooks.com.

13  CR, email correspondence with author.

14  Arnold Rich, typed assessment of *Snapshots of a Daughter-in-Law,* folder 26, AR Papers.

15  AR to DL, Nov. 23, 1964, DL Papers. In this letter, Rich specifically expressed her admiration for Wieners.

16  See Donna Krolik Hollenberg, *A Poet's Revolution: The Life of Denise Levertov* (Berkeley: University of California Press, 2013); and Dana Greene, *Denise Levertov: A Poet's Life* (Urbana: University of Illinois Press, 2012).

17  Hollenberg, *A Poet's Revolution,* 169.

18  AR to Denise Levertov, July 5, 1960, DL Papers.

19  "A Communal Poetry," *WIFT,* 166.

20  AR to DH, Oct. 30, 1953.

21  "A Communal Poetry," *WIFT,* 166.

22  John Dorsey, "Adrienne Rich: 'One Writes Poetry Because It Is Necessary for Him,' Says the Noted Baltimore-Born Author," *Sunday Sun Magazine,* May 15, 1966.

23  "The Academy of American Poets Presents Adrienne Rich and William Stafford," display ad in "Arts & Leisure," *New York Times,* Nov. 17, 1963.

24  Robert Lowell to AR, Feb. 25, 1964. *The Letters of Robert Lowell,* ed. Saskia Hamilton (New York: Farrar, Straus and Giroux, 2005), 443–44.

25  AR to Robert Lowell, Feb. 23 [1965], Robert Lowell Papers.

26  Hollenberg, *A Poet's Revolution,* 213.

27  DL, quoted in Hollenberg, *A Poet's Revolution,* 213.

28  Harry Gilroy, "Pulitzer Winner Is Seeking a Job," *New York Times,* May 6, 1964.

29 Robert Lowell to AR, June 3, 1964, *The Letters of Robert Lowell*, ed. Saskia Hamilton (New York: Farrar, Straus and Giroux, 2005), 450.

30 Richard F. Shepard, "Robert Lowell Rebuffs Johnson as Protest over Foreign Policy," *New York Times*, June 3, 1965.

31 CR, email message to author, Mar. 19, 2020.

32 Hollenberg, *A Poet's Revolution*, 219. Specifically, Levertov was moved by Rich's draft of "After Dark," a poem about Rich's painful relationship with her father. According to Hollenberg, the draft provided some of the impetus behind the "Olga Poems," memorializing Levertov's difficult relationship with her older sister.

33 AR to DL, Mar. 10, 1966, DL Papers.

34 DL, journal entry recorded after Oct. 23, 1966. Series 3.1, box 3, folder 6, Datebook 1966, DL Papers.

35 John H. Fenton, "Read-In for Peace Held at Harvard: Antiwar Poetry Heard at First of National Series, *New York Times*, May 4, 1966.

36 Alfred Conrad to HC, Dec. 26, 1965, HC Papers.

37 AR to Lowell and Hardwick, July 26, 1966, Robert Lowell Papers.

38 Dorsey, "Adrienne Rich," 12.

CHAPTER 11: Like This Together

1 AR to HC and Rose Marie Carruth, Dec. 4, 1966, HC Papers.

2 "Eben Haëzer," *CP*, 209–210.

3 AR quoted in Celia B. Betsky, "Adrienne Rich: Some Kind of Hetaira," *Harvard Crimson*, June 14, 1973.

4 "Autumn Sequence," *CP*, 191–93.

5 "After Dark," *CP*, 186.

6 "Like This Together," *CP*, 174.

7 HC, "To Solve Experience," *Poetry* 109.4 (Jan. 1967): 267–68.

8 Albert J. Gelpi, "Disclosing the 'Secret in the Core,'" *Christian Science Monitor*, Aug. 18, 1966.

9 Robert Lowell, "Modesty Without Mumbling," *The New York Times Book Review*, July 17, 1966.

10 Arnold Rich and HJR, letter to Olga Givens [spelling of last name is uncertain], Aug. 2, 1966, file 14, HJR Papers.

11 AR, correspondence with Elizabeth Lawrence, Cass Canfield, and Frances Munson McCullough, folder 138, AR Papers.

12 AR to HC, Mar. 23, 1967, HC Papers.

13 AR to HC, Oct. 11, 1966, HC Papers.

14 AR to George Becker, Oct. 18, 1966; Becker to AR, Oct. 20, 1966, file 380, AR Papers.

15 AR to HC and Rose Marie Carruth, Dec. 12 [?], 1966, HC Papers.

16 AR to HC and Rose Marie Carruth, Dec. 12 [?], 1966, HC Papers.

17 AR to HC, Dec. 15, 1966, HC Papers.

18  AR to HC and Rose Marie Carruth, Dec. 23, 1966, HC Papers.

19  AR to HC, Dec. 29, 1966, HC Papers.

20  AR to HC, Dec. 31, 1966, HC Papers.

21  AR to HC, Dec. 31, 1966, HC Papers.

22  AR to HC, Mar. 23, 1967, HC Papers.

23  AR to HC, Feb. 14, 1967, HC Papers.

24  AR to HC, Feb. 14, 1967, HC Papers.

25  AR to George Becker, Jan. 6, 1967, and George Becker to AR, Jan. 9, 1967, folder 380, AR Papers.

26  AR to Samuel Hynes, Jan. 12, 1968, folder 380, AR Papers.

27  AR to C. Courtney Smith, president of Swarthmore College, July 31, 1968, folder 380, AR Papers.

28  Rose Marie Carruth, interview with author, Johnson, VT, Mar. 9, 2017.

29  AR to HC and Rose Marie Carruth, Oct. 11, 1966, HC Papers.

30  Beginning in the fall of 1966 and continuing well into 1967, AR sent HC periodic updates on the purchase of the West Barnet property. Her 1967 letter giving history of the area and explaining Conrad's name for the house is dated only "Friday morning."

31  Columbia University MFA syllabuses and reading lists, folder 381, AR Papers.

32  Hugh Seidman, "Will, Change, and Power in the Poetry of Adrienne Rich," *The Virginia Quarterly Review* 82.2 (Spring 2006), vqronline.org.

33  Louise Glück, email message to author, Aug. 14, 2019.

34  CR, email message to author, July 15, 2014.

35  File 1.10, HJR Papers.

36  HJR to Leonel Weil, May 31, 1982, file 1.10, HJR Papers.

37  AR to HC, Apr. 22, 1968, HC Papers.

38  Arnold Rich, typed assessment of *Snapshots of a Daughter-in-Law,* folder 26, AR Papers.

39  HJR to David C. Sabiston, Apr. 8, 1968, file 1.8, HJR Papers.

40  Robert H. Heptinstall, tribute to Arnold Rice Rich, "Department of Pathology History," Johns Hopkins Medicine Pathology. Web.

41  Ella H. Oppenheimer, M.D., *Arnold Rice Rich, 1893–1968* (Washington, D.C.: National Academy of Sciences, 1979), 337.

42  James Shaka, M.D., letter to AR, Dec.1, 1993, file 9.9, HJR Papers.

43  AR to HC, Apr. 22, 1968, HC Papers.

44  CR, email message to author, July 22, 2017.

45  AR to HC, Apr. 22, 1968, HC Papers.

46  CR, email message to author, July 23, 2017.

47  HJR to Evy [no last name given], undated, file 1.8, HJR Papers.

48  AR wrote about her drinking in letters to HC. See, for example, AR to HC, Sept. 27, 1968, HC Papers.

CHAPTER 12: What the Autumn Knew Would Happen

1 AR to HC, Aug. 3, 1968, HC Papers.
2 Peggy Webb Patterson, phone interview with author, May 1, 2016.
3 AR, "Teaching Language in Open Admissions," *LSS*, 53.
4 Gwendolyn Brooks, quoted by Cheryl Clarke in "Rich Recollections: 'Her Love Means Danger,'" *Sinister Wisdom* 87 (Fall 2012): 15.
5 The story of the Columbia protests is available from numerous sources—for example, Frank da Cruz, "Columbia University 1968," columbia.edu.
6 Jack Litewka, speaker at memorial reading, "A Change of World: In Memory of Adrienne Rich," James C. Hormel Gay and Lesbian Center, San Francisco Public Library, Apr. 25, 2012, youtube.com.
7 Louis J. Lumenick, "Arrests Appear Imminent as Vigil Continues," *The Campus*, Nov. 7, 1968.
8 Ronald B. McGuire, phone interview with author, Jan. 20, 2017.
9 Jay Schulman, "Alfred Conrad: A Reminiscence," *Observation Post*, Nov. 6, 1970.
10 AR to HC, Nov. 5, 1968, HC Papers.
11 "Restructuring the University," *Firing Line with William F. Buckley, Jr.,* Feb. 25, 1969, youtube.com.
12 The source of this information was a longtime confidante of Rich's who wishes to remain anonymous.
13 Susan Sontag, *Reborn: Journals and Notebooks, 1947–1963*, ed. David Rieff (New York: Farrar, Straus and Giroux, 2009), Kindle edition, 78–79.
14 Robert Lowell to AR [August 1967], *The Letters of Robert Lowell*, ed. Saskia Hamilton (New York: Farrar, Straus and Giroux, 2005), 490.
15 The source of this information wishes to remain anonymous.
16 "November 1968," *CP*, 299.
17 AR quoted in Celia B. Betsky, Adrienne Rich: "Some Kind of Hetaira," *Harvard Crimson*, June 14, 1973.
18 AR to HC, Jan. 1, 1969, HC Papers.
19 Schulman, "Alfred Conrad: A Reminiscence."
20 AR to HC, Feb. 12, 1969, HC Papers.
21 Schulman, "Alfred Conrad: A Reminiscence."
22 Victor Fuchs, phone interview with author, Sept. 11, 2016.
23 Robert Solow, phone interview with author, Jan. 17, 2016.
24 Christine Nagorski, email message to author, Mar. 16, 2017; Nagorski, phone interview with author, Mar. 18, 2017.
25 Nadezhda Mandelstam quoted in Henry Raymont, "Poetry Translations: Literal or the Mood and Art?" *New York Times*, Mar. 19, 1969.
26 John Berryman to AR, Dec. 27, 1969, folder 126, AR Papers.
27 "7/24/68: I," *CP*, 281.
28 "8/4/68," *CP*, 284.
29 "8/8/68: II," *CP*, 285.

30 AR to family, May 29, 1951, folder 94, AR Papers.

31 AR to HC, Mar. 10, 1969, HC Papers.

32 AR undated letter to HC, filed between letters dated Nov. 6, 1969, and Nov. 13, 1969, HC Papers.

33 "Dr. Alfred H. Conrad, City College Professor, Dies," *New York Times,* Oct. 20, 1970.

34 AR to HC, May 25, 1969, HC Papers.

35 Israel Shenker, "City College Faculty Is Divided Over Dual Admissions," *New York Times*, May 27, 1969.

36 AR to HC, May 25, 1969, HC Papers.

37 AR to HC, Oct. 6, 1971, HC Papers.

38 AR to HC, May 16, 1969, HC Papers.

39 AR to HC, May 25, 1969, HC Papers.

40 AR to HC, Nov. 13, 1969, HC Papers.

41 AR to HC, Dec. 1, 1969, HC Papers.

42 AR to HC, May 16, 1969, HC Papers.

43 AR to HC, Nov. 23, 1969, HC Papers.

## CHAPTER 13: Brilliant, Mad, Human, and Irreplaceable

1 Jay Schulman, "Alfred Conrad: A Reminiscence," *Observation Post*, Nov. 6, 1970.

2 AR to HC, Mar. 27, 1970, HC Papers.

3 Schulman, "Alfred Conrad: A Reminiscence."

4 Henry D. Thoreau, *Walden* (New York: Thomas Y. Crowell & Co., 1940), 118.

5 CR, email message to author, Jan. 12, 2017.

6 "Tear Gas," *CP,* 293–95.

7 AR to HC, Dec. 4, 1969, HC Papers.

8 AR to HC, Dec. 4, 1969, HC Papers.

9 "What Is Effective in the Therapeutic Process? A Round Table Discussion," *American Journal of Psychoanalysis* 75.2 (June 2015). Web.

10 Barbara Moore, "Gordon/Graham: Two Recent Accounts of Psychotherapy with Leslie Farber," *Salmagundi* 123 (Summer 1999): 259. Web.

11 Robin Morgan, phone interview with author, Aug. 25, 2017.

12 "Adrienne Rich," interview by Matthew Rothschild, *The Progressive* 58.1 (Jan. 1994), progressive.org.

13 Rose Marie Carruth, interview with author, Johnson, VT, Mar. 9, 2017.

14 AR to HC, June 5, 1970, HC Papers.

15 AR to HC, June 20, 1970, HC Papers.

16 AR to HC, June 20, 1970, HC Papers.

17 AR to HC, July 3, 1970, HC Papers.

18 AR to HC, July 22, 1970, HC Papers.

19 AR to HC, July 30, 1970, HC Papers.

20 AR to HC, July 30, 1970, HC Papers.

21 Rose Marie Carruth, phone conversation with author.

22 John O'Mahoney, "Poet and Pioneer," *Guardian*, June 14, 2002. Web.

23 Robin Morgan, "Goodbye to All That," in *Dispatches from the Women's Liberation Movement*, ed. Rosalyn Fraad Baxandall and Linda Gordon (New York: Basic Books, 2001), 56.

24 AR to HC, Aug. 6, 1970, HC Papers.

25 Linda Charlton, "Women March Down Fifth in Equality Drive," *New York Times*, Aug. 27, 1970.

26 "Foreword," *BBP*, vii.

27 AR to HC, Aug. 31, 1970, HC Papers.

28 AR to HC, Sept. 18, 1970, HC Papers.

29 AR to HC, Oct. 4, 1970, HC Papers.

30 "Cloudy and Warm with Showers," *Caledonian-Record*, Oct. 13, 1970.

31 "Weather," *Caledonian-Record*, Oct. 13, 1970.

32 AR laid out her theory in a letter to HC, Nov. 10, 1970, HC Papers.

33 AR to HC, Oct. 13, 1970, HC Papers.

34 HC to his mother, Oct. 18, 1970, HC Papers.

35 AR mentioned receiving a bank statement, including the canceled check for Conrad's purchase of the gun, in a letter to HC, Nov. 10, 1970, HC Papers.

36 O'Mahoney, "Poet and Pioneer."

37 HC to AR, Oct. 19, 1970, HC Papers.

38 X. J. Kennedy, phone interview with author, Sept. 6, 2019.

39 John Berryman to AR [dated "Monday," 1970], folder 126, AR Papers.

40 "Alfred H. Conrad, City College Professor, Dies," *New York Times*, Oct. 20, 1970.

41 Several sources have said AR told them about the letters. Her friend Helen Margolis Smelser Daube identified the woman in question as a close mutual friend of hers and AR's who went on to become a Jungian analyst. Tina Smelser (conveying responses from Daube, her mother), email message to author, Feb. 16, 2019.

42 AR to HC, Oct. 24, 1970, HC Papers.

43 Victor Fuchs, phone interview with author, Sept. 11, 2016.

44 Christine Nagorski, email message to author, Mar. 16, 2017; Nagorski, phone interview with author, Mar. 18, 2017.

45 Steve Marcus, "Memorial," *Observation Post*, Nov. 20, 1970.

46 Jonny Neumann, untitled tribute to Alfred Conrad, *Observation Post*, Nov. 6, 1970.

47 "Sources," *CP*, 588.

48 "The Days: Spring," *CP*, 291.

## CHAPTER 14: A Woman of the 1970s

1 AR to HC, Oct. 31, 1970, HC Papers.

2 HC to his mother, Nov. 7, 1970, HC Papers.

3 AR to Audre Lorde, Aug. 15, 1979, AL Papers.

4 Rose Marie Carruth, interview with author, Mar. 9, 2017.

5 AR to HC, Apr. 3, 1971, HC Papers.

6 AR to HC, Sept. 16, 1971, HC Papers.

7 AR to HC, Jan. 19, 1971, HC Papers.

8 AR to HC, Jan. 19, 1971, HC Papers.

9 AR to HC, Jan. 19, 1971, HC Papers.

10 AR to HC, Oct. 31, 1970, HC Papers.

11 AR to Susan Griffin, June 8 [1975], Susan Griffin personal collection.

12 Robin Morgan, phone interview with author, Aug. 25, 2017.

13 Robin Morgan, phone interview with author, Aug. 25, 2017.

14 Kathleen Spivack, interview with author, Watertown, MA, Aug. 15, 2016.

15 AR to Kathleen Fraser, Dec. 10, 1971, Kathleen Fraser Papers.

16 "The Will to Change," *CP*, 330.

17 "Images for Godard," *CP*, 337.

18 "The Burning of Paper Instead of Children," *CP*, 304.

19 Roger Ebert, "Pierrot le Fou," rogerebert.com.

20 AR to HC, Mar. 6, 1971, HC Papers.

21 "Talking with Adrienne Rich," *Ohio Review* 13.1: 43–44.

22 "Talking with Adrienne Rich," *Ohio Review* 13.1: 46.

23 Stanley Plumly, email message to author, May 6, 2017.

24 Mary Dorman, email message to author, Mar. 18, 2019.

25 AR to HC, Mar. 6, 1971, HC Papers.

26 AR to Kathleen Fraser, Dec. 10, 1971, Kathleen Fraser Papers.

27 AR to HC, Jan. 30, 1971, HC Papers.

28 AR to HC, July 12, 1971; AR to HC, July 23, 1971; HC Papers.

29 AR quoted in David Kalstone, "Talking with Adrienne Rich," *Saturday Review*, Apr. 22, 1972, 57.

30 AR to HC, July 19, 1971, HC Papers.

31 AR to HC, Sept. 17, 1971, HC Papers.

32 AR to HC, Oct. 6, 1971, HC Papers.

33 AR to HC, Jan. 10, 1972, HC Papers.

34 AR quoted in Ruth Heimbuecher, " 'Zombies' of Watergate Hollow Inside, Poet Says," *Pittsburgh Press*, Oct. 25, 1973.

35 Robin Morgan, phone interview with author, Aug. 25, 2017.

36 AR to HC, Apr. 10, 1972, HC Papers.

37 AR to HC, Apr. 14, 1972, HC Papers.

38 AR to Anthony Burgess, Mar. 16, 1972, folder 110, AR Papers.

39 "5/4/69," "The Blue Ghazals," *CP*, 312.

## CHAPTER 15: The Book of Myths

1 AR to Elizabeth Hardwick, "Cambridge, Nov. 24" [1972].

2 AR to DH and Jane Kenyon, Jan. 7, 1973, DH Papers.

3 AR to Kathleen Fraser, Dec. 10, 1971, box 13, folder 12, Kathleen Fraser Papers.

4  AR to Elaine Hedges, Nov. 3, 1973, Florence Howe personal collection.

5  AR to Tillie Olsen, Nov. 6, 1972, TO Papers.

6  "From a Survivor," *CP,* 397.

7  "Song," *CP,* 369.

8  Cheryl Walker, phone interview with author, Dec. 13, 2017.

9  AR to DH and Jane Kenyon, Jan. 7, 1973, DH Papers.

10  Eve Zaremba, "Adrienne Rich: Stand Fast and Move Forward," *Broadside,* 2.10 (Aug.–Sept. 1981): 4.

11  "The Anti-Feminist Woman," *The New York Review of Books,* Nov. 30, 1972.

12  Phyllis Chesler, interview with author, New York, NY, Aug. 27, 2014.

13  "Women and Madness," *The New York Times Book Review,* Dec. 31, 1972.

14  "Feminist Poet Walks Out of Signet, Terms the Society 'Male-Dominated,'" *Harvard Crimson,* Dec. 18, 1972.

15  Journal, Nov. 1, 1951, folder 41, AR Papers.

16  "Cambridge Misogyny," *Harvard Crimson,* Jan. 8, 1973.

17  AR to HC, Apr. 17, 1972, HC Papers.

18  AR to HC, Feb. 6, 1973, HC Papers.

19  "The Stranger," *CP,* 368.

20  AR to Elaine Hedges, Nov. 3, 1973, Florence Howe personal collection.

21  Anthony Burgess to AR's attorney, Mortimer Natkins, Apr. 21, 1974, folder 110, AR Papers.

22  "Diving into the Wreck," LP, 370–73.

23  Jong observed that Rich had been "writing for years about the relationship between poetry and the patriarchy"—an astute insight that provides a way of conceptualizing Rich's inventive use of form in poems as disparate as "Aunt Jennifer's Tigers" and "The Burning of Paper Instead of Children." Erica Jong, "Visionary Anger," *Ms.* (July 1973): 30–34.

24  Harvey Shapiro, "Two Sisters in Poetry," *The New York Times,* Aug. 25, 1973.

25  Cheryl Walker, "Trying to Save the Skein," *The Nation,* Oct. 8, 1973, 347.

26  AR to Cheryl Walker, Jan. 3, 1974, Cheryl Walker personal collection.

27  Pritchard showed both mettle and obtuseness in taking on "Rape." The heavy-handed poem imagines a rape victim giving the details of her assault to a policeman who seems like he may be a rapist. The poem does not sound like Rich, as Pritchard implied, yet the conundrum that the poem describes, the unsympathetic law-enforcement officer who intimidates victims rather than assisting them, remains a problem nearly fifty years later.

28  William Pritchard, "Review: Poetry Matters," *The Hudson Review* 26.3 (Autumn 1973): 587, 588. Commenting in 2017 on Rich, Pritchard wrote, "I was turned off when she began to write angry poems about being a woman and its pains. But I think that was mainly me being intolerant back in the early days of the Women's Movement." William Pritchard, email message to author, May 5, 2017.

29  AR to Cheryl Walker, Jan. 3, 1974, Cheryl Walker personal collection.

30 Margaret Atwood, "Diving into the Wreck," *The New York Times Book Review,* Dec. 30, 1973.

## CHAPTER 16: In the Name of All Women

1 Elaine Showalter, phone interview with author, Aug. 18, 2017.

2 Catharine MacKinnon, email message to author, Jan. 22, 2018.

3 "Looking for Life," *Newsweek,* Dec. 24, 1973, unpaginated, file 290, AR Papers.

4 Celia Gilbert, "Everywoman and the Muse," *Boston Phoenix,* Mar. 26, 1974.

5 Joan Nestle, email message to author, June 8, 2014.

6 Jean Valentine, "A Change of World: A Friendship," *The Virginia Quarterly Review* 82.2 (Spring 2006), vqronline.org.

7 W. S. Merwin, "On Being Awarded the Pulitzer Prize," *The New York Review of Books,* June 3, 1971.

8 Robin Morgan, phone interview with author, Aug. 25, 2017.

9 Alice Walker, "Adrienne Rich (1929–2012): Alice Walker & Frances Goldin on the Life of the Legendary Poet & Activist," "Democracy Now!" democracynow.org.

10 Eleanor Lerman, phone interview with author, May 21, 2014.

11 "The Awards: High Drama and Low Comedy," *Publishers Weekly* (May 13, 1974), 41.

12 Rust Hills, "Writing," *Esquire,* Sept. 1974, 66.

13 National Book Foundation, nationalbook.org.

14 "What Did You Think of the NBA?" *Publishers Weekly* (May 13, 1974), 40.

15 "The Awards: High Drama and Low Comedy," *Publishers Weekly,* May 13, 1974, 42.

16 "Poetry Citations," National Book Foundation. Sherrie Y. Young, National Book Foundation director of marketing and special projects, email message to author, Apr. 8, 2015.

17 "Adrienne Rich, Winner of the 1974 National Book Award for *Diving into the Wreck,*" National Book Awards Acceptance Speeches, National Book Foundation, nationalbook.org.

18 "The Awards: High Drama and Low Comedy," *Publishers Weekly,* May 13, 1974, 42.

19 AR to Aida Press, editor of *Radcliffe Quarterly,* July 26, 1974, folder 79, AR Papers.

20 Evelyn C. White, *Alice Walker: A Life* (New York: Norton, 2004), 271.

21 "The Awards: High Drama and Low Comedy," *Publishers Weekly,* May 13, 1974, 42.

22 Alexis De Veaux, *Warrior Poet: A Biography of Audre Lorde* (New York: Norton, 2006), 133–34.

23 AR to Cheryl Walker, Nov. 21, 1974, Cheryl Walker personal collection.

24 Robin Morgan, phone interview with author, Aug. 25, 2017.

25 Robin Morgan, phone interview with author, Aug. 25, 2017.

26 AR to HC and Rose Marie Carruth, Mar. 23, 1974, HC Papers.

27 Robin Morgan, phone interview with author, Sept. 1, 2017.

28 AR to HC, Mar. 20, 1972, HC Papers.

29 Robin Morgan, phone interview with author, Sept. 1, 2017.

30 Don Levine, phone interview with author, July 15, 2017.

31 CR, email message to author, Mar. 14, 2020.

32 Robin Morgan, phone interview with author, Sept. 1, 2017.

33 Susan Rennie, phone interview with author, Sept. 1, 2018.

34 Susan Griffin, phone interview with author, Mar. 25, 2015.

35 Robin Morgan, phone interview with author, Sept. 1, 2017.

36 Susan Griffin, interview with author, Berkeley, CA, June 27, 2015.

37 AR to Tillie Olsen, Mar. 2 [1975], TO Papers.

38 AR to Tillie Olsen, Aug. 4, 1975, TO Papers.

39 "Adrienne Rich, reply by Susan Sontag," *The New York Review of Books*, Mar. 20, 1975, nybooks.com.

40 "Adrienne Rich, reply by Susan Sontag."

41 "Adrienne Rich, reply by Susan Sontag."

42 Blanche M. Boyd, "Interview: Adrienne Rich," *Christopher Street* 1.7 (Jan. 1977): 13–14.

43 Susan Sontag to AR, Mar. 17, 1975, folder 128, AR Papers.

44 The source for this information does not wish to be identified.

45 Robin Morgan, phone interview with author, Sept. 1, 2017.

46 "Twenty-One Love Poems," section I, *CP*, 465.

47 "21 Love Poems," section IV, *CP*, 467.

48 "21 Love Poems," section IX, *CP*, 470.

49 "21 Love Poems," "(The Floating Poem, Unnumbered)," *CP*, 472–73.

50 Lynda Koolish, "The Incendiary Feminism of Lesbian Poetry," *San Francisco Bay Guardian*, Mar. 23, 1976.

51 "21 Love Poems," section XVII, *CP*, 474.

52 "21 Love Poems," section XVIII, *CP*, 475.

53 "21 Love Poems," section XII, *CP*, 471.

CHAPTER 17: I Know My Power

1 AR to Tillie Olsen, Aug. 4, 1975, TO Papers.

2 AR to HC and Rose Marie Carruth, Nov. 23, 1974. Rich told the Carruths that CCNY had wanted her to stay on as an adjunct and teach a class every other semester. The offer would have allowed her to earn a retirement pension. However, she did not return to teach at CCNY.

3 Mary Patterson McPherson, phone interview with author, Apr. 30, 2017.

4 Marjorie Perloff, phone interview with author, Jan. 13, 2015.

5 Kathleen Spivack, interview with author, Watertown, MA, Aug. 15, 2016.

6 Hugh Seidman, "Will, Change, and Power in the Poetry of Adrienne Rich," *Virginia Quarterly Review* 82.2 (Spring 2006), vqronline.org.

7  AR to Kathleen Fraser, Apr. 19, 1975, Kathleen Fraser Papers.

8  Kathleen Barry, phone interview with author, Apr. 27, 2018.

9  AR to Tillie Olsen, Sept. 17, 1976, TO Papers.

10  Walter Clemons, "Adrienne Rich: A Retrospective: Poems," *New York Times,* Apr. 27, 1975.

11  "From an Old House in America," *CP,* 430.

12  June Jordan to Honor Moore and Venable Herndon, Oct. 22, 1977, Honor Moore Papers, box 41, file 2, June Jordan, 1972–1985, Schlesinger Library, Harvard University.

13  Carol Flechner, phone interview with author, May 23, 2017.

14  Opal Palmer Adisa, phone interview with author, Sept. 27, 2016.

15  AR to Tillie Olsen, Sept. 17, 1976, TO Papers.

16  Nancy Kerr, interview with author, Santa Cruz, CA, July 2, 2019.

17  AR to Minnie Bruce Pratt, Aug. 16, 1987, MBP Papers. AR wrote that she and Cliff received Pratt's gift of foot warmers on their eleventh anniversary. The context of the exchange makes it clear the gift had arrived in August.

18  AR to Tillie Olsen, Sept. 17, 1976, TO Papers.

19  Donald Lamm, phone interview with author, Sept. 13, 2017.

20  If AR had chosen to live full-time at the West Barnet house, she would have been sharing it with her middle son. According to her correspondence, Pablo Conrad lived there after high school, worked for local businesses, and attended the University of Vermont. Rose Marie Carruth recalled hosting him for a meal, which she said Pablo happily declared the first time an adult had invited him for dinner. Rose Marie Carruth, interview with author, Johnson, VT, Mar. 9, 2017.

21  Janice Raymond, email message to author, Sept. 30, 2017.

22  AR to Susan Griffin, July 23, 1978, Susan Griffin personal collection.

23  AR to Tillie Olsen, Jan. 25, 1976, TO Papers.

24  Joyce Greenberg, "By Woman Taught," *Parnassus: Poetry in Review 7.2* (Spring/Summer 1979): 91–92.

25  Greenberg, "By Woman Taught," 94.

26  Greenberg, "By Woman Taught," 96.

27  Joyce Greenberg Lott, email message to author, June 10, 2018.

28  Elaine Showalter, phone interview with author, Aug. 18, 2017.

29  Rich's description of her book appears on the back of the tenth anniversary edition of *OWB.*

30  Helen Vendler, "Myths for Mothers," *The New York Review of Books,* Sept. 30, 1976.

31  DH to AR, Feb. 16, 1977, DH Papers.

32  AR to Tillie Olsen, Sept. 17, 1976, TO Papers.

33  Francine du Plessix Gray, "Amazonian Prescriptions and Proscriptions: Of Woman Born," *The New York Times Book Review,* Oct. 10, 1976.

34  AR, opinion column, *The New York Times,* Nov. 20, 1976.

35 "A Slight Woman—with Strong Words," (Rochester, NY) *Democrat and Chronicle* (Nov. 22, 1976), C1, File 360, AR Papers.

36 Blanche M. Boyd, "Interview: Adrienne Rich," *Christopher Street* 1.7 (Jan. 1977): 9.

37 Boyd, "Interview: Adrienne Rich," 9.

38 Andrew Greeley, "Outrageous Lies Sell the Best," *Chicago Tribune,* Apr. 5, 1977.

39 "It Is the Lesbian in Us . . . ," *LSS,* 199.

40 "It Is the Lesbian in Us . . . ," *LSS,* 200–201.

41 Catharine Stimpson, "Adrienne Rich and Lesbian/Feminist Poetry," *Parnassus: Poetry in Review* 12 (Jan. 1985).

42 Carol Kleiman, "Liberation's Latest Cause: Pornography," *Chicago Tribune,* July 17, 1977.

43 AR to Karla Jay, Oct. 5, 1978, Karla Jay Papers.

44 AR to Karla Jay, Oct. 5, 1978, Karla Jay Papers.

45 Patricia Schwartz, "Voice for a New Vision," *Hartford Advocate,* Sept. 28, 1977.

46 "Afterword," *OWB,* 285–86.

CHAPTER 18: Hyacinths Rising Like Flames

1 Hollie I. West, "American Poetry Review: A Bias Charge," *Washington Post,* Feb. 5, 1977, washingtonpost.com.

2 Elizabeth Scanlon, editor of *The American Poetry Review,* email message to author, July 23, 2018.

3 AR to Robin Morgan, May 13, 1978, Robin Morgan Papers.

4 Cheryl R. Devall, "From a Woman's Eye," *Harvard Crimson,* July 13, 1979.

5 Alexis De Veaux, *Warrior Poet: A Biography of Audre Lorde* (New York: Norton, 2004), 187.

6 Rita Mae Brown, phone interview with author, July 15, 2018.

7 De Veaux, *Warrior Poet,* 162.

8 AR to Audre Lorde, Mar. 18 [no year on letter], from Montague, MA, AL Papers.

9 De Veaux, *Warrior Poet,* 129.

10 De Veaux, *Warrior Poet,* 182.

11 Blanche Wiesen Cook, interview with author, New York, NY, Nov. 7, 2014.

12 Rita Mae Brown, phone interview with author, July 15, 2018.

13 AR to Audre Lorde, Jan. 18, 1992, AL Papers.

14 AR to John Benedict, May 23, 1977, AR Papers.

15 De Veaux, *Warrior Poet,* 160–61.

16 "The Meaning of Our Love for Women Is What We Have Constantly to Expand," *LSS,* 225.

17 "The Meaning of Our Love for Women," *LSS,* 224.

18 "The Meaning of Our Love for Women," *LSS,* 229.

19 AR to Susan Griffin, July 21, 1977, Susan Griffin personal collection.

20 De Veaux writes that for a year beginning in 1977, Rich and Cliff met in group sessions with Goodman and her partner and several other lesbian couples to discuss their writing. The other couples included Lorde and Frances Clayton and Clare Coss and Blanche Wiesen Cook. "Though the group started out with good intentions, it proved a mistake to hold their meetings at Goodman's home [in the East Village]. Goodman could not separate her roles as therapist and sister writer. While Goodman maintained her relationship as therapist to all of them, the group, as such, fizzled out a year later." De Veaux, *Warrior Poet*, 182.

21 AR to Susan Griffin, Aug. 10, 1977, Susan Griffin personal collection.

22 Michael S. Winett, "Rich Work Inflames Women, Men," *Daily Iowan*, Sept. 14, 1978.

23 Eric Siegel, "Feminist Poet Declines Loyola Honor," *Sunday Sun,* Sept. 11, 1977.

24 AR, "Claiming an Education," *LSS*, 235.

25 AR to HC, Oct. 5, 1977, HC Papers.

26 CR, email correspondence with author.

27 AR to Diane di Prima, Nov. 18, 1977, Berg Collection, New York Public Library.

28 Carol Smith, phone interview with author, July 12, 2018.

29 AR to Richard Poirier, Mar. 15, 1977, folder 395, AR Papers.

30 Carol Smith, phone interview with author, July 12, 2018.

31 AR to Susan Griffin, Oct. 17, 1977, Susan Griffin personal collection.

32 AR to Carol Smith, Apr. 7, 1978, folder 395, AR Papers.

33 Tom Edwards to AR, Apr. 14, 1978, folder 395, AR Papers.

34 AR to Carol Smith, Apr. 7, 1978, folder 395, AR Papers.

35 AR to John Benedict, Dec. 3, 1977, folder 142, AR Papers.

36 AR to John Benedict, Feb. 25, 1978, folder 142, AR Papers.

37 "Origins and History of Consciousness," *CP,* 448.

38 "Origins and History of Consciousness," *CP,* 449.

39 "Splittings," *CP,* 451.

40 "Upper Broadway," *CP,* 481.

41 "Nights and Days," *CP,* 484–85.

42 AR to John Benedict, May 10, 1978, folder 142, AR Papers.

43 AR to John Benedict, June 5, 1978, folder 142, AR Papers.

44 AR to John Benedict, May 10, 1978, folder 142, AR Papers.

45 Margaret Atwood, "Unfinished Women," *The New York Times Book Review,* June 11, 1978.

46 AR to Karla Jay, Oct. 5, 1978, Karla Jay Papers.

47 AR to Audre Lorde, July 1, 1978, AL Papers.

48 AR to Audre Lorde and Frances Clayton, July 1, 1978, AL Papers.

49 AR to Audre Lorde, Aug. 15, 1979, AL Papers.

50 AR to Catherine Nicholson and Harriet Ellenberger, Apr. 12, 1979, Catherine Nicholson Papers.

51  It was not necessarily a given that Rich's second prose work would be a compilation of previously published essays and revised lectures. Her correspondence suggests she received a sizable advance from Norton for her follow-up to *Of Woman Born* and may have planned to write a completely new book, but what her topic might have been is a matter of speculation.

52  DH to AR, June 17, 1981, DH Papers.

53  Jane Roberta Cooper, phone interview with author, June 21, 2017.

54  AR to Catherine Nicholson and Harriet Ellenberger, July 16, 1979, Catherine Nicholson Papers.

55  Michelle Cliff to Catherine Nicholson and Harriet Ellenberger, Nov. 16, 1979, Catherine Nicholson Papers.

## CHAPTER 19: My True University

1  I'm indebted to Paul Mariani for the historical details about AR's house in Montague. Paul Mariani, email message to author, Oct. 28, 2018.

2  AR to Catherine Nicholson and Harriet Ellenberger, July 16, 1979, Catherine Nicholson Papers.

3  Sara Maitland, "Richer Rewards: Sara Maitland Meets AR," *Observer*, Nov. 2, 1980.

4  Victoria Redel, phone interview with author, Oct. 24, 2018.

5  AR to Margareta Faissler, Dec. 13, 1979, folder 112, AR Papers.

6  AR to Susan Griffin, Oct. 4, 1979, Susan Griffin personal collection.

7  AR to Susan Griffin, Aug. 17, 1979, Susan Griffin personal collection.

8  "Culture and Anarchy," *CP*, 526.

9  "The Spirit of Place," *CP*, 552.

10  AR to Margareta Faissler, Dec. 13, 1979, file 112, AR Papers.

11  Michelle Cliff, "Notes for a Magazine," *Sinister Wisdom* 17 (1981): 3.

12  Ruth Gundle, phone interview with author, Jan. 27, 2017.

13  Maureen Brady, phone interview with author, Sept. 3, 2018.

14  Victoria Redel, phone interview with author, Oct. 25, 2018.

15  Janice Raymond, email message to author, Sept. 30, 2017.

16  "Contradictions: Tracking Poems," *CP*, 642.

17  AR to Karla Jay, Mar. 23, 1980, Karla Jay Papers.

18  Michelle Cliff to Tillie Olsen, Apr.18 [no year date, but probably 1980], TO Papers.

19  I'm grateful to Opal Palmer Adisa for her insights about the trade-off Michelle made when she came out as a lesbian and began writing about race and family matters. Opal Palmer Adisa, phone interview with author, Sept. 26, 2016.

20  Meryl F. Schwartz, "An Interview with Michelle Cliff," *Contemporary Literature* 34.4 (1993): 605.

21  Cecile Weil (Arnold Rich's sister) disapproved of AR's lesbianism, and it fell to HJR to defend AR in a strongly worded letter. It is unknown whether AR ever knew of this exchange between her mother and her aunt.

22 Janice Raymond, email message to author, Sept. 30, 2017.

23 AR to Susan Griffin, Mar. 22, 1980, Susan Griffin personal collection.

24 CR, email message to author, Mar. 19, 2020.

25 CR, letter to HJR, Aug. 31, 1985.

26 CR, email message to author, Dec. 1, 2018.

27 Inside cover, *Sinister Wisdom* 17 (1981).

28 CR, email message to author, Dec. 2, 2018.

29 AR to Susan Griffin, June 26, 1975, Susan Griffin personal collection.

30 Susan Rennie, phone interview with author, Sept. 1, 2018.

31 The magazine folded in 1980. One chronicler of *Chrysalis* writes, "Intended as a quarterly, the collective produced just ten issues over a span of three years, disbanding due to a chronic lack of funds. Yet *Chrysalis* was also mired in the bureaucracy of consensus, as editorial decisions were (for better or worse) the result of a collective process, in which everyone was compelled to agree to get to a decision. This leaderless approach was a syndrome of the feminist process itself, a by-product of the consciousness-raising structure. In making sure everyone had a voice, decision-making became woefully inefficient." Jenni Sorkin, "Second Life: *Chrysalis Magazine*," *East of Borneo*, Oct. 31, 2011, eastofborneo.org.

32 Susan Rennie, phone interview with author, Sept. 1, 2018.

33 Maureen Brady, "Adrienne Rich: Friendship Doubles My Universe," *Sinister Wisdom* 95 (Winter 2015): 62.

34 Brady, "Adrienne Rich," 66.

35 Brady, "Adrienne Rich," 65.

36 AR to Mab Segrest, Oct. 24, 1982, box 2, file 11, MS Papers.

37 Brady, "Adrienne Rich," 73.

38 Susan Robinson, email message to author, Sept. 1, 2019.

39 Brady, "Adrienne Rich," 77–78.

40 Blanche Wiesen Cook, interview with author, New York, NY, Nov. 7, 2014.

41 AR to Tillie Olsen, Aug. 8, 1981, TO Papers.

42 Audre Lorde and AR, "An Interview: Audre Lorde and Adrienne Rich," *Sister Outsider: Essays and Speeches* (Berkeley: Crossing Press, 2007), 103–104.

43 Lorde and AR, "An Interview: Audre Lorde and Adrienne Rich," 105.

44 Elana Dykewomon, phone interview with author, June 21, 2017.

45 AR reading her poems in Coolidge Auditorium, April 7, 1981, Gertrude Clarke Whittall Poetry and Literature Fund, and Archive of Recorded Poetry and Literature. Audio retrieved from the Library of Congress, loc.gov.

46 "Power," *CP*, 443.

CHAPTER 20: Anger and Tenderness

1 "For Memory," *CP*, 536.

2 "Rift," *CP*, 561.

3 "Heroines," *CP*, 546.

4 Terry Everett, "Diving into the Delta and Coming Back Up in Memphis," *Delta Scene* 9.2 (Summer 1982): 21.

5 Leigh Allen, email message to author, July 16, 2014.

6 AR's reading at Delta State College, now Delta State University, Feb. 1981, video, author's personal collection.

7 Leigh Allen, email message to author, July 16, 2014.

8 "1977: Poem for Mrs. Fannie Lou Hamer" is collected in *Directed By Desire: The Collected Poems of June Jordan* (Port Townsend, WA: Copper Canyon Press, 2005).

9 Everett, "Diving into the Delta," 26.

10 AR to Mab Segrest, Oct. 24, 1982, MS Papers.

11 Maureen Brady, phone interview with author, Sept. 3, 2018.

12 Eve Zaremba, "Adrienne Rich: Stand Fast and Move Forward," *Broadside*, 2.10 (Aug.–Sept. 1981): 4.

13 Emily Dickinson, "Tell all the Truth but tell it slant," *The Complete Poems of Emily Dickinson* (Boston: Little, Brown, 1960), 506.

14 Sara Maitland. "Richer Rewards: Sara Maitland Meets AR," *Observer*, Nov. 2, 1980.

15 Erika Sanchez, "Poet Won't Be Token Woman," *Dallas Morning News*, Feb. 10, 1980.

16 In her archives at Harvard, Rich included a report of Cornell University's library rejecting an offer of funding for books related to homosexuality. A Cornell professor writing to protest the decision, Sandy Bem, asserted that Rich was nominated for her visiting position in part because she was a lesbian. Folder 399, AR Papers.

17 AR, Cornell workshop materials, folder 399, AR Papers.

18 Donna Krolik Hollenberg, *A Poet's Revolution: The Life of Denise Levertov*, 339.

19 Evelyn Torton Beck, email message to author, Aug. 30, 2019.

20 "Split at the Root: An Essay on Jewish Identity," *BBP*, 100.

21 "Split at the Root," *BBP*, 103.

22 "Readings of History," *CP*, 133.

23 "Split at the Root," *BBP*, 101.

24 Joyce Antler, *Jewish Radical Feminism: Voices from the Women's Liberation Movement* (New York: NYU Press, 2018), 280.

25 Evelyn Torton Beck, email message to author, Aug. 30, 2019.

26 Antler, *Jewish Radical Feminism*, 279.

27 Evelyn Torton Beck, email message to author, Aug. 31, 2019.

28 Evelyn Torton Beck, email message to author, Aug. 30, 2019.

29 Ruth Gundle, phone interview with author, Jan. 27, 2017.

30 Judith Barrington, email message to author, Dec. 12, 2014.

31 Ruth Gundle, email message to author, Jan. 24, 2017.

32 AR, undated postcard to Harriet Desmoines and Catherine Nicholson, from San Francisco, filed under 1982–1983, Catherine Nicholson Papers.

33 AR to Tillie Olsen [undated but details in letter suggest it's from Dec. 1982], TO Papers.

34 AR to Tillie Olsen, Aug. 25, 1982, TO Papers.

35 "Resisting Amnesia: History and Personal Life," *BBP*, 146.

36 "Resisting Amnesia," *CP*, 147.

37 AR to Audre Lorde, Feb. 21, 1983, AL Papers.

38 Susan Sherman, phone interview with author, Aug. 12, 2017.

39 Margaret Randall, email message to author, Aug. 21, 2017.

40 AR to Tillie Olsen, Apr. 3, 1984, TO Papers.

41 "Integrity," *CP*, 524.

## CHAPTER 21: Words That Blew Our Lives Apart

1 AR to Audre Lorde, Feb. 6, 1985, AL Papers.

2 Dorchen Leidholdt supplied the detail about the "friend of the court" brief submitted by survivors of sexual violence. Leidholdt, email message to author, Jan. 15, 2020.

3 Dorchen Leidholdt, interview with author, New York, NY, May 18, 2018.

4 AR was not involved in FACT until she agreed to sign the FACT brief, according to FACT member Carole Vance, in an email message to author, Feb. 12, 2018.

5 "We Don't Have to Come Apart Over Pornography: A Statement by Adrienne Rich," *off our backs* 15.7 (July 1985): 30.

6 Dorchen Leidholdt, interview with author, May 18, 2018.

7 "We Don't Have to Come Apart Over Pornography," 30.

8 "We Don't Have to Come Apart Over Pornography," 32.

9 "We Don't Have to Come Apart Over Pornography," 30, 32.

10 Dorchen Leidholdt, email message to author, Jan. 15, 2020.

11 "An Open Letter on Pornography: A Critical Response to the FACT Brief," *off our backs* 15.8 (Aug.–Sept. 1985): 28.

12 Catharine MacKinnon, "An Open Letter to Adrienne Rich," *off our backs* 15.9 (Oct. 1985): 18.

13 MacKinnon, "An Open Letter to Adrienne Rich," 18.

14 MacKinnon, "An Open Letter to Adrienne Rich," 26.

15 Catharine MacKinnon, email message to author, Sept. 18, 2017.

16 "For an Album," *CP*, 684–85.

17 AR to Mab Segrest, Sept. 18, 1985, MS Papers.

18 "Notes Toward a Politics of Location," *BBP*, 210–11.

19 "Notes Toward a Politics of Location," 217.

20 "Notes Toward a Politics of Location," 220.

21 I'm indebted to the historian Bonnie J. Morris for emphasizing to me just how important Rich has been to the discipline of women's studies and especially to scholarship on lesbian identity and politics. Bonnie J. Morris, phone conversation with author, Aug. 30, 2019.

22 "Notes Toward a Politics of Location," *BBP*, 231.

23  "Notes Toward a Politics of Location," *BBP*, 221.

24  "Diving into the Wreck," *CP*, 373.

25  "Sources," *CP*, 577.

26  Jane Mayer, "Writing the Life of Mina P. Shaughnessy," *Journal of Basic Writing* 16.1 (1997): 54, wac.colostate.edu.

27  "If Not with Others, How?" *BBP*, 202.

28  "If Not with Others, How?" *BBP*, 203.

29  Rabbi Steve Cohen, "Opinion: An Identity Lost," *U.C. Santa Barbara Daily Nexus*, Jan. 21, 1987.

30  The amount of the Lilly Prize was later increased to $100,000.

31  AR to DH, Mar. 24, 1992, DH Papers.

32  Robin Riviello, interview with author, July 2, 2019; Thom and Nancy Kerr, interview with author, July 2, 2019. Both interviews took place in Santa Cruz, CA. Also, author's visit to 2420 Paul Minnie Avenue, Santa Cruz.

33  Robin Riviello, interview with author, July 2, 2019.

34  Sue Reinhold, phone interview with author, Apr. 30, 2014.

35  Donna Krolik Hollenberg, *A Poet's Revolution: The Life of Denise Levertov*, 339–40.

36  Dana Gioia, phone interview with author, Sept. 4, 2019.

37  Hollenberg, *A Poet's Revolution*, 340.

38  File 408, AR Papers. It's possible Rich assigned Levertov's poetry, even though it did not appear in the compilation of poems students were required to purchase. The packet, divided into sections on music, patterns, traditional forms, imagery, and meter/meaning, includes poems by about forty poets, mostly men. Rich included her own poem "The Roofwalker," dedicated to Levertov, in the section on meter and meaning.

39  Levertov's 1980s correspondence with AR, DL Papers.

40  Bettina Aptheker, interview with author, Santa Cruz, CA, July 1, 2019.

41  Sue Reinhold, phone interview with author, Apr. 30, 2014.

42  Radio interview with Michael Krasny, Feb. 24, 2005, archive.org.

43  AR to Philip Levine, Jan. 25, 1990, Philip Levine Papers.

44  California Department of Conservation, conservation.ca.gov.

45  Gary Young, interview with author, Santa Cruz, CA, July 2, 2019.

46  AR to DL, July 15, 1988, DL Papers.

47  "Love Poem," *CP*, 663–64.

48  "Sleepwalking Next to Death," *CP*, 659–74.

49  Terry Castle, phone interview with author, Aug. 14, 2014.

50  Ron Thomas, email message to author, Feb. 5, 2019.

51  Ron Thomas, email message to author, Feb. 13, 2019.

52  AR to DH, Mar. 24, 1992, DH Papers.

53  "Adrienne Rich (1929–2012): Alice Walker & Frances Goldin on the Life of the Legendary Poet & Activist," *Democracy Now!* Mar. 30, 2012, democracynow.org.

54  Fran Goldin, interview with author, New York, NY, June 14, 2017.

CHAPTER 22: Citizen Poet

1 Dana Gioia, "Can Poetry Matter?" *The Atlantic*, May 1991, theatlantic.com.
2 Ira Sadoff, email message to author, Sept. 18, 2019. Sadoff recalled that in an exchange of letters with AR in the mid-1990s, they shared their dislike of the era's conservative politics and "bemoaned the parallel conservative turn in poetry, including the 'new formalism,' the rigid understanding of rhyme and meter that she'd freed herself from in the late 1950s."
3 "What would we create?" *WIFT*, 16.
4 "What would we create?" *WIFT*, 20.
5 "What would we create?" *WIFT*, 15.
6 "Adrienne Rich," interview by Matthew Rothschild, *The Progressive* 58.1 (June 1994), progressive.org.
7 "Adrienne Rich," interview by Matthew Rothschild.
8 "Adrienne Rich," interview by Matthew Rothschild.
9 "An Atlas of the Difficult World," *CP*, 725–26.
10 Michael Milburn, Review of *An Atlas of the Difficult World, Harvard Review* 1 (Spring 1992), 130, 129.
11 Helen Vendler, "Mapping the Air," *The New York Review of Books*, Nov. 21, 1991, nybooks.com.
12 Esther B. Fein, "Book Awards for Poetry, 'Mating' and 'Freedom,'" *The New York Times*, Nov. 22, 1991.
13 AR to Philip Levine, Jan. 25, 1990, Philip Levine Papers.
14 AR to Philip Levine, Nov. 27, 1991, Philip Levine Papers.
15 Joe-Anne McLaughlin, phone interview with author, Aug. 25, 2019.
16 Ruth Gundle, email message to author, Jan. 23, 2017.
17 AR to DL, July 7, 1992, DL Papers.
18 "Hunger," *CP*, 454.
19 AR to Elly Bulkin, Irena Klepfisz, Minnie Bruce Pratt, Dec. 28, 1992, MBP Papers.
20 Bettina Aptheker, interview with author, Santa Cruz, CA, July 2, 2019.
21 Robin Morgan, interview with author, New York, NY, May 17, 2018.
22 AR to Minnie Bruce Pratt, Aug. 29, 1993, MBP Papers.
23 Tim Warren, "Rich, with Memories and a Passion for Poetry," *Baltimore Sun*, Oct. 16, 1993, baltimoresun.com.
24 "Adrienne Rich," interview by Matthew Rothschild.
25 Robin Riviello, interview with author, Santa Cruz, CA, July 1, 2019.
26 Robin Riviello, interview with author, Santa Cruz, CA, July 2, 2019.
27 Thom and Nancy Kerr, interview with author, Santa Cruz, CA, July 2, 2019.
28 "The Heart of Things," *The Language of Life*, July 28, 1995, billmoyers.com.
29 F. Scott Fitzgerald, *The Great Gatsby*, excerpted in the epigraph to *Dark Fields of the Republic, CP*, 752.
30 "In Those Years," *CP*, 755–56.
31 "Deportations," *CP*, 775–76.

32  Note on "Calle Visión," *CP*, 1135.

33  "Calle Visión," *CP*, 763.

34  "Calle Visión," *CP*, 765.

35  John Simon, "The Multicultural Muse," *The New Criterion* 15.1 (Sept. 1996), newcriterion.com.

36  Sandra M. Gilbert, "The Worst of the Best, or 'Pessoa Schmessoa,'" *Poetry* 174.1 (Apr. 1999): 34.

37  Gilbert, "The Worst of the Best," 38.

38  File 1, Biography, 1976, 1999, AR Papers.

39  AR to Audre Lorde, undated letter [1990?], AL Papers.

40  AR to Helen Margolis Smelser Daube, Dec. 28, 1996, Helen Margolis Smelser Daube personal collection.

41  "Why I Refused the National Medal for the Arts," *AP*, 98–99.

42  "Negotiations," *CP*, 664–65.

43  "Dialogue and Dissonance: *The Letters of Robert Duncan and Denise Levertov*," *HE*, 72.

CHAPTER 23: I Am My Art

1  I'm indebted to Gary Young for this insight. Gary Young, interview with author, Santa Cruz, CA, July 2, 2019.

2  Tina Smelser (recalling what AR told her mother), conversation with author, San Francisco, CA, June 30, 2019.

3  "Memorize This," *CP*, 943.

4  "Bract," *CP*, 948.

5  "Adrienne Rich—ChilePoesía 2001," youtube.com.

6  "Midnight Salvage," *CP*, 811.

7  Mystery Spot, mysteryspot.com.

8  "Waiting for You at the Mystery Spot," *CP*, 888.

9  "Turning," *CP*, 702–703.

10  CR, email message to author, June 3, 2019.

11  AR, "Credo of a Passionate Skeptic," *Los Angeles Times*, Mar. 11, 2001, latimes.com.

12  Magdalena Edwards, "Adrienne Rich in Chile: An Interview," *The Critical Flame: A Journal of Literature and Culture* 35 (Mar.–Apr. 2015), criticalflame.org.

13  "Adrienne Rich—ChilePoesía 2001," youtube.com.

14  Magdalena Edwards, email message to author, Dec. 11, 2019.

15  AR quoted in John Sanford, "Adrienne Rich: In Chile, Poets Are Treasured," *Stanford Report*, Apr. 25, 2001, news.stanford.edu.

16  Heidi Benson, "In a world of violence, inequality and moral chaos, Adrienne Rich's voice will be neither silent nor content," *SFGate*, Mar. 29, 2005, sfgate.com.

17  "USonian Journals 2000," *CP*, 915.

18  Joe-Anne McLaughlin, phone interview with author, Aug. 25, 2019.

19  AR, "Directed by Desire: An Introduction to the Collected Poems of June Jordan," Poetry Foundation, poetryfoundation.org.

20  Louise Glück, phone interview with author, Aug. 15, 2019.

21  "Poetry and the Forgotten Future," *HE,* 143.

22  Marilyn Chin, phone interview with author, Aug. 14, 2019.

23  "Ever, Again," *CP,* 1026–27.

24  "Ever, Again," *CP,* 1027.

25  "Winterface," *CP,* 1088.

26  Thom and Nancy Kerr, interview with author, Santa Cruz, CA, July 2, 2019.

27  Linda Janakos and Doren Robbins, interview with author, Santa Cruz, CA, July 3, 2019.

28  Carol Flechner, phone interview with author, Apr. 23, 2017.

29  Elana Dykewomon, phone interview with author, June 21, 2017.

30  Robin Riviello, interview with author, Santa Cruz, CA, July 2, 2019.

31  Jack Litewka, speaking during 2012 memorial tribute to AR, "A Change of World: In Memory of Adrienne Rich," at the San Francisco Public Library, sfpl.org.

32  Robin Riviello, interview with author, Santa Cruz, CA, July 2, 2019; Linda Janakos, interview with author, July 3, 2019; Cynthia Rich, email message to author, June 24, 2020.

33  Bettina Aptheker, interview with author, Santa Cruz, CA, June 30, 2019.

34  Linda Janakos, interview with author, Santa Cruz, CA, July 3, 2019.

35  "A Long Conversation," *CP,* 846–47.

# BIBLIOGRAPHY

ARCHIVES

Hayden Carruth Papers, Jack and Shirley Silver Special Collections Library, University of Vermont.

The Papers of Professor Sir Bernard Rowland Crick, 1947–1992, Birkbeck Library Archives and Special Collections, University of London.

Kathleen Fraser Papers, UCSD Special Collections, University of California San Diego.

Donald Hall Papers, Library, University of New Hampshire.

Karla Jay Papers, Manuscripts and Archives Division, New York Public Library.

June Jordan Papers, Schlesinger Library, Radcliffe Institute, Harvard University.

Denise Levertov Papers, Department of Special Collections, Stanford University Libraries.

Philip Levine Collection of Papers, Henry W. and Albert A. Berg Collection of English and American Literature, New York Public Library.

Audre Lorde Papers, Spelman College.

Robert Lowell Papers, Houghton Library, Harvard University.

Catherine Nicholson Papers, David M. Rubenstein Rare Book & Manuscript Library, Duke University.

Tillie Olsen Papers, Department of Special Collections, Stanford University Libraries.

Minnie Bruce Pratt Papers, David M. Rubenstein Rare Book & Manuscript Library, Duke University.

Adrienne Rich Papers, Schlesinger Library, Radcliffe Institute, Harvard University.

Cynthia Rich and Barbara Macdonald Papers, Schlesinger Library, Harvard University.

Helen Jones Rich Papers, Schlesinger Library, Radcliffe Institute, Harvard University.

May Sarton Papers, Henry W. and Albert A. Berg Collection of English and American Literature, New York Public Library.

Mab Segrest Papers, David M. Rubenstein Rare Book & Manuscript Library, Duke University.

Papers of John L. (Jack) Sweeney and Máire MacNeill Sweeney, UCD Archives, School of History and Archives, University College Dublin.

### BOOKS BY ADRIENNE RICH

*A Change of World.* Foreword by W. H. Auden. New Haven: Yale University Press, 1951.

*The Diamond Cutters and Other Poems.* New York: Harper & Brothers, 1955.

*Snapshots of a Daughter-in-Law: Poems 1954–1962.* New York: Harper & Brothers, 1963.

*Necessities of Life.* New York: Norton, 1966.

*Selected Poems.* London: Chatto & Windus, 1967.

*Leaflets: Poems 1965–1968.* New York: Norton, 1969.

*The Will to Change: Poems 1968–1970.* New York: Norton, 1971.

*Diving into the Wreck: Poems 1971–1972.* New York: Norton, 1973.

*Poems: Selected and New, 1950–1974.* New York: Norton, 1975.

*Of Woman Born: Motherhood as Experience and Institution.* New York: Norton, 1976.

*Twenty-One Love Poems.* Emeryville, CA: Effie Press, 1976.

*The Dream of a Common Language: Poems 1974–1977.* New York: Norton, 1978.

*On Lies, Secrets, and Silence: Selected Prose 1966–1978.* New York: Norton, 1979.

*A Wild Patience Has Taken Me This Far: Poems 1978–1981.* New York: Norton, 1981.

*Sources.* Woodside, CA: Heyeck Press, 1983.

*The Fact of a Doorframe: Poems Selected and New, 1950–1984.* New York: Norton, 1984.

*Your Native Land, Your Life: Poems.* New York: Norton, 1986.

*Blood, Bread, and Poetry: Selected Prose 1979–1985.* New York: Norton, 1986.

*Time's Power: Poems 1985–1988.* New York: Norton, 1989.

*An Atlas of the Difficult World: Poems 1988–1991.* New York: Norton, 1991.

*Collected Early Poems: 1950–1970.* New York: Norton, 1993.

*What Is Found There: Notebooks on Poetry and Politics.* New York: Norton, 1993.

*Dark Fields of the Republic: Poems 1991–1995.* New York: Norton, 1995.

*Midnight Salvage: Poems 1995–1998.* New York: Norton, 1999.

*Arts of the Possible: Essays and Conversations.* New York: Norton, 2001.

*Fox: Poems 1998–2000.* New York: Norton, 2001.

*The Fact of a Doorframe: Poems Selected and New, 1950–2001.* New York: Norton, 2002.

*The School Among the Ruins: Poems 2000–2004.* New York: Norton, 2004.

*Telephone Ringing in the Labyrinth: Poems 2004–2006.* New York: Norton, 2007.

Poetry and Commitment: An Essay. New York: Norton, 2007.

A Human Eye: Essays on Art and Society, 1997–2008. New York: Norton, 2009.

Tonight No Poetry Will Serve: Poems 2007–2010. New York: Norton, 2011.

Later Poems: Selected and New, 1971–2012. New York: Norton, 2012.

Collected Poems: 1950–2012. Introduction by Claudia Rankine. Edited by Pablo Conrad. New York: Norton, 2016.

Selected Poems: 1950–2012. New York: Norton, 2018.

Essential Essays: Culture, Politics, and the Art of Poetry. New York: Norton, 2018.

OTHER BOOKS

Antler, Joyce. *Jewish Radical Feminism: Voices from the Women's Liberation Movement.* New York: NYU Press, 2018.

Cooper, Jane Roberta, ed. *Reading Adrienne Rich: Reviews and Re-Visions, 1951–81.* Ann Arbor: University of Michigan Press, 1984.

Davison, Peter. *The Fading Smile: Poets in Boston from Robert Lowell to Sylvia Plath.* New York: Norton, 1994.

De Veaux, Alexis. *Warrior Poet: A Biography of Audre Lorde.* New York: Norton, 2004.

DuPlessis, Rachel Blau. *Writing Beyond the Ending: Narrative Strategies of Twentieth-Century Women Writers.* Bloomington: Indiana University Press, 1985.

Gelpi, Barbara Charlesworth, and Albert Gelpi. *Adrienne Rich's Poetry.* New York: Norton, 1975.

Greene, Dana. *Elizabeth Jennings: "The Inward War."* Oxford: Oxford University Press, 2018.

Hollenberg, Donna Krolik. *A Poet's Revolution: The Life of Denise Levertov.* Berkeley: University of California Press, 2013.

Lowell, Robert. *Selected Poems.* Rev. ed. New York: Noonday, 1977.

Lowell, Robert. *The Letters of Robert Lowell.* Edited by Saskia Hamilton. New York: Farrar, Straus and Giroux, 2005.

Middlebrook, Diane Wood. *Anne Sexton: A Biography.* Boston: Houghton Mifflin, 1991.

Plath, Sylvia. *Collected Poems.* New York: Harper & Row, 1981.

Plath, Sylvia. *The Unabridged Journals of Sylvia Plath, 1950–1962.* Edited by Karen V. Kukil. New York: Anchor, 2000.

Rasula, Jed. *The American Poetry Wax Museum: Reality Effects, 1940–1990.* Urbana, IL: National Council of Teachers of English, 1996.

Sontag, Susan. *Reborn: Journals and Notebooks, 1947–1963.* Edited by David Rieff. New York: Farrar, Straus and Giroux, 2009. Kindle edition.

Spivack, Kathleen. *With Robert Lowell and His Circle: Sylvia Plath, Anne Sexton, Elizabeth Bishop, Stanley Kunitz, and Others.* Boston: Northeastern University Press, 2012.

Wagner-Martin, Linda W. *Sylvia Plath: A Biography.* New York: St. Martin's Press, 1987.

White, Evelyn C. *Alice Walker: A Life.* New York: Norton, 2004.

# INDEX

"AR" indicates Adrienne Rich.

## ABOUT THE AUTHOR

HILARY HOLLADAY is a biographer, novelist, poet, and scholar of modern and contemporary American literature. Her books include *Herbert Huncke: The Times Square Hustler Who Inspired Jack Kerouac and the Beat Generation; Tipton: A Novel;* and *Wild Blessings: The Poetry of Lucille Clifton.* She holds a Ph.D. in English from the University of North Carolina at Chapel Hill and lives in Orange County, Virginia.

## A NOTE ON THE TYPE

This book was set in Monotype Dante, a typeface designed by Giovanni Mardersteig (1892–1977). Modeled on the Aldine type used for Pietro Cardinal Bembo's treatise *De Aetna* in 1495, Dante is a modern interpretation of the venerable face.

Typeset by North Market Street Graphics,
Lancaster, Pennsylvania

Printed and bound by Berryville Graphics,
Berryville, Virginia

Designed by Betty Lew